MW01253158

Piety and Politics in the Early Indian Mosque

Oxford in India Readings

DEBATES IN INDIAN HISTORY AND SOCIETY

Series Editors: Sabyasachi Bhattacharya, B. D. Chattopadhyaya, Richard M. Eaton

BISWAMOY PATI (EDITOR) — *The 1857 Rebellion*

SCOTT C. LEVI (EDITOR) — *India and Central Asia*
Commerce and Culture, 1500–1800

BHAIRABI PRASAD SAHU (EDITOR) — *Iron and Social Change in Early India*

SEEMA ALAVI (EDITOR) — *The Eighteenth Century in India* (OIP)

THOMAS R. TRAUTMANN (EDITOR) — *The Aryan Debate* (OIP)

AMIYA P. SEN (EDITOR) — *Social and Religious Reform*
The Hindus of British India (OIP)

DAVID N. LORENZEN (EDITOR) — *Religious Movements in South Asia 600–1800* (OIP)

G. BALACHANDRAN (EDITOR) — *India and the World Economy 1850–1950* (OIP)

BIDYUT CHAKRABARTY (EDITOR) — *Communal Identity in India*
Its Construction and Articulation in the Twentieth Century (OIP)

OXFORD
UNIVERSITY PRESS

YMCA Library Building, Jai Singh Road, New Delhi 110 001

Oxford University Press is a department of the University of Oxford.
It furthers the University's objective of excellence in research, scholarship,
and education by publishing worldwide in

Oxford New York
Auckland Cape Town Dar es Salaam Hong Kong Karachi
Kuala Lumpur Madrid Melbourne Mexico City Nairobi
New Delhi Shanghai Taipei Toronto

With offices in
Argentina Austria Brazil Chile Czech Republic France Greece
Guatemala Hungary Italy Japan Poland Portugal Singapore
South Korea Switzerland Thailand Turkey Ukraine Vietnam

Oxford is a registered trade mark of Oxford University Press
in the UK and in certain other countries.

Published in India
by Oxford University Press, New Delhi

© Oxford University Press 2008

The moral rights of the authors have been asserted
Database right Oxford University Press (maker)

First published 2008

All rights reserved. No part of this publication may be reproduced,
or transmitted in any form or by any means, electronic or mechanical,
including photocopying, recording or by any information storage and
retrieval system, without permission in writing from Oxford University Press.
Enquiries concerning reproduction outside the scope of the above should be
sent to the Rights Department, Oxford University Press, at the address above

You must not circulate this book in any other binding or cover
and you must impose this same condition on any acquirer

ISBN-13: 978-0-19-569512-0
ISBN-10: 0-19-569512-7

Typeset in Giovanni Book 10/12.8
by Eleven Arts, Keshav Puram, Delhi 110 035
Printed in India by De-Unique, New Delhi 110 018
Published by Oxford University Press
YMCA Library Building, Jai Singh Road, New Delhi 110 001

Piety and Politics in the Early Indian Mosque

edited by
Finbarr Barry Flood

OXFORD
UNIVERSITY PRESS

GUELPH HUMBER LIBRARY
205 Humber College Blvd
Toronto, ON M9W 5L7

Contents

List of Plates

Series Editors' Note

The Debates in Indian History and Society series focuses on the diversity of interpretations in historical discourse. The series addresses widely debated issues in South Asian history (including contemporary history) through edited volumes centering around sharply-focused themes or seminal writings that have generated arguments and counter-arguments resulting in worthwhile debates. In this context, the debates represent not simply differences in opinions but also offer important interpretative frameworks, which result in them acquiring a certain historiographic status. The approach encourages the interrogation of history, as distinct from presenting history as a collection of 'given' facts. The aim is to bring to readers significant writings, interpretations, and sources and to open to students bridge-heads into research.

The present volume, edited by an art historian Barry Flood, addresses some of the most charged questions informing the modern history of South Asia. How are we to understand the mosques patronized in the twelfth and thirteenth centuries by north India's earliest Muslim rulers? How did the patrons of these monuments seek to situate themselves with respect to that region's cultural milieu, and especially the built environment that was already there? In the end, do these monuments reflect an alien intrusion, a 'clash of civilizations', or something rather different?

Modern historians have been sharply divided over whether patrons of north India's earliest mosques sought to stamp an essentially foreign, especially Persian, aesthetic vision upon the landscape they ruled, or whether they sought to establish continuity with pre-conquest cultures and traditions. At issue here are not only matters of form and style, but also the builders' intent in re-using material from former temples. Essays included in the present volume provide readers with arguments and evidence supporting both perspectives. They also suggest future directions of research in this on-going debate.

Sabyasachi Bhattacharya
B. D. Chattopadhyaya
Richard M. Eaton

Introduction

FINBARR BARRY FLOOD

Although much of the current academic debate about the nature of South Asian Islam centres on textual constructions of Islam, the popular focus has been on architecture. The demolition of the Baburi Masjid at Ayodhya in 1992 provided a violent illustration of the mosque as a nexus between divergent views of Islam, its culture and history in South Asia. While the medieval past and its histories can often seem arcane and remote, these events demonstrated how both could be mobilized in the service of the present to dramatic effect. In addition, they underlined how medieval monuments could be taken to instantiate tendentious histories, competing narratives that appear to be written in stone.[1]

In his sensitive reading of the Qutb Mosque in Delhi, first published over thirty years ago and republished here, Mohammad Mujeeb warned against permitting 'the rhetoric of the medieval historians and the political slogans of our own times' to provide the lens through which medieval monuments were viewed. Nevertheless, in the past decades, nineteenth and twentieth-century scholarship on early Indo-Islamic architecture has been directly implicated in the targeting of mosques by religious nationalists seeking to replace them with temples, and thereby redress a perceived historical injustice.[2] If, as Richard Eaton has suggested, the project for modern historians of South Asia 'has as much to do with unravelling complicated historiographies as it does with writing histories,' the same is true of pre-modern architecture and its histories.[3]

As a way of exploring the interrelationships between architecture, history, and historiography, this volume brings together divergent voices that have contributed to nineteenth- and twentieth-century scholarship on some of the earliest surviving mosques in South Asia. The chronological and geographical range of the volume is narrow, focusing on four mosques constructed for Turkic patrons in northwest India in the decades between 1192 and 1220. The single exception is the opening essay, which sets the tone for the volume by providing an overview of the (generally scant) material evidence for South Asian mosques in the period before 1192. This date has been considered a watershed in South Asian history, marking the victory of the Shansabanid or Ghurid sultan Mu'izz al-Din Muhammad ibn Sam (better known in modern South Asia as Muhammad Ghuri) over a confederation of Rajput armies led by the Chauhan raja Prithviraja III at Tar'ain (modern Tarori) in Rajasthan. The victory opened up the Gangetic Plain to the armies of the sultan, and by the time that Mu'izz al-Din was assassinated in 603/1206, his Turkic generals had extended the sultan's dominion from Ghazna to the borders of Bengal.[4]

In South Asian historiography Ghurid expansion into north India has traditionally been represented as an (or even *the*) 'Islamic' invasion of India, as it often was in the rhetoric of medieval historians. Implicit in the paradigm is a teleological view of history in which the exploits of the Ghurids continue and culminate a project of 'Muslim' expansion begun by Arab armies in eighth-century Sind, the 'slow progress' of Islam in South Asia as D.R. Bhandarkar famously put it.[5] The teleology operates through a collapse of all possible identities into a unitary sectarian identification.[6] In doing so, it not only ignores ethnic and linguistic differences between the Muslim rulers who engaged with their Rajput counterparts over several centuries, but also aspects of intra-Muslim factionalism that undermine the notion of a monolithic Muslim self, and are directly relevant to the aggrandizement of Ghurid authority.

The rise of the Ghurids (named after the remote mountainous region of central Afghanistan from whence they hailed) had begun in 545/1150 with the sack of Ghazna, the eponymous capital of the Ghaznavid sultanate that had dominated the eastern Islamic world for a century-and-a-half. This dramatic event earned the Ghurid *malik* (chief) 'Ala al-Din Husayn the sobriquet *Jahān-sūz* (World-burner). It also marked the abrupt entry of these mountain chiefs onto the wider political stage. The apogee of the sultanate was reached under Ghiyath al-Din Muhammad ibn Sam (r. 558–99/1163–1203) and Mu'izz al-Din Muhammad ibn Sam (r. 569–602/1173–1206), brothers whose joint rule came to define the apogee of Ghurid power. The brothers ruled in a condominium, the elder partner Ghiyath al-Din overseeing the westward expansion of the sultanate from Firuzkuh in west-central Afghanistan, while Mu'izz al-Din expanded the Ghurid's dominions eastwards from the former Ghaznavid capital. A third line based in Bamiyan was celebrated for its patronage of Persian literati, but is less immediately relevant to the Indian conquests. The floruit of the sultanate was brief (roughly between 1175 and 1205) and its existence ephemeral, for the death of Mu'izz al-Din in 1206 effectively marked the end of Ghurid sovereignty. In its aftermath the neighbouring Khwarazmshahs of Central Asia incorporated large areas of the western Ghurid territories into their domains. In the east, the Turkish slave generals on whom the Ghurids had relied during their Indian campaigns assumed power in their own right, establishing an independent sultanate based in Delhi.

As the ambitions of the Ghurid sultans outgrew the confines of their mountain kingdom, their self-representations grew increasingly bombastic, marked by a dynamic process of self-fashioning designed to project their claims to authority in the wider world. The phenomenon is most apparent in the titulature of the Ghurids who, soon after the sack of Ghazna, assumed of the title of *sulṭān* to complement their traditional but less impressive claim to be *malik al-jibāl* (king of the mountains).

Like many parvenu dynasties, the Ghurids portrayed themselves as purveyors of Sunni orthodoxy. Writing in another context, the Ottoman historian Cemal Kafadar has noted the utility of championing the faith, which constituted 'a form of symbolic capital that could turn a title into (political and economic) entitlement.'[7] The standing of the Ghurid sultans in the *dār al-Islām* was inseparable from their engagement with the territories of the *dār al-ḥarb*, the latter providing both the financial and symbolic capital essential to efforts to refashion and reposition themselves in the late twelfth century. Framed within the rhetoric of idolatry, Indian victories were useful for bolstering the orthodox credentials of the Ghurid sultans in Baghdad and the wider Islamic world. The historians aggrandize Mu'izz al-Din's role as champion of the faith, identifying him as *sultān-i ghāzi* (the sultan of the holy warriors) and depicting the Indian campaigns of the sultan as a confrontation between the army of Islam (*lashkar-i Islām*) and the army of unbelief (*lashkar-i kuffār*).[8] However, campaigns against heterodox co-religionists were no less instrumental to the Ghurids in their endeavour to present themselves as champions of Sunni orthodoxy. Indeed, the titles of the Ghurid sultan

Ghiyath al-Din describe him as 'victor over the unbelievers and the heretics' (*qāhir al-kafara wa'l-mulḥidīn*), enshrining a common linkage between the suppression of heresy and the chastisement of unbelievers.[9]

The self-fashioning of the Ghurid sultans included a major religious realignment when, in 595/1199, they shifted their allegiances away from the Karramiya. This was a rather enigmatic pietistic sect of Sunni Islam that was dominant in the remote mountainous region of medieval Ghur (central Afghanistan) but considered theologically unsophisticated (and even unorthodox) in the wider Islamic world for their anthropomorphist views concerning God's nature. In their stead, the sultans embraced the Shafi'i and Hanafi *madhhabs* (schools of jurisprudence), two of the four orthodox schools of Sunni Islam, which could boast of celebrated thinkers and transregional networks of authority and patronage. Although unpopular in Ghur, this shift aligned the Ghurids more closely with their Sunni contemporaries to the west, a reorientation that was also reflected in the contemporary introduction of coin types based on those then circulating in the eastern Mediterranean.[10]

The erection of congregational mosques was among the normative duties of Muslim kingship, and architectural patronage was integral to the ostentatious promotion of Sunni orthodoxy. The last decade of the sixth/twelfth century saw a major architectural programme undertaken in the name of the Ghurid sultans in both Afghanistan and India. Following a fire, in 597/1200–1 the Great Mosque of Herat, one of the four great cities of Khurasan, was rebuilt and delivered into the hands of the Shafi'is. Ghurid patronage of mosques and funerary shrines in the Indus Valley during the same period may have been intended to encourage outlets for expressions of orthodox Sunni piety in an area known for its strong Isma'ili loyalties.[11]

One of the first acts undertaken after the eastward expansion of the Ghurid sultanate was to build a series of mosques and shrines in the newly-conquered Indian territories. In addition to two Ghurid extant funerary monuments near Multan in the Indus Valley, there is textual evidence for the construction of several madrasas and the refurbishment or reconstruction of the Friday Mosque of Multan and its endowment with a royal *waqf*.[12] The foundation texts of two Ghurid congregational mosques survive from Hansi, an important fortified centre in Haryana, and an inscription in the name of the Ghurid sultan Mu'izz al-Din dated

594/1196 now incorporated into the walls of Nagaur fort in Rajasthan may also have come from a mosque.[13]

The four extant mosques that form the subject of this volume—the Qutb Mosque in Delhi, the Arhai-din-ka-Jhonpra Mosque at Ajmir, and Shahi Mosque at Khatu (both in Rajasthan) and the Chaurasi Kambha Mosque at Kaman—are all congregational mosques designed to accommodate the entire male population of urban centers for Friday prayers.[14] All four were erected at the behest of the Turkic mamluks of the Ghurid sultan. The best-known of the four, the 'Quwwat al-Islam' or Qutb Mosque at Delhi (Plates 1 and 2) bears a series of inscriptions informing us that it was built by the commander Qutb al-Din Aybak on the orders of the Ghurid sultan, Muhammad ibn Sam (d. 1206). The foundation text above the eastern entrance of the mosque gives the date of 587/1191–2, that above northern entrance 592/1195, while the arched screen preceding the pillared prayer-hall (Plate 3) seems to have been added in 594/1198. After its construction by agents of the Ghurid sultan, the mosque was twice enlarged and remodeled by the Delhi sultans Iltutmish (d. 1236) and 'Ala' al-Din Khilji (d. 1316). However, in keeping with the chronological focus of this volume, the essays below concentrate on the initial phase of the mosque's history.

The second of the four extant Ghurid mosques, the Arhai-din-ka-Jhompra Mosque at Ajmir, contains a *mihrab* dated 595/1199. The participation of immigrants from Khurasan in its construction is suggested by the Herati *nisba* (toponymic) of one of those who supervised the work.[15]

A third mosque, the Shahi-Masjid at Khatu in Rajasthan (Plate 4), roughly 50 miles north of Ajmir lacks a foundation text but may be associated with an inscription dated 599/1203 recovered nearby. It is in any case provided with a white marble mihrab (prayer-niche) of virtually identical form to that in the Ajmir mosque (compare Plates 5 and 6), with which it shares many formal features, and can thus be confidently ascribed to the turn of the twelfth century, if not the same workshop.[16] Opinions differ on whether the mosque was built upon the platform of an earlier temple or constructed *de novo*, making extensive reuse of architectural materials.[17]

The fourth of the group, the Chaurasi Kambha mosque at Kaman in Rajasthan (Plate 7), about 70 miles south of Delhi on the route between Ajmir and Sind, bears a damaged foundation text ascribing the foundation to Baha' al-Din Tughril, a mamluk of the Ghurid sultan who held the *iqṭā'* of Bayana between 1195 and 1210. Since Baha' al-Din claims the title of sultan, the mosque probably dates from 600/1204 or later, when Ghurid authority in India began to wane. It contains the earliest surviving minbar in India, a stone structure known locally as 'Krishna's swing.'[18]

The basic form of the four mosques is similar, with a monumental rectangular projecting entrance (elevated at Ajmir, Delhi and Khatu; Plates 8 and 9) leading to a central courtyard, a multi-bayed prayer-hall at its western end and (at Delhi and Kaman) a narrow arcade or *riwāq* surrounding the remaining three sides (compare Plates 1, 4, and 7). The interior spaces are covered by means of corbelled domes and flat slabs supported on trabeate beams borne by pillars composed of discrete sections set vertically on end to achieve the required height. Many but not all of these elements have been reused from earlier pre-conquest monuments (Plate 2). With the exception of the Delhi mosque, where the mihrab or mihrabs does/do not survive, all four structures are provided with a single elaborately carved concave mihrab on the central axis of the building: white marble at Ajmir and Khatu, red sandstone at Kaman.

Despite commonalities of conception, formal differences divide the mosques into two distinct groups. For example, the mosques at Ajmir and Khatu are distinguished from those at Delhi and Kaman by the absence of a colonnade (riwāq) around the courtyard, and the presence of identical white marble mihrabs with a semi-circular profile, in contrast to the rectangular profile of the mihrab at Kaman (the main mihrab of the Delhi mosque does not survive).

The Qutb Mosque in Delhi is further distinguished by the occurrence of a massive tapering red sandstone seventy-five metre high minaret, the Qutb Minar, outside its southeast corner (Plate 10). The minaret is comprised of cylindrical sections with alternating angled and convex flanges, a design that has its origins in earlier minarets of eastern Iran and Afghanistan. None of its extensive Arabic historical texts are dated, but Sanskrit graffiti dated Samvat 1256 (1199 AD) occur on the first storey, and the presence of the Ghurid sultan Ghiyath al-Din's titles on the fourth band of the same storey (their only extant occurrence on a monument east of Ghazna) indicates that the minaret stood up to this height by at least 601/1203, the date of the sultan's death.[19] Work on the minaret thus seems to have begun around the same time as an arched screen was added to the façade of its prayer-hall (Plate 3), a feature that reiterates the arcades and *iwāns* found in the courtyards of contemporary Iranian mosques in a stone medium and trabeate idiom. This was extended as part of sultan Iltutmish's expansion of the Qutb Mosque in the 1220's, when the Ghurid mosque at Ajmir was also remodelled and provided with a spectacular carved stone screen (Plate 11).[20]

Although seldom noted, the foundation of the mosques at Ajmir, Delhi, and elsewhere was co-terminous with the architectural programme undertaken under Ghurid patronage in Afghanistan and Khurasan. In modern scholarship, however, disciplinary, linguistic, and political boundaries have conspired to sunder the Indian mosques from their Afghan contemporaries, with the result that they are usually considered as distinct and self-subsisting. This tendency has been reinforced by their use of an Indic stone medium and trabeate (post-and-lintel) idiom alien to Afghanistan and Iran, where brick predominated and arcuate forms were favoured.

In addition, the extensive reuse and recycling of architectural elements distinguishes Indo-Ghurid mosques from the contemporary mosques of Iran and Afghanistan and from mosques built for communities of Muslims living in Sind and Gujarat before the Ghurid conquest. In stark contrast to the mosques erected in the wake of Ghurid expansion, pre-conquest mosques make no use of recycled materials. Skilled stone masons were surely available in major urban centres such as Ajmir and Delhi after the conquest and, as we will see, may even have been involved in the construction of Ghurid mosques from reused materials. The recycling of architectural materials even when alternatives were available thus seems to represent a conscious choice. Speed may have been a factor, but the same pattern was repeated in the mosques erected later after expansion into the Deccan and Gujarat by the Delhi sultans in the thirteenth and fourteenth centuries, by which date the mosques and shrines of Delhi were being constructed from newly-carved materials.[21]

It has generally been assumed that these materials were purloined from temples destroyed in the wake of the conquest. As Michael Meister points out, however, the range of styles among the constituent materials indicates that not all the materials reused in Indo-Ghurid mosques are of the same date; on the contrary, they represent a synthesis of materials drawn from near-contemporary structures (including but not confined to temples), from those that were antique by this date, and newly-carved stones that often emulate the style of the reused material. Nevertheless, the preference for recycling and the repeated use of specific architectural modules in the post-conquest mosques of the sultanate period has led to suggestions that mosques such as those in Delhi and Rajasthan constitute a distinct type, the 'conquest mosque', which was associated with the expansion of the frontiers of Islamicate polities.[22]

Formal and iconographic differences between the four mosques complicate this scenario, however, indicating that any template was heavily inflected by regional architectural idioms and norms. These differences reflect the way in which regional architectural traditions determined the domestic inscription of any imported conception of the mosque. They may also reflect variables among the mosques' patrons, or even the impact of pre-conquest traditions of mosque architecture. The twelfth-century mosques at Bhadreshvar on the coast of Gujarat discussed in Alka Patel's essay attest to a pre-conquest Muslim presence that was not confined to the coastal regions of north India.[23] In his account of Qutb al-Din Aybek's campaign against the Gahadavalas of Kanauj, the historian Ibn al-Athir notes that Muslim communities had existed in the area since the time of Mahmud of Ghazni, and were steadfast in their adherence to the *sharī'a*, prayer and the giving of charity.[24] At Nagaur in Rajasthan, the survival of a tombstone dated 545/1150 belonging to the son of an Isma'ili missionary (*dā'ī*) indicates the presence of Muslim communities in the decades before the Ghurid conquest, while providing a further reminder that these did not necessarily share the confessional affinities of the Ghurids or their Turkic soldiery.[25] It is in any case possible (if far from certain) that regional pre-conquest traditions of mosque architecture contributed to the development of Indo-Ghurid mosques.

TAXONOMY AND HYBRIDITY

The idea that temple and mosque functioned as mutually antithetical metonymies for 'Hindu' and 'Muslim' cultural forms and practices is an axiom of South Asian historiography, common to colonial and postcolonial scholarship (whether indigenous or not). The current entry on al-Hind in *The Encyclopaedia of Islam* explains, for example, that idol-temples 'were not only anathema to Islam but were its direct antithesis.'[26] The two modalities have thus come to represent extremes of a bipolar historiography, in which difference has been thoroughly naturalized.[27]

These ideas find particularly strident expression in scholarship on the mosques that form the subject of this volume. Because of their assumed or implied associations with conquest and temple desecration (a subject that will be considered below), the recycling of materials to construct them has generally been taken as both a sign of 'Muslim' victory over the 'pagan' Hindus and an expression of contempt for the aesthetic and cultural values represented by the temples that they are assumed to have replaced. In the historiography of pre-modern South Asia, a general tendency to attribute fixed sectarian identities to medieval objects and buildings has also been informed by essentialist and ahistorical ideas about 'Islamic' practices of looting and iconoclasm. Thus the fourth-century iron pillar from a Vishnu temple re-erected by sultan Iltutmish (d. 1236) in the courtyard of the Qutb Mosque in Delhi is referred to as the 'Hindu iron pillar', an object in direct opposition to the adjacent 'Islamic' minaret, ignoring the fact that the terms *stambha* (pillar) and *minār* (minaret) were used interchangeably to refer to the same objects by medieval observers, whether Hindu or Muslim.[28]

The resulting emphasis on disjunction and rupture has been the dominant theme in scholarship on the Ghurid mosques of India since its inception. It is plainly manifest in the earliest modern discussion of any Ghurid monument, James Tod's analysis of the Arhai-din-ka-Jhonpra Mosque at Ajmir in his *Annals and Antiquities of Rajasthan* (1829).[29] Tod's discussion of the Ajmir mosque marks a significant watershed in the nature and tone of writing on Indo-Turkic architecture, departing from descriptions found in earlier Arabic and Persian geographies and histories (which, with a single exception, ignore the question of reuse), while also projecting onto medieval monuments oppositional categories of Turk (or Muslim) and Hindu that were well established even in medieval literary texts.[30] Writing only three decades after Abbé Grégoire popularized the censorious use of the term vandal in the aftermath of the French Revolution, Tod condemns the Turks, the 'Goths and Vandals of Rajasthan':

> Whatever time had spared of the hallowed relics of old, bigotry has destroyed, or raised to herself altars of materials, whose sculptured fragments serve now as disjointed memorials of two distinct and distant eras: that of the independent Hindu, and that of the conquering Muhammadan ...[31]

On occasion, the ability of medieval monuments to materialize sectarian narratives saw them pressed into the service of colonial administrators. Perhaps the most (in)famous instance is the 'Gates of Somnath' episode of 1842, when the doors of the tomb of Mahmud Ghaznavi (r. 388–421/998–1030) were carried off from Afghanistan to India on the orders of the Viceroy, Lord Ellenborough in the belief that they had been looted from the Hindu temple of Somnath in Gujarat when sacked by Mahmud eight centuries previously. This erroneous idea was apparently reinforced by contemporary translations of medieval Persian histories, underlining the centrality of texts to the construction of Indian pasts. In his proclamation announcing the Gates' return, Ellenborough declared that the 'insult of eight hundred years is at last avenged.'[32] The absurdity of the gesture was evident even to contemporaries, who pilloried Ellenborough for his crude attempt 'to retaliate on the Mussulmans' a perceived slight, eight hundred years distant.[33]

Although the 'Gates of Somnath' episode is generally seen as an idiosyncratic adventure of Ellenborough's conceiving, in its interventionist approach to medieval Indo-Islamic monuments the gesture was unique only in the public criticism that it attracted. A more ad hoc variant on Ellenborough's attempt to renegotiate the past by restoring 'Hindu' and 'Muslim' elements to their appropriate domains is manifest in the alterations to a stone monument at Umga in Bihar around 1847, just five years later. The structure is described as a temple, but from its inscriptions was probably a mosque, which later served as a temple (a not uncommon transformation):

> A remarkable feature of this Temple (to which its preservation from the destructive hand of Mahomedan fanatics may be attributed) is its bearing cufic inscriptions over the entrance doorway, as well as those of the two small chambers, also on the eight sides of each pillar and on the architraves, the latter consist simply of the word 'Allah.' The former appears to be extracts from the Koran, but having been chiselled off it is nearly impossible to make them out. This piece of mischievous folly, I regret to record, is attributed to a European officer, at whose suggestion the late Rajah Gunsam Singh of Deo caused it to be done, and the words 'Ramjee,' 'Sri Ram,' 'Sri Gneash,' 'Sri Jugnath,' 'Bulbudrajee,' &c. &c. have been scratched in common Nagree to supply their place, as his European friend suggested that it was not right to allow Mahomedan badges to remain in a Hindu Temple: however, his having at the same time recommended substantial repairs which were executed, may be considered as some slight set-off to such outrageous folly.[34]

The Kufic inscriptions that were said to have preserved the building from Muslim fanatics were thus precisely the features that attracted the violence of British (or British inspired) iconoclasts.

A third variant on these attempts to renegotiate the instantiated past occurred in October 1870, less than three decades after the Somnath episode, when the Viceroy of India, Lord Mayo, held a durbar in the western Indian city of Ajmir in Rajasthan to commemorate the foundation of an elite college bearing his name. As part of the festivities, elaborately carved stone pillars were taken from the Arhai din ka-Jhonpra Mosque at Ajmir (Plates 11 and 14).[35] The pillars were used to construct a triumphal arch under which the viceroy and the local Rajput chiefs were intended to march in procession (although the instability of the structure rendered this impossible, and on the day it was circumnavigated instead). Ironically, the removal of pillars from the Ajmir mosque to honour the viceroy and his guests flew in the face of a notice affixed to the mosque in 1809 by Daulat Rao Sindhia, the Maharaja of Gwalior, forbidding the quarrying of stone from the site, a precocious example of architectural conservation in advance of the earliest British legislation on the subject.[36]

Anticipating the 'historical rectifications' of Hindutva, both Ellenborough's theatrical manipulation of Ghaznavid marquetry and Lord Mayo's appropriation of Chauhan masonry are part of more extensive nineteenth-century experiments with rituals designed to represent British colonial authority to Indian subjects. [37] The utility of medieval monuments as sites for the construction and negotiation of historical memory under the aegis of colonial administrators was directly related to the sectarian meanings ascribed to them in colonial histories and art histories, which figured them as sites for the construction and (re)negotiation of a dyadic past.

Especially after the Mutiny of 1857, contrasts between the arbitrary violence of Muslim rule and the rational benevolence of British administration were often articulated around figurations of a 'Hindu' golden age subject to 'Muslim' rupture. In post-Mutiny scholarship, the perceived violence of the medieval past was often conflated with the memory of more recent strife, with medieval mosques such as the Qutb Mosque in Delhi invoked to conjure the spectre of iconoclastic violence as a potential future of the subcontinent, should it ever slip the bonds of colonial rule. In this way, colonial scholarship on the medieval past often constituted the medieval realities that it sought to describe, establishing a mutually constitutive relationship between histories and monuments.[38]

If, as Pierre Nora has argued, memory is distinguished from history by its attachment to sites rather than events, both could be rendered coincident by the judicious use of texts.[39] A plaque attached to the eleventh-century Sas Bahu temple in Gwalior is inscribed in English:

> This temple was cleaned and stripped of the Chuna [whitewash] with which the Mahomedans had defaced it for centuries by Major J.B. Keith November AD 1881 under the direction of Captain H. Cole R.E. Curator of Ancient Monuments in India.[40]

The gesture materializes a trope found in the work of contemporary architectural historians such as James Fergusson (d. 1886), which figured medieval monuments as lithic books from which the (primarily racial and sectarian) history of India could be read.[41]

As this suggests, the ideologies and methodologies of ethnology and architectural history were closely intertwined in the formative period between 1850 and 1870. The taxonomic structures upon which both nascent disciplines were premised depended upon the ability to read difference, an endeavour facilitated by the endogamous practices associated with the caste system. As a consequence, nineteenth-century ethnologists were at pains to emphasize the absence of 'the disturbing element of crossing' in the Indian objects and subjects of their study.[42] However, as Mayo's manipulation of the Ajmir pillars suggests, the reuse of 'Hindu' carvings in a mosque, and the practice of combining these with elements newly carved for Muslim patrons complicated the project of reading and writing difference.

Although rarely manifest in such a 'hands-on' manner, the attempt to negotiate the resulting 'hybridity' of Indo-Ghurid mosques has been a feature of analysis since its inception. Tod's pioneering description of the Arhai-din-ka-Jhonpra Mosque at Ajmir contrasts the gate of the mosque (composed of newly carved elements) with its prayer-hall (constructed from reused columns). In so doing, it draws from the repertoire of classicizing imagery that both informed and structured colonial responses to the remains of South Asia's past to evoke a graphic epitome of dissimulation and dissonance:

> Separately considered, they are each magnificent; together, it is as if a modern sculptor were (like our actors of the last age) to adorn the head of Cato with a peruke. I left this precious relic, with a malediction upon all the spoilers of art—whether the Thane who pillaged Minerva's portico at Athens, or the Toork who dilapidated the Jain temple at Ajmér.[43]

This remarkable conjuration of a Roman portrait bust capped with an eighteenth-century wig is firmly rooted in an iconography of incongruity drawn from contemporary discourses on cultural mixing. Fortuitously or not, the figure conjured here is that of the quintessential figure of Indian hybridity, the Nabob, a turban perched precariously on his bald pate.[44]

The tone set by Tod inflects the work of most subsequent commentators, for whom the early Indo-Islamic monuments are improbable, unstable, and unsatisfactory hybrids cobbled together from mutually incommensurate traditions. Consequently, the mosques discussed below figure as intrusive anomalies within the basic taxonomic structures of colonial and postcolonial scholarship. In this sense their reception by modern scholars parallels that of certain kinds of vernacular religious texts, which cannot be accommodated within dyadic categories of Muslim and Hindu, and whose 'hybrid' or 'syncretistic' content consequently relegates them to the margins of modern scholarship.[45]

The biological metaphors of hybridity and syncretism that are often used to explain unlikely unions of opposites in both monuments and texts draw upon notions of essence and purity that are deeply embedded in colonial theories of the relationship between culture and race, within which the mixing of forms (as of races) signalled degeneration.[46] Writing in 1870, Lord Napier decried the mixing of Hindu, Mussulman and European styles in India, since Mussulman is 'a perfect style, which can only be debased by alliance.'[47] Concomitant anxieties about miscegenation and the dilution of cultural purity often have distinctly sexual overtones manifest for example in the view that the Ajmir and Delhi mosques show how 'the developing Muslim style was being penetrated by the Indian tradition.'[48]

Inflecting similar sentiments with a different meaning, S.D. Sharma's 1937 history of Islam in India attributes the decline of the Ghaznavid sultanate that dominated the eastern Islamic world and parts of north-west India between 1000 and 1150 to a heady mix of architectural hybridity, transculturation and sexual intermingling:

> Indian architects suggested some of the motifs that Indian artisans forcibly carried off to Ghazni executed for their Muslim masters; Indian captives that were taken in their thousands served to breed enervating habits among the restless and energetic Turks, Afghans, Arabs and Persians who formed the population of Ghazni;

and lastly, Indian women abducted and enslaved also in large numbers sapped the vigour of their ravishers and contributed to their downfall.[49]

The relative weight given to indigenous and 'alien' elements or to the agency of Turkic patron and Hindu mason in evaluations of the 'hybridities' or 'syncretisms' that constitute the distopian style of the Indo-Ghurid monuments has generally depended on the aesthetic predispositions, disciplinary affiliations, and political proclivities of the writer.[50] The essays chosen for this volume reflect the two basic paradigms that have structured scholarship on the monuments since the early nineteenth century: an 'indigenizing' approach that emphasizes continuity with pre-conquest architectural traditions, and a 'foreignizing' emphasis that figures the early mosques as attempts to replicate the architectural norms of Iran, with varying degrees of success.

The indigenist paradigm is the older of the two, associated with scholarship on the monuments from its inception. In a lecture on the study of Indian architecture delivered in London in 1866, for example, James Fergusson espoused a contemporary perception of Islam as a culturally amorphous empty vessel devoid of any distinctive architectural styles, but capable of assimilating those of the cultures it engulfed:

Wherever the Muslims went they introduced no style of their own, but employed the native people to build their mosques for them; and this accounted for the fact that some of the most beautiful Mahommedan buildings in India were purely Hindoo from first to last.[51]

Such sentiments led to a lively debate on whether or not the Qutb Mosque in Delhi (Plate 10) was in fact a converted Hindu temple. Rejected by Walter Ewer in what seems to be the earliest scholarly analysis of the mosque (1832), the notion was championed in Sayyid Ahmad Khan's *Āṣār al-Sanādīd*, an Urdu account of Delhi's monumental architecture first published in 1847 and in a revised edition in 1854.[52]

For those who championed the 'Hindu' origins of the Qutb Mosque, even its foundation texts proved the falsity of their own claims. Writing of the Qutb Mosque in 1872, J.D. Beglar, an engineer commissioned by the newly-formed Archaeological Survey of India to survey the site, notes:

I have shown in a manner that cannot be shaken by any number of lying inscriptions, that this great beautiful structure is essentially Hindu in design, altered to a greater or lesser extent by the Muhammadan conquerors, who could perceive neither the beauty of the whole, nor the harmony of the parts, but deliberately did their best to hide the signs of the Hindu origin of the structure by building in, covering up, whitewashing and plastering, destroying parts and building them up according to their own crude and barbarous notions, and crowned the whole by inserting in the true style of oriental exaggeration in their inscriptions, that they built the structure![53]

Beglar's views were not, however, acceptable to his superior, Alexander Cunningham, the first director of the Archaeological Survey of India. Indeed, the question of the Qutb's origins led to a very public contretemps between the two, which took the form of a written exchange published as a preface to the report containing the passage just quoted. Portions of the exchange are reproduced in this volume: they consist of an extract from Beglar's long report on the Qutb Mosque asserting its Hindu origins, a preface containing Cunningham's rejection of this interpretation, and Beglar's introduction to his essay, which amounts to a humiliating recantation of its assertions regarding the mosque's origins.[54]

The epistemes of colonialist historiography survived well into the twentieth and twenty-first centuries. In the post-independence period, for example, nationalist scholars like D.S. Triveda ignored both the epigraphic evidence and the criticisms of his contemporaries to insist that the lower stories of the Qutb Minar (Plate 10) were the remains of a Hindu observatory built in 280 BC.[55] Recently, the wheel has come full circle in a particularly sinister way, with religious ultra-nationalists asserting that there is no Islamic architecture in South Asia. In an echo of colonialist architectural histories, this school of of thought holds that buildings such as the Qutb Mosque, the Red Fort of Delhi, and Taj Mahal, are all converted Hindu buildings, which should be 'restored' to their original use.[56]

Partly in response to these atavistic readings, over the past decades a handful of scholars have developed more nuanced versions of the indigenist paradigm. These are represented by Michael Meister's contributions to this volume. Rejecting the traditional axes of 'accommodation', 'assimilation', 'synthesis,' which have structured even the most sophisticated discussions, Meister offers 'a different metaphor, that of permeability through a membrane, for the interaction between Islam and Hindu India; which cultural forms prove to be more permeable and which do not may provide a more interesting litmus for cultural interaction than a discussion of "syncretism."'

If the indigenist paradigm of colonialist and nationalist historiography figured the Turkic patron as a kind of decorator crab building a house of prayer from a bricolage of purloined forms and materials, an alternative 'foreignizing' paradigm emphasized the filiation of Indo-Ghurid mosques with the monuments of the eastern Islamic world, despite their inevitable concessions to Indian idioms and media. This 'foreignizing' paradigm developed towards the end of the nineteenth century, but gained momentum in the early decades of the twentieth, with the increasing availability of publications on the medieval architecture of Afghanistan and Iran, and the institutionalized study of Islamic art. Proponents of this approach (represented for example by Robert Hillenbrand's contribution to this volume) see the Indo-Ghurid mosques as epigonous reflections of the brick idiom and vaulted forms favoured in the eleventh— and twelfth-century Seljuq architecture of Iran, products of a compromise between the desires of Turkic patrons and the abilities of Indic craftsmen.

Caught between these two paradigms, the monuments have been subject to a scholarly Gestalt in which Islamicists have recognized what is familiar from the central Islamic lands, while South Asianists have emphasized a (sometimes fractured) relationship to pre-conquest architectural traditions. As the tensions between these positions suggest, the early Indian mosques illustrate what Richard Eaton has described as the 'complex kinds of double-movement between the regional cultures of South Asia and the wider world of Islam' that are characteristic of South Asian Islam.[57]

One problem with both indigenizing and foreignizing paradigms is the priority that they afford to valorized 'originals', whether material temple or conceptual mosque. This problem was noted more than three decades ago by Mohammad Mujeeb in his sensitive appraisal of the Qutb Mosque in Delhi, reproduced in this volume. In it, Mujeeb bemoans the search for borrowed elements in the Qutb Mosque and the ways in which it has detracted from aesthetic appreciation and empirical analysis of the mosque itself.

A good example of this neglect is the treatment of a feature that recurs in the Delhi and Kaman mosques (Plates 1 and 7, visible top right). In both, a richly decorated entrance at the northwest corner of the mosque led to a mezzanine enclosure (Plate 12), a feature that is absent from the mosques at Khatu and Ajmir. Although the importance of this structure has been ignored—indeed it has often been misidentified as a *zenāna* or womens' chamber—it represents a type of royal enclosure referred to in later Persian texts as a *mulūk-khāna*. The feature is an innovation that seems to have first appeared in the Friday Mosque with which Mahmud of Ghazna embellished his capital around 1018–19, and was probably reproduced in the congregational mosques built by the Ghurids in Afghanistan.[58] It is not, however, found in the Seljuk mosques of Iran, which have consistently provided the standard against which the Indian mosques have been measured.

In other words, an over-emphasis on reuse, a failure to recognize the innovative character of Ghaznavid and Ghurid architecture (appreciation of which is hampered by the ruinous state of the few surviving monuments), and the valorization of the Seljuk mosques of Iran as prototypical in modern scholarship have all combined to obscure the significance of this formal feature. Although it left little trace on the mosque architecture of the central Islamic lands, the mulūk-khāna was to become standard in subsequent Indian congregational mosques. The extant chambers at Delhi and Kaman are the earliest surviving examples of this feature, and therefore of great interest not only for the history of South Asian architecture, but for the history of the mosque in general.

CONTINUITY AND RUPTURE

Implicit (and sometimes explicit) in both the indigenizing and foreignizing approaches to architectural history is a broader debate about the nature of the changes wrought by the eastward expansion of Ghurid imperium. The idea of two distinct periods—Hindu and Muslim—already present in Indo-Persian chronicles was adopted and embellished in colonial histories of South Asia: it is clearly manifest in Tod's evaluation of the Ajmir mosque.

That the defeat of the major Rajput houses of northern India by the Ghurids created a cultural and political *tabula rasa* is a shibboleth of modern scholarship:

> Muslims became the ascendant power and the new kings, unlike their Muslim predecessors in the subcontinent, viewed the world more clearly in terms of *dār al-Islām* and *dār al-ḥarb*. Emphatically bent on the expansion of Islamic authority, often through violently iconoclastic conquest, they sought to create an entirely new and Islamic dispensation. In this endeavour, which tried to sweep away all before it, adaptations of the old order of things could find little place.[59]

In such figurations, the 'Islamic dispensation' stands in opposition to the Indic or 'Hindu' modes of governance that it supplanted, figuring a shift from a model of incorporative kingship and ritual hegemony to a radically different paradigm, a unitary Indo-Persian super-state created through the subjugation of pagan polities.[60] Whether this shift was seen in a positive or negative light depended on the ideological sympathies of the viewer: Marxist scholars of the post-independence period represented it as an 'enfranchisement of the Indian city-workers' at the expense of Brahminical hegemony.[61]

Notions of rupture are, however, adumbrated by the hybrid nature of the political arrangements made in the immediate aftermath of Ghurid expansion. In several cases, scions of defeated dynasties were reinstated as tributary subjects of the Ghurids; these included the Chauhan rulers of Ajmir and Delhi, the Parimara rajas of Gwalior, and perhaps also the Gahadavalas of Kanauj.[62] The reinstallation of the sons of defeated foes was perfectly congruent with the practices of pre-Ghurid victors and consonant with the normative ideals of *dharmavijaya*, or righteous conquest, an ideal common to both Buddhist and Hindu codes governing the conduct of conquest and warfare.[63] Indeed, the incorporation of smaller regional centres into larger hierarchical political structures was essential to the process of medieval state formation in India. These arrangements were often cemented by intermarriage, which might explain a curious assertion by the historian Ibn al-Athir that sultan Mu'izz al-Din married the daughter of the Hindu ruler of Āja (Uchch) in the Indus Valley as part of the arrangements that led to the surrender of that city in 569/1174; the princess is reported to have been brought to Ghazna, where her tomb later became a popular shrine.[64]

Reinstated Rajput blood lines were only one element in the post-conquest administration of north India, however. A second (and statistically more significant) factor was the introduction to India of the administrative iqṭā', a type of land or revenue assignment that carried with it military (or more rarely, financial) obligations to the state and that might or might not be hereditary. The territories conquered by Mu'izz al-Din from Ghazna appear to have been considered as part of his personal appanage. Most of the iqṭā's created in India were assigned not to the maliks of Ghur (who played a negligible role in the administration of the Indian territories), but to the mamlūks or manumitted Turkish military slaves upon whom the Ghurids were increasingly dependent, and to whom fell the lot of consolidating and securing the eastern marches of their sultanate.[65]

The post-conquest political arrangements thus combined modes of governance perfectly consonant with the traditions of dharmavijaya and newly introduced administrative institutions such as the iqṭāʿ. In this way, the decade after the Indian conquests saw sultan Muʿizz al-Din ruling over an eclectic combination of manumitted Turkic subordinates collecting revenues and providing service, and vassal Hindu princelings ruling all or part of their ancestral territories reapportioned as appanages.

The heterogeneous constitution of Ghurid administrative authority was not confined to the abstractions of political structures, but was also manifest in more mundane spheres of cultural life. Hasan-i Nizami, our earliest source for the Ghurid campaigns in north India, informs his readers that after the conquest of Benares in 590/1193, temples were converted into mosques and *khanqah*s, the law of Islam was promoted, and 'the face of dinars and dirhams gained fresh luster from the name and titles (*nām va alqāb*) of the king.'[66] While it is indeed true that name of the Ghurid sultan appeared on gold coins issued from Benares or nearby Kanauj after the conquest, it did so in Sanskrit, the language of the north Indian literate elite, shorn of its bombastic Islamic titles. Moreover, any idea that these coins were part of a comprehensive programme to promote the faith of the conquerors is further undermined by the presence of an image of the Hindu deity Lakshmi on their reverse.[67] The divergence between textual and numismatic evidence suggests that the rhetorical claims found in medieval documents should not be read as transparent statements of 'fact', but need to be treated with caution, a point to which I will return below.

The dissemination of coins bearing the sultan's name juxtaposed with Hindu iconography reflects a pragmatic attitude towards economic realities. Ghurid coins struck in India not only continued existing iconographic types, but also conformed to indigenous standards of weight and metallic purity, in contrast to the issues from Ghazna, which conformed to the numismatic norms of the wider Islamic world.[68] The endeavour to minimize the negative economic impact of the conquest was evidently successful, for during this period the Jewish and Muslim traders whose presence is reported in Anahilawad (Patan), the capital of the Solanki or Chalukya rulers of Gujarat, find counterparts in the Indian merchants from the same city who traded in Muʿizz al-Din's capital of Ghazna, and as far west as Bardasir, Jiruft, and Kirman in Iran.[69] Despite the bloody battles upon which it was predicated, Ghurid expansion in the late twelfth century may even have fostered mercantile contacts between north India and Afghanistan along the terrestrial trade routes.

In addition to fostering economic stability, the continuance of indigenous coin types (no less than indigenous modes of administration) was also a means of legitimating Ghurid rule by casting it in a familiar mould, as Sunil Kumar notes in his essay on the Qutb Mosque. The Indian coins of the Ghurids were, however, marked not only by continuities but also by innovations. Shorn of its bombastic Islamic titles, the name of sultan Mu'izz al-Din appeared on the Indian coins of the Ghurids preceded by the hybrid title *Hamīra* or *Śrímad Hamīra*. While the honorific *Śrî* follows protocols rooted in the constitutive and substantive norms of Indic kingship, the presence of Hamīra on Indian coins is an innovation born of diachronic engagements. This was a Sanskritic title derived from the Arabic *amīr*, commander, a title that lay well below the bombastic heights to which Ghurid titulature aspired. Its presence can be attributed not to Ghurid usage, but to its earlier deployment in north Indian texts and inscriptions to designate the Ghaznavid sultans.[70]

Numismatic and textual evidence thus both suggest that the cultural life of the period was marked by a dialectical interplay between continuity and discontinuity, tradition and innovation. As a nexus between 'global' and regional networks of artistic innovation, religious authority, popular piety, political power, and religious sentiment, the mosques discussed in this volume manifest this dialectic in various ways. While the form of the mosques and the graffiti that they contain bear witness to continuities in workshop practices, some if not all of them seem to have been constructed on the sites of temples that were destroyed in the aftermath of Ghurid expansion, and many make use of materials garnered from earlier structures. The question of temple desecration is perhaps the most contentious issue raised by the mosques, not least because of its potential ramifications in the present. The theme of architectural destruction has been central to the construction of sectarian histories in which mosque construction and temple destruction are mutually conditioning activities.[71] Paradoxically perhaps, the demolition of the Baburi Masjid at Ayodhya in 1992 by those attempting to (re)erect a temple dedicated to Rama that the sixteenth-century mosque was assumed to have replaced has also provided the impetus for a number of re-evaluations of this tendentious question.

REWRITING SACRED SPACE

Despite indications of an effort to foster a degree of economic and political continuity in north India after the Ghurid conquest, the exclusively monotheist nature of Islam meant that Indic modes of consolidating authority through the incorporation of regional deities or appeals to a common ideology of sacral kingship manifest in temple cults were not an option for the Ghurid sultan and his agents. The dearth of evidence for the conversion of Hindu or Jain temples into mosques may be explained by the nature of the temple, and its role as a focus for individual rather than congregational prayer. Unlike Syrian basilical churches, which could be converted into mosques by the simple expedient of internal reorientation, or fire temples, which offered a domed chamber that might be adapted for communal prayer, temples with *garbagrihas* and *pradakshinapatha*s designed to accommodate small groups of worshippers were not well suited to this purpose.

In addition to fulfilling the religious needs of the Muslim community, the construction of mosques inscribed a dialectics of absence and presence upon existing urban landscapes. Early thirteenth-century accounts refer to the destruction of idols (*aṣnam*) and idol-houses (*but-khāna*s), and their replacement by mosques, madrasas and khanqahs, in the wake of the conquest.[72] The rhetorical function of such claims mitigates taking them at face value, but some of the post-conquest mosques do appear to have been constructed on the sites of earlier temples. Since the jurists distinguish between non-Muslims who capitulate voluntarily (*ṣulhan*) and those defeated by force (*'anwatan*), the fate of the principal temples of each city may have varied according to the specific circumstances in which it fell into Ghurid hands.[73]

The political utility of destruction can hardly be doubted, especially in light of the temple's role as a nexus between deity, icon, and ruler. This relationship was often expressed through shared nomenclature, ritual, and shared attributes that adduced a constitutive relationship between the tutelary images housed in dynastic temples and the rulers who installed them. According to the *Bṛhat Saṁhitā* (fifth–sixth century AD) for example, silver images will increase their patron's fame, and gold his health, while images of stone will ensure that land accrues to him. Conversely, damage to the image augurs ill for both its patron and the polity over which he presides:

If a pike is seen driven into an image, the master will perish with his family; if there be holes in images, the master will suffer from diseases and never ending troubles.[74]

Within the competitive discourse of Indian kingship, the construction of a temple also communicated the ability to command resources. Consequently, as Inden notes, royal patronage of temples, 'was as much an act of war as it was an act of peace, as much a political as it was a religious act,' one that could be the culmination of a successful military campaign.[75] The centrality of temples to the competitive discourse of Indian kingship was underlined by their use as sites for the recontexualization of images of tutelary deities and the doorkeepers of their shrines looted from rivals during periods of warfare.[76] In certain cases, materials purloined from the temples of a defeated rival were also carried off and incorporated into structures erected by the victor.[77]

The destruction of a rival's cities, forts, and palaces and the erection of commemorative pillars on the sites of destruction was an accepted feature of medieval Indic warfare.[78] Most modern historians and architectural historians have assumed, however, that the Ghurids and their agents were distinguished from their Rajput adversaries by the theological motivations adduced for such acts. Hence, instances of temple desecration that pre-date the Ghurid conquest or that do not involve invading Turks are usually dismissed as anomalies. As Brajadulal Chattopadhyaya has observed, however, to see cases of image destruction and temple desecration in pre-Ghurid South Asia as aberrations is to ignore the evidence that they offer for the relationship between instantiations of sacrality and temporal power.[79] In contrast to those historians who see such acts as anomalies, others have mined medieval texts and inscriptions in order to demonstrate the utility of temple desecration and destruction to the exercise of medieval Indic kingship.

The divergent opinions on the topic are represented by the contributions of André Wink and Richard Eaton to this volume. Wink's approach represents the dominant historiographic tradition, within which a theologically motivated iconoclasm considered essential to Islamic identity is opposed to the iconophilia of Indic cultures, with instances of pre-conquest temple desecration and image destruction consequently seen as aberrations. The iconoclasm of invading Turks is thus assumed to be theologically motivated, in contradistinction to the political acts of indigenous Hindu kings in appropriating the images of their rivals.

Conversely, the political implications of iconoclastic acts undertaken by Muslims appear as unintended consequences of a theological opposition to figuration.

By contrast, Eaton suggests that the expansion of the Ghurid sultanate and its Delhi successor were characterized by the selective desecration or destruction of temples that housed the tutelary deities of defeated ruling houses. According to Eaton, selective destructions served not only to attack the infrastructure of rival religious formations, but also to eradicate a rival's power base and with it the possibility of dynastic revanchism. The perception of a link between the exercise of political power and its constitution in temple patronage can hardly be doubted: it is, for example, evident in a *farmān* (edict) issued by the Delhi sultan Iltutmish in 1217, in which he states that those who consistently oppose the state should be punished by the destruction of their icons and the temples that house them.[80]

More controversial is Eaton's conclusion that 'temples had been the natural sites for the contestation of kingly authority well before the coming of the Muslim Turks to India,' therefore, 'by targeting for desecration those temples that were associated with defeated kings, conquering Turks, when they made their own bid for sovereign domain in India, were subscribing to, even while they were exploiting, indigenous notions of royal legitimacy.' Implicit in this evaluation is the suggestion that, as a tool of military and political expansion, temple desecration represents a point of continuity rather than rupture with pre-conquest royal practices. This suggestion may seem counterintuitive, but finds some support in the treatment of reused materials in the Ghurid mosques themselves. It is now clear, for example, that the re-erection of a fourth-century iron pillar in the centre of Delhi's Qutb Mosque, probably in the 1220s, has less to do with specifically 'Islamic' modes of commemorating victory (and thus a rupture with the preceding order) than with the adoption and continuation of pre-conquest commemorative practices, including the appropriation and re-erection of antique pillars (*lats* and *stambhas*).[81]

Since acts of temple desecration undertaken by 'Hindu' rulers are usually considered cultural anomalies, the empirical, epigraphic, and textual evidence for them and the specific circumstances in which they occur have never been subject to systematic analysis. The dearth of such analysis hampers any attempt to evaluate the impact of temple desecration on the cultural life of north India during the last decades of the twelfth century and first of the thirteenth. However, reports of rulers placing portrait sculptures in front of their temples, their hands joined in supplication as a safeguard against the destruction of their temple by invading rulers suggest that the practice was by no means unknown.[82] In addition, we have the evidence of numerous inscriptions containing imprecations against those who would damage or destroy temples. Although later than the period under discussion here, the foundation text of a Shiva temple found at Kunkali in Goa and dated S. 1501/1579 AD is typical in the inter-sectarian threats and promises that it offers to those who would damage the *linga* that the temple housed:

> He who, being a Musulman, destroys it will incur the sin of the violation of the holy place. He who, being a Marhata (Maratha), destroys it, will incur the sin of killing a Brahmin. By reconstructing it, a Musulman will have the merit of going on a pilgrimage to Mecca. He who, being a Marhata (Maratha), reconstructs it, will have the merit of a pilgrimage to Kashi (Benares).[83]

A brief overview of the textual and epigraphic evidence suggests that acts of temple desecration or destruction can be associated with all of the major political formations of pre-conquest India, north and south: Chalukyas, Rashtrakutas, Pratiharas, Cholas, and Pandyas. The desecration of the Temple of Kalapriya at Kalpi near Kanauj was, for example, included in a record of the accomplishments of the tenth-century Rashtrakuta raja Indra II.[84] The plundering of temple property was almost an established tradition among Kashmiri rulers of tenth and eleventh centuries: among the many examples that might be cited, Ksemagupta of Kashmir (1063–89) had the Jayendra vihara in Kashmir burnt to the ground in pursuit of a political rival. Gathering from it the brass image of Buddha (for its metal content?) and stone from numerous delapidated temples, he built a Shiva temple in a prominent location in Srinagar. His son and successor, Harsha (r. 1089–1111)—who effected the ritual defilement of temple icons by leprous (and therefore ritually impure) mendicants—reportedly planned the desecration of this temple upon his accession, plotting to remove its golden ornaments and to reuse its stones (themselves taken from earlier structures) in the construction of a bridge.[85]

The circumstances in which this was plotted recall reports in the *Prabandhachintamani* that the western Chalukya ruler Ajayapala (r. ca. 1171–6) demolished many of the temples erected by his father and predecessor Kumarapala, a convert to Jainism.[86] Jain temples were peculiarly susceptible to damage and desecration, and the Paramara ruler Subhatavarman (r. 1193–1210) is said to have plundered a number of them at Dabhoi and Cambay.[87] During the same period, the Chola rajas of southeastern India, who had strong Shaivite leanings, not only destroyed Buddhist stupas and Jain temples, but also Vaishnavite shrines, including the celebrated temple at Chidambaram. In Saka 993–4, for example, the Chola king Rajendradeva invaded the western Chalukyan region of Belvola; according to an inscription recording local history, he burned down many temples and defiled the Jain temples that stood there.[88]

This was part of a broader pattern of inter-religious tension and conflict in south India that on more than one occasion led to the desecration or destruction of a place of worship associated with one faith, and its replacement by the shrine of another. The *Cūlavamsa* reports numerous instances of temple desecration in Sri Lanka between the fourth and twelfth centuries, many related to various military encounters between indigenous Buddhist rulers and the Pandyas and Cholas of south India, who looted and burnt temples and monasteries, seizing golden images and breaking open stupas in their search for treasure. In the reign of King Magha (ca. 1214–35), for example, an invading Kalinga army from Kerala destroyed Buddhist shrines, and monasteries, along with their libraries. We also encounter Sri Lankan rulers destroying monasteries and reusing their component elements in the construction of new *vihāras*, while in various internecine struggles for the royal succession temples and monasteries were looted and destroyed, golden images and temple adornments smashed, and their gold purloined.[89]

Similar phenomena are attested in north India: a twelfth- or thirteenth-century inscription from Badaun in Uttar Pradesh, which gives the genealogy of a Shaivite ascetic records that one of his predecessors called Varamshiva who hailed from the Chalukya capital of Anahilawad (Patan), in Gujarat 'destroyed by the efficacy of his mantras a Buddhist idol in Dakṣiṇapatha' as one of the proofs of his piety and superhuman power.[90] Earlier tensions in north India are reflected in the destruction of Buddhist monasteries by Shaivites in the northwest during the seventh and eighth centuries and in a series of ninth- and tenth-century metal and stone sculptures that show Buddhist figures trampling Hindu deities.[91]

Regardless of the rhetorical frames within which such acts were inscribed, they had material consequences directly related to competition for the control of sacred sites and the material and spiritual benefits that flowed from this. A pattern of erasure and reinscription accompanied the conversion of Jain cave temples to Shaivite worship following the conversion of the Pandya ruler from Jainism to Shaivism in seventh-century south India, while the Rashtrakutas of the Deccan converted Buddhist viharas into 'Hindu' shrines, a process that entailed chiselling the Buddhist images found in existing cave shrines. The process repeats itself in the conversion of Jain cave temples to Shaivite (or Vaishnavite) worship in South India, where Jain images were erased and Shaivite images installed in their stead or materials from one shrine used to construct another.[92] These conversions were sometimes rationalized in narratives concerning the 'rediscovery' of sacred sites obscured by impious interlopers, narratives that find interesting counterparts in the encounters between Christians and Muslims in the medieval Mediterranean.

Although the particular circumstances in which these acts occurred merits further investigation, they suggest that pre-Ghurid temple desecration can be associated with three broad types of phenomena, which are not mutually exclusive: territorial expansion or dynastic change; new accessions within the same dynastic line; rivalry between different sectarian groups competing for converts, political patronage or control of sacred sites. The practice appears to have been particularly common during the eleventh and twelfth centuries, on the eve of the Ghurid conquests, but this may just reflect the abundance of sources for these periods.

The destruction of 'pagan' temples and the mosques of 'heretics' was equally instrumental to those seeking to assert their role as champions of Sunni orthodoxy, and one further factor that is rarely considered but that is clearly relevant is the role of architectural destruction in intra-Muslim struggles for authority or territory in eastern Iran and Afghanistan. The instrumentalization of architectural destruction in struggles between the Shi'i Isma'ilis and their Sunni opponents is the obvious example. Around 965, for example, the Isma'ili rulers of Multan destroyed the Sun Temple of that city, and erected a new congregational mosque on its site, abandoning the long-established Sunni Friday Mosque.[93] When Mahmud of Ghazni, an implacable enemy of the Isma'ilis, captured Multan in 1026 (en route to destroy the temple at Somnath), he razed the Isma'ili Friday Mosque which had been constructed on the site of the celebrated Sun Temple of the city six decades earlier, leaving its site vacant (a kind of *spolium* signifying the supercession of a rival dispensation), and restoring the original Sunni congregational mosque to its former pre-eminence.

The destruction of mosques and madrasas was also integral to the factional rivalries between the different sectarian strains of Sunni Islam in the eastern Islamic world during the eleventh and twelfth centuries. In the first decades of the eleventh century, the Karramis (the Sunni sect with which the Ghurids were initially associated) of Nishapur instituted a reign of terror against the Shi'is, destroying their mosque, and even smashing the minbar of at least one respected Sunni imam. A *fitna* (civil disturbance) between Karramis, Shafi'is, and Hanafis in Nishapur in 488–9/1095–6 resulted in the razing of the main Karrami madrasa in the city. Similarly, in 556/1161 the 'Aqil mosque, one of the Shafi'i mosques of the city, was destroyed during factional fighting; around the same time, the Shi'is of Aleppo in nothern Syria destroyed a Sunni madrasa built by Nur al-Din Zangi.[94] Writing of factional rivalries in the Iranian city of Isfahan—whose Friday Mosque suffered significant damage when it was attacked by a heterodox faction in 551/1121–2—the geographer Yaqut reports that each time once faction gained the upper hand it plundered, burnt and ruined the quarter of the other.[95]

These events were not instruments of state policy, but sectarian conflicts with political overtones. Nevertheless, they find analogies with acts of selective destruction during periods of political conflict. For obvious reasons, the destruction of mosques belonging to a Sunni co-religionists was seldom heralded in the Arabic or Persian chronicles of those whose armies carried out such acts; instead, we tend to hear of them either in regional chronicles or histories written by non-Muslims. The destruction of the Friday mosque of Zarang, the rebellious former Saffarid capital of Sistan in 394/1003, by the Indian troop contingents of the sultan Mahmud, the *sālār-i Hinduyān* is a case in point, one that is at odds with Mahmud's role as a champion of Sunni orthodoxy.[96] The sack of the Zarang mosque was far from a unique event. From a Syriac chronicle, for example, we learn that when the Seljuq sultan Tughril Beg sacked the rebellious city of Sinjar in the Jazira region of northern Iraq in 459/1057 he not only destroyed its palaces, but also burnt the Friday Mosque of the city to the ground.[97] Similarly, during the sack of Ghazna in 1150, the Ghurid malik 'Ala' al-Din Husayn razed many of the city's monuments, sparing only the tombs of Mahmud and two of his admired successors.[98] These actions are best understood as both revenge and a means of destroying the traditional power-base of the Ghaznavids.

The replacement of temples with congregational mosques in major adminstrative centres constituted a rewriting of urban space that was both pragmatic (providing the Muslim community with a space to fulfil the requirements of ritual prayer) and ideological (signifying the supercession of the old political order and the permanence of the new). As in other contexts in which the new Muslim rulers were a tiny minority, patronage of large-scale urban mosques formed part of what the art historian Oleg Grabar has dubbed a 'symbolic appropriation' of the land.[99] This was apparently evident to subject communities, for a Persian poem written some time before the seventh/thirteenth century presents the revanchist aspirations of Iranian Zoroastrians in terms of architectural destruction and reversal, using epic frames of demonic mythologisation common to medieval Hindu-Muslim encounter:

> Lo, we shall pull down their mosques and set up again the sacred fires. We shall destroy the idol-temples and purge them from the world, so that the foul offspring of demons shall become invisible and [vanish] from this world.[100]

Such antagonisms may explain the accusation that during the reign of the Solanki ruler Siddharaja Jayasimha (ca. 1094–1143), the Zoroastrian (*Mugh*) community of Cambay incited the Hindus of the town to destroy the Friday mosque of the minority community residing there.[101]

With the benefit of hindsight, the permanency of Turkic hegemony appears inevitable, but this was not a given at the time that the mosques discussed in this volume were constructed. On the contrary, the possibility of dynastic revanchism in the unsettled conditions of the 1190s was a real concern. In, or shortly after, 589/1193 Hariraja, brother of the defeated Prithviraja Chauhan III, led a revolt against Ghurid rule and briefly succeeded in regaining Ajmir, reportedly damaging Muslim shrines there. Chauhan revanchism seems to have destabilized most of northwestern India, for the *Tāj al-Ma'āthir* indicates that Delhi was finally occupied by the armies of the sultan only after the involvement of its ruler in the revolt of Hariraja.[102] Although Ajmir was taken in 588–89/1192, the earliest dated inscription in the Arhai-din-ka-Jhompra hails from 595/1198–9, several years after the original conquest of the city. The persistence of the temples of Chauhan tutelary deities on the site during the period when Prithiviraja's son ruled as a Ghurid vassal might explain the time-lag, in which case the date of the mosque probably marks the end of Chauhan rule at Ajmir.

The architecture and siting of the Indo-Ghurid mosques suggests ambivalence towards the likelihood of perdurance. In Bada'un, Delhi, Hansi, and probably Multan, Ajmir, and Kaman, the first congregational mosques were located within pre-existing forts, a practice followed later as the Delhi sultanate expanded southwards. While the choice of locale represented continuity in sites of administrative and military significance, it also suggests a concern with security. This concern may also be reflected in the defensive appearance of the mosques at Ajmir, Delhi, and Khatu, and the presence of large projecting rectangular entrances like those found in the twelfth-century *ribāts* or fortified halting places along the trade routes of eastern Iran, among them Ribat-i Sharaf on the road between Nishapur and Merv.

While emphasizing that architectural destruction, including the razing of religious monuments, was an integral part of pre-modern warfare in India and the Islamic world, it is also important to highlight differences in the meanings of such acts and the contexts in which they occurred. The destruction of tribal icons and the appropriation of their shrines were integral to the Islamicization of Arabia, providing a powerful precedent to which the reiterative rhetoric of later dynasts, including the Ghaznavids, often laid claim. However, although image destruction and temple desecration were also known in pre-conquest South Asia—and may even have been considered religiously meritorious in certain circumstances—they lacked the powerful imprimatur of a historiographic tradition in which iconoclasm was seen as a defining act of a newly emergent religion. The rapid proliferation of temple desecration at the end of the twelfth century may reflect little more than the unprecedented scale and speed of Ghurid expansion itself, but the shock of these events must have resounded through all levels of society. The Jain writer Jinapala Suri, who was present at the fall of Ajmir to the Ghurid armies in 588/1192, captures something of the chaos and dislocation of that moment.[103] The impact of the post-conquest arrangements on the population, their daily rituals, and experience of familiar cityscapes can hardly be doubted.

As early as the eleventh century, Jain texts tell of icons attacked by Ghaznavid iconoclasts avenging the blows of their attackers, or decamping of their own volition, but such supernatural prophylaxis and protection could not always be relied upon, and the practice of burying or concealing icons to protect them from marauding armies is well documented.[104] A Sanskrit inscription carved in the name of the nephew of Jayachandra, the Gahadavala ruler of Kanauj defeated and killed by the Ghurids in 1193 provides a rare insight into the emotional impact of these events, albeit one framed within the conventions of royal rhetoric. The text commemorates the protective concealment of a Durga icon from Etawah fort by a priest (*ācārya*) in the service of Jayachandra:

> My rationality has been destroyed because of my fear of the Mlecchas. With great sorrow, touching her with my head (to honour her), I place this Durgā, the dweller of the fort and destroyer of bad luck, into this pit, till the god Skanda turns their glory (Sun) to dust. When ill fate meets the Yavanas, she might re-appear, or manifest herself again amidst uproar.[105]

Highlighting elements of congruence in the instrumental deployment of architectural destruction by north Indian rajas and their Ghurid successors should not therefore obscure significant disjunctions in the relationship between the exercise of political authority and the patronage of monumental religious architecture, a point well made in Sunil Kumar's contribution to this volume.

The tension between new and old dispensations is in fact evoked by the foundation text half-obscured in the gloom above the principal (eastern) entrance to the Qutb Mosque in Delhi, which reads:

> This fort was conquered and this congregational mosque built in the months of the year 587 [1191–92] by the amir, the great glorious commander of the army (*ifahsalār ajil kabīr*), Pole of the World and Religion (*Quṭb al-dawlat wa'l-dīn*), the *amīr al-umarā* Aibek *sulṭanī* (i.e. slave of the sultan) may God strengthen his helpers. [The materials of] twenty-seven idol temples (*but-khāna*), on each idol temple two million *diliwāl*s had been spent, were used in this mosque. May God the Great and Glorious have mercy on that slave who prays for the faith of the good builder.[106]

The foundation text thus constitutes the mosque as a *lieu de mémoire* inscribed with the conditions of its own production. It is, however, marked by several idiosyncrasies, including the early use of Persian. However, the Ghurid complex at Chisht (562/1167) has a Persian foundation text, and Persian also occurs on an historical text on the outer tympanum of the same gate that names Qutb al-Din Aybek as the builder of the mosque, and in some of the less formal inscriptions of the Delhi mosque.[107] The commemoration of reuse is also unusual in a foundation text of this period even if the practice was common. In addition, the date given for the foundation is at odds with that of 588/1192, which early thirteenth-century Persian histories give for the capture of Delhi. It is possible, therefore, that the Persian text was in fact set in place later than the date cited within it, perhaps during the reign of Iltutmish (d. 1236).[108] Whether the text was set in place in 587/1191–2 or a decade or so later, the bald facts comunicated to those entering the mosque point to a disjunction in the established order encapsulated by the seizure of the fort, the appropriation of the site, and the reuse of materials (some perhaps taken from Chauhan temples that once stood within the fort) to construct a new place of worship for the new Turkic overlords.

Like the medieval histories into which accounts of temple desecration are inscribed, the text at the entrance to the Delhi mosque has been read as a transparent statement of historical fact, a triumphal statement of disjunction and disruption that locates the reuse of materials within a theology of iconoclasm. Using these texts and inscriptions as factual representations of the past, scholars have often fallen into the trap of conflating historical acts with epigraphic or textual representations of them, ignoring the distinction between the primary act of founding a building and the secondary representation of that act.[109] In fact, despite its emphasis on the mining of pre-conquest temples for structural materials, closer inspection of the foundation text and its content reveals a rather complex relationship between the old and new orders.

Most commentators have taken the given figure of twenty-seven temples mentioned in the foundation text quite literally, at least one demonstrating its veracity by correlating the number of reused pillars in the mosque to the number used in a 'typical' Hindu temple.[110] The figure coincides, however, with the traditional number of *nakshatra*s or lunar mansions in Indic cosmology.[111] Descriptions of Ghurid monuments in Firuzkuh and India in slightly later texts sometimes stress their cosmological significance in numerological terms (the Qutb Minar is, for example, often said to have 365 steps), but here the idea is expressed by drawing upon the norms of Indic cosmology.[112] Furthermore, the manner in which the cost of materials is coded in the Delhi text—in the local currency of *diliwāl*s rather than the dirhams used in Afghanistan and the central Islamic lands—represents another point of continuity with indigenous norms.

The citation of a figure for the value of the constituent materials reportedly reused in the mosque is highly unusual among Islamic foundation texts—indeed I can think of no other example. It conforms, however, to the way in which certain kinds of religious patronage were memorialized in pre-modern Indic texts. For example, the *Rājataraṅgiṇī*, the royal chronicle of the Kashmiri kings compiled just decades before the Ghurid conquest, informs us that Lalitaditya of Kashmir (d. 760) expended 84,000 *tola*s of gold on an icon of Vishnu.[113] Once again, it seems likely that figure should not be taken literally, but was chosen for its auspicious connotations.

The commemoration of cost and value is also integral to descriptions of temples encountered in Arabic and Persian texts even before the Ghurid conquest, manifest for example in al-'Utbi's account of Mahmud of Ghazna's expedition against the city of Mathura, which cites the sultan's *fatḥnāma* (victory dispatch) eulogizing the main temple of the city:

> Should anyone wish to build the equivalent of these edifices, he would be unable to, even if he spent a hundred million dirhams over the course of a hundred years, employing master workmen and craftsmen of magical skill.[114]

The citation of a monetary value for the architectural materials of the temples establishes a relationship with the idols that they contained, and whose constituent metals are similarly parsed in the same text.

The historical inscriptions of Indo-Ghurid mosques have usually been considered as distinct from the prolific Qur'anic texts that they bear, but the content of the historical text on the inner lintel of the eastern entrance of the Delhi mosque suggests that it was intended to be read along with the Qur'anic inscription that accompanies it. The text consists of Qur'an 3:91–9:

> From those who deny and die disbelieving will never be accepted an earthful of gold if proferred by them as ransom. For them is grievous punishment, and none will help them. You will never come to piety unless you spend of things you love; and whatever you spend is known to God.[115]

These verses evoke an economy of piety in which hoarding and accumulation of gold was proscribed in favour of its circulation for the benefit of the *umma*, the Muslim community. Exegetical traditions amplify this theme, identifying an association between hoarding and the economy of unbelief. Moreover, a cultural predisposition towards accumulation is a marked feature of Arabic and Persian writings on India, a quality that is often given a negative spiritual gloss.[116]

The juxtaposition of historical and Qur'anic texts appears to locate the reuse of architectural materials within the broader context of this economy of piety. Just as the material resources encapsulated in looted icons could be freed for circulation in the service of Islam (often by funding the construction of mosques), so the constituent materials of demolished temples or derelict structures could be recycled to the same end. However, the emphatic stress on the need for this to be a gesture made not under duress but from belief and renunciation is striking and (questions of linguistic access notwithstanding) may have been intended as an invitation to conversion, an end that Qur'anic epigraphy sometimes served in other post-conquest situations.

Employing tropes associated with the representation of royal patronage in pre-conquest Sanskrit texts, the content of this Persian inscription raises questions of cognition, continuity, and transmission that are no less relevant to the adjoining mosque. The architecture of the mosque is characterized by a complex interplay between past and present, tradition and innovation common to Indo-Ghurid coinage and the political arrangements made in the wake of the conquest.[117] This aspect of the mosques has, however, been occluded by a scholarly tradition that has generally denied the very possibility that temple and mosque might share any aesthetic, formal, or iconographic values. Failing to consider reuse as a positive mode of reception, for example, nineteenth—and twentieth-century observers who lauded the quality of the carvings from which the Indo-Ghurid mosques were constructed generally denied the same appreciation to their Muslim patrons. On the contrary, the act of reuse was even portrayed as an anti-aesthetic gesture. An account of the Qutb Mosque complex in Delhi written by J.D. Beglar and quoted to the Second Congress of Orientalists in London in 1874 makes clear the contemporary reasoning:

> Indeed, on *à priori* grounds, we should expect this want of appreciation of truthful ornamentation among the Mahomedans, a barbarous and warlike people, whose religion narrowed their minds, naturally none of the most liberal, and demanded the suppression of aesthetic feelings .... It is only after the Mughal conquest that Mahomedan architecture begins to be beautiful.[118]

Twentieth-century scholarship took this idea one step further, identifying the screen added to the Qutb Mosque at Delhi in 1198 (Plate 3), and that added to the Ajmir mosque three decades later (Plate 11) as unsuccessful attempts to veil the alien appearance of the earlier prayer-halls that lay behind them, comprised as they were of 'Hindu' materials.[119] Indeed, the Delhi screen (rather than the mosque with which it is associated) has been hailed as the true beginning of Islamic architecture in India, although its corbelled arches and domes are routinely described as false or pseudo versions of the real (Iranian, arcuate) thing.[120]

With the different values that they ascribe not only to reused materials (Plates 2 and 14) but also to the practice of recycling itself, the papers in this volume by Robert Hillenbrand and Michael Meister represent divergent approaches to the question of reuse. Articulating what has been the dominant view, the former reads the fact and manner of reuse as both a pragmatic way of capitalizing on temple desecration and a triumphal gesture, a derogation of cultural traditions materialized in carved stones whose recontextualization and recarving expressed 'Muslim' victory by means of a metonymy. By contrast, Meister's essays note that while some of the material used to construct the mosques may have come from temples targeted as symbols of the *ancien régime*, the majority of it was redeployed in a manner congruent with pre-conquest architectural practice. Instead of a violent rejectionism, Meister sees in the carvings of the mosques at Ajmir and Kaman evidence 'of a sort of empathetic response of local workmen,' whose work for Turkic patrons was informed by a search for similes between Indic and Persianate architectural forms, a process that implies the ascription of positive value to recycled materials.

As Carl Ernst has pointed out, Muslims who wrote about Hindu temples (and presumably also those observers who never committed their impressions to paper), 'had complex reactions based as much on aesthetic and political considerations as on religion.'[121] The rupture and reinscription noted by each author may, therefore, be part of the same phenomenon and not only the mutually exclusive products of modern analysis. The dialectical nature of the foundation text above the main entrance to the Qutb Mosque suggests this, and (paradoxically perhaps) the point can also be made by reference to the treatment of figural imagery on reused materials.

Like the larger phenomenon of temple desecration, the question of figuration has served as a touchstone of alterity, pitting a monolithic indigenous iconophilia against an Islamic iconophobia constructed as its foil. Although figural imagery proliferated in Ghaznavid and Ghurid palaces and on portable objects, for cultural and religious reasons figuration was generally avoided in the embellishment of medieval mosques.[122] Rare exceptions include pre-Islamic monuments converted for use as mosques after campaigns of conquest: the enduring presence of figural imagery in the Sasanian structures converted for use as mosques after the Arab conquest of Iran in the seventh century is frequently remarked upon in the medieval sources.[123] The construction of mosques from richly carved architectural materials that proliferated with a myriad of celestial nymphs (*apsaras*), dwarfs (*pramathas*) radiant lion faces (*kīrttimukhas*) and occasional deities (*murtis*) presented patrons and builders with a problem that had not arisen in pre-Ghurid Indian mosques—which adopt the simple expedient of substituting vegetal ornament and inscriptions for anthropomorphic and zoomorphic imagery—or in Ghurid monuments constructed from fired brick in the Indus Valley.

Assertions about the treatment of images in Indo-Ghurid mosques have often been underwritten by unexamined assumptions about the nature of Islam itself. Puzzled as to the visibility of figural ornament on the exterior lintels of the windows at the Qutb Mosque, the nineteenth-century archaeologist James Cunningham concluded: '... as it is very unlikely that these figures would have been exposed to the sight of the early Musalmâns, I conclude that these stones must have also been carefully plastered over.'[124] The voluptuous semi-naked bodies that appear throughout the mosque may have led Victorian gentlemen scholars and their successors to conclude that the images on reused materials were originally covered, but defaced as they are, they were perfectly acceptable from a theological point of view.[125]

The extent to which a pre-existing figural vocabulary was considered problematic can in fact be determined from the degree and nature of the alterations to it. These suggest a differential approach, with anthropomorphic imagery standing at one end of a spectrum that ranges from obliteration to toleration. Alterations to anthropomorphic imagery are ubiquitous. Concentrated on the most affective aspects of the images—their face and eyes—they range in nature from total erasure to the ubiquitous gouging of the face, and from careful retooling to crude chiseling of facial features. This focus on the head and face conforms to the spirit and letter of proscriptions on figuration in Islam and to iconoclastic practice in other areas of the medieval Islamic world.[126]

The treatment of zoomorphic imagery reveals a more ambivalent attitude: although animal figures are occasionally defaced they are just as often left intact, with the result that birds and mythological creatures such as *maqaras* appear alongside headless torsos and noseless faces.[127] Similarly, on the pillars of the Ajmir mosque and in the interiors of the corbelled domes found in Delhi and Khatu paired birds or narrow friezes of *haṃsas* (auspicious geese) continue to exist unaltered. The preservation of these friezes in Khatu is particularly striking, for this is the most starkly aniconic of the mosques, a quality achieved by the sparing use of material bearing figural carving.

The most dramatic evidence for a selective approach to figuration is provided by the reception of the radiant horned lion face (kīrttimukha), a ubiquitous figure in pre-conquest iconography. In the Friday mosque of Delhi, the image of the kīrttimukha appears more than thirty times on the trabeate lintels that still remain in place (roughly fifty per cent of the original number), and innumerable more times on the reused columns that support them. Not only the form but the logic of the image is preserved, for it often appears above windows and doors, as prescribed in Sanskrit treatises on architecture and witnessed in numerous surviving medieval temples.[128] In several instances, the face of the kīrttimukha remains untouched, while those of the apsaras flanking it have been chiselled or hammered away (Plate 13).

The proliferation of this figure throughout the mosques contravenes both the spirit of the proscriptions relating to images in Islam and established architectural practice, while adumbrating any notion of an essential and undifferentiated iconophobia. The disembodied nature of the kīrttimukha image might have facilitated its adoption, for the hadiths (prophetic traditions) prescribe decapitation as a means of rendering an image acceptable, but it may also have been valued for its talismanic qualities.

This selective approach to figuration included the differential deployment of figural material. For example, the confinement of reworked figural material to the upper levels of the mosque at Ajmir points to a spatial hierarchy governing the deployment of figural pillars and beams, with the most exuberantly iconic shafts obscured by reuse in the upper registers of the multi-tiered columns, the most aniconic reserved for the lower and more visible shafts (Plate 14). Similarly, in the Shahi Mosque at Khatu, the most starkly aniconic of any of the four mosques considered here, the *nalamandapa*, the pavilion facing the prayer-hall, is replete with images of the horned lion (kīrttimukha) that have generally been effaced on the trabeate beams reused in the construction of the prayer-hall itself. As at Ajmir, even here kīrttimukhas are still visible at points on the carved ceiling slabs hidden in the upper reaches of the superstructure.

Particularly striking is the careful erasure of the kīrttimukha figures carved on the columns that flank the mihrab of the Shahi Masjid at

Khatu (Plate 6), another point of similarity to the Arhai-din-ka-Jhonpra Mosque at Ajmir. This reticence about the use of figural ornament in the qibla area is common to other mosques in the group. In the Qutb Mosque in Delhi, for example, the pillars reused in the qibla bay contain fewer figural carvings than those found in many other areas of the mosque, and their figural capitals are more thoroughly defaced than those in other locations.

In addition to this stratification of interior space by the selective alteration and location of figural carving, exterior space could also be differentiated by the massing of richly carved figural material. Examples include the exterior entrances to the mulūk khānas, the royal chambers in the northwestern corners of the mosques at Delhi and Kaman (visible in Plates 1 and 7, top right). In Delhi, an entire door-frame was appropriated and reused in toto (Plate 12), whereas in Kaman we are dealing with a collage of reused materials distinguishing the entrance to the mulūk khāna. In both cases, antique slabs carved with lions were chosen for the threshold, while at Kaman large elephant capitals project from the elevated porch that leads to it. As royal beasts, elephants, and lions were evidently considered appropriate adornments for these royal chambers.

The hierarchization of space through the selective deployment of reused carvings is equally evident, if less immediately apparent, in the creative reimagining of an aniconic vocabulary to stratify sacred space, providing potential insights into how these spaces were conceived and how they functioned. Although it is evident in all of the surviving Indo-Ghurid mosques, this phenomenon is most apparent in the Chaurasi Kambha Mosque at Kaman near Bharatpur in Rajasthan. As Meister notes in his essay on this mosque, 'the pattern of re-use of pillars and other parts suggests a defined attempt to create a hierarchy of ornament within the new mosque.' Meister sees in the enterprise not the death-knell of indigenous architectural traditions, but evidence for a reconceptualization of established architectural iconographies and idioms under the exigencies of new patterns of patronage.[129]

PATRON AND MASON

The nexus between guild, ruler, and religion that is a pronounced feature of pre-Ghurid architectural patronage was undoubtedly disrupted by the conquest and the new conditions prevailing in its aftermath, but just as continuities in Indian coin issues suggest continuity in mint personnel, empirical and epigraphic evidence points to continuities in workshop practices. The names of the *shilpīs* (craftsmen or architects) and *sūtradhāras* (masons) preserved in the twelfth—to fourteenth-century graffiti on the Qutb Minar (Plate 10) are all Hindu. A Sanskrit inscription of Samvat 1426/1369 AD on the Qutb Minar, invokes Viśvakarma, the divine architect of the universe and ultimate source of architectural knowledge.[130] The invocation of Viśvakarma is a standard element in mason's inscriptions on pre—and post-Ghurid Indian temples, and its appearance here underlines the degree of continuity in the working practices (and indeed cognitive categories) of the masons comprising the guilds.

In his study of transcultural elites and their architectural patronage in the Deccan during the fourteenth century, Phillip Wagoner makes two points that are equally relevant to the twelfth-century mosques under consideration here: first, that whether expansive or minimal, the masons' comprehension of the patron's brief 'would have been mediated through a series of cognitive filters provided by the conceptual categories upon which Indic architectural practice was based;' second, this process of mediation was dependent upon 'the discovery of fortuitous areas of convergence between the two cultures in question.'[131] The fortuitous convergences that Wagoner notes are cognates for the similes between different traditions that Meister, in his essay on the mosques at Kaman and Khatu, suggests shaped the 'translation' of architectural forms in the Ghurid mosques of India.

The processes of mediation through which this translation was effected are usually imagined as a simple negotiation between Muslim patron or overseer and Hindu master mason (sūtradhāra), with the relative agency of each varying in accordance with the predilections and sympathies of those representing this imagined exchange.[132] In his essay, Fritz Lehmann envisions a division of labour in which formal and decorative elements were assigned to different agents:

> The Turkish patrons clearly were firm on overall design, the fairly standardized layout of a mosque, the use of arches, mihrab niche and mimbar, but seem to have been free to local suggestions on decoration and execution, and perhaps did not know enough about building technology in the older Islamic centres to be able to provide instruction in the techniques of building the exotic Muslim forms.

By contrast, a recent variant of the indigenist paradigm emphasizes the agency of the indigenous craftsmen and their role in determining the parameters of translation. Although offering a corrective to the emphasis on rupture in colonial histories, this approach tends to marginalize the potential contribution of Muslim patrons.[133]

Texts reveal little about the organization of labour in Indo-Ghurid mosques beyond the use of elephants for both construction and destruction, but epigraphic evidence, and the empirical evidence of the mosques themselves provide some insights into the modus operandi of patron and craftsman. The foundation of the text above the eastern entrance to the Qutb Mosque in Delhi gives the name of the Ghurid sultan Mu'izz al-Din Muhammad ibn Sam, but it is unlikely that the sultan was actively involved in the project. In Ghaznavid Afghanistan and Seljuq Anatolia patrons reportedly had some role in the process of design, although the major part of the burden usually fell upon a royal agent acting as supervisor.[134] The recurrence of Qutb al-Din Aybek's name throughout the foundation texts of the Qutb Mosque indicates that here (as in Indo-Ghurid mosques at Hansi, Kaman, and elsewhere) the commissioning patron was usually a member of the *bandagān-i khāṣṣ*, the elite cadre of manumitted Turkic slaves upon whom the sultan depended for the administration of his Indian territories.

Inscriptions in the Arhai-din-ka-jhonpra mosque at Ajmir and the Qutb Mosque in Delhi tell us that some or all of the work took place under the supervision of (*fī tawallīyyat*) Abu Bakr ibn Ahmad Khalu (?) al-Harawi and Fadl ibn Abi'l-Ma'ali respectively. The latter is named twice, on both the arched screen of the mosque and on the lowest storey of the Qutb Minar.[135] The *nisba* (toponymic) of the former suggests that he may have hailed from Herat, a major artistic center within the Ghurid sultanate whose denizens also seem to have contributed to the decoration of Ghurid monuments around Multan. These were constructed from brick, however, the dominant medium in both regions; the predominance of a monumental stone medium in north Indian presumably limited the contribution that any Herati craftsmen could make.

The formula used in these inscriptions is among the earliest occurrences of a cognate expression, *bi-tawallī*, that appears in twelfth- and thirteenth-century foundation texts from Anatolia, the central Islamic lands, and Syria, where it refers to individuals who occupied the position of *mutawallī* or Supervisor of Works.[136] The mutawallī was responsible for keeping accounts and finances, hiring labour, acquiring raw materials, and commissioning a master mason. Ibn Battuta's account of the mosque planned by 'Ala al-Din Khilji in his new capital of Siri (ca. 1311) suggests that the master mason was also responsible for estimating the cost of construction.[137] The mutawallī was usually a member of the *'ulamā'* or religious class, often a *qadī* (religious judge) or *khaṭīb* (preacher): the mutawallī of the mosque that the Ghurid sultan Mu'izz al-Din endowed at Multan was also the Sheikh al-Islam.[138] The mutawallī ensured that the legal aspects of the project conformed to the Shari'a, negotiated the linguistic divide between the language of the chancery (Persian) and of foundation texts (Arabic) and sometimes provided the draft of the latter.

Epigraphic and comparative ethnographic material thus enables us to establish a chain of command from the nominal patron (the Ghurid sultan), to his agent (the Turkic slave generals), and hence to the mutawallī or supervisor of works. This distribution of labour is perfectly commensurate with what can be reconstructed for pre-conquest India, a fact that no doubt facilitated the adaptive restructuring necessitated by post-conquest conditions. The involvement of military commanders as agents of the ruler is, for example, attested in pre-conquest temple construction, as is the role of the *sthāpaka* or ācārya, the priest who ensured conformity to religious norms and sometimes functioned as a superintendent of works, the equivalent of the mutawallī. Both sthāpaka and mutawallī dealt directly with a master mason (sūtradhāra) who could also function as designer/architect, a position comparable to that of *mi'mar* in the Islamic world.[139] At the end of this chain stood the members of the guilds (*śreni*), the masons, and sculptors (shilpīs) who executed the commands of the sūtradhāra.

Despite their position at the end of this hierarchical chain, the masons seem to have had a certain leeway to exercise their initiative, as was the case with pre-conquest architectural projects.[140] The range and variation in alterations to figural imagery range, for example, suggest that while the impetus for neutralizing it derived from the patrons, the parameters of implementation were left to the agency of the individual mason. A group of identical dwarf (pramatha) capitals reused together in the southeastern corner of the Qutb Mosque in Delhi makes the point. Despite their formal affinities and proximity, their facial features have been altered in various ways: while some display jagged irregular surfaces that are clearly the result of a blow, others display a careful retooling of the effaced surface to produce an attractive smooth finish. The only common factor to the process of alteration is the attention paid to the face, a constant of the alterations to anthropomorphic carvings manifest througout the mosques.

Inspection of the monuments provides more specific insights into the order of construction. At both Ajmir and Khatu, rectangular projections on the exterior of the qibla wall indicate that the mosques—which appear to be products of a single workshop—were originally planned with three mihrabs each preceded by a single dome. In their final forms, however, both mosques were provided with only a single mihrab, albeit a spectacular example in white marble. The discrepancy suggests that the qibla wall was the first part of the mosque to be erected, as was the practice in other areas of the medieval Islamic world. The same pattern is seen in sultanate architecture: the Friday Mosque ordered by 'Ala al-Din Khalji for his capital of Siri (ca. 1311) was never constructed beyond the mihrab and qibla wall, while the Tughluqid Friday Mosque constructed in the former Kakatiya capital of Warangal in the Deccan (ca. 1323–34) never proceeded beyond the qibla bay.[141]

CONCLUSION

As noted at the outset, the Indian mosques of the Ghurids formed part of a programme of architectural patronage that also included the western cities of the Ghurid sultanate. One of the problems in conceptualizing the relationship between the Afghan and Indian monuments has been an anachronistic tendency to envisage north India and the territories of the sultanates to the northwest as possessed of boundaries analogous to those of the modern nation state. The rhetorical posturing of the medieval Arabic and Persian histories has tended to affirm this impression by reifying cultural and religious difference, depicting the boundaries between the eastern sultanates of the dār al-Islām and the neighbouring kingdoms of al-Hind as a kind of medieval iron curtain.

Although obscured by the taxonomic structures and disciplinary divisions of modern scholarship, the interrelationships between the newly conquered Indian territories and the Afghan heartlands of the Ghurid sultanate at the end of the twelfth century reveal themselves in a variety of ways. Epigraphy represents the least visible (and most unremarked) facet of this relationship. The foundation text of the Chaurasi Kambha Mosque at Kaman refers to the structure as 'an agreeable place' (*buq'at al-laṭīf*), for example, employing a phrase that also seems to have appeared in the foundation text of the Friday Mosque built by the Ghurids in Herat (599/1200).[142] Similarly, the Qutb Mosque in Delhi is described as a blessed spot (*buq'a-yi mutabarrak*) in the early thirteenth-century *Tāj al-Ma'āthir*.[143] The recurrence of these cognate phrases is significant, establishing a relationship between epigraphic and textual representations of sacred space. In fact, although the question of reuse has dominated the modern reception of Indo-Ghurid mosques, for medieval observers who wrote about their experience of the Qutb Mosque in Delhi (the only mosque of which pre-modern descriptions survive), the extraordinary ubiquity of inscriptions left a far greater impression than the recycled architectural materials from which the mosques were constructed.[144]

The proliferation of Qur'anic inscriptions in the Ghurid monuments of the Indus Valley and north India follows a precedent established in the Ghurid heartlands, whose monuments have been compared to 'huge billboards proclaiming various messages at those who enter them.'[145] The programatic nature of the Qur'anic inscriptions on Ghurid monuments has long been recognized (even if imperfectly understood). The essay by Anthony Welch, Hussein Keshani, and Alexandra Bain reproduced below demonstrates the careful selection of Qur'anic quotations to adorn the Ajmir and Delhi mosques (Plates 15–16), suggesting that what was exported to India in the last decade of the twelfth century was not only a penchant for monumental epigraphy, but also an established tradition of employing Qur'anic quotations discursively.[146]

There is a noted emphasis on idolatry and unbelief in these inscriptions, suggesting that their content was chosen to reflect the context in which they appeared. The authors of this careful study distinguish, however, between the tone and content of Qur'anic verses on the interior and exterior of the Delhi mosque (Plates 15–16), seeing the former as an address to non-Muslims and the latter selected for their relevance to those using the mosque. This raises interesting questions about access (physical, linguistic, conceptual) that are central to understanding the discursive role of Qur'anic epigraphy not only in twelfth-century India, but also in other cross-cultural contexts.

Also relevant is a fundamental linkage between campaigns against and rhetoric about heresy and unbelief, which informed the earlier selection of Qur'anic citations for inscription on Ghurid coins and monuments in Afghanistan.[147] These texts were sometimes chosen for their ability to bolster or champion specific theological doctrines contended between rival Sunni factions. The frequent references to idolatry that they contain should be understood not as allusions to those who were literally outside the fold of Islam, but as part of a contemporary polemic within which proponents of rival positions were often depicted as espousing heterodoxy or even heresy. Doctrinal schism and its correlates in architectural violence continued to be part of the cultural life of the Muslim communities of north India well into the sultanate period, following a pattern familiar from Khurasan in the preceding two centuries.[148] These and other conflicts within the Muslim community are minimized and only referred to in passing in the thirteenth-century chronicles upon which we depend for our knowledge of the period, and which present the Muslim community led by the Turkic elite as a unified monolith, despite contemporary ethnic, intra-sectarian and political tensions within it. The success of the endeavor can be measured from the fact that only recently has any attempt been made to deconstruct this monolith, and to reconstruct the complex histories of the intense rivalries out of which the Delhi sultanate emerged.[149] Seen in this light, allusions to error, falsity, and unbelief in the Qur'anic inscriptions of the Indian mosques may have constituted an address to audiences that included but also extended beyond the Hindu unbeliever.

The interrelationships between the western and eastern domains of the Ghurid sultanate are perhaps most clearly manifest in the material culture of the period. The westward circulation of Ghurid coins minted in India and the emulation of their Sanskrit inscriptions on Afghan coin issues points, for example, to transregional flows that undermine any notion of two hermetically sealed cultural spheres.[150] These flows included raw materials, crafted objects, and artisans. In addition, some of the capital used to fund the rebuilding of the Friday Mosque of Herat derived from Ghiyath al-Din's share of the golden booty taken after the fall of Ajmir, capital of the Chauhans of Śakambhari in 588/1192. The use of Indian booty to underwrite an architectural programme designed to foster Sunni orthodoxy in Khurasan reflects the increasingly complex imbrications of both regions.

Among the Chauhan booty from Ajmir were two golden birds set atop the Ghurid palace in Firuzkuh, a site usually identified with the minaret of Jam, the preeminent monument of the dynasty.[151] Whatever their original function (Garuda eagles perhaps), the golden birds recontextualized in Firuzkuh were identified as *humās*, the royal bird of Persian iconography. It was presumably this identification that rendered them desirable crowning ornaments for the Ghurid palace. The physical transposition of these representational forms was thus accompanied by a translation of their meaning, based on an assumption that they were common signifiers of royalty within Indic and Persianate iconographies of kingship. In this respect, the golden beasts in Firuzkuh suggest themselves as analogues for the antique elephants and stone lions (royal beasts *par excellence*) that were chosen during the same period to adorn the entrances to the mulūk khānas (the royal chambers) in the Qutb Mosque of Delhi (Plate 12) and the Chaurasi Kambha Mosque at Kaman (Plate 7, top right). The relationship between the content of reused carvings and the contexts in which they were redeployed implies an hermeneutic dimension to reception, a carrying over not only of material but also of meaning. This may be equally true of the haṁsa friezes or kīrttimukha images that proliferate in the Indian mosques erected for the Ghurids or their Turkic patrons, even if their transcultural meanings or the precise mechanisms by which they were assimilated is less obvious.

That this was something more than a passive acceptance and more like an active engagement with the figural vocabulary of north Indian architecture is underlined by the appearance of both haṁsa and kīrttimukha around the entrance and interior of a small stone shrine of the late twelfth or early thirteenth century at Larvand in Afghanistan, south of the ancestral homelands of the Ghurids. The shrine (a tomb or mosque) appears to have been built by Indian stonemasons working in the Maru-Gurjara style of northwest India even as their compatriots were building mosques for Ghurid patrons (or, rather, their Turkic agents) in India.[152] The simultaneous and selective co-option of an Indic figural vocabulary in both Afghanistan and north India complicates the notion of Ghurid patrons as violent iconoclasts driven by a visceral response to Hindu iconolatry.

In addition, evidence for the reception of elements drawn from the Maru-Gurjara architecture of western India (including *purnaghata* capitals, ringed columns and *padmalatā* friezes) may be found in a series of dated marble stele from sultan Mu'izz al-Din's capital of Ghazna in eastern Afghanistan (the second city of the Ghurid sultanate), and the site of Bust in south-central Afghanistan, near the palace of Lashkari Bazaar (possibly sultan Ghiyath al-Din's winter residence).[153] The dated carvings from Bust and Ghazna range across the period between 1190 and 1206, the height of the eastward expansion of the Ghurid sultanate, indicating that the sudden appearance of these elements is closely related to contemporary cultural flows.[154]

The contemporaneous reception of Indic forms in Afghanistan and the selective redeployment of figural material to hierarchize and stratify space in the mosques at Delhi and Kaman call into question the widespread assumption that the Indian mosques are the product of a grudging compromise between the desires of Turkic patrons and the abilities of Indian masons. Taken together, these phenomena point instead to a more active engagement with Indic architectural traditions than the indigenizing and foreignizing paradigms of traditional scholarship allow for. As Melikian-Chirvani notes in respect of the mosques at Ajmir and Delhi:

> ... the combination of an Iranian plan ... and Indian details found in architecture is not just down to some practical necessity of using what manpower happened to be available. It was at least as much, if not even entirely, the result of an aesthetic option.[155]

Underlining aesthetic and iconographic dimensions to the reuse of architectural materials, contemporary cultural flows mitigate against the choice of visual 'language' being determined by the contingencies of geography alone. In doing so, they underline the need for a transregional approach to Indo-Ghurid architecture, one that transcends the limits of national boundaries and sectarian taxonomies.

NOTES

1. Nandini Rao, 'Interpreting Silences: Symbol and History in the Case of Ram Janmabhoomi/Babri Masjid', in George Clement Bond & Angela Gilliam, (eds), *Social Construction of the Past: Representation as Power* (London: Routledge, 1994), pp. 154–64; Peter van der Veer, *Religious Nationalism: Hindus and Muslims in India* (Berkeley: University of California Press, 1994) pp. 152–62; Tapati Guha-Thakurta, *Archaeology as Evidence: Looking Back from the Ayodhya Debate*, Occasional Paper No. 159 (Calcutta: Centre for Studies in Social Sciences, 1997). The divergence between different historiographies of the site may be seen by comparing Koenraad Elst, *Ram Janmabhoomi vs. Babri Masjid: A Case Study in Hindu–Muslim Conflict* (New Delhi: Voice of India, 1990) with Harbans Mukhia, *Perspectives on Medieval History* (New Delhi: Vikas Publishing House Pvt Ltd, 2003), pp. 46–54.

2. See the many secondary sources (including some of those discussed here) that are drawn upon in Sita Ram Goel, *Hindu Temples: What Happened to Them?*

(New Delhi: Voice of India, 1991). On the way in which scholarship is implicated in contemporary political developments see Barbara D. Metcalf, Presidential Address, 'Too Little, Too Much: Reflections on Muslims in the History of India', *Journal of Asian Studies* (54, 1995), p. 95.

3. Richard Eaton, *Essays on Islam and Indian History* (New Delhi: Oxford University Press, 2001), 159. See also Peter van Veer, *Religious Nationalism: Hindus and Muslims in India* (Berkeley: UCLA Press, 1994), pp. 144–5.

4. Charles M. Kieffer, *Les Ghorides: Une grande dynastie nationale* (Kabul: Historical Society of Afghanistan, 1962); C.E. Bosworth, 'Ghūrids', *The Encyclopaedia of Islam*, new (ed.), (Leiden, 1960), Vol. 2, pp. 1099–1104; 'Atiq Allah Pazhvak, *Ghūriyan* (Kabul: Anjuman-i Tarikh-i Afghanistan, 1966 [1345s]); Mahdi Rawshanzamir, *Tārīkh-i Siyāsī wa Nizamī-yi Dūdmān-i Ghūri* (Tehran: Danishgah-i Milli-yi Iran, 1978); K. Nizami, 'The Ghurids', in C.E. Bosworth and M.S. Asimov, (eds), *History of Civilizations of Central Asia*, Vol. 4, The Age of Achievement: AD 750 to the End of the Fifteenth Century, Part One: The History, Social and Economic Setting (Paris: UNESCO Publishing, 1998), pp. 177–90; Peter Jackson, *The Delhi Sultanate: A Political and Military History* (Cambridge: Cambridge University Press, 1999), 3–26.

5. D.R. Bhandarkar, 'Indian Studies No. 1: Slow Progress of Islam Power in Ancient India', *Annals of the Bhandarkar Oriental Research Institute* (19, 1930), pp. 25–44.

6. Peter Gottschalk, *Beyond Hindu and Muslim: Multiple Identities in Narratives from Village India* (Oxford: Oxford University Press, 2000), p. 17; David Gilmartin & Bruce B. Lawrence, 'Introduction', in idem., (eds), *Beyond Turk and Hindu: Rethinking Religious Identity in Islamicate South Asia* (Gainesville: University Press of Florida, 2000), p. 3.

7. Cemal, Kafadar, *Between Two Worlds: The Construction of the Ottoman State* (Berkeley: University of California Press, 1995), p. 91.

8. Peter Hardy, 'Force and Violence in Indo-Persian Writing on History and Government in Medieval South Asia', in Milton Israel & N.K. Wagle (eds), *Islamic Society and Culture, Essays in Honour of Professor Aziz Ahmad* (Delhi: Manohar, 1983), p. 169.

9. Finbarr Barry Flood, 'Ghurid monuments and Muslim identities: Epigraphy and exegesis in twelfth-century Afghanistan', *Indian Economic and Social History Review* (42/3, 2005), pp. 267–9.

10. Ibid., pp. 283–6.

11. Holly Edwards, 'The Ribāt of 'Alī b. Karmakh', *Iran* (29, 1991), pp. 85–94; Finbarr Barry Flood, 'Ghurid Architecture in the Indus Valley: the Tomb of Shaykh Sadan Shahid', *Ars Orientalis* (36, 2001), pp. 129–66.

12. 'Ain al-Din 'Ain al-Mulk Abdullah ibn Mahru, *Inshā'-i-Māhrū* (*Letters of 'Ain ud-Din 'Ain al-Mulk Abdullah bin Mahru*), (eds) 'Abdur Rashid and Muhammad

Bashir Hussain (Lahore: Research Society of Pakistan, 1965), p. 38; Ahmad Nabi Khan, *Development of Mosque Architecture in Pakistan* (Islamabad: Lok Virsa Publishing House, 1991), pp. 34, 51–3.

13. Paul Horn, 'Muhammadan Inscriptions from the Sūba of Dihlī', *Epigraphia Indica* (2, 1894), pp. 429–30; Z.A. Desai, 'A New Inscription of Muhammad bin Sam', *Epigraphia Indica Arabic and Persian Supplement* (1968), pp. 1–3; Mehrdad Shokoohy, *Haryana I: The Column of Fīrūz Shāh and other Islamic Inscriptions from the District of Hisar, Corpus Inscriptionum Iranicarum Part IV: Persian Inscriptions down to the Early Safavid Period. Volume XLVII: India, State of Harayana* (London: School of Oriental and African Studies, 1988), pp. 30–1, pls. 75–7; Mehrdad Shokoohy & Natalie H. Shokoohy, *Ḥiṣār-i Fīrūza: Sultanate and Early Mughal Architecture in the District of Hisar, India* (London: Monographs on Art, Archaeology and Architecture, South Asian Series, 1988), pp. 88–92; Mehrdad Shokoohy, *Rajasthan I, Corpus Inscriptionum Iranicarum* (CII), *Part IV, Persian Inscriptions down to the Safavid Period*, Vol. (London: Lund Humphries, 1986), pp. 29–31, 69, pls. 62b, 75–9. The Nagaur inscription is unusual among Ghurid inscriptions in being incised, a common practice in north India.

14. In addition, it has been suggested that the congregational mosque at nearby Bayana (now known as the Ukha Mandir) dates from the same period: Mehrdad & Natalie H. Shokoohy, 'The Architecture of Baha al-Din Tughrul in the Region of Bayana, Rajasthan', *Muqarnas* (4, 1987), pp. 14–32. While it resembles the Kaman mosque in its formal aspects, the flat, two-dimensional, geometricized style of the mosque's stone carvings, especially around the mihrab, is quite different from those found at Kaman, finding analogies in the style of the carving on the screens added to the mosques at Ajmir and Delhi by sultan Iltutmish (d. 1236). Based on these analogies, it seems likely that at least parts of the Bayana mosque should be dated to the 1220s.

15. J. Horovitz, 'The Inscriptions of Muḥammad ibn Sām, Quṭbuddin Aibeg and Iltutmish', *Epigraphia Indo-Moslemica* (1911–12), pp. 13–16; J.A. Page, *An Historical Memoir on the Qutb: Delhi*, Memoirs of the Archaeological Survey of India, No. 22 (Calcutta: Government of India Central Publication Branch, 1926), p. 29; Shokoohy, *Rajasthan*, pp. 12–13.

16. Shokoohy, *Rajasthan* I, pp. 55–6; Mehrdad Shokoohy & Natalie H. Shokoohy, *Nagaur: Sultanate and Early Mughal History and Architecture of the District of Nagaur, India* (London: Royal Asiatic Society, 1993), pp. 107–10.

17. Shokoohy, *Rajasthan*, pp. 55–6; Shokoohy & Shokoohy, *Nagaur*, pp. 107–10. See also the essay of Michael Meister reprinted as Chapter 11 in this volume.

18. Pandit Bhagwanlal Indraji, 'Inscription from Kāmā or Kāmāvana', *Indian Antiquary* (10, 1881), pp. 34–6; Shokoohy & Shokoohy, 'The Architecture of Baha al-Din Tughrul'; Shokoohy, *Rajasthan*, pp. 50–4, and Chapter 11 by Michael Meister in this volume.

19. Page, *Memoir*, p. 39; Pushpa Prasad, *Sanskrit Inscriptions of the Delhi Sultanate 1191–1256* (New Delhi: Oxford University Press, 1990), pp. 1–2; *Repértoire Chronologique d'Épigraphie Arabe*, No. 3619, where the sultan's *kunya* (damaged in the inscription) is erroneously given as Abū'l-Muẓaffar rather than Abū'l-Fath.

20. Horovitz, 'The Inscriptions of Muḥammad ibn Sām', pp. 23, 29–30, 33–4.

21. Alka Arvind Patel, *Building Communities in Gujarat: Architecture and Society During the Twelfth Through Fourteenth Centuries* (Leiden: E.J. Brill, 2004), pp. 133.

22. Phillip B. Wagoner, and John Henry Rice, 'From Delhi to the Deccan: Newly Discovered Tughluq Monuments at Warangal-Sulṭānpūr and the Beginnings of Indo-Islamic Architecture in Southern India', *Artibus Asiae* (31/1, 2001), pp. 89–90.

23. Mehrdad Shokoohy, *Bhadreśvar, the Oldest Islamic Monuments in India* (Leiden: E.J. Brill, 1998). See also Brajadulal Chattopadhyaya, *Representing the Other? Sanskrit Sources and the Muslims (8th to 14th Century)* (New Delhi: Manohar, 1998).

24. Ibn al-Athir, *Al-Kāmil fi'l-Tā'rīkh*, 13 vols, (ed.) C.J. Tornberg, (Beirut: Dar Sadr, 1965–67), Vol. 12, p. 105.

25. Shokoohy & Shokoohy, *Nagaur*, p. 8.

26. J. Burton-Page, 'Hind', *The Encyclopaedia of Islam*, Vol. 2 (Leiden: E.J. Brill, 1965), p. 441. See also A.B. Rajput, *Architecture in Pakistan* (Karachi: Pakistan Publications, 1963), p. 6.

27. Among numerous examples see Forbes Watson, *Report on the Illustration of the Archaic Architecture of India* (London: Indian Museum, 1869), p. 25; Mohammad Habib, 'Indian Culture and Social Life at the Time of the Turkish Invasions', *Journal of the Aligarh Historical Research Institute* (2–3, 1946), pp. 1–125, especially p. 61.

28. Finbarr Barry Flood, 'Pillars, Palimpsests and Princely Practices: Translating the Past in Sultanate Delhi', *Res* (43, 2003), pp. 95–116.

29. James Tod, *Annals and Antiquities of Rajast'han or, the Central and Western Rajpoot States of India*, Vol. 1 (London: Smith, Elder and Co., 1829), pp. 778–82.

30. Of the four extensive thirteenth—and fourteenth-century descriptions of the mosque that survive the sole exception is the earliest, the *Tāj al-Ma'āthir* (begun ca. 602/1205–6), which refers to the golden domes of the idol temples (*qubbāha-yi zārīn-i but-khāna*) formerly associated with the site: Tāj al-Dīn Ḥasan ibn Nizāmī Nīshāpūrī, *Tāj al-Ma'āthir*, British Library, India Office Library, ms. 15 (Ethé No. 210), fol. 114b; Syed Hasan Askari, 'Taj-ul-Maasir of Hasan Nizami', *Patna University Journal* (18/3, 1963), p. 72; Bhagwat Saroop, tr., *Tajud Din Hasan Nizami's Taj ul Ma'athir [The Crown of Glorious Deeds]* (Delhi, 1998), p. 142.

31. Tod, *Annals*, Vol.1, p. 778.

32. Cited in John William Kaye, *History of the War in Afghanistan*, 2 vols, Vol. 2 (London: Richard Bentley, 1851), p. 650. See also, Richard D. Davis, *Lives of*

Indian Images (Princeton: Princeton University Press, 1997), p. 202; Romila Thapar, *Somanatha: The Many Voices of a History* (Delhi: Penguin India, 2001).

33. Thomas Babington Macaulay, *The Miscellaneous Writings and Speeches of Lord Macaulay* (London: Longman, Green, Reader & Dyer, 1871), p. 638.

34. M. Kittoe, 'On the Temples and Ruins of Oomja', *Journal of the Royal Asiatic Society of Bengal* (16/2, 1847), pp. 657–8.

35. James Fergusson, *A History of Indian and Eastern Architecture* (London: John Murray, 1876), p. 513; Har Bilas Sarda, *Ajmer: Historical and Descriptive* (Ajmer: Fine Art Printing Press, 1941), pp. 221–3.

36. Sarda, *Ajmer*, p. 71. The Mayo durbar was followed by a campaign of restoration to the mosque between 1875–8: Anon., 'Restoration Work in Ajmīr', *Archaeological Survey of India Reports* (1902–3), pp. 80–1.

37. Bernard S. Cohn, 'Representing Authority in Victorian India', in J. Hobsbawm and T. Rangers, (eds), *The Invention of Tradition* (Cambridge: Cambridge University Press, 1983), pp. 165–210.

38. Finbarr B. Flood, 'Signs of Violence: Colonial Ethnographies and Indo-Islamic Monuments', *Australian and New Zealand Journal of Art* (5/2, 2004), pp. 33–8. The dyadic vision of pre-colonial Indian history championed in colonial narratives was already adopted by some nineteenth-century indigenous historians, who contrasted the darkness of 'Muslim' rule with the light of British governance: Partha Chatterjee, *The Nation and its Fragments: Colonial and Postcolonial Histories* (Delhi: Oxford University Press, 1997), p. 94.

39. Pierre Nora, 'Between Memory and History: *Les Lieux de Mémoire*', *Representations* (26, 1989), pp. 8–9.

40. Recorded during a visit to the temple in December 1999.

41. Flood, 'Signs of Violence', p. 26.

42. Nicholas B. Dirks, 'Reading Culture: Anthropology and the Textualization of India', in E.V. Daniel and J. Peck, (eds), *Culture/Contexture* (Berkeley: University of California Press, 1996), p. 292; Flood, 'Signs of Violence', pp. 28–30.

43. Tod, *Annals*, Vol. 1, p. 782.

44. Finbarr Barry Flood, 'Correct Delineations and Promiscuous Outlines: Envisioning India at the Trial of Warren Hastings', *Art History* (29/1, 2006), pp. 47–78.

45. Tony K. Stewart, 'In search of equivalence: Conceiving Hindu–Muslim encounter through translation theory', *History of Religions* (40/3, 2001), pp. 260–87.

46. For the broader European context see Nancy Stepan, 'Biological Degeneration: Races and Proper Places', in J. Edward Chamberlain and Sander L. Gilman, (eds), *Degeneration: The Dark Side of Progress* (New York: Columbia University Press, 1985), pp. 97–120; Robert J.C. Young, *Colonial Desire: Hybridity in Theory, Culture and Race* (London: Routledge, 1995).

47. Lord Napier, 'Modern Architecture in India', *The Builder* (1870), p. 722.

48. Doğan Kuban, *Muslim Religious Architecture*, Part 2: *Development of Religious Architecture in Later Periods* (Leiden: E.J. Brill, 1985), p. 15.

49. S.D. Sharma, *The Crescent in India* (Bombay: Karnataka Publishing House, 1937), p. 63.

50. Writing in 1959, the Pakistani scholar Muhammad Chaghatai noted of the Qutb Mosque in Delhi, 'How much precisely this Indo-Islamic art owes to India and how much to Islam remains a controversial point:' Muhammad Abdullah Chagatai, 'Turkish Architectural Ornament in Indo-Pakistani Architecture', *First International Congress of Turkish Art, Ankara 19th–24th October, 1959* (Ankara, 1961), p. 75.

51. James Fergusson, *On the Study of Indian Architecture* (London: John Murray, 1867), p. 32. For later elaborations of the same theme see E.B. Havell, *Indian Architecture, its Psychology, Structure and History from the first Muhammedan Invasion to the Present Day* (London: John Murray, 1913), pp. 42–4; idem., *The Ancient and Medieval Architecture of India: a Study of Indo-Aryan Civilisation* (London: John Murray, 1915), p. 218.

52. Walter Ewer, 'An Account of the Inscriptions on the *Cootub Minar*, and on the Ruins in its Vicinity', *Asiatic Researches* (14, 1832), p. 485; Sayyid Aḥmad Khān, *Āthār ul-Sanādīd* (Delhi, 1847 and 1854), tr. M. Garcin de Tassy as 'Descriptions des monuments de Dehli en 1852 d'après le texte Hindustani de Saïyid Ahmad Khan', *Journal Asiatique* (August–September, 1860), pp. 238–50. For an English calque see R. Nath, *Monuments of Delhi: Historical Survey* (New Delhi: Ambika, 1979). See also R. Nath, 'The Quṭb Mīnār of Delhi and its Symbolism (1200–1215)', *Studies in Medieval Indian Architecture* (New Delhi: M.D. Publications, 1995), pp. 1–17.

53. J.D. Beglar, 'Dehli', in *Archaeological Survey of India Reports* Volume 4, *Report for the Year 1871–72*, p. 45.

54. J.D. Beglar and Alexander Cunningham, 'Preface', *Archaeological Survey of India Reports*, Vol. 4, *Report for the Years 1871–72* (Varanasi, 1966 [1872]), pp. i–xvii.

55. D.S. Triveda, 'Vishnudhvaja or Kutub Minar', *Annals of the Bhandarkar Oriental Research Institute*, (40, 1960), pp. 241–61. For contrary views see S.K. Banerji, 'The Qūwat-ul-Islām Mosque in Delhi', *Journal of the Royal Asiatic Society of Bengal, Letters* (4, 1938), pp. 293–307; Muhammad Yasin, 'Origin and Authority of Qutb Minar', *Journal of Indian History* (54, 1976), pp. 399–405.

56. Sita Ram Goel, *Hindu Temples: What Happened to Them?* (New Delhi: Voice of India 1991), especially pp. 232–3.

57. Richard M. Eaton, 'Introduction', *India's Islamic Traditions, 711–1750* (New Delhi: Oxford University Press, 2003), p. 9. See also S.C. Misra, 'Indigenisation and Islamization in Muslim Society in India', *Transactions of the Indian Institute of Advanced Study* 6 (1971), pp. 366–71.

58. For a description see Muḥammad b. 'Abd al-Jabbār al-'Utbī, *Al-Tārīkh al-Yamīnī*, printed in the margin of Aḥmad ibn 'Alī al-Manīnī, *Al-Fatḥ al-wahabī 'alā tārīkh Abī Naṣr al-'Utbī* (Bulaq: al-Matba'ah al-wahadiyah, 1869), Vol. 2, pp. 296–7. See also Shokoohy and Shokoohy, *Hiṣār-i Fīrūza*, pp. 33–7; Finbarr Barry Flood, 'Lost in Translation: Architecture, Taxonomy and the Eastern "Turks"', *Muqarnas* (24, 2007), pp. 79–116.

59. Michael D. Willis, 'An Eighth Century Miḥrāb in Gwalior', *Artibus Asiae* (46/3, 1985), p. 245.

60. Richard H. Davis, 'Three Styles in Looting India', *History and Anthropology (Great Britain)* (6/4, 1994), p. 303.

61. Mohammad Habib, 'The Urban Revolution in Northern India', reprinted in Jos. J.L. Gommans and Dirk H.A. Kolff, (eds), *Warfare and Weaponry in South Asia 1000–1800*, (New Delhi: Oxford University Press, 2001), p. 46.

62. Hasan Nizami, *Tāj al-Ma'āthir*, fols. 49a–b, 80b, 137a; Askari, 'Taj ul-Maasir', pp. 62, 67–68; Rama Shankar Tripathi, *History of Kanauj to the Moslem Conquest* (Delhi: Motilal Banarsidass, 1989), pp. 333–5; Pushpa Prasad, *Sanskrit Inscriptions of the Delhi Sultanate 1191–1256* (New Delhi: Oxford University Press, 1990), pp. 58–70; H.M. Elliott, & John Dowson, *The History of India as told by its Own Historians*, 4 vols, (Delhi: Low Cost Publications, 1990 [1867–77]), Vol. 2, pp. 216, 223; Saroop, *Crown of Glorious Deeds*, pp. 67–8, 70; Sunil Kumar, *The Emergence of the Delhi Sultanate 1192–1286* (New Delhi: Permanent Black, 2007), pp. 109–10.

63. Kautilya, *The Arthashastra*, tr. L.N. Rangarajan (New Delhi: Penguin Books, 1992), p. 613; Peter Hardy, 'Growth of Authority over a Conquered Political Élite: Early Delhi Sultanate as a Possible Case Study' in J.F. Richards, (ed.), *Kingship and Authority in South Asia* (Delhi: Oxford University Press, 1998), p. 231.

64. Ibn al-Athir *Al-Kāmil fi'l-Tārīkh*, Vol. 11, pp. 171–2. For later examples of such relationships see Cynthia Talbot, *Precolonial India in Practice: Society, Region and Identity in Medieval Andhra* (Oxford: Oxford University Press, 2001), pp. 155–6.

65. Peter Jackson, 'The Mamlūk Institution in Early Medieval India', *Journal of the Royal Asiatic Society* (2/1990), pp. 340–58; Irfan Habib, 'Formation of the Sultanate Ruling Class of the Thirteenth Century', *Medieval India 1: Researches in the History of India 1200–1750* (New Delhi: Oxford University Press, 1992), pp. 6–7; Sunil Kumar, *The Emergence of the Delhi Sultanate*, pp. 63–77.

66. Hasan Nizami, *Tāj al-Ma'āthir*, fol. 134b.

67. Hirananda Sastri, 'Devanāgarī and the Muhammadan rulers of India.' *Journal of the Bihar and Orissa Research Society* (23, 1937), pp. 492–7.

68. John S. Deyell, *Living without Silver, the Monetary History of Early Medieval North India* (New Delhi: Oxford University Press, 1990), pp. 195–206.

69. Muhammad b. Ibrahim, *Tārīkh-i Saljūqiyān-i Kirmān*, (ed.) M.T. Houtsma,

Recueil de texts relatives à l'histoire des Seljoucides I (Leiden: Brill, 1886), pp. 25–6, 49; S.D. Goitein, 'From the Mediterranean to India: Documents on the Trade to India, South Arabia, and East Africa from the Eleventh and Twelfth Centuries', *Speculum* (29, 1954), p. 193; Ahmad, S. Maqbul, *India and the Neighbouring Territories in the* Kitāb Nuzhat al-Mushtāq fi Khtirāq al-'Āfāq *of Al-Sharīf al-Idrīsī* (Leiden: E.J. Brill, 1960), p. 60; Elliott & Dowson, *The History of India*, Vol. 2, p. 201.

70. M.S. Ahluwalia, 'References to the Muslims in Sanskrit Inscriptions from Rajasthan during the Sultanate Period', *Indian History Congress, Proceedings of the 31st Session, Varanasi 1969* (Patna, 1970), p. 163; Brajadulal Chattopadhyaya, *Representing the Other? Sanskrit Sources and the Muslims (8th to 14th Century)* (New Delhi: Manohar, 1998), p. 30.

71. Gyanendra Pandey, 'The Culture of History', *In Near Ruins: Cultural Theory at the End of the Century*, (ed.) Nicholas B. Dirks (Minneapolis: University of Minnesota Press, 1998), p. 31. See also Elst, *Ram Janmabhoomi*, p. 83: 'The old Muslim records and temples-turned-mosques keep on testifying with one voice that the 'Muslim period' of Indian history was a blood-soaked catastrophe, a marathon of persecution and religious war, inciting thousandfold temple desecration'.

72. See, for example, Muhammad b. Mansur Fakhr-i Mudabbir, *Ta'rīkh-i Fakhr al-Dīn Mubārakshah*, (ed.), E. Denison Ross (London: Royal Asiatic Society, 1927), p. 26, fol. 17b.

73. Ann K.S. Lambton, *State and Government in Medieval Islam* (Oxford: Oxford University Press, 1991), p. 204; Jackson, *Delhi Sultanate*, p. 20.

74. N.C. Iyer, *The Bṛhat Saṃhitā of Varāha Mihira* (Delhi: Sri Satguru Publications, 1987), p. 295. See also Granoff, 'The Jina Bleeds', pp. 122–7.

75. Ronald Inden, *Imagining India* (Oxford: Blackwell, 1990), p. 230; John E. Cort, 'Who is a King? Jain Narratives of Kingship in Medieval Western India', in John E. Cort, (ed.), *Open Boundaries, Jain Communities and Cultures in Indian History* (Albany: State University of New York Press, 1998), p. 89.

76. Narayan Chandra Bandyopadhyaya, *Development of Hindu Polity and Political Theories* (New Delhi: Munshiram Manoharlal Publishers Pvt Ltd, 1980), pp. 292–3; Richard H. Davis, *Lives of Indian Images* (Princeton: Princeton University Press, 1997), pp. 51–87.

77. D. Dayalan, 'The Role of War-Trophies in Cultural Contact', *Tamil Civilisation* (3/2–3, 1985) p. 136.

78. E. Hultzsch, *South-Indian Inscriptions*, Vol. 3, part 1 (Madras: Government Press, 1899), pp. 52, 64.

79. Brajadulal Chattopadhyaya, *The Making of Early Medieval India* (Delhi: Oxford University Press, 1997), p. 201. See also Sanjay Subrahmanyam, 'Before the Leviathan: Sectarian Violence and the State in Pre-Colonial India', in Kaushik

Basu and Sanjay Subrahmanyam, (eds), *Unravelling the Nation—Sectarian Conflict and India's Secular Identity* (New Delhi: Penguin Books, 1996), pp. 44–80.

80. Iqtidar Husain Siddiqui, *Perso-Arabic Sources of Information on the Life and Conditions in the Sultanate of Delhi* (New Delhi: Munshiram Manoharlal, 1992), p. 170.

81. Flood, 'Pillars, Palimpsests and Princely Practices'.

82. C.H Tawney, *The Prabandhacintāmaṇi or Wishing-Stone of Narratives* (New Delhi: Indian Book Gallery, reprinted 1982), p. 90. See also Karl-Heinz Golzio, 'Das Problem von Toleranz in Indischen Relgionen anhand epigraphischer Quellen', in Helmut Eimer, (ed.), *Frank-Richard Hamm Memorial Volume, October 8, 1990* (Bonn: Indica et Tibetica Verlag, 1990), pp. 89–102.

83. V.T. Gune, 'Meaning of "Marhata Houni"', *Maratha History Seminar May* p. *28–31 1970.* (Kolhapur: Shivaji University, 1971), p. 1. For a similar tenth-century text see J.F. Fleet, 'An Inscription at Devageri', *Epigraphia Indica* (11, 1911), p. 7, l.18.

84. Michael D. Willis, 'Religious and Royal Patronage in North India', in Vishaka N. Desai & Darielle Mason, (eds), *Gods, Guardians, and Lovers, Temple Sculptures from North India* AD *700–1200* (New York: The Asia Society, 1993), p. 59.

85. M.A. Stein, Kalhaṇa's *Rājataraṅgiṇī: A Chronicle of the Kings of Kaśmīr*, 3 Vol. (Delhi: Motilal Banarsidass Publishers, 1990), 6: 170–3, 7:1077, 7:1089–95.

86. Tawney, *The Prabandhacintāmaṇi*, pp. 90–1, 151; Asoke Kumar Majumdar, *Chaulukyas of Gujarat* (Bombay: Bharatiya Vidya Bhavan, 1956), p. 127.

87. Harbans Mukhia, 'Medieval Indian History and the Communal Approach', in Romila Thapar, Harbans Mukhia, and Bipan Chandra, (eds), *Communalism and the Writing of Indian History* (Delhi: People's Publishing House, 1969), p. 31.

88. Bhattanatha Svamin, 'The Cholas and the Chalukyas in the Eleventh Century', *The Indian Antiquary* (41, 1912) p. 225; Lionel D. Barnett, 'Two Inscriptions from Gawarwad and Arnigeri, of the Reign of Somesvara II: Saka 993 and 994', *Epigraphia Indica* (15, 1919–20), pp. 338, 345–6. See also R. Rangachari (tr.), *Saint Sekkizhar's Periya Puraanam (Thirutthondar Puraanam)* (Tiruvanamalai: Sri Ramanarraman, 1992), pp. 115, 124.

89. Wilhelm Geiger, *Cūlavamsa* Being the More Recent Part of the Mahāvamsa, Parts I and II (Colombo: The Ceylon Government Information Department, 1953), Part I, pp. 3, 86–7, 140–1, 182, 188, 219, 222; Part II, pp. 114, 133.

90. F. Kielhorn, 'Badâun Stone Inscription of Lakhanapala', *Epigraphia Indica* (1, 1892), pp. 61–6.

91. Stein, Kalhaṇa's *Rājataraṅgiṇī*, 1, p. 307; B.P. Sinha, 'Some reflections on Indian sculpture (stone or bronze) of Buddhist deities trampling Hindu deities', in *Dr Satkari Mookerji Felicitation Volume*, (Varanasi: Chowkambha Sanskrit Series Office, 1969), pp. 97–107.

92. A. Ghosh, *Jaina Art and Architecture*, 3 vols (New Delhi: Bharatiya Jnanpith, 1975), Vol. 2, p. 208; R. Champakalakshmi, 'Religious Conflict in the Tamil Country: a Reappraisal of Epigraphic Evidence', *Journal of the Epigraphic Society of India* (5, 1978), pp. 69–81; Romila Thapar, *Cultural Transaction and Early India: Tradition and Patronage* (Delhi: Oxford University Press, 1994), pp. 17–18, 34. See also Subrahmanyam, 'Before the Leviathan', pp. 49–52, 66.

93. Edward C. Sachau, *AlBeruni's India*, 2 vols (London: Kegan Paul, Trench, Trubner and Co., 1910), Vol. 1, p. 117. Around the same time, a mosque in the vicinity of Herat was destroyed by a marauding army from Ghur, then still largely pagan; Bertold Spuler, 'Afghanistans Geschichte und Verwaltung in Früh-Islamischen Zeit', in Erwin Gräf, (ed.), *Festschrift Werner Caskel* (Leiden: E.J. Brill, 1968), p. 356.

94. Yasser Tabbaa, *The Transformation of Islamic Art during the Sunni Revival* (Seattle and London: The University of Washington Press, 2001), p. 21.

95. Wilferd Madelung, *Religious Trends in Early Islamic Iran* (Albany, N.Y; Persian Heritage Foundation, 1988), p. 36; Richard W. Bulliet, *Islam: The View from the Edge* (New York: Columbia University Press, 1994), pp. 141, 187–9; Oleg Grabar, *The Great Mosque of Isfahan* (London: I.B. Tauris & Co. Ltd, 1990), pp. 26–7, 56–7, 69.

96. Milton Gold, *The Tārīkh-e Sistān* (Rome: Istituto Italiano per il medio ed estremo Oriente, 1976), pp. 291–2; Clifford Edmund Bosworth, *The History of the Saffarids of Sistan and the Maliks of Nimruz (247/861 to 949/1542–3)* (Costa Mesa & New York: Mazda, 1994), pp. 277, 299, 382, 348–9.

97. Ernest A. Wallis Budge, *The Chronography of Gregory Abû'l-Faraj 1225–1286* (Amsterdam: APA-Philo Press, 1976), Vol. 1, p. 210.

98. Minhaj al-Din Abu 'Umar al-Uthman Juzjani, *Ṭabaqāt-i Nāṣirī*, (ed.), 'Abd al-Hayy Husayni Habibi, 2 volumes (Kabul: Anjuman-i Tarikh-i Afghanistan, 1963–4), Vol. 1, p. 344; H.G. Raverty, *Ṭabaḳāt-i-Nāṣirī: A General History of the Muhammedan Dynasties of Asia, Including Hindustan*, 2 vols (New Delhi: Oriental Books Reprint Corporation, 1970 [1881]), pp. 353–4.

99. Oleg Grabar, *The Formation of Islamic Art* (New Haven: Yale University Press, 1987), pp. 43–72.

100. François de Blois, 'A Persian Poem Lamenting the Arab Conquest', in Carole Hillenbrand, (ed.), *Studies in Honour of Clifford Edmund Bosworth*, Vol. 2, *The Sultan's Turret: Studies in Persian and Turkish Culture* (Leiden: E.J. Brill, 2000), p. 92.

101. Sadid al-Din Muhammad 'Awfi, *Jawāmī al-Hikāyāt fi Lawāmī' al-Riwāyāt*, (ed.), M. Nizam'ud-din (Hyderabad: Dairatu'l-Ma'arif-ul-Osmania Press, 1967), pp. 207–8; W.H. Siddiqi, 'Religious Tolerance as Gleaned from Medieval Inscriptions', *Proceedings of Seminar in Medieval Inscriptions (6–8th February*

1970) (Aligarh: Centre of Advanced Study Aligarh Muslim University, 1974), pp. 50–8.

102. Hasan Nizami, *Tāj al-Ma'āthir*, fols. 81a, 148a–b; Askari, 'Taj ul-Maasir', pp. 68–9, 80–2; Saroop, *Crown of Glorious Deeds*, pp. 125, 184, 192.

103. Dasaratha Sarma, 'The Kharataragaccha Paṭṭāvalī Compiled by Jinapāla', *Indian Historical Quarterly* (11, 1935), p. 780.

104. Phyllis Granoff, 'Tales of Broken Limbs and Bleeding Wounds: Responses to Muslim Iconoclasm in Medieval India', *East and West* (41, 1991), pp. 189–204; Granoff, 'When Miracles Become Too Many: Stories of the Destruction of Holy Sites in the Tapi Khanda of the Skanda Purana', *Annals of the Bhandarkar Oriental Research Institute,* (77, 1992), pp. 556–7; Granoff, 'The Jina Bleeds: Threats to the Faith in Medieval Jain Stories', in Richard Davis, (ed.), *Images, Miracles and Authority in Asian Religious Traditions* (Boulder Colorado: Westview Press, 1998), pp. 130–3.

105. Prasad, *Sanskrit Inscriptions*, pp. 92–4.

106. Horovitz, 'Inscriptions', p. 13; Page, *Memoir*, p. 29; Anthony Welch, Hussein Keshani, Hussein, & Alexandra Bain, 'Epigraphs, Scripture, and Architecture in the Early Delhi Sultanate', *Muqarnas* (19, 2002), p. 18 (reprinted as chapter 8 in this volume). For a discussion of some of these peculiarities see Alka Arvind Patel, *Islamic Architecture of Western India (mid-12th–14th Centuries): Continuities and Interpretations*, unpublished D. Phil. thesis, (Harvard University, 2000), pp. 104–11.

107. Sheila S. Blair, 'The Madrasa at Zuzan: Islamic Architecture in Eastern Iran on the Eve of the Mongol Conquest', *Muqarnas* (5, 1985), p. 82.

108. As suggested by Horovitz, 'Inscriptions', p. 14. Pinder-Wilson suggests that the Persian text replaces an Arabic original with an original date of 589 misread as 587. The confusion between the reading of the Arabic for seven and nine is common in the absence of diacritical marks, although why it might have been felt necessary to replace the orginal text is unclear: Ralph Pinder-Wilson, *Studies in Islamic Art* (London: The Pindar Press, 1985), p. 102n. For a full discussion see Finbarr Barry Flood, *Objects of Translation: Material Culture and 'Hindu-Muslim' Encounter, 800–1250* (Princeton: Princeton University Press, forthcoming), Chapter 6.

109. Phillip B. Wagoner, 'Fortuitous convergences and essential ambiguities: Transcultural political elites in the medieval Deccan', *International Journal of Hindu Studies* (3/3, 1999), p. 253.

110. Alexander Cunningham, 'Delhi', *Archaeological Survey of India Reports, Four Reports Made During the Years 1862–63–64–65* (1, 1871), pp. 177–8.

111. Michael W. Meister, 'Mystifying Monuments', *Seminar* (364, December, 1989) p. 25.

112. M. Reinard, *Géographie d'Aboulféda*, Vol. II. 2 (Paris: Imprimerie nationale, 1848), p. 120.

113. Stein, Kalhaṇa's *Rājataraṅgiṇī*, Vol. 1, p. 142.

114. Al-'Utbi, *Al-Tārīkh al-Yamīnī*, Vol. 2, pp. 274–5. I am grateful to Everett Rowson of New York University for permitting me to use his unpublished translation of al-'Utbi's text.

115. Welch *et al.*, 'Epigraphs, Scripture, and Architecture', p. 18.

116. Julie Scott Meisami, *The Sea of Precious Virtues (Bāḥr al-Favā'id): A Medieval Islamic Mirror for Princes* (Salt Lake City: University of Utah Press, 1991), p. 211. For an extended discussion see Flood, *Objects of Translation*, Chapter 2.

117. For empirical analyses of the Qutb Mosque in Delhi that emphasize this dialectic between continuity and discontinuity as well as the idea of the mosque as a space of mediation see Sunil Kumar's essay in this volume; Monica Juneja, 'Spaces of Encounter and Plurality: Looking at Architecture in Pre-Colonial North India', in Jamal Malik and Helmut Reifeld, (eds), *Religious Pluralism in South Asia and Europe* (New Delhi: Oxford University Press, 2005), pp. 245–67.

118. Address by Grant Duff to the Archaeological Section, *Transactions of the Second Session of the International Congress of Orientalists*, (ed.) Robert K. Douglas (London: Trübner & Co., 1876), p. 300. See also Finbarr Barry Flood, 'Refiguring Iconoclasm in the Early Indian Mosque', in Anne Maclanan & Jeffrey Johnson, (eds), *Negating the Image: Case Studies in Iconoclasm* (Aldershot: Ashgate, 2005), pp. 15–40. James Fergusson was a notable exception to this tendency: Thomas R. Metcalf, *An Imperial Vision: Indian Architecture and Britain's Raj* (Berkeley: Uninversity of California Press, 1989), pp. 38–9.

119. John Marshall, 'The Monuments of Muslim India', in Wolseley Haig, (ed.), *Cambridge History of India*, Vol. 3: *Turks and Afghans* (Cambridge: Cambridge University Press, 1928), p. 576. See also Robert Hillenbrand's essay in this volume.

120. John Terry, *The Charm of Indo-Islamic Architecture: an Introduction to the Northern Phase* (London: A. Tiranti, 1955), p. 7; Flood, 'Lost in Translation'.

121. Carl Ernst, 'Admiring the Works of the Ancients: The Ellora Temples as Viewed by Indo-Muslim Authors', in David Gilmartin & Bruce B. Lawrence, (eds), *Beyond Turk and Hindu: Rethinking Religious Identity in Islamicate South Asia* (Gainesville: University Press of Florida, 2000), p. 99. See also Patel, *Islamic Architecture of Western India*, p. 322.

122. Finbarr Barry Flood, 'Between Cult and Culture: Bamiyan, Islamic Iconoclasm and the Museum', *Art Bulletin* (84/4, 2002), pp. 641–59.

123. Gautier H.A. Juynboll, *The History of al-Ṭabarī, Vol. 23: The Conquest of Iraq, Southwestern Persia, and Egypt* (Albany: State University of New York Press, 1989), pp. 23, 30; J. Pedersen, 'Masdjid', *The Encyclopaedia of Islam*, new edition, Vol. 6 (1991), p. 650.

124. Cunningham, *Four Reports*, p. 187.

125. Flood, 'Between Cult and Culture'.

126. Flood, 'Refiguring Iconoclasm'.

127. As noted by Mehrdad and Natalie H. Shokoohy, 'Indian Subcontinent III, 6(iii)(b): 11th–16th Century Indo-Islamic Architecture: North', *Dictionary of Art*, Vol. 15 (New York: MacMillan Publishing Limited, 1996), p. 338.

128. Stella Kramrisch, *The Hindu Temple*, 2 vols (Delhi: Motilal Banarsidas Publishers, 1996 [1946]), pp. 322–31.

129. See also Patel, *Building Communities in Gujarat*, pp. 104, 155–6. For a full discussion of this phenomenon see Flood, *Objects of Translation*, chapter 5.

130. Prasad, *Sanskrit Inscriptions*, pp. 21–2, 32–5; Carl W. Ernst, *Eternal Garden: Mysticism, History, and Politics at a South Asian Sufi Center* (Albany: State University of New York Press, 1992), p. 32.

131. Wagoner, 'Fortuitous convergences and essential ambiguities', p. 259.

132. See Monica Juneja, 'Introduction' in Monica Juneja, (ed.), *Architecture in Medieval India: Forms, Contexts, Histories* (Delhi: Permanent Black, 2001), pp. 49–50. Also Juneja, 'Spaces of Encounter and Plurality'.

133. See, for example, Patel, *Islamic Architecture of Western India*, pp. 160, 190, 199–200; Patel, 'Toward Alternative Receptions of Ghurid Architecture in North India (late twelfth–early thirteenth century ce)', *Archives of Asian Art* (54 2004), p. 40.

134. Flood, *Objects of Translation*, Chapter 6.

135. Horovitz, 'Inscriptions', pp. 13, 15, 19.

136. J. Michael Rogers, 'Waqf and Patronage in Seljuk Anatolia. The Epigraphic Evidence', *Anatolian Studies* (26, 1977), pp. 70, 91, 93, 95–6, 98–9.

137. H.A.R. Gibb, *The Travels of Ibn Baṭṭūṭa* AD *1325–1354*, 4 vols. (Cambridge: Cambridge University Press, 1958–94), Vol. 3, p. 624.

138. Ibn Mahru, *Inshā'-i-Māhrū*, p. 38; Khan, *Development of Mosque Architecture*, p. 51.

139. Stella Kramrisch, 'Traditions of the Indian Craftsman', *The Journal of American Folklore* (71, 1958), p. 229; R.N. Mishra, 'Artists of Ḍāhala and Dakṣina Kosala: A Study Based on Epigraphs', in Frederick M. Asher and G.S. Gai, (eds), *Indian Epigraphy, its Bearing on the History of Art* (New Delhi: Oxford University Press and IBH Publishing Co., 1983), pp. 185–90.

140. Alice Boner, 'Economic and Organizational Aspects of the Building Operations of the Sun Temple at Koṅārka', *Journal of the Economic and Social History of the Orient* (13/3, 1970), p. 268.

141. Gibb, *Travels*, Vol. 3: 624; Wagoner and Rice, 'From Delhi to the Deccan', pp. 90–1. For contemporary Anatolian parallels see Rogers, 'Waqf and Patronage', p. 72.

142. Z.A. Desai, *Published Muslim Inscriptions of Rajasthan* (Jaipur: The Directorate of Archaeology and Museums, 1971), p. 96. The phrase is used in al-Isfizari's description of the Ghurid inscriptions in the Great Mosque of Herat, suggesting that it occurred among them: Mu'in al-Din Muhammad al-Zamji al-Isfizari, *Rawḍāt al-Jannāt fī awṣāfi madīnat-i Harāt* (Aligarh: Aligarh Muslim University, 1961), p. 27.

143. Hasan-i Nizami, *Tāj al-Ma'āthir,* fols. 114a-b; Askari, 'Taj ul-Maasir', pp. 71-2.

144. Flood, *Objects of Translation,* Chapter 6.

145. Robert Hillenbrand, 'The Architecture of the Ghaznavids and Ghurids', in Carole Hillenbrand, (ed.), *Studies in Honour of Clifford Edmund Bosworth,* Vol. 2, *The Sultan's Turret: Studies in Persian and Turkish Culture* (Leiden: E.J. Brill, 2000), p. 173.

146. For an analysis of the calligraphy on the screens see Shah Muhammad Shafiqullah, 'Calligraphic Ornamentation of the Quwwat al-Islam Mosque: an Observation on the Calligraphy of the Screens of Qutb al-Din and Iltutmish', *Journal of the Asiatic Society of Bangladesh,* Humanities Volume (39/2, 1994), pp. 61-7.

147. Flood, 'Ghurid Monuments and Muslim Identities', pp. 288-90.

148. Juzjani, *Ṭabaqāt-i Nāṣirī,* Vol. 1, p. 461; Khaliq Ahmad Nizami, *Religion and Politics in India during the Thirteenth Century* (New Delhi: Oxford University Press, 2002 [1961]), pp. 309-10.

149. Jackson, *Delhi Sultanate,* p. 31; Kumar, *The Emergence of the Delhi Sultanate,* pp. 87-97, 105-25, 135.

150. Deyell, *Living Without Silver,* pp. 201-7.

151. E. Denison Ross, 'The Genealogies of Fakhr-ud-dīn Mubārakshāh', in T.W. Arnold & Reynold A. Nicholson, (eds), *Ajaib Nāma: A Volume of Oriental Studies* (Cambridge: Cambridge University Press, 1922), p. 398; Fakhr-i Mudabbir, *Ta'rikh-i Fakhr al-Dīn Mubārakshah,* pp. 22-3; Juzjani, *Ṭabaqāt-i Nāṣirī,* Vol. 1, pp. 408-9; Raverty, *Ṭabaḳāt-i-Nāṣirī,* Vol. 1, p. 488; Askari, 'Taj ul-Maasir', p. 68; Saroop, *Crown of Glorious Deeds,* p. 110.

152. Gianroberto Scarcia & Maurizio Taddei, 'The Masğid-i sangī of Larvand', *East and West* (N.S. 23, 1973), pp. 89-108; Warwick Ball, 'Some notes on the Masjid-i Sangi at Larwand in Central Afghanistan', *South Asian Studies* (6, 1990), pp. 105-10.

153. Hillenbrand, 'The Architecture of the Ghaznavids and Ghurids', pp. 157, 164.

154. Flood, 'Ghūrid Architecture in the Indus Valley', pp. 153-4; Flood, *Objects of Translation,* Chapter 5.

155. A.S. Melikian-Chirvani, 'Islamic Metalwork as a Source on Cultural History', *Arts and the Islamic World* (1/1, 1982-3), p. 42.

PART I

Mercantile Communities and Early Mosques

The Mosque in South Asia

Beginnings

Alka Patel

THE EVIDENCE

Few scholarly works have treated the surviving architectural, textual and epigraphic evidence for the presence of Muslim communities in South Asia before the establishment of long-term Ghurid presence east of the Indus in 1192–93. Despite this oversight, physical remnants attest to the presence of Muslim settlers in the subcontinent by the eighth century, and textual descriptions of their activities date even earlier to a few years after the Hijra in the seventh century. While architectural remains of Muslim groups have been found in parts of modern north India and Pakistan, the textual and inscriptional references place them along the western and eastern seaboards of the subcontinent all the way to Sri Lanka. Since the early Islamic architectural remains and textual and epigraphic references to Muslim communities span the seventh to twelfth centuries, this *corpus* inevitably engages with current scholarly debates surrounding trade and urbanization in early medieval South Asia.

Proponents of decline in trade during the seventh through twelfth centuries hold that South Asia's economy devolved from one based in international trade, principally supported by Indo-Roman contacts during the first few centuries CE, to one reliant on local small-scale transactions. This drastic change was brought about by under-monetization, and its major ramification was pan-Indic de-urbanization, or the atrophy of urban centres throughout the subcontinent to small outposts or exclusively religious centres.[1] Other scholars argue that, while economic changes are evident between ca. 600–1100, under-monetization was not so extensive as to deter long-distance trade, and urban centres continued to function as nodes of intra-regional exchange and even international commerce.[2] In light of these debates, the pre-Ghurid architectural and textual evidence of early Muslim groups in the subcontinent can contribute valuable insights to the larger historiography of early medieval South Asia.

The Islamic buildings and other physical remains known to belong to the centuries prior to Ghurid expansion in the Indus Valley and eastward are dispersed throughout a wide geographical expanse. In Pakistan, these remains are found at the two extremes of the nation's political boundaries, in lower Sindh and in the Swat valley, Northwest Frontier Province (NWFP). In India, pre-Ghurid buildings and fragments are located on the coast of Kachh, Gujarat, as well as far inland at Gwalior in the region historically known as Madhyadesha.

The surviving pre-Ghurid architectural evidence clearly shows large chronological and geographical gaps. Fortunately, textual and inscriptional sources partially remedy these *lacunae*. Although no pre-twelfth-century Islamic buildings survive along the Konkan and Malabar coasts of the subcontinent, travelling Arab merchants and geographers of the ninth through eleventh centuries described several Muslim communities there. Indeed, mercantile contacts between Arab traders and South Asia's western and southwestern coasts pre-dated the Islamic era. Muslim merchants continued to rely on these conduits virtually without interruption, establishing enclaves on the western and southwestern coasts within a few years of the Hijra.[3] The Arab merchants also give accounts of well-established Muslim traders in Sri Lanka, accounts supported by recent archaeological discoveries.[4] Tenth- and eleventh-century Arabic descriptions[5] are corroborated by Sanskrit epigraphs of the Rashtrakutas and Shilaharas, providing glimpses into the politico-economic prominence attained by Muslims (probably of southern Arabian origin) in the realms of these powerful rulers. Inscriptions from the reigns of the Rashtrakuta kings Krishna II (r. 875–914) and Indra III (r. 914–929) mention the *tajika* Sugatipa Madhumati, son of Sahariyara—the Sanskritized form of Muhammad ibn Shahriyar—as governor of the important port city of Samyana-pattana, or Sindhan in Arabic and Persian sources (now Sanjan). Similarly, a later Shilahara donatory inscription of Shaka *samvat* 956/1034 CE names Alliya, Mahara, and Madhumata—all Sanskritized Arabic names—as the officials involved in regional governance. It is probable that the inland-based Rashtrakuta and Shilahara rulers granted high administrative positions to the Muslim settlers in port cities due to the latter's prosperity and to ensure that these coastal magnates maintained the ports in harmony with the central power.[6]

Flourishing Muslim groups did not settle along coastal areas alone. Akin to the surviving architectural evidence at such inland locales as Swat and Madhyadesha, textual and epigraphic evidence also places Muslim groups far from the seaboards at inland sites. For example, three bilingual inscriptions of the ninth century from the Tochi Valley, south of Peshawar (NWFP, Pakistan), not only make clear reference to an Islamic presence in the area by the 840s but also hint at the negotiations of power between the Muslims and the area's Hindu Shahi rulers. A fragmentary Arabic-Sanskrit inscription names one Hayy ibn 'Amr, likely a man of some prominence, as the commissioner of a tank.[7] The inscription's redaction in Arabic and Sanskrit indicates that the large donation was deemed relevant to both the Muslim and indigenous communities. Moreover, the fragmentary Bactrian version of a bilingual Bactrian-Sanskrit inscription dated 862 CE is a panegyric to the *shahi*, a title used by the Turk and Hindu Shahi dynasties established in the region since the sixth century CE. These inscriptions together convey the impression of a delicate balance of power between the Muslim governor/settler Hayy ibn 'Amr—most probably part of a larger Muslim community—and the Shahis.[8]

While the Gujarat coast held a preëminent position in Indian Ocean trade since the first centuries CE and constantly attracted mercantile groups from the Near East, its inland areas were also frequented by Muslim traders during the eleventh and twelfth centuries and probably earlier, long before the short-lived Ghurid occupation of Patan in 1197.[9] Simultaneously, significant numbers of Muslim groups resided at the key locales of Kanauj and Banaras in the heart of the Indo-Gangetic plain. Gahadavala inscriptions of the eleventh and twelfth centuries indicate that these settlers were merchants and traders who profited from the exchange between various commodities of indigenous origin and prized foreign goods such as horses.[10] Indeed, it has been suggested that the intense activity and success of these groups caused the ruling powers no small discomfort, so that the earlier Gurjara-Pratiharas (ninth–tenth centuries) altogether discouraged Muslim merchants from trading in their domains in order to protect the interests of local mercantile guilds. Their successors the Gahadavalas adopted a more pragmatic approach: inscriptions from the reigns of Chandradeva and Jayachandra, spanning ca. 1090 through 1170, record the levying of the famous *turushkadanda*, most likely a tax on Muslim merchants.[11]

No major Islamic power directly held sway anywhere east of the Indus until the late-twelfth century Ghurid occupations of the Delhi–Rajasthan area. Muhammad ibn Qasim's campaign to Sindh on behalf of the Umayyads in 711/12 began the process of Islamization of the population and initiated a series of Sunni and Isma'ili dynasties based either in the north or south of Sindh. However, the campaign did not lead to a long-term Umayyad annexation. Furthermore, Sindh's later 'Abbasid governors and independent amirs constantly confronted local elite interests and tribal groups.[12] Nevertheless the surviving physical remains, together with textual and inscriptional references, convey the impression of an uninterrupted presence of Muslim groups at various locales throughout the subcontinent, ranging from the seashores to inland capitals, likely beginning in the seventh century and continuing unabated after the Ghurid campaigns of the 1190s. It would seem that the vast majority of these groups had come eastward primarily for trade-related pursuits, following the well-plied pre-Islamic commercial conduits between the Near East and South Asia.

If we accept that commercial interests determined Muslim merchant groups' emigrations to South Asia and their residence there for medium- to long-term periods, we must revisit the larger arguments surrounding the decline of trade and urbanization in South Asia between ca. 600 and 1100. Both sides of this debate have been considerably fleshed out and do not bear repetition here. The evidence put forth here indicates the presence of Muslim mercantile enclaves throughout the subcontinent from the seventh through early twelfth centuries, and therefore falls in favour of continued, vigorous inter- and intraregional commercial exchanges with and within South Asia and the continuation of a monetary economy. Trade is, moreover, a largely urban endeavour. While proponents of deurbanization have focused on the archaeological and textual evidence indicating the abandonment of cities and towns ca. 600–1100, little attention has been accorded the creation of new urban centres.[13] Evidently, commerce continued to be a major factor in its own conduits and nodes.

SINDH (EIGHTH-NINTH CENTURIES)

In AH 92/711 CE Yusuf ibn Hajjaj, the governor of Iraq, put his nephew and son-in-law Muhammad ibn Qasim al-Thaqafi at the head of a military campaign to Sindh. This was ostensibly a punitive expedition: Muslim pilgrims and other travellers on a boat from Sarandib (Sri Lanka) westward had been intercepted by pirates operating off the Sindhi coast and held for ransom at the riverine port of Daibul, near the Indus' debouchement into the Arabian Sea. The captives appealed directly to Yusuf ibn Hajjaj for rescue, and Hajjaj asked the ruler of Sindh, Dahir of the Rai dynasty, to do the needful. When Dahir refused to intercede on behalf of the captives, claiming helplessness in the face of frequent pirate raids along his kingdom's coastlines, Hajjaj took a drastic step: he placed his most favoured general in command of an important military campaign that was not only to rescue the travellers but also reprimand Dahir for his unwillingness to acquiesce to Hajjaj's requests and help the travellers.[14]

The dramatic narration of this incident in the thirteenth-century Persian version of an earlier Arabic text known as the *Chach-nama* serves as a convenient 'handle' for a much grander historical design. Indeed, the actual impetus behind this Arab-Umayyad campaign to Sindh emerges upon examination of the wider geo-political realities of the early eighth century. The previous 100 years had witnessed fierce competition between the Arabs and Tibetans as each side attempted to monopolize the overland trade routes linking China to West Asia and beyond.[15] We recall that another capable military commander, Qutaiba ibn Muslim, was campaigning in Central Asia also during the early 700s for control of the legendary 'Silk Routes'. Arab-Tibetan confrontations had largely reduced the traffic of commodities and people to maritime routes via Sri Lanka (alluded to in the *Chach-nama*'s story above). Sindh, with its strategic coastline on the Arabian Sea and the navigability of the Indus far inland, and Central Asia with its extensive overland links connecting the eastern and western extremes of the vast continent, would together constitute a formidable trade empire.[16]

It is noteworthy that the *Chach-nama* repeatedly emphasized Muhammad's leniency after the occupation of a city, especially toward its 'commonfolk, the traders, the artisans and the cultivators'.[17] On the orders of Hajjaj, the young general also offered the choice of Islam or *jizya* to his new subjects, and extended the rights of *dhimmi* to those who continued in their faiths, including the protection of property and places of worship.[18] These administrative policies suggest that Muhammad ibn Qasim—and ultimately the Umayyads—prioritized the continuity of social and economic infrastructures and sought to minimize disruption. They further underscore the principally commercial interests behind the Arabs' entry into Sindh. With the success of Muhammad's campaigns, Sindh became the first region of South Asia to be occupied, albeit for a short period, by representatives of an expansionist Islamic empire in the west.

The earliest datable mosques of the subcontinent survive in Sindh at Banbhore, probably the ancient Daibul 40 miles east of Karachi, and at Mansura, likely built atop or in the close vicinity of the erstwhile Rai capital Brahmanabad in central Sindh.[19] Although identifiable foundation inscriptions for these buildings have not been unearthed, it is believed that each city's congregational mosque was founded shortly after its takeover, Daibul-Banbhore being occupied in 711 and Mansura founded ca. 738.[20] Daibul-Banbhore continued to serve as an important harbour city on the Indus river through the late twelfth century, gradually declining to a minor military outpost by the 1200s. Mansura's trajectory was the inverse, beginning as a small cantonment town in the 730s and becoming the capital of the Habbari amirate in 883. The latter city was annexed by Mahmud Ghaznavi and his forces in 1026. Thereafter it also shared the fate of Daibul-Banbhore, diminishing considerably in prominence by the time of Ibn Battuta's travels in Hindustan in the 1330s.[21] Both cities saw steady Islamic occupation from the early eighth through thirteenth centuries, and their mosques were maintained, altered and expanded as needed by their Muslim communities.

The eighth-century Daibul-Banbhore mosque (Plate 17) was located in the centre of a fortified enclosure. Its finely dressed limestone perimeter walls measure 122 feet north-south and 128 feet east-west. Archaeologists have surmised that a square, block-like minaret—akin to those of early North African mosques—graced the building's southeast corner. The plan of the building, however, is recognizably similar to the plans of the early Umayyad hypostyle mosques such as those of Kufa (rebuilt ca. 670) and Wasit (702). The building consisted of a covered prayer area (oriented west in South Asia) measuring 113 feet north-south and 34 feet east-west, an open baked-brick central courtyard, and roofed double aisles running down the north, south, and east perimeters.[22]

The prayer area was configured in three aisles of ten columns each. Fragments of decayed wood here indicate that the roof was upheld on wooden columns. These were each set atop stone bases, many of which had carved ornamentation. Disturbance of the *qibla* area made identification of a mihrab difficult. However, the qibla wall was the thickest (4 feet 9 in.) of the four perimeter walls, so that the mihrab might have been carved out and capped by a semi-circular stone measuring 2 x 2.5 feet, also found in the prayer area. The three double aisles (*riwaq*) containing the courtyard were also delineated by parallel rows of wooden pillars on stone bases, and divided into small 'cloisters' or cells measuring 11 x 9 feet each. The precinct had two principal entrances on the north and the east, the latter perhaps fronted by a monumental gateway on the exterior. It was near the north entrance that a group of Kufic inscription slabs were found, though none of these was the foundation inscription.[23] The Daibul-Banbhore mosque's affinity with certain Umayyad and North African traditions is consistent with the probable origins of the majority of Muhammad's forces. With no architectural precedents available in Sindh—only recently integrated into Dar al-Islam—the mosque likely took shape according to the conquerors' memories of mosques in their homelands.[24]

The Daibul-Banbhore mosque's stratigraphy suggests a foundation date in the early eighth century, perhaps ca. 714/15 after the Arabs' consolidation of their conquest, and indicates that the mosque underwent four phases of major reconstruction between its foundation and the twelfth century. All of these subsequent constructions took place atop the remains of previous walls, showing a clear pattern of deterioration in the quality of masonry and workmanship in the later three phases. It would seem that this decline in quality, together with a growing paucity of building stone, led to the reuse of materials from the mosque's own earlier fabrics. Indeed, this is demonstrated by the use of a slab with an Arabic inscription in Kufic script dated AH 109/854 CE as a pillar base in the outer northwestern riwaq.[25]

Although a chronology of the mosque's reconstructions is unclear from the stratigraphy alone, one significant event provides some clues as to the approximate date of when repairs to the building might have been undertaken. It is plausible that a devastating earthquake in 892/3, said to have destroyed half the city of Daibul, occasioned at least one of the mosque's entire or partial reconstructions. Not far from this date is another Arabic inscription of AH 294/906–7 CE, carved in floriated Kufic on a dressed sandstone slab (find spot visible on the left side of Plate 17). Due to the writing's fragmentary state, only the names of 'Umar ibn 'Abd Allah and Muhammad ibn 'Abd Allah are decipherable. 'Umar was probably the Habbari who led a successful rebellion in 854/5, and Muhammad was his grandson. The death of the last 'Abbasid governor Harun ibn Muhammad (mentioned in the 854 inscription above) in this rebellion led to 'Umar's recognition as the *de facto* governor of Sindh. Eventually, an independent Habbari amirate emerged in the second half of the ninth century with its capital at Mansura.[26]

The foundation of Mansura in about 738 is generally attributed to 'Amr ibn Muhammad ibn Qasim when he returned to Sindh as one of the adherents of the new governor of the province, 'Awana ibn Kalbi. The town began its life as a modest cantonment located between Daibul and Alor. Additionally, the fact that the ancient Rai capital of Brahmanabad was nearby—at a distance of only 'two farsakhs'[27]—likely influenced 'Amr's choice of the site. Although founded in the first half of the 700s, the cantonment grew into a prominent city of commerce and learning only in the second half of the 800s under the patronage of the Habbari amirs. Excavations of the site yielded remains dating primarily to its zenith as the Habbari capital, including a brick fortification wall running four miles around the city and four city gates. Among the remains within these confines were residential structures, two impressive buildings of palatial scale that archaeologists dubbed the State Assembly and the Dar al-Imara, and what was presumably the city's congregational mosque. It is noteworthy that, unlike Daibul-Banbhore, Mansura's buildings evidence virtually no reused material from previous structures. The Habbari capital continued to command importance through the third decade of the eleventh century, when two factors conspired in its *dénouement*. Another damaging earthquake in 1020 began the gradual decline of the city, which was accelerated with Mahmud Ghaznavi's siege of 1026 under the pretext that it harboured Isma'ili sympathies.[28]

The choice of Mansura as the new Habbari capital may appear illogical in light of Daibul-Banbhore's centrality to the maritime and overland trade traversing Sindh. However, the realities of controlling a vast territorial empire had become apparent already to the 'Abbasids and their provincial governors. Indeed, within Sindh itself vigilance over the routes and trails criss-crossing its coastal areas and its harsh deserts was essential if any rulership was to survive and benefit from the abundant commercial opportunities the region represented. The Habbaris' economic and political base in Sindh necessitated the move to Mansura in the region's centre, whence both the maritime traffic of Daibul and its overland passage through the region could be closely observed and controlled.[29] The Habbaris' concentration on central, southern, and coastal Sindh resulted in the loss of Multan and upper Sindh by the tenth century. Thereafter, an

Ismaiʻli *daʻwa* established itself in the city and undertook active campaigns of conversion to Ismaiʻlism and Fatimid political allegiance. The Ghaznavids conducted several raids in the area and finally annexed Multan to their territories in 1005/6, supposedly because of the city's heterodoxy.[30]

With the precedent of the Daibul-Banbhore mosque of two decades earlier, the initial Mansura congregational mosque probably followed a similar hypostyle plan. The building was then expanded and embellished after the declaration of the amirate of the Habbaris in 861 and the rising stature of Mansura throughout the ninth century. What survives today of the mosque dates principally to the second half of the ninth century. The building was considerably larger than its predecessor at Daibul-Banbhore, measuring 150 feet north-south and 250 feet east-west. But similar to Daibul-Banbhore, the open central courtyard was contained on the north and south by cloistered aisles. The prayer area consisted of thirteen aisles—the central one being the widest—delineated with sixty wood columns on stone bases. The single mihrab here also was carved out of the qibla wall, though it was semi-circular rather than square on plan. There were also indications that the interior dado of the entire building was of carved teak.[31] Overall, the remnants of Mansura's mosque and other buildings of the second half of the 800s convey a luxury not evidenced at Daibul-Banbhore but in keeping with the city's new-found status as the capital of the Habbari amirate.

Even with the political prominence of Mansura, however, Daibul-Banbhore and the lower Indus delta region continued to be the basis for Sindh's unabated 'international' commercial prominence. Although now a semi-submerged site awaiting excavation, during the ninth through eleventh centuries Jam Jaskars Goth was a sizeable town, as indicated by the dimensions of its fortified enclosure (270 x 264 feet) and the adjacent mosque (180 x 144 feet). Moreover, the accomplished quality of its ornamental Kufic epigraphy indicates the regional importance and labour resources commanded by the inhabitants. Indeed, while the deltaic mosques were still constructed according to familiar hypostyle plans, the distinctively Sindhi stone columns and iconographic details indicate the hand of local architectural practitioners in their execution.[32] Finally, akin to Daibul-Banbhore and Mansura, surface analyses of the deltaic sites have also revealed Iraqi ceramic imports, thereby connecting them with the long-distance trade that continued to flourish through at least the eleventh century.[33]

The continued importance of the lower Indus delta as a region central to global mercantilism visited by merchants, scholars and others from all over the Islamic realms is best underscored by some of the Daibul-Banbhore congregational mosque's fragmentary Kufic epigraphs. Even here, the reversal of the 'Abbasids' prior policy of support toward the Mu'tazalites, enacted during the reign of the caliph al-Mutawakkil (r. 861), was proclaimed to all who frequented the port in the building's anti-Mu'tazalite inscriptional programmes.[34] The choice of inscriptions not only indicates that the Habbaris essentially followed 'Abbasid policies, it also implies that any changes therein were communicated by means of the travelers from throughout the Islamic world frequenting this distant port city.

MADHYADESHA (CA. 750)

The fortified palace of Gwalior (ancient Gopagiri) known as the Man Mandir was commissioned by the later Tomara Rajput rulers of Madhyadesha between 1486 and 1516. Intriguingly, sometime during or after the complex's construction, a niche was affixed to the wall adjacent to the Hathi Pol, one of the Man Mandir's ceremonial entrances. Analysis of this architectural fragment has revealed that it was likely a mihrab, carved *ex novo* in the latter half of the eighth century using the same architectural iconography of the contemporaneous temples of Madhyadesha.[35] The original location of the mihrab is a mystery, as are the reasons for the niche's incorporation into the fifteenth-century palace complex. It is nonetheless reasonable to believe that the mihrab was originally part of a mosque or open prayer area (*musalla*) somewhere within the confines of Gopagiri/Gwalior or its vicinity.

The accepted dating of the Gwalior mihrab to the later eighth century has greater significance for our purposes. It strongly suggests that this town, located at the core of the domains of the declining Mauryas and their successors the Gurjara-Pratiharas and one of their principal urban centres, was home to a Muslim community at least by the 700s. The mihrab's manufacture according to the prevailing style of temple architecture and its articulation with aniconic elements of the region's temple iconography further indicate that this community patronized local craftspeople for its carving, and perhaps also for the structure originally housing it. The Muslim community worshipping at Gwalior was likely well established in the city and, from the evidence of their patronage, they intended to remain there for the foreseeable future. The reasons for their presence in the heart of Madhyadesha can at least partially be explained by Gopagiri/Gwalior's role within the overall economy of the region.

Gwalior was an important market settlement as early as the seventh century, and a fortified town by the late ninth century. It was administered by the Gurjara-Pratiharas as a commercial and military centre. Gwalior's Sanskrit inscriptions of the ninth and tenth centuries indicate that this important settlement's economic activities were frequently directed by merchants and traders. Indeed, most of the town's temples were patronized by merchant guilds rather than the Maurya or later Gurjara-Pratihara rulers. The prominence of these commercial interests in Gwalior is understandable in light of the town's function as an important entrepôt on the well traversed overland routes linking the Coromandel, Malabar, and Gujarati coasts with areas north of the Vindhyas.[36]

It is possible that Gwalior's Muslim community consisted of local converts, who continued patronizing local building traditions even after their adoption of another ritual practice. But a cohesive Muslim community in the heart of Madhyadesha at this early date, possessing the economic wherewithal to patronize local architectural traditions, was more likely of non-Indic roots. The Gwalior mihrab's manufacture is similar to the architectural patronage of the later Muslim communities in neighbouring Gujarat.[37] Muslim groups immigrated to and settled in the Gujarat for reasons of trade, residing there on a more or less permanent basis. Since these groups were likely small and specialized in commerce rather than craft, they relied on local architectural labour for the construction of their ritual and other buildings. The Gujarat example is applicable to Gwalior as well, particularly since the eighth-century mihrab was executed in the style and iconography recognizable in neighbouring temples; this suggests that an immigrant Muslim group commissioned local stoneworkers to provide what was required to fulfil ritual necessities. Moreover, Gwalior's commercially and strategically important location would have attracted such mercantile communities, in the same vein as the subcontinent's coastal and other areas.

Whether the Gopagiri/Gwalior community did in fact remain in the city is uncertain due to the lack of additional evidence. However, textual and inscriptional remains from the neighbouring Gahadavala and northern Rashtrakuta territories (discussed above) indicates not only the presence of Muslim communities in the areas of Kanauj and Banares through the eleventh and twelfth centuries, but also their competitiveness and prosperity in mercantile pursuits. The well-established trade and travel routes along with other realities of successfully engaging in commerce likely continued to attract Muslim trading communities to the northern and central regions of India well after the Ghurids' establishment at Ajmer and Delhi in the late twelfth century.

UDEGRAM, SWAT (MID-ELEVENTH CENTURY)

Until recently, the work of Albert Foucher on the routes between northwestern India (ancient Gandhara) and Central Asia was accepted as doctrine. Foucher held that overland communications between these two regions primarily occurred via Bactria, as the awesome mountain massifs to the north and northwest of Gandhara and Kashmir—most notably the western Himalayas, the Pamirs, and the Hindu Kush—were virtually impassable for much of the year. Thus, the vast majority of traffic in people, goods and ideas must have flowed toward the west before circling around northward to the major arteries of the so-called Silk Routes. This overall pattern meant that Swat (ancient Uddiyana), while perhaps serving as a way station for local travellers, was largely isolated from the mainstream of cultural and commercial exchanges taking place between South, Central, and West Asia.[38]

Recent epigraphic discoveries have shed new light on the flow of cultural exchange along South Asia's northwestern borders. Studies of these new finds have modified Foucher's conclusions, proposing that Swat was much better connected with surrounding regions than previously believed. During recent years, the gradual discovery of about 30,000 petroglyphs and over 5,000 Karoshthi, Brahmi, Soghdian, and Hebrew inscriptions and graffiti throughout the Upper Indus, Gilgit, and Hunza river valleys demonstrate that merchants, pilgrims and other travelers braved the mountain passes providing more direct access to Central Asia than the routes via Bactria.[39] Apparently, the mountain massifs were not as impassable as they appear and were intricately knit together by means of many seasonal capillary routes. Thus, rather than being a remote and isolated area, the Swat valley was in direct communication with Central Asia and farther east. It served as an important passage between the Silk Routes and the overland networks of the subcontinent, ultimately connecting with the riverine and maritime conduits of the entire Indian Ocean world. Swat's local prominence was even greater, as it served as a regional market and exchange place for the groups and individuals descending from or ascending to the northern river valleys.[40]

The larger regional relevance of Swat adds another dimension to the early eleventh-century Ghaznavid campaigns of conquest there: Swat's annexation to the Ghaznavid territories farther west was essential not only for the final eradication of Hindu Shahi belligerence, but also for Ghaznavid control over the important routes of communication connecting the area directly with Central Asia and beyond. Furthermore, the settlement of a sizeable Muslim community at Udegram by the mid-eleventh century—indicated by the construction of a mosque there—is also understandable in light of Swat's importance. By this time, not only had the region been integrated into the larger Ghaznavid territories, but its commercially strategic location had made it attractive for what was likely a mercantile Muslim community, not dissimilar to the settlement of such groups at other prominent nodes of trade networks since the very beginning of the Islamic era.[41]

The mosque was not built within the insulated and well fortified settlement on Raja Gira hill, which was likely a royal quarter of the Hindu Shahis at Udegram, one of their capital cities.[42] Rather, the mosque formed part of an unprotected residential area 100 metres below the fortification close to the highways, further hinting at the mercantile pursuits of its congregation. An Arabic inscription engraved on a white marble slab in *naskh* script was found within the mosque precinct, dating the building to AH 440/1048–49 CE. The record attributes the mosque's construction to the *amir* and *hajib* Abu Mansur Nushtegin, perhaps the same Nushtegin who was appointed governor of the Indian territories by the Ghaznavid sultan 'Abd al-Rashid ibn Mahmud (r. 1049). Like the earlier inscriptions discussed above, the grammatical errors in this record indicate that its carvers were not wholly literate in Arabic. Intriguingly, the nearly square slab was obviously reused, as its reverse consists of a carved lotus medallion within a beaded frame stylistically belonging to eighth- or ninth-century Shahi architectural iconography.[43]

The Udegram mosque is rectangular on plan, measuring 63 feet north-south and 84 feet east-west. The construction material is schist, whose slabs are deployed in the corbelled method typical of Gandhara since at least the early centuries CE. The schist-paved courtyard with its ablution pool is slightly lower than the stamped-earth prayer area. A central mihrab was inset in the qibla wall. It is square on plan but arched into niche form with Gandharan corbelling. Rows of stone column bases throughout the building indicate that not only the prayer area but the whole structure was roofed. Similar to the earlier Sindhi mosques, the pillars here seem to have been of wood. Also like its Sindhi forebears, the north side of the building was separated into an aisle that was partitioned into three small cells.[44]

Various characteristics of the building demonstrate that it was the result of architectural translation: the Islamic concepts of the hypostyle mosque and the *ribat* were here rendered in the regional architectural language. In addition to the use of locally found schist in its construction and the typically Gandharan corbelling mentioned above, the southwestern and northwestern corners of the building—that is, those facing away from Raja Gira Hill and toward the highways and valley beyond—were reinforced with circular buttresses. These elements not only relate the mosque to prior and contemporaneous Shahi architecture, they also give it a fortified and defensive appearance. However, the proximity of the building to busy highways and its full exposure to the valley below indicate that fortification was not a priority. Rather, these components of military architecture were most likely symbolic, hearkening to the idea of the frontier of Dar al-Islam. For despite Ghaznavid annexation of the region one-half century before, it is unlikely that the area's inhabitants were fully Islamized. Nevertheless, as we saw before with the intrepid Muslim mercantile groups settling at the coastal and inland locales throughout the subcontinent ever since the first years of the Hijra, differences in religious practice did not deter the commercial pursuits of this stalwart and adventurous group in the Swat valley.

BHADRESHVAR (MID-TWELFTH CENTURY)[45]

Sometime during the first half of the twelfth century, a Muslim community undertook extensive building activity on the outskirts of Bhadreshvar, on the Kachh coast of Gujarat.[46] It appears that this group emigrated from the western Islamic lands and settled at this new locale sometime during the reign of the Chaulukya king Jayasimha Siddharaja (r. 1094–1144). Epigraphic and textual evidence indicates that the community and its descendants called Bhadreshvar their home through the fourteenth century, and perhaps later.[47] Such a migration is explained at least in part by the strategic advantages Kacch offered: placed precisely between Sindh and the subcontinent's western seaboard, Kachh was a port of call for the voluminous maritime and overland commercial traffic so profitable to the region. The community was quite prosperous, as their two mosques, tombs, stepwell, and numerous cenotaphs would indicate. These architectural remains stylistically belong to the mid-twelfth century, probably within a few years of the community's arrival.[48]

As indicated by the cenotaph inscriptions,[49] this group consisted largely of merchants and their families engaged in the flourishing Indian Ocean commerce spanning the Mediterranean through Southeast Asia. However, it is possible that profit from trade was not the only motivation behind this community's settlement at Bhadreshvar. It has been suggested that the group was also affiliated with the Shi'a da'wa (mission) of Multan, and engaged in proselytizing activities.[50]

Bhadreshvar's Chhoti and Solakhambhi mosques have plans that were derived from southern Iranian precedents, as were the styles of the Arabic monumental and cenotaph inscriptions. It is equally clear, however, that the plans and elevations of the buildings were executed by craftspeople trained in indigenous building practices. Moreover, the relatively accomplished quality of the Bhadreshvar remains suggests that these builders had past experience in the construction of Islamic buildings. Judging from the orthographic and other errors in the inscriptions, these are also attributable to local carvers who were not fully literate in Arabic.[51] The application of local building canons to Islamic buildings is not surprising in the light of the many textual descriptions of Muslim communities along the subcontinent's western coasts, discussed above.

The Chhoti mosque exemplifies the rootedness of all the Bhadreshvar buildings in indigenous structural and iconographic traditions, demonstrated in the low trabeate construction and non-figural decorative elements. But though the Bhadreshvar mosques are structurally and iconographically decipherable, their plans do show unusual characteristics. Both the Chhoti and Solahkhambhi mosques have two parallel qiblas, effectively forming two prayer areas. Since there is no indication of different phases of construction, the mosques were apparently designed with this peculiarity from their inception. Additionally, the Chhoti mosque has no open central courtyard, though the preceding portico could have served as a functional substitute.[52] While the Solahkhambhi mosque has a central courtyard (albeit proportionally small) surrounded by aisles and a double-aisled, covered prayer area, it also has a prominent preceding portico with its own mihrab.[53] This double-mihrab configuration diverges from the traditional hypostyle plan, and has no other known parallels in the Islamic lands.

The mosques accommodated the performance of rituals, so it is probable that these requirements affected their layouts. Since no other documented mosque has a double qibla, the Chhoti and Solahkhambhi mosques then also indicate possible differences between the religious practices of at least some of the Bhadreshvar inhabitants and those of the larger *umma*. It is, of course, possible that one of the prayer areas served as the women's section (*zenana*). However, in other mosques this section is conventionally smaller than the main one for men, being also raised and grilled and having its own entrance for gender segregation and hierarchy. Although textual and other evidence regarding the nature of the Bhadreshvar community's rituals is not available, their intriguing built forms urge us nonetheless to question their conformity with ritual practices elsewhere in the Islamic lands.

Bhadreshvar's shrine of Ibrahim and baldachin, or *chhatri*, are also datable to the mid-twelfth century. Based on comparisons with similar structures in neighbouring Sindh, it is probable that the Bhadreshvar chhatri served a commemorative/funerary function. As for the shrine of Ibrahim, the structure is in essence a closed chhatri with a mihrab, suggesting a commemorative function as well.[54]

Although perhaps not apparent at first view, the Bhadreshvar chhatri and shrine of Ibrahim hearken to the formal conventions governing the construction of Islamic tombs. The domed cube had become the preponderant form for the commemorative structure in Iran and Central Asia, particularly by the time of the Bhadreshvar tombs' construction in the mid-twelfth century.[55] The octagonal core of the traditional tomb, where squinches effected the transition of the square plan into the dome above, is also present here but with one notable difference: the squinches here are splayed flat on the columns placed between the corners. The corbelled concentric ceilings of both buildings clearly evoke the domical cap of the archetypal tomb.

This transformation of the traditional Islamic commemorative structure had to occur in the hands of local craftspeople. These workers, who were charged with building not only the chhatri and shrine but also the two surviving mosques, possessed technical tools that were the results of generations of building within the indigenous architectural tradition. The local buildings were constructed mostly in stone, which required the trabeate method of construction. Thus, the Bhadreshvar tombs, while constructed within the local architectural vocabulary, conformed to the well established conventions directing the form of the commemorative structure in Islam.[56]

CONCLUSIONS AND FUTURE DIRECTIONS

The architectural evidence for Muslim communities in South Asia prior to Ghurid presence east of the Indus is relatively scarce. It is chronologically and geographically dispersed over a wide expanse, punctuating the eighth, mid-eleventh and twelfth centuries and dotting Sindh, Madhyadesha, Swat, and the Kacch coast. The physical evidence is thankfully supplemented by textual and inscriptional sources. While Arab merchants and other travellers' accounts fill in the temporal and spatial gaps in the architectural evidence by shedding light on the presence of Muslim communities along the coasts and inland areas of the subcontinent, the many Arabic, Persian, Sanskrit, Bactrian, and bilingual inscriptions reveal the types of social and economic interactions between the newly arrived Muslims and the peoples among whom they sought to create a home. In many cases—exemplified by the Rashtrakuta and Shilahara epigraphs—these interactions were intimate economic and political contracts for the reciprocal benefit of the Muslims and the other regional inhabitants. The architectural, textual, and epigraphical sources, together convey impressions of sizeable and flourishing Muslim communities throughout the subcontinent, engaged primarily in mercantile activities.

The early Muslim communities of the subcontinent were important participants not only in 'international' maritime and overland trade, they also contributed to local economies. In this regard the architectural evidence of their settlements is telling. With the possible exception of eighth-century Sindh, all the other surviving buildings these groups commissioned for ritual and other purposes clearly relied on local labour and architectural conventions. As we have seen, these new foundations were essentially translations of buildings remembered from their points of origin into indigenous architectural practice. With this translation, these early Muslim communities contributed to a vigorous local economy and also to the expansion and creativity of local building styles.

The similarities and—perhaps more significantly—the differences between the early mosques examined here and their Ghurid counterparts of the late-twelfth and early-thirteenth centuries help elucidate the changing interactions among the Muslim and other communities of South Asia. Both the pre- and post-1190 mosques show the continued use of indigenous building styles and techniques, but there are marked differences in scale and reuse of older building materials.

With the exception of the Banbhore and Mansura mosques in Sindh, the other early mosques were generally built on a modest scale when compared to their Ghurid successors: while the mid-eleventh-century Udegram mosque measured 63 x 84 feet, the 1192–3 Qutbi mosque was 214 x 180 feet, and the 1198–9 Ajmer congregational mosque 350 feet on each side. Furthermore, the early mosques reveal a rare and utilitarian recycling of older materials, seen in the first two reconstructions of the Daibul-Banbhore mosque. The Ghurid patrons, however, very prominently used materials recycled from older buildings, uniting pragmatism with the proclamation of a new political order.[57]

The architectural evidence indicates, then, that after 1192–3 the disparate Muslim mercantile groups who had settled in South Asia to pursue the profits of trade were brought under the aegis of a recently established Islamic government that anticipated influxes of additional Muslim groups. Despite these perceivable changes in political affiliations and religio-social hierarchies—changes which appear all-encompassing—only further investigation will reveal whether they effected material alterations in the way that mercantilism was carried out both within South Asia and without.

NOTES

1. See esp. R.S. Sharma, *Urban Decay in India (c.300–c.1000)* (New Delhi: Munshiram Manoharlal, 1987); and R.S. Sharma, *Early Medieval Indian Society: A Study in Feudalisation* (Kolkata: Orient Longman, 2001).

2. These views are expounded esp. by John S. Deyell, *Living without Silver: A Monetary History of Early Medieval North India* (Delhi: Oxford University Press, 1990); and B.D. Chattopadhyaya, *The Making of Early Medieval India* (Delhi: Oxford University Press, 1994). Derryl N. Maclean, *Religion and Society in Arab Sind* (Leiden: E.J. Brill, 1989), though geographically and historically more focused, is also relevant to the debate.

3. See R. Champakalakshmi, *Trade, Ideology and Urbanization: South India 300 BC to AD 1300* (Delhi: Oxford University Press, 1996), pp. 49, 223, 313; and 'Ceylon', and 'Malabar', in *Encyclopaedia of Islam* 1999 (henceforth EI[2]). The Coromandel or southeastern coast of the subcontinent (Ar. Ma'bar) was less frequented by Arab-Muslim traders and travellers. See 'Ma'bar' in EI[2]. The sailor and author Buzurg ibn Shahriyar (ca. 900–953) further underscores this in his description of India, where there is no reference to the eastern coasts of the subcontinent. See *The Book of the Wonders of India*, trans. G.S.P. Freeman-Grenville, (London: East-West Publications, 1981), esp. p. xxiii.

4. The excavations in Sri Lanka revealing an Islamic cultural presence in the eighth- and ninth-century levels were directed by John Carswell. Cited in Michael Willis, 'An Eighth-Century Mihrab in Gwalior,' *Artibus Asiae* XLVI, 3 (1989), p. 242, n. 28. See also 'Sarandib' in EI[2]. If we are to rely on the thirteenth-century *Chach-nama*, a Persian translation of an eighth-century Arabic account of the conquest of Sindh, there was a well established and sizeable Muslim population in Sri Lanka by the first decade of the 700s, perhaps already there since about the 680s. See Ali ibn Hamid al-Kufi (fl. 1216), *Chach-nama, an Ancient History of Sind*, trans. Mirza Kalichbeg Fredunbeg, (Delhi: Idarah-i Adabiyat-i Delhi, 1979, reprint), p. 69. See also the section on Sindh in this article.

5. Among the second-hand accounts are those collected by Buzurg ibn Shahriyar in *The Book of the Wonders of India*, trans. G.S.P. Freeman-Grenville, for example, pp. 2–3, 27, 37, 49–50, 61–2, 67. Al-Mas'udi's travels to the subcontinent in ca. 915 make his accounts of the Muslim communities there even more compelling. See *Murūj al-dhahab wa ma'ādin al-jawāhir*, 3 vols (Beirut: Publications de l'université libanaise), I: 202–3. Finally, the anonymous *Ḥudūd al-'Ālam* (ca. 982) should be mentioned: Anon., *Ḥudūd al-'Ālam* Tehran: (Tehran University Press, 1341/1961–2), p. 66.

6. See, for example, D.C. Sircar, 'Rashtrakuta Charters from Chinchani,' *Epigraphia Indica* 32,2 (1957), pp. 45–69; the wider historical implication of these inscriptions is explored by Ranabir Chakravarti, 'Monarchs, Merchants and a Matha in Northern Konkan (ca. 900–1053),' in Chakravarti, ed., *Trade in Early India* (New Delhi: Oxford University Press, 2001), pp. 257–81. See also Brajadulal Chattopadhyaya, *Representing the Other? Sanskrit Sources and the Muslims* (New Delhi: Manohar, 1998), pp. 10ff.; and Alka Patel, *Building Communities in Gujarat: Architecture and Society during the Twelfth through Fourteenth Centuries* (Leiden: E.J. Brill, 2004), pp. 37n, 64n.

7. Ahmad Hasan Dani, Helmut Humbach and Robert Gobl, 'Tochi Valley Inscriptions in the Peshawar Museum', *Ancient Pakistan* I (1964), p. 130.

8. Sanskrit continued to be the administrative and literary language in Indian inscriptions at least through the sixteenth century, while Bactrian was associated especially with the Shahi rulers. See Dani *et al.*, 'Tochi Valley Inscriptions', p. 126. See also Hem Chandra Ray, *The Dynastic History of Northern India* (2 vols), (Delhi:

Munshiram Manoharlal, 1973, first published 1936), pp. 55–101; Abdur Rehman, *The Last Two Dynasties of the Śahīs*, (Delhi: Renaissance Publishing House, 1988 reprint); and Abdur Rahman, 'New Light on the Khingal, Turk and the Hindu Shahis', in *Ancient Pakistan* 15 (2002), pp. 37–42.

9. See S.D. Goitein, 'From the Mediterranean to India: Documents on the Trade to India, South Arabia and East Africa from the Eleventh and Twelfth Centuries', *Speculum* 29 (1954), pp. 181–97; V.K. Jain, *Trade and Traders in Western India* (Delhi: Munshiram Manorarlal, 1990), p. 75; and Alka Patel, (ed.), *Communities and Commodities: Western India and the Indian Ocean, Ars Orientalis* XXXIV (2004). A Persian inscription of 1215 commemorates a mosque foundation at Patan, indicating that a sizeable Muslim community was already established in the city. See Z.A. Desai, *Arabic, Persian, and Urdu Inscriptions of West India: A Topographical List* (New Delhi: Sundeep Prakashan, 1999), p. 189; and Patel, *Building Communities*, pp. 12, 70.

10. See Deyell, *Living Without Silver*, p. 25.

11. See Sten Konow, 'Sarnath Inscription of Kumaradevi', *Epigraphia Indica* IX (1907–8), pp. 319–28; Ray, *Dynastic History*, Vol. I, pp. 507–36; and Lallanji Gopal, *The Economic Life of Northern India c.* AD *700–1200* (Delhi: Motilal Banarsidass, 1989) pp. 48–53, 117.

12. For a brief overview of Sindh's pre-Islamic socio-political landscape and its confrontation with Islamization see Sarah F.D. Ansari, *Sufi Saints and State Power* (Cambridge: Cambridge University Press), 1992, pp. 13–17.

13. Deyell, *Living without Silver*, esp. pp. 4–5, 65–6, 188–91; and Chattopadhyaya, *Early Medieval India*, pp. 134–43.

14. See *Chach-nama*, pp. 69–73.

15. This competition also had effects on the travel routes of Buddhist pilgrims, merchants, and travellers during the seventh century. See Shoshin Kuwayama, 'Pilgrimage Route Changes and the Decline of Gandhara', in *Gandharan Buddhism: Archaeology, Art, Texts*, Pia Brancaccio and Kurt Behrendt, eds, (Vancouver: UBC Press, 2006), esp. p. 124.

16. Francesco Gabrieli, 'Muhammad ibn Qasim ath-Thaqafi and the Arab Conquest of Sind', in *East and West* 15, 3–4 (1965), pp. 281–95; Maclean, *Religion and Society*, pp. 59–64; and K.N. Chaudhuri, *Asia before Europe* (Cambridge: Cambridge University Press), 1990, pp. 307–308.

17. For example, the conquest of Brahmanabad and its administration, *Chach-nama*, esp. pp. 161ff.; and the conquest of Sikkah, *Chach-nama*, p. 188.

18. See *Chach-nama*, pp. 101–2, 165–6, 168–9; Gabrieli, 'Muhammad ibn Qasim', pp. 286–7; and Maclean, *Religion and Society*, pp. 38, 40.

19. See F.A. Khan, *Banbhore*, (Karachi: Department of Archaeology and Museums, Government of Pakistan, 1960 second 1963); Ahmad Nabi Khan, *Al-Mansurah:*

a Forgotten Arab Metropolis in Pakistan (Karachi: Department of Archaeology and Museums, Government of Pakistan, 1990), p. 23; and Maclean, *Religion and Society*, p. 72n.

20. The stratigraphic analysis of excavations at Daibul-Banbhore largely supports ca. 715 as marking the beginning of the mosque's first building phase. See Khan, *Banbhore*, pp. 21–22; and S.M. Ashfaque, 'The Grand Mosque of Banbhore', *Pakistan Archaeology* 3 (1969), pp. 191, 201–4. No such analysis is available for Mansura. Some scholars, however, hold that the Banbhore structure was not the eighth-century congregational mosque of the city, but rather the famed Shiva temple converted into a prison in the ninth century under the 'Abbasid governors, and used as a mosque only in the early 10th century. See Muhammad Ishtiaq Khan, 'The Grand Mosque of Banbhore: a Reappraisal', *Ancient Pakistan*, XV (2002), pp. 1–9.

21. See 'al-Mansura', in EI[2].

22. Ashfaque, 'Mosque of Banbhore', pp. 206–7.

23. M.A. Ghafur, 'Fourteen Kufic Inscriptions of Banbhore, the Site of Daybul', in *Pakistan Archaeology* 3 (1966), pp. 65–90.

24. It is held that Muhammad ibn Qasim settled 4,000 Arab families in their own quarter at Daibul. It is possible that among these were builders and other crafts people, particularly since Sindh's early Arab architecture 'had little indigenous input'. See Maclean, *Religion and Society*, p. 73; and also 'Daybul', in EI[2].

25. Khan, *Banbhore*, pp. 13, 21; and Ashfaque, 'Mosque of Banbhore', pp. 191, 201–3. The 854 inscription slab was likely not *in situ* when found. This surmise is supported by what can be gleaned from the writing's contents. Its six lines of Arabic in simple Kufic characters on dressed sandstone mention some type of construction commissioned by Harun ibn Muhammad and executed by 'Ali ibn 'Isa. This type of commemorative/foundation inscription would have likely been placed above the main entrance into the building's precinct, or perhaps over the principal mihrab if it commemorated a mosque. See Ghafur, 'Fourteen Kufic Inscriptions', pp. 76–81.

26. Ghafur, 'Fourteen Kufic Inscriptions', pp. 81–4.

27. Maclean, *Religion and Society*, p. 72n.

28. Khan, *Al-Mansurah*, pp. 1, 7, 8–9, 35, 38–42; and Maclean, *Religion and Society*, pp. 140–1.

29. See Jean Deloche, *Transport and Communications in India Prior to Steam Locomotion*, 2 vols, trans. James Walker (Delhi: Oxford University Press, 1993), Vol. I: *Land Transport*, Map II; Maclean, *Religion and Society*, pp. 59–61; Deyell, *Living without Silver*, p. 46.

30. Maclean, *Religion and Society*, pp. 138–9.

31. Khan, *Al-Mansurah*, p. 38.

32. The stone examples are from the nearby mosque of Thamban Waro, less than one kilometre to the northeast of Jam Jaskars Goth. See Monique Kevran, 'Le port multiple des bouches de l'Indus: Barbariké, Deb, Daybul, Lahori Bandar, Diul Sinde', in *Sites et monuments disparus d'après les témoignages des voyageurs, Res Orientales* VIII, (Paris: Groupe pour l'Étude de la Civilisation du Moyen-Orient, 1996), p. 47, & figs 9–14. The dialogue between ninth-tenth century stone carving in Sindh and neighbouring Gujarat continued in force through the 16th century and later. See Patel, *Building Communities*, pp. 112–3, and Plates 53–5; and the section on Bhadreshvar below.

33. For the deltaic sites see, Kevran, 'Le port multiple des bouches', pp. 45–7 ; and also Asma Ibrahim and Kaleem Lashari, 'Recent Archaeological Discoveries in the Lower Deltaic Area of Indus', in *Journal of Pakistan Archaeology Forum* 2, i–ii (1993), pp. 1–44. Ceramics identifiably from Fustat, Samarra, and China were unearthed in the ninth- and tenth-century strata of Daibul-Banbhore and Mansura, alongside coins with mint marks from Egypt, Samarqand, and Wasit. See Khan, *Banbhore*, pp. 33–47; Ashfaque, 'Mosque of Banbhore', pp. 210–4; and Maclean, *Religion and Society*, pp. 69–70. For an analysis of the coinage, see Pervin T. Nasir, 'Coins of the Early Muslim Period from Banbhore', in *Pakistan Archaeology* 6 (1969), pp. 117–81; and Deyell, *Living without Silver*, pp. 45–50. Mansura remained an integral part of this network, as indicated by Near Eastern and Chinese potteries. See R.L. Hobson, 'Potsherds from Brahminabad', in *Transactions of the Oriental Ceramic Society* 1928–30, pp. 21–3.

34. Ghafur, 'Fourteen Kufic Inscriptions', pp. 85–88, 90.

35. Willis, 'Eighth Century Mihrab', pp. 228, 239–40.

36. See Chattopadhyaya, *Making of Early Medieval India*, pp. 137–43; and Anjali Malik, *Merchants and Merchandise in Northern India* AD *600–1000*, Delhi: Manohar, 1998, pp. 51, 61–2. For overland routes, see Deloche, *Land Transport*, p. 53, Map VIII.

37. As elaborated in Patel, *Building Communities*. Gujarat is discussed below in the section on Bhadreshvar.

38. Alfred Foucher, *La vielle route de l'Inde de Bactres à Taxila, Memoires de la délégation archéologique française en Afghanistan* Vols I–II, (Paris: Les editions d'art et d'histoire, 1942–7).

39. Jason Neel, '*La Vielle Route* Reconsidered: Alternative Routes for the Early Transmission of Buddhism', Paper presented at the University of Wisconsin-Madison South Asia Conference, October 6–9, 2005; see also Kuwayama, 'Pilgrimage Route Changes'.

40. Giuseppe Tucci, 'Preliminary Report on an Archaeological Survey in Swat', in *East and West* N.S. 9, 4 (December 1958), esp. p. 280; Giorgio Gullini, 'Udegram' in *Reports on the Campaigns 1956–1958 in Swat (Pakistan)*, Vol. I of *Reports and Memoirs* (Rome: Istituto italiano per il medio ed estremo oriente, 1962), pp.

173–335. See also Muhammad Nazir Khan, 'A Ghaznavid Historical Inscription from Udegram, Swat', in *East and West* n.s. 35, 1–3 (1985), pp. 153–66; and Umberto Scerrato, 'Research on the Archaeology and History of Islamic Art in Pakistan: Excavation of the Ghaznavid Mosque on Mt. Raja Gira, Swat', *East and West* n.s. 35 (1985), pp. 439–50. Additionally, I am grateful to Dr Jason Neelis of Florida State University for his thoughts on the Udegram fort and mosque.

41. Only about 100 metres above the mosque lie the remains of a fortified hillock which was evidently destroyed in the course of Ghaznavid campaigns in Swat during the first decade of the 11th century. It was reoccupied, however, and continued in use through the 13th century until the threat of Mongol incursions in the 1230s again led to its depopulation. For the Ghaznavid campaigns in Swat, see Abdur Rahman, 'The Zalamkot Bilingual Inscription', *East and West* 48, 3–4 (December 1998), esp. pp. 472–3; and *idem*, 'Arslan Jadhib, Governor of Tus: the First Muslim Conqueror of Swat', in *Ancient Pakistan* 15 (2002), pp. 11–14.

42. Tucci, 'Preliminary Report', p. 286.

43. Khan, 'Ghaznavid Historical Inscription', pp. 157–60, 164–6.

44. Ibid., pp. 154, 161, 163–6; and Scerrato, 'Research on the Archaeology and History', pp. 445–7.

45. The most thorough documentation of this site, including architectural drawings, continues to be Mehrdad Shokoohy and Natalie Shokoohy, *Bhadreśvar, the Oldest Islamic Monuments in India, Studies in Islamic Art and Architecture* Vol. II, (Leiden: E.J. Brill, 1988). See also Patel, *Building Communities,* esp. pp. 105–24; and Alka Patel, 'Merchants, *Ghazis*, and the Inception of an 'Islamic' Architecture in India', in *Monuments, Myths, Motifs: the Aesthetic Discourse in Asia and its Artistic Expression*, Kapila Vatsyayan and H.P. Ray, eds, (New Delhi: Manohar, 2007), pp. 81–106.

46. See also Patel, *Building Communities,* esp. pp. 105–24; and Patel, 'Merchants, *Ghazis*'.

47. For the epigraphic evidence from the site, informative of the occupation dates, see: 1–8; Shokoohy et al., *Bhadreśvar,* pp. 1–8; Sheila S. Blair, Review of *Bhadreśvar: The Oldest Islamic Monuments in India,* in *The Journal of the Society of Architectural Historians* 48, 4 (December 1989), pp. 390–1; and Patel, *Building Communities*, pp. 57–58, 107–11. Mention of the Muslims of Bhadreshvar comes to us again in the 14th-century *Jagaducarita*. See Sarvananda, *Jagaducarita*. Vol. V, *Indian Studies,* G. Bühler (ed.), and commentary, (Vienna: Akademie der Wissenschaften, 1892).

48. Further discussed in Patel, *Building Communities*, pp. 36, 57–8, 107ff. See also Z.A. Desai, 'Kufi Epitaphs from Bhadreswar', *Epigraphia Indica Arabic and Persian Supplement* (1965), p. 2; and Shokoohy, *Bhadreśvar*, pp. 10 & *passim*.

49. For example, the cenotaph of one Abu al-Faraj al-Sirafi (d. 1174) indicates that the origins of the deceased were in the port city of Siraf, southwestern Iran.

Siraf had been flourishing in trade with India, Southeast Asia, and the Mediterranean since at least the mid-ninth century. But an earthquake in 977 led to a shift in shipping patterns in the Gulf, with Qais replacing Siraf as the principal port of call on Iran's southwestern coast. Thereafter, Siraf gradually declined until it was abandoned by the early thirteenth century. It is plausible that Abu al-Faraj, together with his family, left Siraf during the period of the city's *dénouement*, and eventually settled at Bhadreshvar to continue in trade. See David Whitehouse, 'Excavations at Siraf: First Interm Report', in *Iran* VI (1968), pp. 2–3; Desai, 'Kufi Epitaphs'; Shokoohy, *Bhadreśvar*, pp. 16–17, 55–9; and Manijeh Bayani-Wolpert, 'A Study of the Islamic Inscriptions in Bhadreshvar', in *Bhadreśvar* (*op. cit. supra*), pp. 58–9.

50. See Samuel Stern, 'Isma'ili Propaganda and Fatimid Rule in Sind', *Islamic Culture* 23, 4 (1949), pp. 298–307; Stern, 'Cairo as the Center of the Isma'ili Movement', *Colloque international sur l'histoire du Caire* (Cairo: Ministry of Culture, Arab Republic of Egypt, 1972), pp. 437–51; and S.C. Misra, *Muslim Communities in Gujarat* (New York: Asia Publishing House), 1964, esp. pp. 19–20, 55ff.

51. Shokoohy, *Bhadreśvar*, pp. 3ff.; and Bayani-Wolpert, 'Study of Islamic Inscriptions', pp. 53–4. See also Patel, *Building Communities*, pp. 105–24.

52. Possible precedents for the closed plan without a courtyard can be found in the Yemen. These buildings often had porticos, though none had double qiblas. See Robert Hillenbrand, *Islamic Architecture* (New York: Columbia University Press, 1994), pp. 90–1, and line drawings 2.152, 2.155, 2.159, 2.160, 2.168.

53. Pointed out in Mehrdad Shokoohy, *Muslim Architecture of South India* (London: Routledge Curzon), 2003, p.14.

54. Bayani-Wolpert, 'A Study of the Islamic Inscriptions', pp. 53–9; and Patel, *Building Communities*, pp. 112–15.

55. See Oleg Grabar, 'The Earliest Islamic Commemorative Structures, Notes and Documents', in *Ars Orientalis* VI (1966), pp. 7–46.

56. Patel, *Building Communities*, esp. pp. 111–12.

57. For this interpretation of the extensive Ghurid reuse of older building materials, see Richard M. Eaton, 'Temple Desecration and Indo-Muslim States', in *Beyond Turk and Hindu: Shaping Indo-Muslim Identity in Pre-Modern India*, D. Gilmartin and B. Lawrence, eds, (Gainesville, Fla.: University of Florida Press, 2000), pp. 246–81 reprinted as Chapter 3 in this volume.

PART II

Temple, Mosque, and Conquest

The Idols of Hind*

André Wink

The establishment of Islamic rule in north India did not entail any systematic attempts at conversion of the native Indian population, and whatever conversion occurred in the eleventh to thirteenth centuries mostly fell outside the scope of the conquest state. Islamic conquest resulted in the formation of new urban centres under the aegis of Muslim immigrants, and an expansion of the money economy, but no great demographic shifts or widespread Islamicization. Unlike the Middle East, which converted to Islam almost entirely, in the settled societies of *al-Hind* a non-Islamic substructure survived.

But without the independent Hindu king, the intimate connection of kingship, temple building, and Hindu religious worship was lost in the areas which were conquered. If the temples were not destroyed, patronage dried up, and few great temples were built in north India after the thirteenth century. Even without conversion, India's sacred geography was uprooted by the Islamic conquest, and the newly evolving Indo-Islamic polity transcended it in the name of the new universal religion. Thus, the fusion of frontier and settled society became engraved in the architectural landscape as well. Most importantly perhaps, Islamic iconoclasm—a religious phenomenon of the frontier—undermined the potential power of the icons as communal symbols, as expressions of the communal life of the peasantry. For the veneration of icons and relics was a collective experience of a mass of believers, exciting powerful emotions, while the power exhibited by icons, through miracles, like

*Previously published as Chapter IX in André Wink, *Al-Hind: The Making of the Indo-Islamic World, The Slave Kings and the Islamic Conquest, 11th–13th Centuries*, Vol.II, Brill, Leiden, 1997, pp. 294–333. In the present version, some portions of the text and notes have been removed. For the complete text see the original version.

that of relics, was overwhelmingly public.[1] The present chapter aims to explore how Islamic iconoclasm in India reflects the structural urge for social atomization and the attempt to integrate the authority of the Muslim emperor among local polities and elevate it above them.

KINGS AND TEMPLES: INDIAN RELIGION AND ARCHITECTURE ON THE EVE OF THE TURKISH CONQUEST

Let us first look again into the relationship of kingship and religion as it existed in pre-Islamic India. It has been shown in the previous volume that, by the time that the Turks arrived, the building of monumental temples in stone for congregational worship and theistic cults had become a characteristic feature of kingdoms throughout *al-Hind.*[2] Such temples arose from the Gupta period onward, expressing new vertical patterns of social and political organization which brought the brahman priesthood to ascendancy and which superseded the loose, 'imperial' organization of Buddhism as supported by itinerant traders and monks. The building in stone reflected a pattern of increased sedentarization and agricultural expansion. Permanent materials were used in the new building style—not without betraying its origin in wood and bamboo architecture—and many of the earliest stone buildings, in effect, survived to the present day, wholly or partially intact, with the detail of their surface decoration still showing. The building of temples marks the early medieval period as an especially creative one. From the beginnings of this period we also have texts on temple building: the *Bṛhat-Samhitā* of Varāhamihira,[3] and the *Vishnudharmottara Purāna.*[4]

Henceforward, temples continued to be built in stone. Or, when suitable stone was not easily available, in brick, with mortar, as in central and eastern India, the Himalayas, and parts of mainland Southeast Asia and the Indonesian Archipelago. Many of the great brick temples, of Bengal for instance, have not survived.[5] Others did: the small, isolated brick temples of the Majapahit period in eastern Java are still standing; while those of Bali, with carved stone lintels and cornices and with wooden superstructures, dating from perhaps as early as the eleventh century, were levelled by earthquakes. Many of the most famous buildings in north India at the time of the Turkish invasions must have been built entirely of brick, and were decorated with terracotta ornaments and alto-relievos.[6] [...] It was in stone, however, that Hindu architecture found its most durable, as well as typical, expression. [...] The building pattern of all known styles was trabeate, with horizontal and vertical components only, and in the total absence of true arches, vaults and domes could always easily be distinguished from Islamic architecture. If we can speak of a Hindu arch, it was one in which the voussoirs were placed end to end, instead of face to face, as in a true arch.[7] This type of arch, although strong enough for small domes, was defective, as each ring of bricks formed a distinct and separate arch, which had no bond with its neighbours, and the outer ring was therefore always liable to peel away or fall from the face of an arch.

The monumental temples with their image shrines—which, needless to say, existed side by side with numerous smaller structures of merely local significance—provided the setting for elaborate royal cults, especially of Shiva and Vishnu. The buildings themselves came about mainly as a result of royal patronage. Temple styles and art, therefore, closely follow dynastic developments rather than variations of cult.[8] Royal patrons fostered the rise of regional styles, which often acquired dynastic appellations. In competition with rivals, kings sought to erect the most splendid structures, the dimensions of which would reflect their political ambitions.

It is all the more remarkable, with this in mind, that we have very little information from inscriptions about the builders of most temples in India. The information which the Muslim conquerors of the eleventh century were able to gather concerning the antiquity of icons and temples is mostly useless: 'an inscription declared the great stone idol (*budda*) at Nārdīn to be 40,000 years old';[9] 'at Kanauj there were about 10,000 temples, which the infidels believed had been in existence for 200,000 to 300,000 years';[10] and so on. There is historical evidence about the dynasties which patronized particular temples, and it is also clear that the resources needed to start and successfully complete these grandiose projects could only be found by kings with extensive dominions. An unique manuscript from Orissa, written in an antiquated Oriyā script of the thirteenth century, lists the day-to-day expenses which were incurred in the construction of the gigantic Sun temple at Konārka.[11] This account shows how the building was completed, thanks to skillful organization and adherence to a strict time schedule, in less than thirteen years. And that, while the work progressed, many spontaneous donations came in from wealthy people throughout the region, but that the main patrons always remained the royal family. It is striking that everywhere in South

Asia representations or portraits of these royal patrons in the temples were rather rare. What we have are depictions of scenes of enthronement, warfare, and so on, in the form of temple decoration, providing evidence of the close association of the lives of the rulers with the activity of temple building. Everyone, too, was free to see the Candella kings appear in the erotic scenes of Khajuraho. We read that in Gujarat, Siddharāja built a temple in Siddhapura, where

the king caused to be made figures of distinguished kings, lords of horses, lords of elephants, and lords of men, and so on, and caused to be placed in front of them his own statue *(svām mūrttim), w*ith its hands joined in an attitude of supplication ...'[12]

Images of kings represented as worshippers in Hindu or Jain temples were not uncommon in Gujarat, as were those of their ancestors, and of merchants and ministers.[13] Hiuen Tsang observed representations of kings and queens in mansions and shrines, probably pictures of them painted on the walls opposite the entrance, of a type that was familiarly observed in small temples by all travellers in India.[14] But the religious identification of these kings with the temples they built normally went no further than that. [...]

Yet, either way, whether he was merely the patron-builder of the temple or whether the temple was actually dedicated to god *and* king, the vital constituent of these religious complexes was the Hindu or Buddhist king. What this means is that, before the conquests of Islam, the temples were an integral part of the regional polity because of their embeddedness in the authority structure. Kings, great and small, shared their sovereignty with the deities installed in the temple, the community of worshippers overlapping with the political community.[15] In the most important temples, kings would devote their daughters to service in prostitution.[16] The temples were not only associated with kingship, but they were the locus where kingship was contested and revitalized. With their sovereign status, temples became, like courts, centres of intellectual and artistic life, accumulated treasure and landed wealth, acted like wealthy patrons or employers, enjoyed tax exemptions, and, not infrequently, independent jurisdiction, and inviolability or immunity from military attack, while in South India they also served as fortresses.[17] If temples came to control increasing amounts of revenue, they also accumulated fixed assets such as jewels, bullion, and a variety of paraphernalia, like image frames, thrones, parasols, crowns, and vestiments of the deity.[18] The *devāpūja* or devotional cult of the image or symbol of the deity installed in the 'womb-chamber' of the temple also encompassed the temple itself, the components of which evoked the presence of the divine. Images were carved in relief in niches on the outer side of the temple walls. And as much as the images and symbols of Hindu religious art were temporary receptacles for gods and goddesses, the temple itself—often built at a sacred site where the gods might easily reveal themselves—became a temporary abode of the gods on earth: the deity would take up residence, if the appropriate rituals were performed, as a royal guest in the temple.[19] The act of *pranāma,* prostration or bowing, was made to images of gods and great persons alike. It was a way in which the association of royalty with the divine was expressed in worship. And it was in the ritual, meant to persuade the deity to accommodate itself in the image of the temple as a king, that the role of the brahman temple-priests became essential.

If in the Hindu icon we find the expression of the shared sovereignty of king and deity, or of the (semi-) divinity of the king, and if the temple, constituted by the king, could become the temporary accommodation of the deity on earth, Islamic iconoclasm in India could not fail to have a political dimension. Students of iconoclasm in the Judeo-Christian context are quite familiar with this. In ancient Israel, where images were symbols of a hated ruling elite, prophetic iconoclasm was politically motivated as well. And in Byzantium, during the Controversy, victorious military campaigns were inextricably entwined with iconoclastic theology. Islamic iconoclasm in the Middle East appears to have been typically associated with successful political and military expansionism. This was also the case in *al-Hind*. It accompanied the Islamic conquest, but once the conquest was becoming consolidated, iconoclasm became relatively rare. What Islamic iconoclasm in India achieved was a new fusion of universalism and particularism, transcendent authority and local power, of mobility and sedentariness, nomadic space, and cultivated realm.

THE POWER OF IMAGES

From early times, the religion of *Hind* or *Hinduism* developed as an 'image-making' tradition, the fundamental tenet of which was that divinity could express itself in a multiplicity of transient forms in the visible world.[20] The divine world could become manifest in images, but also in people and sacred places. Hinduism is embedded in a sacred iconography, a sacred prosopography, and a sacred geography, all of which are bound up with pilgrimage and mythology. Mountain ranges are the abodes of gods; there are sacred rivers, foremost the Ganges, and sacred springs and lakes; and sacred caves, providing the idea of the sanctuary in the temple. The temple itself was regarded as a mountain, an idea which was especially developed in the northern building style. In the Indianized states of Southeast Asia, the temple represented the sacred mountain of Meru, which had a universal significance, associated with Shiva, the 'lord of the mountain'.[21] While the Hindu religion is the product of a 'polytheistic imagination'[22] which is polycentric and pluralistic, the actual fabrication of images, like the building of temples, became a carefully regulated art form and was not left to the imagination of individual artists. The general principles of Hindu iconography and iconometry, the techniques of iconoplastic art, developed along with architecture and town-planning in the so-called *shilpashāstra* literature, the texts of artists who made icons and who were called *shilpins*.[23] This body of literature took form in the course of centuries, and even though only a portion of what was composed survived, became so vast that no single scholar could ever treat it exhaustively. The oldest texts of an iconographic or iconometric character, of the sixth-century *Bṛhat-saṃhitā*, incorporate orally transmitted material of a much earlier period. In the earliest period of Hindu art, and in the Gupta period, there was still considerable variation and latitude permitted in image-making. But in the early medieval period the images became more and more stylized, with general principles being applied by the brahman theologians to the choice of image, execution, dress, posture, proportions of the body (the face-length mostly determining the size of the figure), gestures of the hands (*mudrās*), emblems and weapons, and the appropriate animal mount of each particular deity. The more naturalistic images of the earlier period were now left behind, and, while the temples became larger, the increasing number of images in stone and precious or non-precious metal became, like the temples themselves, subject to strict mathematical control and canons of prescribed rules, the neglect of which would render worship fruitless. Hindu iconography in its broadest sense became the interpretative knowledge of the religious, largely figural, art of Hinduism, the religious tradition of Hind, in which Buddhism too became absorbed, primarily an art of sacred icons of gods, goddesses, demons, and semi-divine beings. [...]

In the Indian tradition in its widest sense, major deities thus take a whole range of images and forms, each of which communicates different aspects of the divine. The most significant element in Hindu worship is 'seeing' the divine image, *darshan*, and what is most characteristic about this worship is not merely the multitude of images that meets the eye but the sensuousness of it, the way it relates to the senses: seeing, but also touching, smelling, tasting and hearing.[24] The Greek *eikoon* (Latin *īcon*), meaning 'figure', 'representation', 'likeness', 'image', especially of deities meant for worship, has a close parallel in the Sanskrit *arcā, bera, vigraha*, and other terms; these, in effect, denote sensible representations of gods and saints which are worshipped.[25] And these icons are described as the body or form *(tanu, rūpa)* of the gods or saints. Such 'representations', 'forms', or 'images' were and are mainly anthropomorphic or theriomorphic, or a composite thereof, with arms and heads multiplied to communicate their superhuman character. In addition, side by side with the icons, existed, from a very early period, the aniconic symbols which are not 'forms' or 'images' and do not aim to be a representational likeness. Early Vedic religion, like early Buddhism, was entirely aniconic, just as it had no permanent temples or sanctuaries. Image worship in India dates from before the first century AD, and phallicism, the worship of the *lingam* (which is the most prevalent of aniconic Hindu symbols), is attested as a part of Shiva worship at the time of the Kushanas by the ithyphallic feature of the god on a gold coin.[26] Its counterpart, the display of the female *yoni*, in combination with the depictions of ritual copulation, is also attested for early times, while eroticism in general came to be perceived as auspicious in ritual and temple art, generating an uniquely Indian eroto-religious context for all forms of worship, which came to include (as already indicated) temple prostitution.

The importance of the visibility of the image is confirmed even in those cases where it is restricted by limited access to the temple. Often, a god or goddess would be secluded from the gaze of particular impure sections of the population. Even then, however, the visibility of the god would be restored during processions, on specific occasions, with the aid of portable god-images or 'moving images' (*calantī pratimā*) replicas, usually smaller, of original cult images (*mūla bera*) which remained fixed in the temple.[27] During major temple festivals, the image itself or the portable replica with which it was temporarily identified could be brought out from the sanctuary on a chariot in which it was carried around as in a mobile temple, for the duration of the festival. At certain times of the year, images were carried around in procession to tanks, where they were placed in floating shrines.[28] Such enhanced visibility could have an electrifying impact on the assembled worshippers, as can still be observed in India. It is probable that in Angkor the *devarāja* was such a portable image of Shiva and was worshipped as a substitute for the original lingam which was established in 802 AD at the foundation of the state by Jayavarman II.[29]

IDOLATRY

Just as it would be an impossible task to survey everything that has been written on iconography in the polytheistic tradition of India, so it would be an equally impossible task to survey everything that was written against images in the monotheistic tradition. The word *idolatry* is formed from the Greek *eidoolon,* 'image', and *latreia,* 'adoration'. Hence, from a strictly etymological point of view, idolatry would mean nothing more than 'adoration of images'. However, the concept of idolatry originated in the context of the monotheism of Israel, that is, in the application of the Second Commandment, forbidding the making of representations of the divinity.[30] Idolatry is what was to be censured of the pagan cults by the prophets of Israel. As such the concept passed into the New Testament and early Christianity, and, ultimately, into Islam, with the result that all three great monotheisms censured idolatry. In other words, it was through Greek translators of the Bible that eidoolon acquired the meaning of 'false god': nothing but vanity, moulded metal, and carved wood.

For Judeo-Christianity, to worship as God things which are not God is, hence, idolatry. But there was, next to the infinite variations in the interpretation of the Second Commandment, also a theology of images which defended an iconodule position.[31] Thus the common *apologia* of Byzantine authors was essentially the pagan argument that images or statues are men's teachers and can direct men's minds towards the divinity, or that they were 'copybooks through which man engraves on his memory the lineaments of the divinity'.[32] This pragmatic point of view closely connected the icons with their prototypes: they would direct the mind from the visible to the invisible, they were the books of the illiterate. This was the educationalist point of view which found easy acceptance in the theologically less sophisticated Christianity of early

Europe, and it was the view which triumphed in Byzantium in 843 AD, after intense theological debate and the Iconoclast Controversy, providing continuity not only with the pagan worship of statues but also with earlier anti-Jewish apologetics.[33] All of the arguments used among the Byzantines in the debates about whether Christian images were or were not different from pagan idols, reappear among the Reformation critics of images, when again theological arguments had a direct bearing on iconoclastic practice.[34] When the first European traders and travellers came to India in the sixteenth century, they were frequently appalled by the overwhelming multitude of images, which they saw, indeed, as mere 'idols'. In this vein, Ralph Fitch wrote about Benares: 'The town is a vast museum of idols—and all of them crude, misshapen, and ugly. They flash through one's dreams at night, a wild mob of nightmares'.[35]

However, it might be pointed out that the Hindu position on images was that they were not intrinsically sacred, and likewise that there is a Hindu theological view which was perhaps in essence not very different from the Christian iconodule position which regarded the images as useful because they led from the visible to the invisible, because they were 'aids' in contemplating the divine. If in India the icons were more than statues and were connected with a divine prototype while becoming the abode of deities, it would be with the implicit understanding that the divine lay behind appearances. Gods and goddesses would assume the outer form of images in order to aid the defective imagination of the worshippers. The image had the function of a *yantra,* an 'instrument' which allowed the worshipper to glimpse a reflection of the deity whose effulgence transcends what the physical eye can see.[36] The *Vishnudharmottara Purāna* defends image worship with the argument that 'in the former three ages, Kṛta, Tretā, and Dvāpara, men were able to see a god directly but in the Kali age men have lost that faculty; therefore they have to worship them (the gods) in an image'.[37] Elsewhere the same text explains:

> Vishnu's ... image is made not for his satisfaction because he is always satisfied, but for the satisfaction of his devotee. He does not want his image but he concedes his image to his devotees only to satisfy their devotion (*bhakti*). It is for favouring (*anugraha*) the devotees that he has allowed his images to be made. He who has no body comes to assume a body in order that his devotee can meditate upon him (*bhaktalakshana bandārtham*) because it is very difficult to concentrate on what is formless, while it is easy to do so on what has forms. So Mārkandeya has instructed as to how his form is to be made and how he is to be inducted. After

meditating on god through a particular form (*sākāra*), a man becomes capable of meditating on him without the aid of any form (*anākāra*).[38]

Almost a millennium later, in the early seventeenth century, an Indo-Persian text, the *Dabistān al-Madhāhib*, dismissed the charge of idolatry in the same way:

Strangers to their [the Hindus'] faith supposed them to look upon the idol as God which is by no means the case, their belief being as follows: 'The idol is merely a *qibla*, and they adore under that particular form the Being who has neither accident nor form'.[39]

Put in another way, it could be said that in Hinduism we find all possible forms of image worship, from the didactic notion to the notion that an image or statue could possess divine powers, dispense life and death, pleasure and pain, reward and punish, cure disease, and so on. Especially the latter were, however, characteristic only, as al-Biruni writes, of 'the uneducated', 'the common people (*al-'āmmī, al-'awāmm*), since the popular mind leans towards the concrete (*maḥsūs*) only, and is incapable of abstraction, which is the domain of the highly educated few. For this reason, al-Biruni continues, the leaders of many religious communities, including the Hindus, have introduced pictorial representations which then began to be venerated. Uneducated Muslims would be prone to do the same thing if they would be offered a picture of the Prophet, for example, or of Mecca and the Ka'ba. Whatever absurd views on image worship among the Hindus he is about to recount, al-Biruni adds, they are merely the notions of the ignorant crowd. Philosophers and theologians, those who seek liberation, worship nothing but God alone and would not dream of worshipping an image made to represent Him (*'an sūrati-hi al-ma'mūla*). To illustrate this, al-Biruni offers some quotations from the Bhagavad Gita.[40]

For all that, it seems safe to conclude that Hinduism never produced a theology of iconoclasm. Of course, just as in Christian Europe, and in Byzantium and the Islamic world, in India people can be seen to have engaged in acts of destruction, of buildings and statues, for purely utilitarian reasons, especially in times of economic hardship, or to enable themselves to erect new buildings, or when conquering the dominions of rivals, or in attempts to obliterate the architectural heritage of a previous dynasty, or in acts of aggression (thus Hindus destroying mosques).[41] Marble works of art from Amarāvatī, for instance, appear to have been brought down by the local people to supply them with lime.[42] But these remained incidental or random acts which were not backed up by any iconoclastic motivation as such. The same can be said about the incidental confiscations of temple treasure or lands by Hindu kings, or the periodic 'purifications' of the Buddhist sangha, which primarily served financial or political purposes and should be distinguished from iconoclasm. The well-known 'looting' of images which was pervasive in early medieval India and the Buddhist mainland of Southeast Asia should be seen in the same light. Thai chronicles refer to certain Buddha images which were regarded as the palladia of principalities, acting as their protectors and guardians of prosperity. When a ruler was dethroned, he would surrender his palladium and send it to the conqueror's capital. Here however it would be held as a hostage and treated with respect. It also happened within the context of Buddhist polities that rulers demolished each other's temples before carrying off famous Buddha images and relics. In the destruction of Ayuthaya, in the years following 1767, monasteries were looted, images and texts were destroyed or lost, and monks were forced to flee. And many similar incidents are recorded in South Asia in the early medieval period. As Richard Davis reminds us,

> We would certainly be wrong to picture Islamic iconoclasm or European commoditization, however profound their impact, as impinging on a previously static Hindu domain, where all such [sacred] objects occupied and remained in their own fixed places, recognized and respected by all.[43]

The appropriations of sculpted images by medieval Indian rulers can be seen as political acts. These rulers often proudly and repeatedly proclaimed their expropriation of objects from other kings. Such 'looting' was a normal and public aspect of war, directed towards symbolic objects, a matter of 'victory' not theft.[44] Commodities such as gold and silver and all regalia and images were reserved for the king, the centre of a redistributive network involving expropriated objects. Here too, 'the appropriation of Indian images recasts their significance without altering what they are and fundamentally represent'.[45] Intentional defilement or public mutilation of divine images is rarely mentioned in Hindu texts as a politically meaningful act.[46]

Apologists for Islam, as well as some Marxist scholars in India, have sometimes attempted to reduce Islamic iconoclasm in India to a gratuitous 'lust for plunder' on the part of the Muslims, unrelated in any direct way to the religion itself, while depicting Hindu temples as centres of political resistance which had to be suppressed.[47] Concomitantly, instances have been described in the popular press of Hindu destruction of Buddhist and Jain places of worship, and the idea was promoted that archaeological evidence shows this to have happened on a large scale, and hence that Hindu kings could be placed on a par with the Muslim invaders. The fact is that evidence for such 'Hindu iconoclasm' is incidental, relating to mere destruction, and too vague to be convincing. Shashānka, for instance, the wicked king of Karnasuvarna in eastern India in the early seventh century, a precursor of the Palas, is described by Hiuen Tsang as a persecutor of Buddhism.[48] Among other things, Shashānka is said to have attempted to remove the Buddha's footprints from a stone located near Pātaliputra, but he failed to do so and then had the stone thrown into the Ganges, from where however it miraculously returned to its original place. Shashānka also cut down the Bodhi Tree at Bodh Gaya, destroyed its roots down to the water, and burned the remainder; but the tree was resuscitated by Pūrnavarman, 'the last descendant of Ashoka', and in one night the tree became above three metres high again. Shashānka also attempted to replace the image of Buddha in the Mahābodhi temple—but only to replace it by one of Shiva. Another incidence is the one described by Taranatha of the reign of Dharmapala in the mid-ninth century: the Hindu sect of Saindhava Shrāvakas, joined by Hinayana Buddhists, breaking the silver image of Heruka at Bodh Gaya.[49] An inscription mentions the destruction of a Buddhist image in Dakshināpatha by king Varmashiva in the first half of the twelfth century, by the efficacy of his *mantras*.[50] In Kashmir, the kings Shankaravarman (883–902) and Harsha (1089–1101) acquired iconoclastic reputations. But, Shankaravarman merely confiscated treasure and lands of temples; the temples themselves he left intact, with their icons.[51] In Harsha's case, statues of gods were defiled by 'naked mendicants whose noses, feet and hands had rotted away', and these were dragged along the streets 'with ropes around their ankles, with spittings instead of flowers'.[52] There was hardly a temple in Kashmir whose images were not despoiled by this king, and reconverted into treasure. But in all likelihood, Harsha—who employed Turkish officers in his army—had followed the Muslim example, as the epithet applied to him, *Harsharājaturushka,* seems to indicate. In the same way, when the Kashmiri poetess Lalla criticized the worship of idols ('the temple is but stone;

from top to bottom all is stone') she appears to be influenced by Islamic notions of iconoclasm.[53] And, to take a final example, when the Jain sect of the Lonkagachcha (or its later offshoots) claimed that there was no mention of image-worship in the canonical scriptures, this was the result of Islamic influence on its founder in the fifteenth century; and the same holds for Kabir and Nanak when they tried to establish the main principle of their religion as devotion to an attributeless god, or what is known in Hindi as *nirguna upasana*.[54] [...]

THE ISLAMIC THEOLOGY OF ICONOCLASM

In spite of attempts to link Islamic iconoclasm and iconomachy to a Zoroastrian influence which made itself felt from the ninth century,[55] the evidence seems overwhelming that Muhammad's view of idolatry, like the concept of idolatry in its very origin, as well as the later Islamic opposition to images, developed from a Judeo-Christian inheritance. Here the monotheistic tradition can be opposed to the Indo-Iranian tradition in its entirety—even though in practice religious labels like Muslim or Hindu have historically not been markers of exclusive groups or understandings of cultural symbols.

The Second Commandment forbids the making of representations of the divinity (Ex. 20: 4–6; Dt 4: 15–19 & 5: 6–9; Lv. 26:1). The Biblical God Yahveh simultaneously forbids the worship of false gods and the worship of images that are claimed to represent Him, on the ground that it is impossible to represent the God of Israel. The repeated condemnation of idol-worship by various Old Testament prophets has been taken, quite plausibly, as evidence of the ongoing popularity of iconolatry. When considering the uncompromising Muslim attitude to images, however, it is important to note that Islam evolved from the Judaism of the Christian period, when the earlier permissive attitudes of Hellenistic Judaism had been shed in the confrontation with the Christians.[56] Uncompromisingly, the Qur'ān denies validity to any form of image worship, including the didactic form, which, it says, is favoured by those who say they worship images 'only that they may bring us near to Allāh' (*illā li-yaqribūna ilā allāh*).[57]

The Qur'ān makes Abraham the progenitor of the monotheistic faith which Muhammad espouses and which sees idols as the enemies of God and His worshippers, condemning these along with the whole Semitic ancestral tradition which is at the origin of their worship and which is radically opposed to the worship of the, one true God (26: 69–83). The Qur'ān also tells how Abraham smashed the idols which were being worshipped by his countrymen (21: 52/53–70). These idols were without substance and could not create anything (25: 3–4/5). Moses had to interfere against the sons of Israel as they had begun to worship idols after their flight from Egypt (7:134–138). Even the turning away from Jerusalem was justified by an appeal to the 'religion of Abraham'.[58] About one-and-a-half years after the Hijra, when the good relations with the Jews had begun to fail, the *Ka'ba* and the *Hajj* are mentioned in the revelations. In the Qibla edict, the faithful are exhorted no longer to turn towards Jerusalem in the salāt but to the *Ka'ba.* It is argued that the religion of Abraham, the prototype of Judaism and Islam, was obscured by the Jews but brought back to light by Muhammad: thus the Ka'ba was presented as the first sanctuary founded on earth (3: 90), the sanctuary of the Meccan cult, the sanctuary of which Ibrāhīm and Ismā'īl had laid the foundations (2: 121), 'the Holy House' (5: 98), 'the Ancient House' (22: 30, 34). From now on, the eyes of the Muslims were turned to Mecca, while an ancient pagan cult was given a foundation in religious history—not without making the Muslims vulnerable to the charge of idolatry by non-Muslims. Such a charge was, in effect, repeatedly made. Germanus, the Patriarch, pronounced the Arab worship of the Black Stone (*al-hajar al-aswad*)—which was made of lava or basalt—inside the Ka'ba as idolatrous, after which 'Umar is said to have had qualms about kissing it.[59] Similarly, Hindus are reported to have made the point that Muslims should not reproach the 'adorers of idols' as they themselves worship the Ka'ba.[60]

The Qur'ān opposes idols, idolatry, and idolaters throughout, and most forcefully. Ibn Ishaq, the first Arabic biographer of the Prophet, devotes many pages to a description of Arab polytheism before the rise of Islam. In Mecca there was an idol in every house. Ibn al-Kalbi, in his *Kitāb al-asnām,*[61] describes the prevalent cult-objects in the *Jāhilīyā: ansāb,* raised stones; *jaris,* stones upon which sacrificial blood was poured; sacred trees; small statues, 'which were bought and sold at markets'. For 'idol' these texts use the word *sanām* (pl. *asnām*), which is also found in the Qur'ān (6: 74, 7: 134, 14: 36, 21: 58, 26: 1) and in Qur'ānic commentary, 'an object venerated next to God'. In the Qur'ān we also find the word *shirk* in the Madina verses, describing Muhammad's attacks on the 'associators', *mushrikūn* (6:94, 10:19, 30:12, 39:4). Shirk designates the act of associating a person with divinity; or 'polytheism'. In the Qur'ān and hadīth, shirk is the opposite of Islam, 'worship of God'.

In addition to this, the Qur'ān demands from the Muslims that they fight against idolaters (9: 36), or turn away from them (15: 94), as they are nothing but liars (16: 86/88–88/90), who will be treated like their idols (10: 28/29), and so on. Idolaters are distinguished from Jews and Christians, however, who are 'unbelievers' (*kāfirs*) but possessors of scripture. Idolatry is an insult to God as it confers on creatures the honour and worship reserved for the Creator. The Qur'ān however nowhere speaks out against representation of living beings as such. It is silent on images (*sūra*), except as idols. The latter prohibition is only found in the hadīth, the traditions attributed to the Prophet and his followers, the oral law of Islam, which were recorded in the eighth and ninth centuries. The Islamic prohibition, moreover, may have been concerned, at first, primarily with sculpture—which could lead mankind back into idolatry.[62] In the hadīth, representations of living beings, those that have a *rūḥ*, are forbidden on the ground that the making of them is harām, because it is an imitation of Allah's creative activity.[63]

Iconoclasm, then, became an integral part of the theology of Islam. But with regard to secular art the situation is ambiguous and complex. Manuscripts of the Qur'ān and hadīth were never illustrated, but their calligraphy sometimes assumed an almost iconic quality.[64] Until recently, objections were often made to photography. Hardly any sculptural art developed in Islam, but arabesques and calligraphy may be regarded as a substitute for it. In secular buildings there was an abundance of representations of kings, musicians, or dancers, and so on. Illustrative painting developed, predominantly in Iran, especially after the Mongol occupation in the thirteenth century, when the influence of the 'picture house' of China grew. Islamic painting reached its peak in Iran and India in the sixteenth and seventeenth centuries. Human faces are shown, portraits of Sufis are frequent, and even the Prophet is depicted with his face uncovered; sometimes however these are found mutilated by later critics. Maps to guide Indian Muslims around places of pilgrimage exist in abundance, as they do for Jains or Hindus.[65] Islamic hostility to images was, it appears, limited to artistic expression which were directly and exclusively related to religion and the religious legitimation of the polity. Thus, mosques in Kerala, for example, while in most respects virtually identical to neighbouring temples, lack decoration of any kind of human or animal representation in sculpture, frieze, or painting.[66] In Bengal, the similarities between the brick mosques of the early Islamic period and the Hindu brick temples are striking; but the mosques were equipped with multiple mihrabs—as many as there are entrances in the mosque—which aimed to dilute the resemblance of the single mihrab with the image niche of a temple.[67] The central tradition of Islamic art always downplayed respresentations of living bengs.[68] Islamic culture did develop a visual symbolic system and an argument about representation which was a form of 'aniconism' rather than 'iconoclasm': images were irrelevant because the truth or reality of anything alive did not lie in its shape or physical character, but in its inner worthiness which is hidden by its accidental shape.[69]

ISLAMIC ICONOCLASM IN INDIA

The universalism of Islam—itself born in the desert, the locus of revelation and religious vision—soon acquired its operational and high-profile iconoclastic dimension on the frontier of conquest. Iconoclastic activity can, in effect, be dated from the very beginning of the religion of Islam. The Prophet himself, according to Ibn Ishaq, ordered all idols around the Ka'ba to be destroyed. We have sporadic evidence of the removal and destruction of idolatrous objects, for example the Christian cross, or images, from the early conquests on.[70] In 721 AD, Yazid II issued an iconoclastic decree, alleged in the non-Muslim sources to have led to a systematic destruction of Christian crosses and images, even in churches and private homes.[71] Iconoclasm was, however, as the archaeological evidence shows, more characteristic of the Abbasids than the Umayyads. Unlike Christian iconoclasm, Islamic iconoclasm was virtually always directed against non-Muslim objects, with the exception of the late defacing of miniatures in manuscripts by pious librarians.[72]

The archaeological and literary evidence of Islamic iconoclastic activity does not become substantial until the eleventh century, when the Ghaznavids penetrate into India. It probably reached its highest pitch then, but remained a recurrent phenomenon until much later—Nadir Shah is still seen directing his artillery against the Buddhas at Bamiyan—, and into modern times. 'Skilled image-makers,' writes Taranatha, 'abounded in every place wherever the Law of the Buddha flourished. In the regions that came under the influence of the mlecchas the art of image making declined.'[73] As the following will show, it seems highly probable that al-Hind was more affected by Islamic iconoclastic activity, at least in the eleventh to thirteenth centuries, than any other metropolitan area which was conquered by Muslims.

Byzantium went through an Iconoclast Controversy in the period from 726 to 824 AD, that is, several decades before the Abbasids rose to power; and here an important Islamic influence has been postulated, or it has been seen as a response to Islam, by both contemporary and modern historians.[74] Others have seen it as 'a Near Eastern movement' or 'a Semitic movement' rather than as a strictly Byzantine one which originated within the Church or with the Emperor Leo III.[75] There was, in any case, a coincidence in time between Byzantine iconoclasm and the rise and expansion of Islam. And in the arguments used by the Byzantine iconoclasts the same Judaic condemnation of idolatry turned up. In the Controversy, religious, economic, military, and political factors were inextricably entwined.[76] The iconodules ultimately prevailed in 843 AD. The pagan legacy was, once again, linked to the Christian tradition, and Byzantium was to be the bridge between the Greco-Roman world and medieval Europe. Later, during the Turkish conquests of the eleventh and twelfth centuries, there is some evidence in the sporadic chronicles that considerable damage was done to ecclesiastical foundations throughout Anatolia.[77] Even before the battle of Manzikert, the Turkish raids had resulted in the pillaging of the churches of St Basil at Caesareia and of the Archangel Michael at Chonae.[78] In the decade after 1071 the destruction of churches and the flight of clergy became widespread.[79] When Antioch was taken by Sulayman in 1085, many of the churches were desecrated, the priests driven out, and the churches were used as stables. William of Tyre presents one of the earliest descriptions of the destruction and defacing of religious pictures.[80] In Antioch, he writes, the Turks removed or covered the pictures of the saints on the walls, gouging out the eyes and mutilating the noses; occasionally churches were converted into mosques.[81]

What we see in Persia in the wake of the Muslim conquest is the gradual evanescence of the Zoroastrian fire cult in most places. To all appearances, iconoclastic activity by the early Muslims was directed against some major targets, but was far from systematic. Its impact, as far as we can tell, was patchwise. Fire temples in Khurasan and Transoxania, for instance those of Nishapur and Bukhara, were demolished by the Arabs.[82] Ubaidallah

b. Abi Bakra, the later general of al-Hajjaj, had been assigned to Fars and Sistan specifically to take charge of the suppression of the sacred fires and the confiscation of temple treasure—tasks which he performed with great diligence.[83] In Sistan, however, mosques remained scarce until the tenth century, and during the first four centuries of Muslim rule Zoroastrian religious centres remained present in large number, falling into disuse before the tenth century only in the cities. In many areas, urban and rural, of eastern Iran the Zoroastrian institutions declined between the tenth and twelfth centuries due to conversion. In Sistan, Muslims did not become the numerically dominant community before the mid-thirteenth century. Above all, iconoclastic activity in Persia appears to have been tempered by the Muslim belief that Zoroastrians were People of the Book.[84]

This was not the case in Hind. Or, rather, the idea of treating Hindus as protected subjects, while it was advanced during the conquest, could not claim Qur'ānic authority, nor could it be found in classical Qur'ānic interpretation or in hadīth.[85] The account of the conquest of Sind points at a practical compromise with idolatry, but in general there is nothing more striking in the Arabic literature on *Sind* and *Hind* than its constant obsession with the idol worship and the polytheism of the Indians.[86] Islamic tradition almost equates Indian culture with idolatry.[87] One hadīth holds that India was the first country in which idolatry was practised, and that the ancient Arabian idols were of Indian origin. Another has it that the brahmans of India in pre-Islamic times used to travel to Mecca to do worship at the Ka'ba, which was the best place for worship. After the rise of Islam, Mu'āwiya is said to have sent golden idols which he had obtained in Sicily for sale in India.[88]

Iconoclastic activity is already in evidence in Sind and Afghanistan under the Arabs. Unfortunately, for a long time it has been all too common among Sindi archaeologists to explain almost every ruin as the result of Arab iconoclasm.[89] The evidence, dating from this early period, is in fact still quite limited. At Debal, the budd temple was destroyed, and in the construction of a mosque, the earliest inscription of which goes back to 727–8 AD, Shaivite lingams were used as a step in front of the threshold.[90] In other cities of Sind we know that mosques were built to replace 'idolhouses'.[91] In the shrine of Zun, an Arab general broke off a hand from the idol and plucked out the rubies which were its eyes.[92] Muhammad al-Qasim is reported to have hung a piece of cow's flesh on the neck of the great budd statue at the Sun-temple of Multan, while he confiscated its wealth and made captives of its custodians.[93] Later Muslim governors always threatened to break the idol or mutilate it when they were confronting the hostility of neighbouring Hindu powers; until in the late tenth century the Ismāʿīlīs finally did break it and killed its priests, erecting a mosque on its site.[94] The Arab chiefs who ruled Sind in the ninth and tenth centuries, rather than transmitting revenue, on occasion sent cartloads of idols to Baghdad.[95] This is about all we know. And it is in contrast to the general practice of the Arabs in Sind which allowed for old temples to be rebuilt, new ones erected, and Hindu/Buddhist practices to be continued.

Such piecemeal evidence which we have, then, on Arab iconoclasm in Sind, can be set off against what we know of the wholesale and far more systematic onslaught launched by the Muslim Turks against the major religious sites of north India. As already indicated, iconoclastic motives can be distinguished from economic and political motives only with the greatest difficulty, if at all. Iconoclasm escalated, no doubt, because the Indian temple cities still contained vast amounts of immobilized treasure. But the Ghaznavid reputation throughout the Islamic world was based on two interrelated accomplishments: the 'breaking of the idols' and the de-hoarding of the temple treasure of *al-Hind*.

Iconoclastic motives are already interwoven in the early life stories of both Sabuktigin and Mahmud. On the first we read in the *Pandnama*:

> I was taken to the tribe of the Bakhtiyans. They were idol-worshippers and had, in the plain, carved out a stone in human form which they said had grown of itself on the spot. They used to prostrate themselves before this stone at all times, and it was a place of pilgrimage for them. They had sent me to tend their sheep, and I used to remain in the plain where I passed that idol every day. God put it into my heart that those Bakhtiyans were a miserable people who prostrated themselves every day before a stone. One day I said to myself that I should offend against that idol in order to see if I was punished. I looked about me and finding nearby filth and droppings of animals which were sacrificed to that idol, I placed them on a piece of wood and daubed them on the face and body of that image. I came to no harm on the following day, and in fact what harm could come from inert stone? I did this every day, and my belief in the existence of God increased.[96]

Concerning Mahmud, we read that in the same night that he was born, 'an idolhouse in Hind' (*butkhānā bi-hind*), which was situated on the confines of Barshābūr, on the bank of the Sind [Indus] river, split asunder spontaneously.[97] Mahmud replaced, it is also recorded, many thousands of idol-houses with mosques.[98] Alone among his contemporaries and successors, Mahmud described himself (on his coins, issued at Lahore in the seventh year of his reign) and was described by others as *Mahmūd butshikan*, 'Mahmud the breaker of idols'.[99]

What is often not easy to make out is to what extent temples were demolished and then replaced with mosques, or whether they were sometimes just converted into mosques. Or to what extent already ruined temples were disassembled and used for the construction of new buildings. Obviously, the Muslims had no qualms about reusing materials from destroyed temples, although many Muslims refer to the Qur'ān as the source for a prohibition against this.[100] In many of the early Islamic monuments in India, plunder from Hindu or Jain temples appears to have been a common source of building material. In one case, that of the early thirteenth-century Caurāsī (or Causat) Kambhā Masjid at Kāmān, Rajasthan, (Plates 9, 13, and 21) one of the earliest Indian monuments of the Ghurids, dating from before the establishment of the Slave Kingdom by Aybak in 1206, we find elements in use which were taken not from recent Hindu structures, but rather from monuments which were built four or five centuries earlier.[101] This appears to have been done with calculated consistency; and, possibly, the practice may have been much more widespread. Building materials for the Kāmān mosque were removed from pavilions (*mandapīkas*) and monasteries (*mathas*) and a variety of other structures, including temples, which were built during the rule of the Shūrasena dynasty in the seventh and eighth centuries and the Pratiharas in the ninth century. The resulting mosque still substantially expresses a Hindu sensibility, and, built by Hindu craftsmen (at least in part) under Muslim patronage, integrates Hindu architectural design with Islamic ornament and use.[102]

Most of the mosques which were built from the materials of, and on the sites of, demolished Hindu temples, are known to the Archaeological Survey of India, and their histories are related in local traditions. What replaced the images which were effaced, destroyed, or removed was God's Word, in calligraphic Arabic—in the way that the Decalogue came to rule in the churches of the West in the later sixteenth and seventeenth centuries. Inscriptions in Arabic, quoting the Qur'ān, state the date and founder of the mosque as well.[103] The seventh to eighteenth centuries have also generated an enormous mass of literary evidence of Islamic iconoclasm in the area from Transoxania and Afghanistan to Tamil Nadu and Assam, the whole of which is littered with ruins of temples and monasteries.[104] These texts speak of the destruction of 'places of worship' (*ma'ābid, biya'*), 'idol-houses' *(buyūt al-asnām, butkhānahā)*, 'fire-temples' (*kunishthā, ātashkhānahā*), and their budda stone idols, 'deaf and dumb idols', and so on.[105] Or, at some more length, we are told, for example, that

> Aybak built the jāmi' masjid at Delhi, and adorned it with stones and gold obtained from the temples which had been demolished by elephants, and covered it with inscriptions in Toghra, containing the divine commandments.[106]

Such texts survived from all periods of Indo-Islamic history, indicating that, while iconoclasm was at its peak in the eleventh to thirteenth centuries, there are many instances which occurred in a context which was otherwise characterized by all kinds of accommodation between Hindus and Muslims (which often included patronage of each others' shrines and religious complexes). What happened in historical times in areas like Sinkiang, Transoxania, Sistan, and Afghanistan—which converted almost entirely to Islam and eradicated all vestiges of Hinduism and Buddhism—, happened still recently in Pakistan and Bangladesh, where many temples were destroyed by Muslims as recently as 1989, and, still continuing, in Kashmir.

In the thirteenth century and afterwards, large temples continued to be built, but not with the same frequency. The Islamic conquest put temples at risk, and the power of Indian ruling elites to patronize temple construction became increasingly circumscribed.[107] In the temples that were built after 1200 AD, as for example at Ranakpur in Rajasthan, the emphasis shifted from carving to the articulation of grand spaces. In north India this resulted, after 1200, in a significant dearth of well-carved sculptures. The temples that survived the thirteenth and fourteenth centuries are now abandoned and stand as hollow shells in secluded spots, but some of the greatest temple complexes of the north obviously survived the Muslim invasions intact. This was the case with about twenty-five of the approximately eighty temples of Khajuraho, built by the Candellas. These, however, appear to have occupied a site which had already been abandoned before the Muslims penetrated the area.

After the thirteenth century, then, the building of monumental Hindu temples became more and more a feature of the south of India, the area which for many centuries longer remained beyond the frontier of Islamic expansion.[108] [...]

It was only in south India that the building of large temple complexes remained embedded in a Hindu polity and continued to be organically linked to the other institutions of kingship and social organization in a variety of complex ways. Hindu temples in south India show a relatively unbroken, linear development, from the earliest rock-cut temples of the Pallavas in the seventh century to the great Cola structures of the eleventh century and then to the sprawling urban temple ensembles, with their *gopurams* or 'gates', of the sixteenth- and seventeenth-century Vijayanagara and Nayaka dynasties. This tradition did not decline before the seventeenth century, under the impact of Muslims and Europeans. And even modern temples of the south are still done in a style that continues the earlier tradition. In north India, by contrast, the Muslim invasions, apart from destroying many temples, interrupted the evolution of Hindu temple architecture. If temples continued to be built in the Northern style (as developed by the Candellas or the Solankis), it was on a much reduced scale. Parallel to developments in Gwalior and Khajuraho, we find that temples continued to be built in a related style in the west of India and in Kathiawar. Here the Jain temple cities stand out. These were built, with elaborate ornamentation, from the tenth century on, and they are built in the same style to this day. The city of Satrunjaya, Palitana, is the most sacred of the Jain temple cities: most of its nearly 900 temples date from the sixteenth century; but the original temples, built in the eleventh century, were completely destroyed by the Muslims. Similarly, the town of Ajmer, founded by Ajaipal, one of the Cauhan kings, was sacked in 1024 AD by Mahmud of Ghazna, and again by Muhammad Ghuri in 1193; it had a Jain college, built in 1153, which was turned into a mosque by putting a massive screen of seven arches in front of the pillared hall which was left standing: 'the hut of two-and-a-half days', built supernaturally, according to Muslim tradition, in two-and-a-half days. Other great Jain temples, like the one at Rānakpur, in Rajasthan, built around 1439, were equipped with holes in the ground leading to cellars where the images could be hidden from the Muslim iconoclasts. We know of underground Jain temples which were built for the protection of images in Mughal times, and it is quite likely that these existed in our period as well, or that underground portions were beginning to be added to temples, with narrow passages as their entrance.[109] Of the great Buddhist establishments, Vikramashila had been completely destroyed before 1206, its foundation stones hurled into the Ganges. Nalanda was severely damaged by 1234 (when visited by Dharmasvamin) and abandoned. In Bodh Gaya at that time—deserted by all except four monks—an ancient image had been walled up by a brick wall and a new one had been put up in the ante-chamber. The old image had already been despoiled of its emerald eyes earlier. With the departure of the Muslim force, people returned to the site, removed the wall, and again made the old image accessible to devotees.[110] In a Jain poem we hear of another image, which was fashioned in the city of Kannanaya in the Cola country in 1176; when in 1192 AD Pṛthiviraja, the Cauhan leader, was killed, Ramadeva sent a letter to the Jains, stating: 'the kingdom of the Turks has begun; keep the image of Mahavira hidden away'.[111] This image, accordingly, was kept concealed in the sand at Kayamvasatthala and remained there for about sixty years.

Some of the oldest temples, for example at Pushkar, eleven kilometres to the west of Ajmer, on the bank of the most sacred lake of India (described as such in the fifth century by Fa Hsien), were not destroyed before the time of Aurangzeb. Mathurā, the birthplace of Krishna, was destroyed again and again. Aurangzeb ultimately raised a great red sandstone mosque on the ruins of its Kesava Deo temple. Chitorgarh, the most famous of Rajput fortresses, founded about 728 AD, was taken by Muslim armies three times: the first by 'Alā' ad-Dīn Khalajī in 1303, the second by Bahādur Shāh in 1535, and the third by Akbar in 1567. Here again we find many temples dating back to the fifteenth century, when a revival of Jain architecture took place. But often, like in the case of the Temple of Mirabai, erected in 1449 by Rana Kumbha of the Mewar dynasty, they were built on an eighth- or ninth-century substructure which was demolished centuries earlier. Another example is the sun-temple in Chitorgarh, probably dating to the eighth century, where Sūrya is defaced by the Muslim iconoclasts on one side of the temple, while left intact on the other side; the temple itself was rededicated to Kali, after having been destroyed by the Khalajīs and again by later Muslims. Nowhere in the north did the Hindu temple building tradition perpetuate itself without hindrance. Even in the east, in Orissa, the climax of the Hindu architectural tradition was clearly reached with the thirteenth-century Sūrya temple at Konarkā, after which stylistic decline set in, imitative of earlier forms, but less flamboyant and without the same quality of surface decoration as for instance can be seen in the Jagannath temple at Puri.

The temples, with their incumbent images, rather than being turned into mosques directly, most often appear to have been destroyed, after their portable wealth was taken, and then replaced with mosques or Muslim shrines built from the rubble.[112] Icon pieces were sent to Ghazna to be trodden under foot by the believers, or to be fastened into doors and walls of the Jami' Masjid; fragments of religious statues were also sent to Mecca, Madina, and Baghdad for propaganda purposes.[113] On first discovery, temples and icons would immediately be stripped of their valuable parts, gold or red gold, silver, precious stones, the eyes made of jewels being picked out first.[114] Temples were destroyed with 'nafta and fire' (*nafta wa-l-dirām*), and with the aid of elephants. The greatest statues, like the one at Somnath, which was almost five metres in height, were first mutilated by the Sultan himself with a mace, and then destroyed—like any temple—by lighting fire around it so that it would burst into pieces.[115]

Comprehensive destruction, clearly, was not always the aim. It was essential to render the images powerless, to remove them from their consecrated contexts. Selective delapidation could be sufficient to that purpose. It is hard to gauge the depth of religious convictions here. Did fear play a role in the iconoclastic destruction of the early Muslim conquerors in India? Were the images destroyed, desecrated, or mutilated because they were potent or impotent? Mathura is described in the contemporary Muslim sources as 'the work of demons (jinn)', while the images themselves as well as the image-worshippers are referred to as 'devils' (*shāyatīn*), indicating the association of idolatry with evil. Hand in hand with iconoclasm and the destruction of temples went the hounding of temple priests, brahmans, as also Buddhist monks, who were seen as proponents of images and the ritual specialists which made image worship possible. This is also what happened in Sind, where many of the custodians of the budd temples were either made captives or killed by the Arab conquerors.[116] In the late tenth century the Ismā'ilis who occupied Multan and smashed the image of the Sun-god also killed its officiant priests.[117] The Ghaznavids too 'struck at the idol-worshippers (*butparastān*)', especially at Somnath, where the casualties are reported to have been as high as 50,000. Whether other objects which were associated with image worship were destroyed is not easy to determine; but the destruction of books, so familiar in European history and known from pre-Islamic India as well,[118] probably occurred during attacks on the Buddhist viharas in the early thirteenth century and elsewhere.

It seems beyond doubt that, in India too, Islamic iconoclasm was almost always directed against non-Islamic objects. When Mahmud attacked the Ismā'īlīs of Multan he did not destroy their mosque, but just left it to decay. The Ghaznavid expeditions, from the time of Sabuktigin onwards, are described in the sources as a *jihād* against the inhabitants of *Hind* who are all 'worshippers of images and idols' (*mu'abbid-i-ausān-o-asnām*).[119] Rhetorically, the texts describe the aim of the Ghaznavid operations as 'to extinguish the sparks of idolatry', 'to humiliate the sinners, Hindu unbelievers, the idol-worshippers', 'to destroy the deaf and dumb idols of al-Hind', and to replace the idolatrous belief by Islam, 'to spread the carpet of Islam', 'to cleanse the country of the odiousness of the idolatrous', and so on.[120]

The Turkish invaders were certainly familiar with Hindu sacred geography. The main religious sites were easily identified and taken out serially in the first quarter of the eleventh century. An unknown number of temples were destroyed by Sabuktigin, while nothing has survived of the mosques which he erected, largely in *Lamghān* and adjacent areas, as appears from the literary material. As Mahmud's first great triumph against the idolatrous religion is recorded the expedition of 1008 AD against *Bhīm-naghar*, 'the storehouse of a great idol', which was full of precious goods and metals and jewels donated by neighbouring kings, and which was situated in the foothills of the fort of *Nagarkot*.[121] *Thāneswar* or *Tānesar*, a city about 48 km west of Delhi, called *Tāneshar* by Biruni, came next, in 1011 AD. This was a city which 'was held in the same veneration by idolaters as Mecca by the faithful'.[122] Without doubt it was an important place of worship, but it was left undefended, and plundered by the Muslims with ease, while many of the icons were broken, and the chief icon *Yugasoma* or *Cakrasvāmin*, made of bronze and nearly the size of a man, was despatched to Ghazna—where it was put in the hippodrome.[123] It was only after Tānesar, however, that the major religious sites were reached. There were three of these, and it is in their destruction that the systematic nature of Islamic iconoclastic activity in India is most apparent.

Mathura

This city, *Mathurá* or *Mathurā*, Biruni's *Māhurā*,[124] present-day *Muttra*, was already an important religious site in ancient times—Ptolemy's 'Madoura of the Gods'—, due to its location on the Yamuna, at the very centre of the Ganges–Yamuna Doab. 'Utbī calls it *Mahrah al-Hind.*[125] No Ashokan inscriptions have been found in the area, although archaeology suggests that the first transition to urbanism was made in the area in the Mauryan period. According to Hiuen Tsang there existed in his time three stupas of Ashoka at Mathura. We merely know from inscriptions that there were Buddhists in Mathura by the first century BC, but also that there were probably more Jains than Buddhists in these early times. The city appears to have retained its Buddhist-Jaina imprint up to 300 AD, with a great increase of Buddhist relics being noticeable under Kanishka. Unprecedented urban growth occurred when it became the principal capital of the Kushanas in India. With close relations developing between Gandhara and Mathura, Hellenistic and Parthian elements, were passed on and many new elements of iconography were incorporated. In later times, Mathura became a centre of the Krishna cult, a transformation to which Ābhīra and Gujar pastoralists, following the transhumance route from Saurashtra, probably contributed a great deal.[126]

Mathura was the first city in India to be destroyed by the Muslims. This happened in 1018 AD. 'Utbī, again, describes the extraordinary 'buildings' (*mabāni*) and 'mansions' (*mughānī*) which Mahmud saw there, and the one thousand 'idolhouses' (*butkhānahā*), built in compounds with stone walls (*az sang-i-banyād*), raised on high ground to protect them from the water of the Yamuna.[127] The main temple of Mathura, according to 'Utbī, represented a total cost of 100,000,000 dinars and could not have been built in less than 200 years. In it were five idols (asnām, *sanamhā*), in red gold (*adh-dhahab al-ahmar, zar-i-sarkh*), five metres high, one of which had eyes of rubies worth 50,000 dinars; another contained a blue sapphire which weighed 450 mishqāl. There were 'many thousands' of smaller idols in the city. We are told that the Sultan ordered all the temples to be devastated with fire and laid waste, after collecting vast amounts of gold and silver as well as jewels.

Kanauj

Kanauj was the most important of the religious centres of early medieval India, the brahmanical capital of Madhyadesha, a very large city, consisting of seven fortresses (*qilā, qalʿajāt*), with a total of 10,000 'idolhouses' (*buyūt al-asnām, butkhānahā*), 'in which enormous treasure was collected', on the west bank of the Ganges, where 'kings and brahmans' (*rāyān-o-barāhima*) from far away came to seek religious liberation and do worship 'in the tradition of their ancestors' (*bi-taqlīd-i-aslāf*).[128] 'Utbī refers to the Kanauj ruler as 'the chief (*muqaddam*) of the kings of Hind'. It was, in effect, the capital of the Gurjara-Pratiharas from 815 to 1019 AD, when it was sacked by Mahmud. By then the dynasty was already powerless. But Kanauj may well have been the wealthiest of Indian cities still.

When the Muslim army approached, most of the inhabitants had taken refuge 'with the gods', that is, in the temples. The city was taken possession of in one day, and emptied of its treasure. The 'idols' were destroyed; the 'infidels', 'worshippers of the sun and fire' (*ʿubbād ash-shams wa-l-nār*), fleeing, were pursued by the Muslims, and great numbers of them were killed. Kanauj probably never recovered its status as sacred capital of the brahmans. In Biruni's time, Kanauj was still in ruins, and the reigning king had removed himself to the town of Bari, east of the Ganges. Later in the eleventh and twelfth centuries the city revived under a northern branch of the Rashtrakutas and then the Gahadavalas; it ceased to be of any real importance by 1193 AD, when the last of the Gahadavala kings was defeated.

Somnath

The temple and town of *Somnāth*, Biruni's *Somnāt*, differs from Mathura and Kanauj in that it was not located on either of the sacred rivers of the Yamuna and Ganges. Away from the land-routes, on the peninsula of Kathiawar, it was thought to be relatively safe from Muslim interference. Not being on a sacred river, fresh Ganges water was brought daily for the god's bath.[129] On a narrow strip of land, it was fortified on one side, and washed on three sides by the sea, while the tide was looked upon as the worship paid to the god by the sea.[130] Somnāth (Skt. *Soma-nātha*, 'lord, of the moon') owed its name to the ebb and flow of the sea.[131] During lunar eclipses, the crowd of pilgrims visiting the temple could swell to 200,000 or 300,000.[132] The nearby town of the same name had become famous because of its maritime connections;[133] it was a station (*manzil*) for 'those who travelled back and forth between Sufāla al-Zanj and as-Sīn'.[134] Due to its maritime connections, the temple of Somnāth could be built on columns of teakwood imported from Africa.[135] For the same reason, we find Muslims living in Somnāth before Mahmud's expedition of 1025 AD.

Somnāth was 'the greatest of the idols of al-Hind'.[136] Thousands of villages had been donated to its upkeep, 1,000 or 2,000 brahmans served as its priests, hundreds of sacred prostitutes and musicians belonged to it, and it owned more jewels and gold 'than any royal treasury had ever contained'.[137] The great idol was a phallic representation of Mahadeva—next to which there were thousands of smaller images, wrought in gold or silver—and was brought, according to some, from Mecca in the time before the Prophet (but this was denied by the brahmans, according to whom it had stood near the harbour of Dew since the time of Krishna).[138]

Ibn al-Athir writes that when the other icons failed to fulfil their apotropaic functions the Hindus alleged that this was because Somnāth was displeased with them.[139] Now, however, Somnāth had drawn the Muslims to it in order to have them destroyed and to avenge the destruction of the gods of India.[140] But Mahmud destroyed this idol too, scattering its parts to Ghazna, Mecca, and Madina, and taking booty to the amount of two million dinars.[141] Its destruction was publicized, by both contemporary and later authors, as the crowning glory of Islam over idolatry, elevating Mahmud to the status of a hero. It is not possible any longer to identify the exact site of the icon which was thus destroyed, as the whole coastline of this area is littered with ruins. Moreover, there has been a succession of later Muslim invaders who tried to raze the temple to the ground. Time and again the Hindus started rebuilding the monument. This went on for 400 years, until the shrine was finally abandoned. In 1842, the British, after attacking the Afghans at Ghazna, decided to bring back 'the gates of Somnāth' to India. Lord Allenborough proclaimed, on that occasion, that he had restored to the princes of India their honour by presenting them with these gates. The gesture, however, merely angered the Muslim princes, while the Maharajas did not want the 'polluted' portal.[142]

The destruction of Somnāth was clearly regarded as the climax of Muslim iconoclastic activity in Hind, and iconoclastic events after 1025–6 receive less attention in our sources. This is true even of the raids on Benares. We do not know much about the first Muslim raid on Benares, by Ahmad Nāyaltigin in 1033 AD, which appears merely to have been a plundering expedition.[143] When Muhammad Ghuri marched on the city, we are merely told that 'after breaking the idols in above 1,000 temples, he purified and consecrated the latter to the worship of the true God'.[144] Numerous other iconoclastic incidents are recounted throughout the eleventh–thirteenth centuries, indicating that in some cases new icons were introduced by the Hindus where the earlier ones were destroyed, and also that sometimes Hindu kings were allowed to retain their dominion on the condition that they demolished their own temples themselves.[145] Most significant, by the late twelfth and in the thirteenth century, was doubtlessly the destruction by the Turks of the Buddhist monasteries of Uddandapura, Vikṛamashila, and Nalanda, all in eastern India.[146] The Turkish invasions proved fatal to the existence of Buddhism as an organized religion in the country of its origin. Here again, conversion played no role. The Buddhist religion disappeared from north India because it had been almost exclusively concentrated in a few major monastic centres and these centres were destroyed by the Muslims. Insofar as Buddhism survived the thirteenth century, outside the orbit of Islamic conquest, in Sri Lanka, Tibet, and in mainland Southeast Asia, it was as a religion with roots in the peasant societies of these areas.

NOTES

Abbreviations used in these notes are listed below:

FS A. M. Husain (ed.), *Futūḥ as-Salāṭin of 'Iṣāmī* (Agra, 1938).

KT C. J. Tornberg (ed.), *Ibn al-Athir, Al-Kāmil fi'l-Ta'rīkh*, 12 vols (Leiden, 1853–1869).

TB W. H. Morley (ed.), *Ta'rīkh-i-Baihaqi* (Calcutta, 1862).

TF *Ta'rīkh-i-Firishta* (Lucknow, 1864).

TM *Tāj al-Ma'āthir: BM: Add. 7623.*

TMS M. Hidayat Hosaini (ed.), *Ta'rīkh-i-Mubārakshāhī of Yaḥya bin Aḥmad bin 'Abdullāh as-Sirhindi* (Calcutta, 1931).

TN N. Lees et al. (eds), *Ṭabaqāt-i-Nāṣirī of Ābū 'Umar al-Jūzjāni* (Calcutta, 1894).

TYA Al-'Utbī, *Ta'rīkh al-Yamīnī* (Delhi, 1847).

TYP Al-'Utbī, *Ta'rīkh-i-Yamīnī: Persian translation by Jurbādqāni (1206 AD)* (Teheran, 1334 H.).

ZA M. Nazim (ed.), *Zayn al-Akhbār of Gardizi* (Berlin, 1928).

*

1. Cf. A.P. Kazhdan and Ann Wharton Epstein, *Change in Byzantine Culture in the Eleventh and Twelfth Centuries* (Berkeley, Los Angeles, and London, 1985), pp. 12–13.

2. André Wink, *Al-Hind: The Making of the Islamic World*, Vol. I (Leiden, 1990), pp. 226–30.

3. A. Tripathi (ed.), *The Bṛhat-Samhitā of Varāhamihira* (Varanasi, 1968).

4. P. Shah (ed.), *Vishnudharmottara Purana, Khanda III*, 2 vols (Baroda, 1958–61).

5. Cf. *Al-Hind*, Vol. I, p. 264.

6. Cf. A. Cunningham, *Report of Tours in the Gangetic Provinces from Badaon and Bihar in 1875–6 and 1877–8 (Archaeological Survey of India, Vol. Xl*) (Varanasi, 1968), p. 42.

7. Cunningham, *Report of Tours*, p. 43.

8. Cf. G. Michell, *The Hindu Temple: An Introduction to its Meaning and Forms* (Chicago and London, 1988), pp. 18, 50, 53, 89, 92; S. Kramrisch, *The Hindu Temple* (Delhi, 1980).

9. *TYA*, pp. 335–6.

10. Ibid., p. 403; *TYP*, p. 245.

11. A Boner, 'Economic and Organizational Aspects of the Building Operations of the Sun Temple at Konārka', *Journal of the Economic and Social History of the Orient*, XIII (170), pp. 257–72.

12. C.H. Tawney, tr., *The Prabandhacintāmani or Wishing Stone of Narratives*, (Calcutta, 1899) pp. 149–50.

13. J. Burgess and H. Cousens, *The Architectural Antiquities of Northern Gujarat* (*1902*) (Varanasi, 1975), pp. 5, 17.

14. Thomas Watters, *On Yuan Chwang's Travels in India, 629–645 AD* (London, 1904–5), II, pp. 2–3.

15. Cf. B. Stein (ed.), *South Indian Temples: An Analytical Reconsideration* (New Delhi, 1978).

16. As, for example, in Somnāth (*TF*, p. 33).

17. Cf. Michell, *Hindu Temple*, p. 58.

18. Cf. M.D. Willis, 'Religious and Royal Patronage in North India', in V.N. Desai and D. Mason (eds), *Gods, Guardians, and Lovers: Temple Sculptures from North India, AD 700–1200* (New York, 1913), p. 51.

19. Ibid., pp. 62–8.

20. Michell, *Hindu Temple*, p. 36; D.L. Eck, *Darshan: Seeing the Divine Image in India* (Chambersburg, 1985), p. 10.

21. *Al-Hind*, Vol. I, p. 338.

22. Eck, *Darshan*, pp. 22–4.

23. Cf. *Al-Hind*, Vol. I, p. 297; J.N. Banerjea, *The Development of Hindu Iconography* (Calcutta, 1956).

24. Cf. Eck, *Darshan*, esp. pp. 2, 11, and 17.

25. Banerjea, *Hindu Iconography.* p. 1.

26. Ibid., p. 152.

27. Shah, *Vishnudharmottara Purāna, Khanda III,* Vol. II, pp. 190–1; Hermann Kulke, *The Devarāja Cult* (Ithaca, 1978) esp. pp. xvi, 24–9; Michell, *Hindu Temple,* p. 65; R. Inden, 'The Temple and the Hindu Chain of Being', in J-C. Galey (ed.), *L'Espace du Temple,* Vol. I (Paris, 1985), p. 65.

28. Cf. John M. Fritz and George Michell, *City of Victory: Vijayangara, The Medieval Hindu Capital of Southern India* (New York, 1991), p. 7.

29. Kulke, *Devarāja Cult.*

30. J. Ries, 'Idolatry', *The Encyclopaedia of Religion,* Vol. 7 (New York, 1987), pp. 72–82.

31. L. Barnard, 'The Theology of Images', in: A. Bryer and J. Herrin (eds), *Iconoclasm: Papers given at the Ninth Symposium of Byzantine Studies* (Birmingham, 1975), pp. 7–13.

32. Ibid., p. 13.

33. Ibid.; *Al-Hind,* Vol. I, p. 40.

34. D. Freedberg, 'The Structure of Byzantine and European Iconoclasm', in Bryer and Herrin (eds), *Iconoclasm,* pp. 116–77.

35. Quoted in Eck, *Darshan,* p. 17.

36. S. Kramrisch, 'Hindu Iconography', *The Encyclopaedia of Religion,* Vol. 7 (New York, 1987), p. 40.

37. Shah, *Vishnudharmottara Purāna, Khanda III,* Vol. I, adhyāya 93; II, pp. 1–2.

38. Ibid., Vol. I, adhyāya 103–8; Vol. II, p. 189.

39. D. Shea and A. Troyer (trans.), *Dabistān al-Madhāhib* (Lahore, 1973), p. 199. See for a comparable view: Law de Lauriston, 'Les Indiens ne sont pas idolatres', in Guy Deleury, *Les Indes Florissantes: anthologie dẹs voyageurs,Français, 1750–1820* (Paris, 1991), pp. 706–9: '... il n'êst pas moins vrai que la religion des Indiens originaires est pure dans son principe, sans mélange de ce que nous nommes idolatrie .... Elle ne reconnait qu'un être supreme avec ses attributs qui sont adorés sous diverses emblemes ou figures .... c'êst que la religion des Gentils dans 1'Inde n'est pas une idolatrie ....' See also: K. Narayan, *Storytellers, Saints, and Scoundrels: Folk Narrative in Hindu Religious Teaching* (Philadelphia, 1989), p. 33: 'If you want to reach the formless, you can only go from what has form [sākār] to what has no form. First form, then the formless.'

40. Al-Biruni, *Kitāb fī Taḥqīqi ma li-l-Hind* (Hyderabad, India, 1958), pp. 84–95.

41. For an example of the latter: M. Nizam ad-Din (ed.), *Jawāmi' al-Hikāyat,* (Hyderabad, Deccan, 1966), Vol. I, pt. II, pp. 255–8. For an example of a Hindu king destroying temples of his father, see Tawney, *Prabandhācintāmani,* p. 245: 'Ajayadeva was set on the throne [in Gujarat] .... When he began to destroy the temples set up by his predecessor .... Hearing that his younger son had quickly destroyed them, he said: "Why even His Majesty Ajayadeva did not destroy his

father's religious edifices, until his father had gone to the next world, but you are the lowest of the low, for you destroy mine while I am still alive"'.

42. Banerjea, *Hindu Iconography*, p. 33.

43. R. H. Davis, 'Indian Art Objects as Loot', *Journal of Asian Studies*, 52, 1 (1993), p. 22.

44. Ibid., p. 27.

45. Ibid., p. 28.

46. Ibid., pp. 28–9, 42.

47. For an example of this Marxist view, see K.A. Nizami (ed.), *Politics and Society during the Early Medieval Period: Collected Works of Professor Mohammad Habib*, 2 vols (New Delhi, 1974–81). Nizami writes: '... His [M. Habib's] study of Mahmud of Ghazni led him to the conclusion that the Sultan's Indian campaigns were not inspired by any religious objective but were motivated by a desire for economic exploitation.' (p. xi; see also p. xiii).

48. *Al-Hind*, Vol. I, p. 264; Watters, *Yuan Chwang*, Vol. I, p. 343; Vol. II, pp. 43, 92, 115–6.

49. D. Chattopadhyaya, *Tāranātha's History of Buddhism in India* (Calcutta, 1980), p. 279.

50. *Epigraphia Indica*, I (1892), p. 61–6.

51. Cf. *Al-Hind*, Vol. I, p. 249; M.A. Stein, tr. *Rājataranginī*, (London, 1900) Vol. V. 166–70.

52. Stein, *Rājataranginī*, Vol. VII, 1092–5.

53. Cf. M. Ishaq Khan, 'The impact of Islam on Kashmir in the Sultanate period (1320–1586)', *The Indian Economic and Social History Review*, XXIII, 2 (April–June 1986), pp. 197–9.

54. A.K. Roy, *A History of the Jainas* (New Delhi, 1984), pp. 4, 144–5.

55. For example M. Boyce, 'Iconoclasm among the Zoroastrians', in J. Neusner (ed.), *Christianity, Judaism and other Greco-Roman Cults: Studies presented to Morton Smith*, Vol. 4 (Leiden, 1975), pp. 93–111, suggests that an iconoclastic movement in Zoroastrianism 'may well have played a part' in inspiring Christian and Islamic iconoclasm and iconomachy. This however remains purely hypothetical, and moreover would lead us to suppose that the formation of Islamic iconoclast theology did not begin before the ninth century—which seems too late.

56. P. Crone, 'Islam, Judeo-Christianity and Byzantine Iconoclasm', *Jerusalem Studies in Arabic and Islam*, Vol. II (Jerusalem, 1980), p. 66, note 30.

57. *Qur'ān*, 39: 4.

58. *Qur'ān*, 2: 129; 3: 89, etc.

59. A.A. Vasiliev, 'The Iconoclastic Edict of the Caliph Yazid II, AD 721', *Dumbarton Oaks Papers*, 9 (1955), p. 27.

60. For example, Shea and Troyer, *Dabistān al-Madhāhib*, p. 199.

61. Cairo, 1914.

62. A Schimmel, 'Islamic Iconography', *The Encyclopaedia of Religion, Vol. 7* (New York, 1987), p. 65.

63. R. Paret, 'Textbelege zum islamischen Bilderverbot', in *Das Werk des Kunstlers. Studien zur Ikonographie und Formgeschichte H. Schrade dargebracht* (Stuttgart, 1960).

64. Schimmel, 'Islamic Iconography', pp. 64–7.

65. J.B. Harley and D. Woodward (eds), *The History of Cartography, Volume Two, Book One: Cartography in the Traditional Islamic and South Asian Societies* (Chicago and London, 1992), p. 303.

66. S.F. Dale, 'Islamic architecture in Kerala', in A,L. Dallapiccola and S. Zingel-Avé Lallemant (eds), *Islam and Indian Regions*, 2 vols (Stuttgart, 1993), Vol. I, pp. 491–5.

67. P. Hasan, 'Temple niches and mihrabs in Bengal', in A.L. Dallapiccola and S. Zingel-Avé Lallemant (eds), *Islam and Indian Regions*, 2 vols (Stuttgart, 1993), Vol. I, pp. 87–94.

68. O. Grabar, 'Islam and Iconoclasm', in A. Bryer and J. Herrin (eds), *Iconoclasm: Papers given at the Ninth Symposium of Byzantine Studies* (Birmingham, 1975), p. 49.

69. Ibid., p. 51.

70. Crone, 'Islam', p. 68.

71. Vasiliev, 'Iconoclastic Edict'; Crone, 'Islam', p. 69. Grabar, 'Islam and Iconoclasm', p. 46 denies the historical validity of Yazid's document.

72. Grabar, 'Islam and Iconoclasm', p. 45.

73. Chattopadhyaya, *Tāranātha's History*, p. 348.

74. *Al-Hind*, Vol. I, p. 40; Crone, 'Islam'.

75. J. Herrin, 'The Context of Iconoclast Reform' in A. Bryer and J. Herrin (eds), *Iconoclasm: Papers given at the Ninth Symposium of Byzantine Studies* (Birmingham, 1975), p. 20.

76. Ibid.

77. S. Vryonis, Jr, *The Decline of Medieval Hellenism in Asia Minor and the Process of Islamization from the Eleventh through the Fifteenth Century* (Berkeley, 1971), p. 195.

78. Ibid.

79. Ibid.

80. Ibid., p. 196.

81. Ibid., pp. 196–7.

82. J.K. Choksy, 'Conflict, Coexistence, and Cooperation: Muslims and Zoroastrians in Eastern Iran during the Medieval period', *The Muslim World*, LXXX, 3–4 (1990), pp. 213–33; J.K. Choksy, 'Zoroastrians in Muslim Iran: Selected Problems of Coexistence and Interaction during the Early Medieval Period', *Iranian Studies*, XX, 1 (1987), pp. 17–30.

83. *Al-Hind*, Vol. I, pp. 121–2.

84. Ibid., p. 143.

85. Ibid., p. 193.

86. Ibid., p. 5.

87. Y. Friedmann, 'Medieval Muslim Views of Indian Religions', *Journal of the American Oriental Society,* 95, 2 (1975), pp. 214–5. [...]

88. Friedmann, 'Medieval Muslim Views', pp. 214–5.

89. D.N. Maclean, *Religion and Society in Arab Sind* (Leiden, 1989), p. 24.

90. F.A. Khan, *Banbhore* (Karachi, 1969), pp. 24–30.

91. *Al-Hind,* Vol. I, p. 203.

92. Ibid., p. 120.

93. Ibid., pp. 186–7.

94. Ibid., pp. 187–8.

95. Ibid., p. 212.

96. M. Nazim, ed. and tr., 'The Pand-Namah of Sabuktigin', *Journal of the Royal Asiatic Society* (1933), pp. 611–12 (tr. p. 622).

97. *TN,* p. 9.

98. Ibid.

99. For example, *TF,* p. 33.

100. It is explicitly forbidden in the Hindu shastras. The materials used for a Hindu temple could only function effectively in their original context; for a new building all materials had to be made or collected expressly—a rule which was however frequently violated.

101. M.W. Meister, 'Indian Islam's lotus throne: Kaman and Khatu Kalan', in A.L. Dallapiccola and S. Zingel-Avé Lallemant (eds), *Islam and Indian Regions,* 2 vols (Stuttgart, 1993), Vol. I, pp. 445–52, reproduced in this volume as Chapter 11.

102. Ibid.

103. Most of these texts are collected in the *Epigraphia Indica—Arabic and Persian Supplement* and *Epigraphia Indo-Moslemica.*

104. On this, see also (with caution): S.R. Goel, *Hindu Temples: What happened to them, pt. II: The Islamic Evidence* (New Delhi 1991).

105. *TYA,* pp. 402–4; *TYP,* pp. 31, 38, 187, 244; *ZA,* p. 75.

106. *TM,* p. 222.

107. Willis, 'Religious and Royal Patronage in North India', pp. 49–65.

108. Cf. Stein, *South Indian Temples,* pp. 1–31; Michell, *Hindu Temple,* pp. 18, 131, 149–51, 183. For the effects of the early Muslim raids on a major temple complex in Shrirangam, south India, see G.W. Spencer, 'Crisis of Authority in a Hindu Temple under the Impact of Islam', in: B.L. Smith (ed.), *Religion and the Legitimation of Power in South Asia* (Leiden, 1978), pp. 14–27.

109. Cf. K.C Jain, *Jainism in Rajasthan* (Sholapur, 1963), p. 128.

110. Roerich, *Dharmasvamin,* pp. xix, xxxii, 64.

111. K. Mitra, 'Historical references in Jain poems', *Proceedings of the Indian History Congress,* 5 (1941), p. 299.

112. *TYP*, pp. 38, 179; *TF*, pp. 26–7.

113. *TYP*, p. 250; TF, pp. 27, 32–3.

114. *TF* p. 27; *TYA*, p. 402; *TYP*, p. 244; *ZA*, pp. 75–6.

115. *TF*, pp. 32–3.

116. Cf. p. 426; *Al-Hind*, Vol. I, pp. 203, 205.

117. *Al-Hind*, Vol. I, p. 188.

118. For example, Tantra treatises, which were burnt in the reign of Dharmapala because of their content (Chattopadhyaya, *Tāranātha's History*, p. 279).

119. TYP, pp. 31–9; *TYA*, pp. 258–61,

120. See esp. *TYA* and *TYP passim*.

121. *TYA*, pp. 278–82; *TYP*, p. 187; *TF*, pp. 26–7.

122. *TF*, p. 27.

123. Ibid.; *TYA*, pp. 336–8; al-Bīrūnī, *Kitāb al-Hind*, p. 89.

124. Cf. *Al-Hind*, Vol. I, p. 299.

125. *TYA*, pp. 395, 401.

126. Cf. *Al-Hind*, Vol. I, p. 280; Srinivasan, *Mathurā;* Van Lohuizen-De Leeuw, *The 'Scythian' Period*.

127. *TYP*, pp. 242–4; *TYA*, pp. 401–3; and cf. *ZA*, pp. 74–8.

128. *TYA*, pp. 403–7; *TYP*, pp. 244–5; *ZA*, p. 76.

129. *TF*, p. 32; al-Bīrūnī, *Kitāb al-Hind*, p. 430.

130. *TF*, p. 32; *KT*, Vol. IX, p. 241; al-Bīrūnī, *Kitāb al-Hind*, p. 431.

131. al-Bīrūnī, *Kitāb al-Hind*, p. 431.

132. *TF*, p. 32; *KT*, Vol. IX, p. 241.

133. Cf. *Al-Hind*, Vol. I. pp. 185, 218, 199, 307; and *supra*, pp. 271, 275.

134. al-Bīrūnī, *Kitāb al-Hind*, pp. 430–1.

135. *KT*, Vol. IX p. 241.

136. Ibid.

137. *TF*, pp. 31–3; *KT*, Vol. IX, p. 241; *ZA*, p. 86.

138. *TF*, p. 32.

139. *KT*, Vol. IX, p. 241.

140. *TF*, p. 32.

141. *KT*, Vol. IX, p. 241; al-Bīrūnī, *Kitaāb al-Hind*, p. 429.

142. On Somnāth, see also R.H. Davis, 'Unmiraculous Images: Early Muslim Encounters with the Idols of India' (Unpublished paper read at the meeting of the Association for Asian Studies, April 1991).

143. *TB*, p. 497.

144. *TF*, p. 58.

145. For example, *TF*, pp. 44–5, 65; *FS*, vs. 1546–99; Siddiqui, *Perso-Arabic Sources*, p. 170; *TMS*, p. 20.

146. Cf. *TN*, pp. 147, 151; Chattopadhyaya, *Tāranātha's History*, pp. 318–9; Roerich, *Dharmasvamin*, intro, pp. xli–xliv; text, pp. 64, 90.

Temple Desecration and Indo-Muslim States*

RICHARD M. EATON

FRAMING THE ISSUE

In recent years, especially in the wake of the destruction of the Baburi Mosque in 1992, much public discussion has arisen over the political status of South Asian temples and mosques, and in particular the issue of temples desecrated or replaced by mosques in the pre-British period. While Hindu nationalists have endeavoured to document a pattern of wholesale temple destruction by Muslims in this period,[1] few professional historians have engaged the issue, even though it is a properly historical one. This essay aims to examine the evidence of temple desecration with a view to asking: Which temples were desecrated in India's pre-modern history? When, and by whom? How, and for what purpose? And above all, what might any of this say about the relationship between religion and politics in pre-modern India? This is a timely topic, since many in India today are looking to the past to justify or condemn public policy with respect to religious monuments.

Much of the contemporary evidence on temple desecration cited by Hindu nationalists is found in Persian material translated and published during the rise of British hegemony in India. Especially influential has been the eight-volume *History of India as Told by Its Own Historians,* first published in 1849 and edited by Sir Henry M. Elliot, who oversaw the

*Previously published as Chapter X in David Gilmartin and Bruce B. Lawrence (eds), *Beyond Turk and Hindu, Rethinking Religious Identities in Islamicate South Asia,* The University Press of Florida, Gainesville, 2000, pp. 246–81. In the present version, some portions of the text and notes have been removed. For the complete text see the original version.

bulk of the translations, with the help of John Dowson. But Elliot, keen to contrast what he understood as the justice and efficiency of British rule with the cruelty and despotism of the Muslim rulers who had preceded that rule, was anything but sympathetic to the 'Muhammadan' period of Indian history. As he wrote in the book's original preface:

> The common people must have been plunged into the lowest depths of wretchedness and despondency. The few glimpses we have, even among the short Extracts in this single volume, of Hindus slain for disputing with Muhammadans, of general prohibitions against processions, worship, and ablutions, and of other intolerant measures, of idols mutilated, of temples razed, of forcible conversions and marriages, of proscriptions and confiscations, of murders and massacres, and of the sensuality and drunkenness of the tyrants who enjoined them, show us that this picture is not overcharged.[2]

With the advent of British power, on the other hand, 'a more stirring and eventful era of India's History commences ... when the full light of European truth and discernment begins to shed its beams upon the obscurity of the past.'[3] Noting the far greater benefits that Englishmen had brought to Indians in a mere half century than Muslims had brought in five centuries, Elliot expressed the hope that his published translations would 'make our native subjects more sensible of the immense advantages accruing to them under the mildness and the equity of our rule.'[4]

Elliot's motives for delegitimizing the Indo-Muslim rulers who had preceded English rule are thus quite clear. Writing on the pernicious influence that this understanding of pre-modern Indian history had on subsequent generations, the eminent historian Mohammad Habib once remarked,

> The peaceful Indian Mussalman, descended beyond doubt from Hindu ancestors, was dressed up in the garb of a foreign barbarian, as a breaker of temples, and an eater of beef, and declared to be a military colonist in the land where he had lived for about thirty or forty centuries... The result of it is seen in the communalistic atmosphere of India today.[5]

Although penned many years ago, these words are especially relevant in the context of current controversies over the history of temple desecration in India. For it has been through a selective use of Elliot and Dowson's selective translations of pre-modern Persian chronicles, together with a selective use of epigraphic data, that Hindu nationalists have sought to find the sort of irrefutable evidence—one of Sita Ram Goel's chapters is entitled 'From the Horse's Mouth'—that would demonstrate a persistent pattern of villainy and fanaticism on the part of pre-modern Indo-Muslim conquerors and rulers.

In reality, though, each scrap of evidence in the matter requires careful scrutiny. Consider an inscription dated 1455 and found over the doorway of a tomb-shrine in Dhar, Madhya Pradesh, formerly the capital of Malwa. The inscription, a Persian *ghazal* of forty-two verses, mentions the destruction of a Hindu temple by one 'Abdullah Shah Changal during the reign of Raja Bhoja, a renowned Paramara king who ruled over the region from 1010 to 1053. In *Hindu Temples: What Happened to Them?* Goel accepts the inscription's reference to temple destruction more or less at face value, as though it were a contemporary newspaper account reporting an objective fact.[6] Unlike Goel, however, the text is concerned not with documenting an instance of temple destruction but with narrating and celebrating the fabulous career of 'Abdullah Shah Changal, the saint who is buried at Dhar. A reading of a larger body of the text reveals, in fact, a complex historiographical process at work:

> This centre became Muhammadan first by him [i.e., 'Abdullah Shah Changal], (and) all the banners of religion were spread. (I have heard) that a few persons had arrived before him at this desolate and ruined place. When the muazzin raised the morning cry like the trumpet-call for the intoxicated *sufis*, the infidels (made an attack from) every wall (?) and each of them rushed with the sword and knife. At last they (the infidels) wounded those men of religion, and after killing them concealed (them) in a well. Now this (burial place and) grave of martyrs remained a trace of those holy and pious people.
>
> When the time came that the sun of Reality should shine in this dark and gloomy night, this lion-man ['Abdullah Shah Changal] came from the centre of religion to this old temple with a large force. He broke the images of the false deities, and turned the idol-temple into a mosque. When Rai Bhoj saw this, through wisdom he embraced Islam with the family of all brave warriors. This quarter became illuminated by the light of the Muhammadan law, and the customs of the infidels became obsolete and abolished.
>
> Now this tomb since those old days has been the famous pilgrimage-place of a world. Graves from their oldness became levelled (to the ground), (and) there remained no mount on any grave. There was also (no place) for retirement, wherein the distressed *darvish* could take rest. Thereupon the king of the world gave the order that this top of Tur [Mount Sinai] be built anew. The king of happy countenance, the Sultan of horizons (i.e., the world), the visitors of whose courts are Khaqan (the emperor of Turkistan) and Faghfur (the emperor of

China), 'Ala-ud-din Wad-dunya Abu'l-Muzaffar, who is triumphant over his enemies by the grace of God, the Khilji king Mahmud Shah, who is such that by his justice the world has become adorned like paradise, he built afresh this old structure, and this house with its enclosure again became new.[7]

The narrative divides a remembered past into three distinct moments. The first is the period before the arrival of the Hero, 'Abdullah Shah Changal. At this time a small community of Muslims in Malwa, with but a tenuous foothold in the region, were martyred by local non-Muslims, their bodies thrown into a well. The narrative's second moment is the period of the Hero, who comes from the 'centre of religion' (Mecca?), smashes images, transforms the temple into a mosque, and converts to Islam the most famous king of the Paramara dynasty—deeds that collectively avenge the martyred Sufis and (re)establish Islam in the region. The narrative's third moment is the period after the Hero's lifetime when his grave, although a renowned place of pilgrimage has suffered from neglect. Now enters the narrative's other hero, Sultan Mahmud Khalaji, the 'king of the world' and 'of happy countenance', to whose court the emperors of China and Central Asia pay respect, and by whose justice the world has become adorned like paradise. His great act was to patronize the cult of 'Abdullah Shah by (re)building his shrine, which we are told at the text's end included a strong vault, a mosque, and a caravanserai. The inscription closes by offering a prayer that the soul of the benevolent sultan may last until Judgment Day and that his empire may last in perpetuity.

Although Indo-Muslim epigraphs are typically recorded soon after the events they describe, the present one is hardly contemporary, as it was composed some four hundred years after the events to which it refers. Far from being a factual account of a contemporary incident, then, the text presents a richly textured legend elaborated over many generations of oral transmission until 1455, when the story of 'Abdullah Shah Changal and his deeds in Malwa became frozen in the written word that we have before us. As such, the narrative reveals a process by which a particular community at a particular time and place—Muslims in mid-fifteenth-century Malwa—constructed their origins. Central to the story are themes of conversion, martyrdom, redemption, and the patronage of sacred sites by Indo-Muslim royalty, as well as, of course, the destruction of a temple. Whether or not any temple was actually destroyed four hundred years before this narrative was committed to writing, we cannot know with certainty. However, it would seem no more likely that such a desecration had actually occurred than that the renowned Raja Bhoja had been converted to Islam, which the text also claims.

In any event, it is clear that by the mid-fifteenth century the memory of the destruction of a temple, projected into a distant past, had become one among several elements integral to how Muslims in Malwa—or at least those who patronized the composition of this *ghazal*—had come to understand their origins. The case thus suggests that caution is necessary in interpreting claims made in Indo-Muslim literary sources to instances of temple desecration. It also illustrates the central role that temple desecration played in the remembered past of an Indo-Muslim state or community.

Early Instances of Temple Desecration

It is well known that, during the two centuries before 1192, which was when an indigenous Indo-Muslim state and community first appeared in north India, Persianized Turks systematically raided and looted major urban centres of north India, hauling immense loads of movable property to power bases in eastern Afghanistan.[8] The pattern commenced in 986, when the Ghaznavid sultan, Sabuktigin (r. 977–97), attacked and defeated the Hindu Shahi raja who controlled the region between Kabul and northwest Punjab. According to Abu Nasr 'Utbi, the personal secretary to the sultan's son, Sabuktigin marched out towards Lamghan [located to the immediate east of Kabul], which is a city celebrated for its great strength and abounding in wealth. He conquered it and set fire to the places in its vicinity which were inhabited by infidels, and demolishing the idol-temples, he established Islam in them.'[9] Linking religious conversion with military conquest—with conquest serving to facilitate conversion, and conversion to legitimize conquest—'Utbi's brief notice established a rhetorical trope that many subsequent Indo-Muslim chroniclers would repeat, as for example in the case of the 1455 inscription at Dhar, just discussed.

Notwithstanding 'Utbi's religious rhetoric, however, subsequent invasions by Sabuktigin and his more famous son, Mahmud of Ghazni (r. 998–1030), appear to have been undertaken for purely material reasons. Based in Afghanistan and never seeking permanent dominion in India, the earlier Ghaznavid rulers raided and looted Indian cities, including their richly endowed temples loaded with movable wealth, with a view to financing their larger political objectives far to the west in Khurasan.[10] The predatory nature of these raids was also structurally integral to the Ghaznavid political economy: their army was a permanent, professional one built around an elite core of mounted archers who, as slaves, were purchased, equipped, and paid with cash derived from regular infusions of war booty taken alike from Indian and Iranian cities.[11] From the mid-eleventh century, however, Mahmud's successors, cut off from their sources of military manpower in Central Asia first by the Seljuqs and then by the Ghurids, became progressively more provincial, their kingdom focused around their capital of Ghazni in eastern Afghanistan with extensions into the Punjab. And, while the later Ghaznavids continued the predatory raids of the Indian interior for booty, these appear to have been less destructive and more sporadic than those of Sabuktigin and Mahmud.[12]

The dynamics of north Indian politics changed dramatically, however, when the Ghurids, a dynasty of Tajik (eastern Iranian) origins, arrived from central Afghanistan toward the end of the twelfth century. Sweeping aside the Ghaznavids, Ghurid conquerors and their Turkish slave generals ushered in a new sort of state quite unlike that of the foreign-based Ghaznavids. Aspiring to imperial dominion over the whole of north India from a base in the middle of the Indo-Gangetic plain, the new Delhi Sultanate signalled the first attempt to build an indigenous Indo-Muslim state and society in north India. [...]

Temple Desecration and State Building

By effectively injecting a legitimizing 'substance' into a new body politic, royal patronage of Chishti Shaikhs contributed positively to the process of Indo-Muslim state building. Equally important to this process was its negative counterpart: the sweeping away of all prior political authority in newly conquered and annexed territories. When such authority was vested in a ruler whose own legitimacy was associated with a royal temple—typically one that housed an image of a ruling dynasty's state deity, or *raṣṭra-devatā* (usually Vishnu or Śiva)—that temple was normally desecrated, redefined, or destroyed, any of which would have had the effect of detaching a defeated raja from the most prominent manifestation of his former legitimacy. Temples that were not so identified, or temples formerly so identified but abandoned by their royal patrons and thereby rendered politically irrelevant, were normally left unharmed. Such was the case, for example, with the famous temples at Khajuraho south of the middle Gangetic Plain, which appear to have been abandoned by their Candella royal patrons before Turkish armies reached the area in the early thirteenth century.[13]

It would be wrong to explain this phenomenon by appealing to an essentialized 'theology of iconoclasm' felt to be intrinsic to the Islamic religion. While it is true that contemporary Persian sources routinely condemned idolatry (*but-parastī*) on religious grounds, it is also true that attacks on images patronized by enemy kings had been, from about the sixth century AD on, thoroughly integrated into Indian political behaviour. With their lushly sculpted imagery vividly displaying the mutual interdependence of kings and gods and the commingling of divine and human kingship, royal temple complexes of the early medieval period were thoroughly and preeminently political institutions. It was here that, after the sixth century, human kingship was established, contested, and revitalized.[14] Above all, the central icon housed in a royal temple's 'womb-chamber' and inhabited by the state deity of the temple's royal patron expressed the shared sovereignty of king and deity. Moreover, notwithstanding that temple priests endowed a royal temple's deity with attributes of transcendent and universal power, that same deity was also understood as having a very special relationship, indeed a sovereign relationship, with the particular geographical site in which its temple complex was located.[15] As revealed in temple narratives, even the physical removal of an image from its original site could not break the link between deity and geography.[16] The bonding between king, god, temple, and land in early medieval India is well illustrated in a passage from *Bṛhatsaṃhitā*, a text from the sixth century AD:

> If a Śiva linga, image, or temple breaks apart, moves, sweats, cries, speaks, or otherwise acts with no apparent cause, this warns of the destruction of the king and his territory.[17]

In short, from about the sixth century on, images and temples associated with dynastic authority were considered politically vulnerable.

Given these perceived connections between temples, images, and their royal patrons, it is hardly surprising that early medieval Indian history abounds in instances of temple desecration that occurred amidst interdynastic conflicts. In 642 AD, according to local tradition, the Pallava king, Narasimhavarman I, looted the image of Ganesha from the Chalukyan capital of Vatapi. Fifty years later, armies of those same Chalukyas invaded north India and brought back to the Deccan what appear to be images of Ganga and Yamuna, looted from defeated powers there. In the eighth century, Bengali troops sought revenge on King Lalitaditya by destroying what they thought was the image of Vishnu Vaikuntha, the state deity of Lalitaditya's kingdom in Kashmir. In the early ninth century the Rashtrakuta king, Govinda III, invaded and occupied Kanchipuram, which so intimidated the king of Sri Lanka that he sent Govinda several (probably Buddhist) images representing the Sinhala state. The Rashtrakuta king then installed these in a Śaiva temple in his capital. About the same time the Pandyan king, Srimara Srivallabha, also invaded Sri Lanka and took back to his capital a golden Buddha image—'a synecdoche for the integrity of the Sinhalese polity itself'—that had been installed in the kingdom's jewel palace. In the early tenth century, the Pratihara king, Herambapala, seized a solid gold image of Vishnu Vaikuntha when he defeated the Sahi king of Kangra. A few years later, the same image was seized from the Pratiharas by the Candella king, Yaśovarman, and installed in the Lakshmana temple of Khajuraho. In the early eleventh century the Chola king, Rajendra I, furnished his capital with images he had seized from several prominent neighbouring kings: Durga and Ganesha images from the Chalukyas; Bhairava, Bhairavi, and Kali images from the Kalingas of Orissa; a Nandi image from the eastern Chalukyas; and a bronze Śiva image from the Palas of Bengal. In the mid-eleventh century, the Chola king, Rajadhiraja, defeated the Chalukyas and plundered Kalyani, taking a large black stone door guardian to his capital in Thanjavur, where it was displayed to his subjects as a trophy of war.[18]

While the dominant pattern here was one of looting royal temples and carrying off images of state deities,[19] we also hear of Hindu kings destroying the royal temples of their political adversaries. In the early tenth century, the Rashtrakuta monarch, Indra III, not only destroyed the temple of Kalapriya (at Kalpa near the Jamuna River), patronized by the Rashtrakutas' deadly enemies, the Pratiharas, but they took special delight in recording the fact.[20]

In short, it is clear that temples had been the natural sites for the contestation of kingly authority well before the coming of Muslim Turks to India. Not surprisingly, Turkish invaders, when attempting to plant their own rule in early medieval India, followed and continued established patterns. Table 3.1 gives dates and places, which are keyed to maps that follow. These cannot give the complete picture of temple desecration after the establishment of Turkish power in upper India. Undoubtedly, some temples were desecrated, but the facts were never recorded, or the facts were recorded but the records themselves no longer survive. Conversely, later Indo-Muslim chroniclers, seeking to glorify the religious zeal of earlier Muslim rulers, sometimes attributed acts of temple desecration to such rulers even when no contemporary evidence supports the claims.[21] As a result, we shall never know the precise number of temples desecrated in Indian history. Nonetheless, by relying strictly on evidence found in contemporary or near-contemporary epigraphs and literary evidence spanning more than five centuries (1192–1729), one may identify eighty instances of temple desecration whose historicity appears reasonably certain. Although this figure falls well short of the 60,000 claimed by some Hindu nationalists,[22] a review of these data suggests several broad patterns.

First, acts of temple desecration were almost invariably carried out by military officers or ruling authorities; that is, such acts that we know about were undertaken by the state. Second, the chronology and geography of the data indicate that acts of temple desecration typically occurred on the cutting edge of a moving military frontier. From Ajmer—significantly, also the wellspring of Chishti piety—the post-1192 pattern of temple desecration moved swiftly down the Gangetic Plain as Turkish military forces sought to extirpate local ruling houses in the late twelfth and early thirteenth centuries (see table 3.1 and map 3.1: nos. 1–9). In Bihar, this included the targeting of Buddhist monastic establishments at Odantapuri, Vikramasila, and Nalanda. Detached from a Buddhist laity, these establishments had by this time become dependent on the patronage of local royal authorities, with whom they were identified. In the 1230s, Iltutmish carried the Delhi Sultanate's authority into Malwa (nos. 10–11), and by the onset of the fourteenth century the Khalaji sultans had opened up a corridor through eastern Rajasthan into Gujarat (nos. 12–14, 16–17).

Delhi's initial raids on peninsular India, on which the Khalajis embarked between 1295 and the early decades of the fourteenth century (nos. 15, 18–19), appear to have been driven not by a goal of annexation but by the Sultanate's need for wealth with which to defend north India from Mongol attacks.[23] For a short time, then, peninsular India stood in the same relation to the north—namely, as a source of plunder for financing distant military operations—as north India had stood in relation to Afghanistan three centuries earlier, in the days of Mahmud of Ghazni. In 1323, however, a new north Indian dynasty, the Tughluqs, sought permanent dominion in the Deccan, which the future Sultan Muhammad bin Tughluq established by uprooting royally patronized temples in western Andhra (nos. 20–22). Somewhat later Sultan Firuz Tughluq did the same in Orissa (no. 23).

From the late fourteenth century, as the tide of Tughluq imperialism had receded from Gujurat and the Deccan, newly emerging successor states sought to expand their own political frontiers in those areas. This, too, is reflected in instances of temple desecration, as the ex-Tughluq governor of Gujarat and his successors consolidated their authority there (see table 3.1 and map 3.2: nos. 25–6, 31–2, 34–5, 38–9, 42), or as the Delhi empire's successors in the south, the Bahmani sultans, challenged Vijayanagara's claims to dominate the Raichur doab and the Tamil coast (nos. 33, 41). The pattern was repeated in Kashmir by Sultan Sikandar (nos. 27–30) and in the mid-fifteenth century when the independent sultanate of Malwa contested renewed Rajput power in eastern Rajasthan after Delhi's authority there had waned (nos. 36–7). [...]

All of these instances of temple desecration occurred in the context of military conflicts when Indo-Muslim states expanded into the domains of non-Muslim rulers. Contemporary chroniclers and inscriptions left by the victors leave no doubt that field commanders, governors, or sultans viewed the desecration of royal temples as a normal means of decoupling a Hindu king's legitimate authority from his former kingdom, and more specifically, of decoupling that former king from the image of the state deity that was publicly understood as protecting the king and his kingdom. This was accomplished in several ways. Most typically, temples considered essential to the constitution of enemy authority were destroyed. Occasionally, temples were converted into mosques, which more visibly conflated the disestablishment of former sovereignty with the establishment of a new one.[24]

The form of desecration that showed the greatest continuity with pre-Turkish practice was the seizure of the image of a defeated king's state deity and its abduction to the victor's capital as a trophy of war. In February 1299, for example, Ulugh Khan sacked Gujarat's famous temple of Somnath and sent its largest image to Sultan 'Ala al-Din Khalaji's court in Delhi (no. 16; map 3.1). When Firuz Tughluq invaded Orissa in 1359 and learned that the region's most important temple was that of Jagannath located inside the raja's fortress in Puri, he carried off the stone image of the god and installed it in Delhi 'in an ignominious position' (no. 23). In 1518, when the court in Delhi came to suspect the loyalty of a tributary Rajput chieftain in Gwalior, Sultan Ibrahim Lodi marched to the famous fortress, stormed it, and seized a brass image of Nandi evidently situated adjacent to the chieftain's Śiva temple. Brought back to Delhi, it was installed in the city's Baghdad Gate (no. 46; map 3.2). Similarly, in 1579, when Golconda's army, led by Murahari Rao, was campaigning south of the Krishna River, Rao annexed the entire region to Qutb Shahi domains and sacked the popular Ahobilam temple, whose ruby-studded image he brought back to Golconda and presented to his sultan as a war trophy (no. 51). Although the Ahobilam temple had only local appeal, it had close associations with prior sovereign authority, since it had been patronized and even visited by the powerful and most famous king of Vijayanagara, Krishna Deva Raya.[25]

In each of these instances, the deity's image, taken as war trophy to the capital city of the victorious sultan, was radically detached from its former context and transformed from a living to a dead image. However, sacked images were not invariably abducted to the victor's capital. [...]

Whatever form they took, acts of temple desecration were never directed at the people but at the enemy king and the image that incarnated and displayed his state deity. [...]

Temple Desecration and State Maintenance

It seems certain that Indo-Muslim rulers were well aware of the highly charged political and religious relationship between a royal Hindu patron and his client-temple. Hence, even when former rulers or their descendants had been comfortably assimilated into an Indo-Muslim state's ruling class, there always remained the possibility and hence the occasional suspicion, that a temple's latent political significance might be activated and serve as a power base to further its patron's political aspirations. Such considerations might explain why it was that, when a subordinate non-Muslim officer in an Indo-Muslim state showed signs of disloyalty—and especially if he engaged in open rebellion—the state often desecrated the temple(s) most clearly identified with that officer. After all, if temples lying within its domain were viewed as state property, and if a government officer who was also a temple's patron demonstrated disloyalty to the state, from a juridical standpoint ruling authorities felt justified in treating that temple as an extension of the officer and hence liable for punishment.

Thus in 1478, when the Bahmanis' garrison in Kondapalle mutinied, murdered its governor, and entrusted the fort to Bhimraj Oriyya, who until that point had been a Bahmani client, the sultan personally marched to the site and, after a six-month siege, stormed the fort, destroyed its temple, and built a mosque on the site (no. 40). A similar event occurred in 1659, when Shivaji Bhonsle, the son of a loyal and distinguished officer serving the 'Adil Shahi sultans of Bijapur, seized a government port on the northern Konkan coast, thereby disrupting the flow of external trade to and from the capital. Responding to what it considered an act of treason, the government deputed a high-ranking officer, Afzal Khan, to punish the Maratha rebel. Before marching to confront Shivaji himself, however, the Bijapur general first proceeded to Tuljapur and desecrated a temple dedicated to the goddess Bhavani, to which Shivaji and his family had been personally devoted.

We find the same pattern with the Mughals. In 1613 while at Pushkar, near Ajmer, Jahangir ordered the desecration of an image of Varaha that had been housed in a temple belonging to an uncle of Rana Amar of Mewar, the emperor's arch-enemy. In 1635 his son and successor, Shah Jahan, destroyed the great temple at Orchha, which had been patronized by the father of Raja Jajhar Singh, a high-ranking Mughal officer who was at that time in open rebellion against the emperor. In 1669, there arose a rebellion in Benares among landholders, some of whom were suspected of having helped Shivaji, who was Aurangzeb's arch-enemy, escape from imperial detention. It was also believed that Shivaji's escape had been initially facilitated by Jai Singh, the great-grandson of Raja Man Singh, who almost certainly built Benares's great Vishvanath temple. It was against this background that the emperor ordered the destruction of that temple in September 1669.[26] About the same time, serious Jat rebellions broke out in the area around Mathura, in which the patron of that city's congregational mosque had been killed. So in early 1670, soon after the ringleader of these rebellions had been captured near Mathura, Aurangzeb ordered the destruction of the city's Keshava Deva temple, and he built an Islamic structure (*'id-gāh*)on its site.[27] Nine years later, the emperor ordered the destruction of several prominent temples in Rajasthan that had become associated with imperial enemies. These included temples in Khandela patronized by refractory chieftains there, temples in Jodhpur patronized by a former supporter of the emperor's brother and arch-rival, and the royal temples in Udaipur and Chitor patronized by Rana Raj Singh after it was learned that that Rajput chieftain had withdrawn his loyalty to the Mughal state.

Considerable misunderstanding has arisen from a passage in the *Ma'athir-i 'Alamgiri* concerning an order on the status of Hindu temples that Aurangzeb issued in April 1669, just months before his destruction of the Benares and Mathura temples. The passage has been construed to mean that the emperor ordered the destruction not only of the Vishvanath temple at Benares and the Keshava Deva temple at Mathura but of all temples in the empire.[28] The passage reads as follows:

> Orders respecting Islamic affairs were issued to the governors of all the provinces that the schools and places of worship of the irreligious be subject to demolition and that with the utmost urgency the manner of teaching and the public practices of the sects of these misbelievers be suppressed.[29]

The order did not state that schools or places of worship be demolished; rather, it said that they were *subject* to demolition, implying that local authorities were required to make investigations before taking action.

More important, the sentence immediately preceding this passage provides the context in which we may find the order's overall intent. On 8 April 1669, Aurangzeb's court received reports that in Thatta, Multan, and especially in Benares, Brahmans in 'established schools' *(mudāris-i muqarrar)* had been engaged in teaching false books *(kutub-i bātila)* and that both Hindu and Muslim 'admirers and students' had been travelling over great distances to study the 'ominous sciences' taught by this 'deviant group.'[30] We do not know what sort of teaching or 'false books' were involved here, or why both Muslims and Hindus were attracted to them, although these are intriguing questions. What is clear is that the court was primarily concerned, indeed exclusively concerned, with curbing the influence of a certain mode of teaching *(ṭaur-i dars-o-tadrīs)* within the imperial domain. Far from being, then, a general order for the immediate destruction of all temples in the empire, the order was responding to specific reports of an educational nature and was targeted at investigating those institutions where a certain kind of teaching had been taking place.

In sum, apart from his prohibition on building new temples in Benares, Aurangzeb's policies respecting temples within imperial domains generally followed those of his predecessors. Viewing temples within their domains as state property, Aurangzeb and Indo-Muslim rulers in general punished disloyal Hindu officers in their service by desecrating temples with which they were associated. How, one might then ask, did they punish disloyal Muslim officers? Since officers in all Indo-Muslim states belonged to hierarchically-ranked service cadres, infractions short of rebellion normally resulted in demotions in rank, while serious crimes like treason were generally punished by execution, regardless of the perpetrator's religious affiliation.[31]

No evidence, however, suggests that ruling authorities attacked public monuments like mosques or Sufi shrines that had been patronized by disloyal or rebellious officers. Nor were such monuments desecrated when one Indo-Muslim kingdom conquered another and annexed its territories. To the contrary, new rulers were quick to honour and support the shrines of those Chishti shaikhs that had been patronized by those they had defeated. Babur, upon seizing Delhi from the last of the city's ruling sultans, lost no time in patronizing the city's principal Chishti tomb-shrines. The pattern was repeated as the Mughals expanded into the provinces formerly ruled by Muslims. Upon conquering Bengal in 1574, the Mughals showered their most lavish patronage on the two Chishti shrines in Pandua—those of Shaikh 'Ala al-Haq (d. 1398) and Shaikh Nur Qutb-i 'Alam (d. 1459)—which had been the principal object of state patronage by the previous dynasty of Bengal sultans.[32] And when he extended Mughal dominion over defeated Muslim states of the Deccan, the dour Aurangzeb, notwithstanding his reputation for eschewing saint cults, made sizable contributions to those Chishti shrines in Khuldabad and Gulbarga that had helped legitimize earlier Muslim dynasties there.

Temples and Mosques Contrasted

Data presented in the foregoing discussion suggest that mosques or shrines carried very different political meanings than did royal temples in independent Hindu states or temples patronized by Hindu officers serving in Indo-Muslim states. For Indo-Muslim rulers, building mosques was considered an act of royal piety, even a duty. But all actors, rulers and ruled alike, seem to have recognized that the deity worshipped in mosques or shrines had no personal connection with a Muslim monarch. Nor were such monuments thought of as underpinning, far less actually constituting, the authority of an Indo-Muslim king. This point is illustrated in a reported dispute between the emperor Aurangzeb and a Sufi named Shaikh Muhammadi (d. 1696). As a consequence of this dispute, in which the shaikh refused to renounce views that the emperor considered theologically deviant, Shaikh Muhammadi was ordered to leave the imperial domain. When the Sufi instead took refuge in a local mosque, Aurangzeb claimed that this would not do, since the mosque was also within imperial territory. But the shaikh only remarked on the emperor's arrogance, noting that a mosque was the house of God and therefore only His property. The stand-off ended with the shaikh's imprisonment in Aurangabad fort—property that was unambiguously imperial.[33]

This incident suggests that mosques in Mughal India, though religiously potent, were considered detached from both land and dynastic authority and hence politically inactive. As such, their desecration could have had no relevance to the business of disestablishing a regime that had patronized them. Not surprisingly, then, when Hindu rulers established their authority over territories of defeated Muslim rulers, they did not as a rule desecrate mosques or shrines, as when Shivaji established a Maratha kingdom on the ashes of Bijapur's former dominions in Maharashtra, or when Vijayanagara annexed the former territories of the Bahmanis or their successors.[34] In fact, the rajas of Vijayanagara, as is well known, built their own mosques, evidently to accommodate the sizable number of Muslims employed in their armed forces.

By contrast, monumental royal temple complexes of the early medieval period were considered politically active, inasmuch as the state deities they housed were understood as expressing the shared sovereignty of king and deity over a *particular* dynastic realm.[35] Therefore, when Indo-Muslim commanders or rulers looted the consecrated images of defeated opponents and carried them off to their own capitals as war trophies, they were in a sense conforming to customary rules of Indian politics. Similarly, when they destroyed a royal temple or converted it into a mosque, ruling authorities were building on a political logic that they knew placed supreme political significance on such temples. That same significance, in turn, rendered temples just as deserving of peacetime protection as it rendered them vulnerable in times of conflict.

Temple Desecration and the Rhetoric of State Building

Much misunderstanding over the place of temple desecration in Indian history results from a failure to distinguish the rhetoric from the practice of Indo-Muslim state formation. Whereas the former tends to be normative, conservative, and rigidly ideological, the latter tends to be pragmatic, eclectic, and non-ideological. Rhetorically, we know, temple desecration figured very prominently in Indo-Muslim chronicles as a necessary and even meritorious constituent of state formation.[36] In 1350, for example, the poet-chronicler 'Isami gave the following advice to his royal patron, 'Ala al-Din Hasan Bahman Shah, the founder of the Bahmani kingdom in the Deccan:

> If you and I, O man of intellect, have a holding in this country and are in a position to replace the idol-houses by mosques and sometimes forcibly to break the Brahmanic thread and enslave women and children—all this is due to the glory of Mahmud [of Ghazni] .... The achievements that you make to-day will also become a story to-morrow.[37]

But the new sultan appears to have been more concerned with political stability than with the glorious legacy his court poet would wish him to pursue. There is no evidence that he converted any temples to mosques. After all, by carving out territory from lands formerly lying within the Delhi Sultanate, the founder of the Bahmani state had inherited a domain void of independent Hindu kings and hence void, too, of temples that might have posed a political threat to his fledgling kingdom.

Unlike temple desecration or the patronage of Chishti shaikhs, both of which appear in the contemporary rhetoric on Indo-Muslim state building, a third activity, the use of explicitly Indian political rituals, occupied no place whatsoever in that rhetoric. Here we may consider the way Indo-Muslim rulers used the rich political symbolism of the Ganges River, whose mythic associations with imperial kingship had been well established since Mauryan times (BC 321–181). Each in its own way, the mightiest imperial formations of the early medieval peninsula—the Chalukyas, the Rashtrakutas, and the Cholas—claimed to have 'brought' the Ganges River down to their southern capitals, seeking thereby to legitimize their claims to imperial sovereignty. Although the Chalukyas and the Rashtrakutas did this symbolically, probably through their insignia, the Cholas literally transported pots of Ganges water to their southern capital.[38] And, we are told, so did Muhammad bin Tughluq in the years after 1327, when that sultan established Daulatabad, in Maharashtra, as the new co-capital of the Delhi Sultanate's vast, all-India empire.[39] In having Ganges water carried a distance of forty days' journey from north India 'for his own personal use', the sultan was conforming to an authentically Indian imperial ritual. Several centuries later, the Muslim sultans of Bengal, on the occasion of their own coronation ceremonies, would wash themselves with holy water that had been brought to their capital from the ancient holy site of Ganga Sagar, located where the Ganges River emptied into the Bay of Bengal.[40]

No Indo-Muslim chronicle or contemporary inscription associates the use of Ganges water with the establishment or maintenance of Indo-Muslim states. We hear this only from foreign visitors: an Arab traveller in the case of Muhammad bin Tughluq, a Portuguese friar in the case of the sultans of Bengal. Similarly, the image of a Mughal official seated in a canopied chariot and presiding over the Jagannath car festival comes to us not from Mughal chronicles but from an English traveller who happened to be in Puri in 1633.[41] Such disjunctures between the rhetoric and the practice of royal sovereignty also appear, of course, with respect to the founding of non-Muslim states. We know, for example, that Brahman ideologues, writing in chaste Sanskrit, spun elaborate tales of how warriors and sages founded the Vijayanagara state by combining forces for a common defense of *dharma* from assaults by barbaric *(mleccha)* Turkic outsiders. This is the Vijayanagara of rhetoric, a familiar story. But the Vijayanagara of practical politics rested on very different foundations, which included the adoption of the titles, the dress, the military organization, the ruling ideology, the architecture, and the political economy of the contemporary Islamicate world.[42] As with Indo-Muslim states, we hear of such practices mainly from outsiders—merchants, diplomats, travellers—and not from Brahman chroniclers and ideologues.

CONCLUSION

One often hears that between the thirteenth and eighteenth centuries, Indo-Muslim states, driven by a Judeo-Islamic 'theology of iconoclasm', by fanaticism, or by sheer lust for plunder, wantonly and indiscriminately indulged in the desecration of Hindu temples. Such a picture cannot, however, be sustained by evidence from original sources for the period after 1192. Had instances of temple desecration been driven by a 'theology of iconoclasm', as some have claimed,[43] such a theology would have committed Muslims in India to destroying all temples everywhere, including ordinary village temples, as opposed to the strategically selective operation that seems actually to have taken place. Rather, the original data associate instances of temple desecration with the annexation of newly conquered territories held by enemy kings whose domains lay in the path of moving military frontiers. Temple desecrations also occurred when Hindu patrons of prominent temples committed acts of treason or disloyalty to the Indo-Muslim states they served. Otherwise, temples lying within Indo-Muslim sovereign domains, viewed normally as protected state property, were left unmolested.

Finally, it is important to identify the different meanings that Indians invested in religious monuments and the different ways these monuments were understood to relate to political authority. In the reign of Aurangzeb, Shaikh Muhammadi took refuge in a mosque believing that the structure—being fundamentally apolitical, indeed above politics—lay beyond the Mughal emperor's reach. Contemporary royal temples, on the other hand, were understood as highly charged political monuments, a circumstance that rendered them fatally vulnerable to outside attack. Therefore, by targeting for desecration those temples that were associated with defeated kings, conquering Turks, when they made their own bid for sovereign domain in India, were subscribing to, even while they were exploiting, indigenous notions of royal legitimacy. Contemporary Sanskrit inscriptions never identified Indo-Muslim invaders in terms of their religion, as Muslims, but most generally in terms of their linguistic affiliation (most typically as Turk, 'turushka'). That is, they were construed as but one ethnic community in India amidst many others.[44] In the same way, B.D. Chattopadhyaya locates within early medieval Brahmanical discourse an 'essential urge to legitimize' any ruling authority so long as it was effective and responsible. This urge was manifested, for example, in the perception of the Tughluqs as legitimate successors to the Tomaras and Cahamanas; of a Muslim ruler of Kashmir as having a lunar, Pandava lineage; or of the Mughal emperors as supporters of Ramarajya (the 'kingship of Lord Rama').[45] It is likely that Indo-Muslim policies of protecting temples within their sovereign domains contributed positively to such perceptions.

In sum, by placing known instances of temple desecration in the larger contexts of Indo-Muslim state building and state maintenance, one can find patterns suggesting a rational basis for something commonly dismissed as irrational, or worse. These patterns also suggest points of continuity with Indian practices that had become customary well before the thirteenth century. Such points of continuity in turn call into serious question the sort of civilizational divide between India's 'Hindu' and 'Muslim' periods first postulated in British colonial historiography and subsequently replicated in both Pakistani and Hindu nationalist schools. Finally, this essay has sought to identify the different meanings that contemporary actors invested in the public monuments they patronized or desecrated, and to reconstruct those meanings on the basis of the practice, and not just the rhetoric, of those actors. It is hoped that the approaches and hypotheses suggested here might facilitate the kind of responsible and constructive discussion that this controversial topic so badly needs.

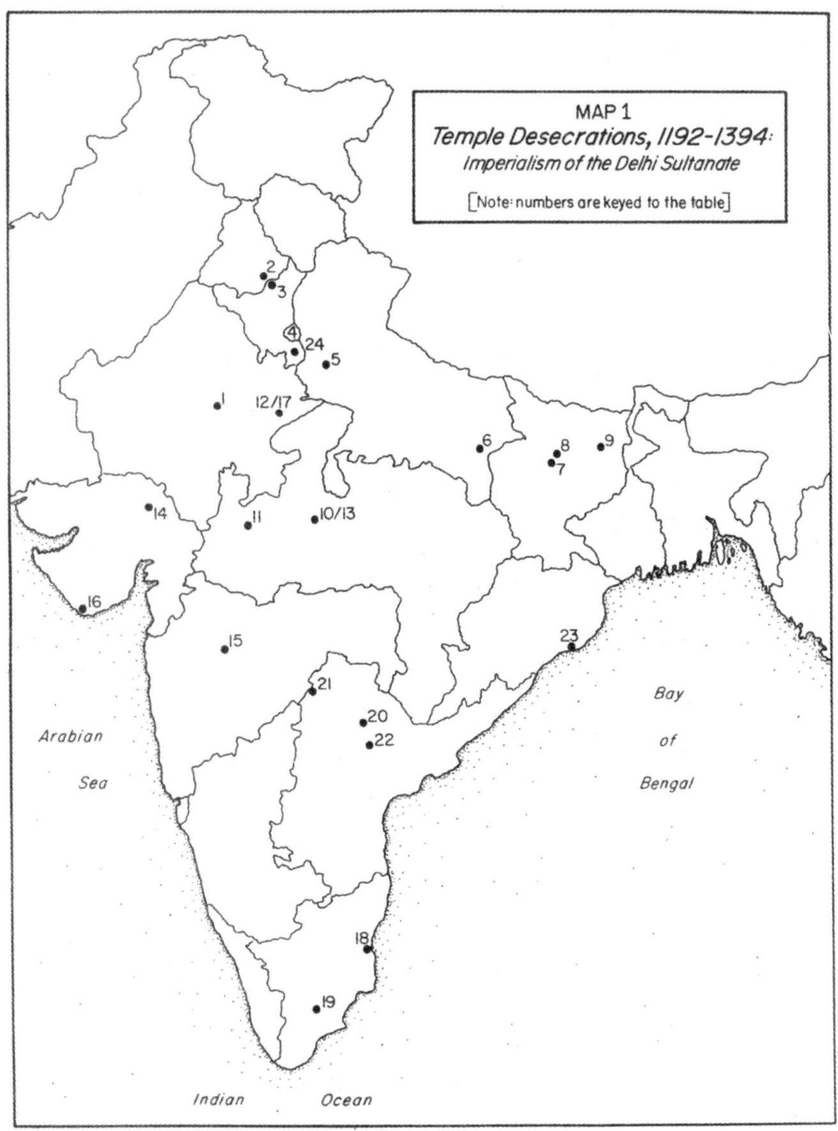

Map 3.1. Temple Desecrations, 1192–1394: Imperialism of the Delhi Sultanate
[Note: Numbers are keyed to the table.]

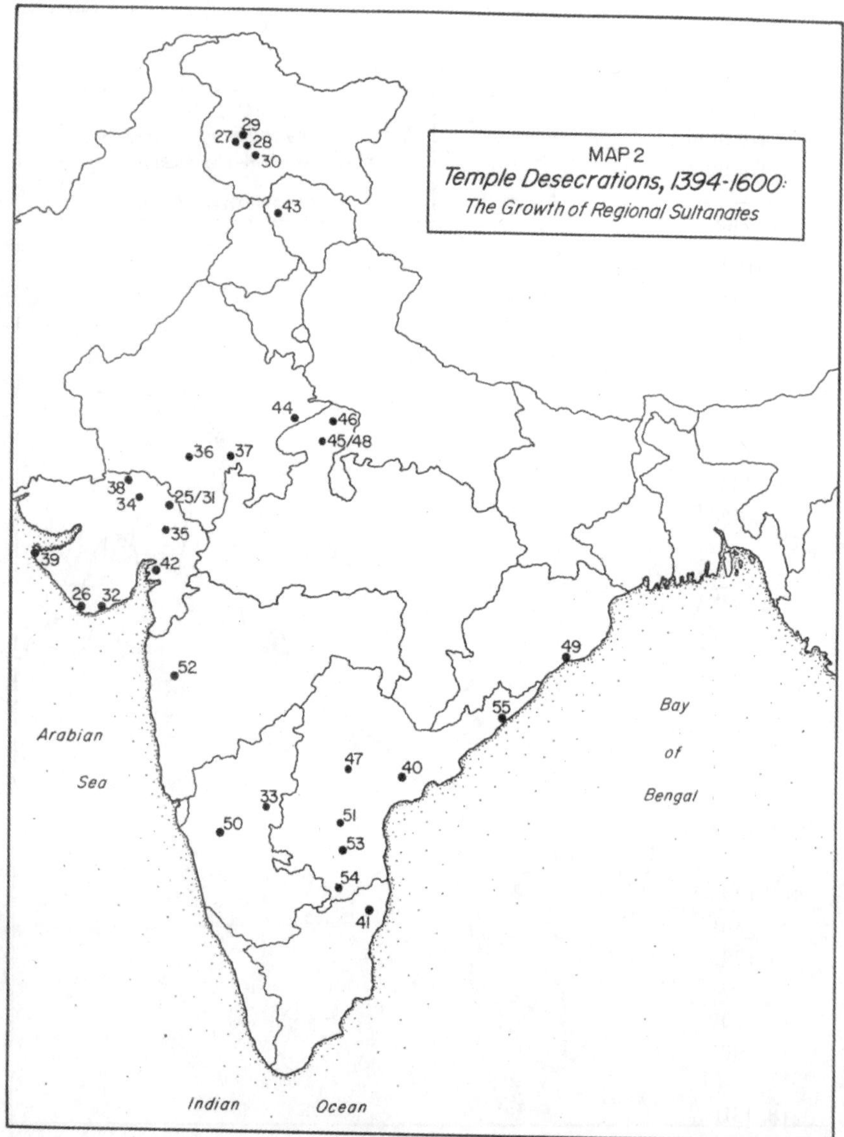

Map 3.2. Temple Desecrations, 1394–1600:
The Growth of Regional Sultanates

Table 3.1. Instances of Temple Desecration, 1192–1760

(e) = emperor; (s) = sultan; (g) = governor; (c) = commander;
(p) = crown prince
For numbers 1–24, see map 3.1.
For numbers 25–55, see map 3.2.

No.	Date	Site	District	State	Agent	Source
1.	1193	Ajmer	Ajmer	Rajast.	Md. Ghuri(s)	23: 215
2.	1193	Samana	Patiala	Punjab	Aibek	23: 216–17
3.	1193	Kuhram	Karnal	Haryana	Aibek(g)	23: 216–17
4.	1193	Delhi		U.P.	Md. Ghuri(s)	1(1911): 13; 23: 217, 222
5.	1194	Kol	Aligarh	U.P.	Ghurid army	23: 224
6.	1194	Benares	Benares	U.P.	Ghurid army	23: 223
7.	c. 1202	Nalanda	Patna	Bihar	Bakhtiyar Khalaji(c)	20: 90
8.	c. 1202	Odantapuri	Patna	Bihar	Bakhtiyar Khalaji	22: 319; 21: 551–52
9.	c. 1202	Vikramasila	Saharsa	Bihar	Bakhtiyar Khalaji	22: 319
10.	1234	Bhilsa	Vidisha	M.P.	Iltutmish(s)	21: 621–2
11.	1234	Ujjain	Ujjain	M.P.	Iltutmish	21: 622–3
12.	1290	Jhain	Sawai Madh.	Rajast.	Jalal al-Din Khalaji(s)	27: 146
13.	1292	Bhilsa	Vidisha	M.P.	'Ala al-Din Khalaji	27: 148
14.	1298–1310	Vijapur	Mehsana	Gujarat	Khalaji invaders	2(1974): 10–12
15.	1295	Devagiri	Aurangabad	Mahara.	'Ala al-Din Khalaji(g)	24: 543
16.	1299	Somnath	Junagadh	Gujarat	Ulugh Khan(c)	25: 75
17.	1301	Jhain	Sawai Madh.	Rajast.	'Ala al-Din Khalaji(s)	25: 75–6
18.	1311	Chidambaram	South Arcot	Tamilnad	Malik Kafur(c)	25: 90–1
19.	1311	Madurai	Madurai	Tamilnad	Malik Kafur	25: 91

(contd.)

Table 3.1 (contd.)

No.	Date	Site	District	State	Agent	Source
20.	c. 1323	Warangal	Warangal	A.P.	Ulugh Khan(p)	33: 1–2
21.	c. 1323	Bodhan	Nizamabad	A.P.	Ulugh Khan	1(1919–20): 16
22.	c. 1323	Pillalamarri	Nalgonda	A.P.	Ulugh Khan	17: 114
23.	1359	Puri	Puri	Orissa	Firuz Tughluq(s)	26: 314
24.	1392–3	Sainthali	Gurgaon	Haryana	Bahadur K. Nahar(c)	3(1963–4): 146
25.	1394	Idar	Sabar-K.	Gujarat	Muzaffar Khan(g)	14-3: 177
26.	1395	Somnath	Junagadh	Gujarat	Muzaffar Khan	6-4: 3
27.	c. 1400	Paraspur	Srinagar	Kashmir	Sikandar(s)	14-3: 648
28.	c. 1400	Bijbehara	Srinagar	Kashmir	Sikandar	34: 54
29.	c. 1400	Tripuresvara	Srinagar	Kashmir	Sikandar	34: 54
30.	c. 1400	Martand	Anantnag	Kashmir	Sikandar	34: 54
31.	1400–1	Idar	Sabar-K.	Gujarat	Muzaffar Shah(s)	14-3: 181
32.	1400–1	Diu	Amreli	Gujarat	Muzaffar Shah	6-4: 5
33.	1406	Manvi	Raichur	Karn.	Firuz Bahmani(s)	2(1962): 57–8
34.	1415	Sidhpur	Mehsana	Gujarat	Ahmad Shah(s)	29: 98–9
35.	1433	Delwara	Sabar-K.	Gujarat	Ahmad Shah	14-3: 220–1
36.	1442	Kumbhalmir	Udaipur	Rajast.	Mahmud Khalaji(s)	14-3: 513
37.	1457	Mandalgarh	Bhilwara	Rajast.	Mahmud Khalaji	6-4: 135
38.	1462	Malan	Banaskantha	Gujarat	'Ala al-Din Suhrab(c)	2(1963): 28–9
39.	1473	Dwarka	Jainnagar	Gujarat	Mahmud Begdha(s)	14-3: 259–61
40.	1478	Kondapalle	Krishna	A.P.	Md. II Bahmani(s)	6-2: 306
41.	c. 1478	Kanchi	Chingleput	Tamilnad	Md. II Bahmani	6-2: 308

(contd.)

Table 3.1 (contd.)

No.	Date	Site	District	State	Agent	Source
42.	1505	Amod	Broach	Gujarat	Khalil Shah(g)	1(1933): 36
43.	1489–1517	Nagarkot	Kangra	Him. P.	Khawwas Khan(g)	35: 81
44.	1507	Utgir	Sawai Madh.	Rajast.	Sikandar Lodi(s)	14–1: 375
45.	1507	Narwar	Shivpuri	M.P.	Sikandar Lodi	14–1: 378
46.	1518	Gwalior	Gwalior	M.P.	Ibrahim Lodi(s)	14–1: 402
47.	1530–31	Devarkonda	Nalgonda	A.P.	Quli Qutb Shah(s)	6–3: 212
48.	1552	Narwar	Shivpuri	M.P.	Dilawar Khan(g)	4 June 1927): 101–4
49.	1556	Puri	Puri	Orissa	Sulaiman Karrani(s)	28: 413–15
50.	1575–6	Bankapur	Dharwar	Karn.	'Ali 'Adil Shah(s)	6–3: 82–4
51.	1579	Ahobilam	Kurnool	A.P.	Murahari Rao(c)	6–3: 267
52.	1586	Ghoda	Poona	Mahara.	Mir Md. Zaman (?)	1(1933–34): 24
53.	1593	Cuddapah	Cuddapah	A.P.	Murtaza Khan(c)	6–3: 274
54.	1593	Kalihasti	Chitoor	A.P.	I'tibar Khan(c)	6–3: 277
55.	1599	Srikurman	Visakh.	A.P.	Qutb Shahi general	32–5: 1312

Sources: 1. *Epigraphia Indo–Moslemica.*

2. *Epigraphia Indica, Arabic and Persian Supplement.*

3. *Annual Report of Indian Epigraphy.*

4. *Indian Antiquary.*

5. Jahangir, *Tuzuk-i-Jahangiri,* Vol. 1, trans. A. Rogers (Delhi, 1968).

6. Firishta, *Tarikh-i Firishta,* trans. J. Briggs, *History of the Rise of the Mahomedan Power in India* (Calcutta, 1971), 4 vols.

7. Kanbo, *'Amal-i Salih* (Lahore, 1967), Vol. 2.

8. A. Butterworth and V. Chetty, *A Collection of the Inscriptions on Copper–Plates and Stones in the Nellore District* (Madras, 1905), Vol. 3.

9. Khafi Khan, *Khafi Khan's History of 'Alamgir,* trans. S. Moinul Haq (Karachi, 1975).

10. A. Cunningham, *Four Reports made during 1862–65* (Varanasi, 1972).

11. S.N. Sinha, *Subah of Allahabad under the Great Mughals* (New Delhi, 1974).

12. Saqi Must'ad Khan, *Maasir-i 'Alamgiri,* trans. J. Sarkar (Calcutta, 1947).

13. Saqi Must'ad Khan, *Maasir-i 'Alamgiri* (Calcutta, 1871).

14. Nizamuddin Ahmad, *Tabaqat-i Akbari,* trans. B. De (Calcutta, 1973), 3 vols.

15. Ishwardas Nagar, *Futuhat-i 'Alamgiri,* trans. T. Ahmad (Delhi, 1978).

16. Surendranath Sen (ed. and trans.), *Siva Chhatrapati* (Calcutta, 1920), Vol. 1.

17. P. Sreenivasachar, (ed.), *Corpus of Inscriptions in the Telingana Districts of H.E.M. the Nizam's Dominions,* pt. 2 (Hyderabad, 1940).

18. Shah Nawaz Khan, *Maathir-ul-Umara,* Vol. 1, trans. H. Beveridge (Patna, 1979).

19. Z.A. Desai, *Published Muslim Inscriptions of Rajasthan* (Jaipur, 1971).

20. G. Roerich, trans. *Biography of Dharmaswamin* (Patna, 1959).

21. Minhaj-i Siraj, *Tabakat-i Nasiri,* Vol. 1, trans. H. Raverty (New Delhi, 1970).

22. Debiprasad Chattopadhyaya (ed.), *Taranatha's History of Buddhism in India* (Calcutta, 1980).

23. Hasan Nizami, *Taj al-maasir,* in Henry M. Elliot and John Dowson, (eds), *The History of India as Told by Its Own Historians* (Allahabad: Kitab Mahal, n.d.), Vol. 2.

24. Amir Khusrau, *Miftah al-futuh* in Elliot and Dowson, *History of India,* Vol. 3.

25. Amir Khusrau, *Khaza'in al-futuh,* in Elliot and Dowson, *History of India,* Vol. 3.

26. Shams-i Siraj, *Tarikh-i Firuz Shahi,* in Elliot and Dowson, *History of India,* Vol. 3.

27. Zia al-Din Barani, *Tarikh-i Firuz Shahi,* Elliot and Dowson, *History of India,* Vol. 3.

28. Khwajah Ni'mat Allah, *Tarikh-i Khan-Jahani wa makhzan-i-Afghani* (Dacca, 1960), Vol. 1.

29. Sikandar bin Muhammad, *Mirat-i Sikandari,* in E.C. Bayley, *Local Muhammadan Dynasties: Gujarat,* (ed.) N. Singh (New Delhi, 1970).

30. Azad al-Husaini, *Nau-Bahar-i Murshid Quli Khani,* trans. Jadu Nath Sarkar, *Bengal Nawabs* (1952; reprint, Calcutta, 1985).

31. 'Abd al-Hamid Lahori, *Badshah-nama,* in Elliot and Dowson, *History of India,* Vol. 7.

32. *South Indian Inscriptions* (New Delhi: Archeological Survey of India).

33. George Michell, 'City as Cosmograph', *South Asian Studies* 8 (1992).

34. Jonaraja, *Rajatarangini,* (ed.) S.L. Sadhu, trans. J.C. Dutt (New Delhi, 1993).

35. Iqtidar Husain Siddiqui, trans., *Waqi 'at-e-Mushtaqui of Shaikh Rizq Ullah Mushtaqui* (New Delhi, 1993).

36. Jagadish Narayan Sarkar, *Life of Mir Jumla* (Calcutta, 1952).

NOTES

1. See Sita Ram Goel, *Hindu Temples: What Happened to Them?* Vol. 1, *A Preliminary Survey* (New Delhi: Voice of India, 1990); Vol. 2, *The Islamic Evidence* (New Delhi: Voice of India, 1991).

2. Henry M. Elliot and John Dowson, trans. and (eds), *The History of India as Told by Its Own Historians,* 8 vols (1849; Allahabad: Kitab Mahal, n.d.), Vol. 1, p. xxi.

3. Ibid., Vol. 1, pp. xvi.

4. Ibid., Vol. 1, pp. xxii, xxvii.

5. K.A. Nizami (ed.), *Politics and Society during the Early Medieval Period: Collected Works of Professor Mohammad Habib,* 2 vols (New Delhi: People's Publishing House, 1974), Vol. 1, p. 12.

6. Goel, *Hindu Temples,* Vol. 2, pp. 115–16. Goel does, however, consider it more likely that the event took place during the reign of Raja Bhoja II in the late thirteenth century than during that of Raja Bhoja I in the eleventh century.

7. G. Yazdani, 'The Inscription of the Tomb of 'Abdullah Shah Changal at Dhar', *Epigraphia Indo-Moslemica* (1909), pp. 1–5.

8. A good summary of the political history of this period is found in André Wink, *Al-Hind: The Making of the Indo-Islamic World,* Vol. 2: *The Slave Kings and the Islamic Conquest, 11th–13th Centuries* (Leiden: Brill, 1997), pp. 111–49.

9. 'Utbi, *Tarikh-i Yamini,* in Elliot and Dowson, *History of India,* Vol. 2, p. 22. For a Persian translation of 'Utbi's original Arabic, made in 1206, see Abu Sharaf Nasih al-Jurfadqani, *Tarjuma-yi Tarikh-i Yamini* (Tehran: Bangah-i Tarjomeh va Nashr-i Kitab, 1926–7), p. 31.

10. C.E. Bosworth, *The Later Ghaznavids, Splendour and Decay: The Dynasty in Afghanistan and Northern India,* 1040–1186 (1977; reprint, New Delhi: Munshiram Manoharlal, 1992), pp. 32, 68.

11. Mahmud did not hesitate to sack Muslim cities. His plunder of the Iranian city of Ray in 1029 brought him 500,000 dinars' worth of jewels, 260,000 dinars in coined money, and over 30,000 dinars' worth of gold and silver vessels. India, however, possessed far more wealth than the more sparsely populated Iranian plateau. Somnath alone brought in twenty million dinars' worth of spoil. C.E. Bosworth, *The Ghaznavids: Their Empire in Afghanistan and Eastern Iran, 994–1040* (Edinburgh: Edinburgh University Press, 1963), p. 78.

12. 'Ali Akbar Fayyaz (ed.), *Tarikh-i Baihaqi* (Mashshad: University of Mashshad, 1971), p. 517. The contemporary historian Baihaqi recorded the first attack on Benares conducted by a Muslim army, carried out in 1033 by the Ghaznavid governor of Lahore. 'He marched out with his warriors and the army of Lahore,' wrote Baihaqi, 'and exacted ample tribute from the Thakurs. He crossed the river Ganges and went down the left bank. Unexpectedly (*nā-gāh*) he arrived at a city which is called Banāras, and which belonged to the territory of Gang.

Never had a Muslim army reached this place.... The markets of the drapers, perfumers, and jewellers were plundered, but it was impossible to do more. The people of the army became rich, for they all carried off gold, silver, perfumes, and jewels, and got back in safety.' Baihaqi, *Tarikh-i Baihaqi*, in Elliot and Dowson, *History of India*, Vol. 2, pp. 123–4.

13. Wink, *Al-Hind*, Vol. 2, pp. 324.

14. 'The need to link one's royal origins to religious and divine forces led to the extraordinary temple building of this period.' B.D. Chattopadhyaya, 'Historiography, History, and Religious Centers: Early Medieval North India, circa AD 700–1200', in Vishakha N. Desai and Darielle Mason (eds), *Gods, Guardians, and Lovers: Temple Sculptures from North India, AD 700–1200* (New York: Asia Society Galleries, 1993), p. 40.

15. Michael Willis suggests that one of the reasons the imperial Pratiharas did *not* build great monumental temple complexes was precisely their determination to avoid the localization of sovereign power that temples necessarily projected. According to this reasoning, the most active patrons of temple construction in this period were subordinate kings who did not have such vast imperial pretensions as did the Pratiharas. Willis, 'Religion and Royal Patronage in North India,' in Desai and Mason (eds), *Gods, Guardians, and Lovers*, pp. 58–9.

16. Richard H. Davis, *Lives of Indian Images* (Princeton: Princeton University Press, 1997), pp. 122,137–8. Davis here cites David D. Shulman: 'A divine power is felt to be present *naturally* on the spot. The texts are therefore concerned with the manner in which this presence is revealed and with the definition of its specific attributes.' Shulman, *Tamil Temple Myths: Sacrifice and Divine Marriage in the South Indian Saiva Tradition* (Princeton: Princeton University Press, 1980), p. 48. Emphasis mine.

17. Cited in Davis, *Lives*, p. 53.

18. Davis, *Lives*, pp. 51–83, passim. The same pattern continued after the Turkish conquest of India. In the 1460s, Kapilendra, the founder of the Suryavamshi Gajapati dynasty in Orissa, sacked both Śaiva and Vaishnava temples in the Kaveri delta in the course of wars of conquest in the Tamil country. See Phillip B. Wagoner, *Tidings of the King: A Translation and Ethnohistorical Analysis of the Rāyavācakamu* (Honolulu: University of Hawaii Press, 1993), p. 146. Somewhat later, in 1514, Krishna Deva Raya looted an image of Bala Krishna from Udayagiri, which he had defeated and annexed to his growing Vijayanagara state. Six years later he acquired control over Pandharpur, where he seems to have looted the Vittala image and carried it back to Vijayanagara, with the apparent purpose of ritually incorporating this area into his kingdom. Davis, *Lives*, pp. 65, 67.

19. In the late eleventh century, the Kashmiri king, Harsha, even raised the plundering of temples to an institutionalized activity, and in the late twelfth and early thirteenth centuries, while Turkish rulers were establishing their rule in north India, kings of the Paramara dynasty were attacking and plundering Jain

temples in Gujarat. See Romila Thapar, Harbans Mukhia, and Bipan Chandra, *Communalism and the Writing of Indian History* (Delhi: People's Publishing House, 1969), pp. 14, 31.

20. Willis, 'Religion and Royal Patronage', p. 59.

21. In 1788, for example, the author of the *Riyaz al-salatin* claimed that Muhammad Bakhtiyar demolished local temples after he conquered Bengal in 1204, although no contemporary evidence suggests that he did so. Ghulam Hussain Salim, *Riyazu-s-Salatin: A History of Bengal,* trans. Abdus Salam (1903; reprint, Delhi: Idarah-i Adabiyat-i Delli, 1975), p. 64. Even contemporary sources could make false claims. An inscription on a mosque in Bidar, dated 1670, claims that the Mughal governor, Mukhtar Khan, had destroyed a temple and built the mosque on its site. 'But as a matter of fact,' noted the epigraphist who published the inscription, 'the mosque is a new construction, and the Hindu shrine [to the lion-god Narasimha] which existed inside the rock does not seem to have been disturbed, for it still survives.' *Epigraphia Indo-Moslemica, 1927–28* (Calcutta: Government of India, 1931), p. 32.

22. Entry for the date 1688 in 'Hindu Timeline,' *Hinduism Today* (December 1994), cited in Cynthia Talbot, 'Inscribing the Other, Inscribing the Self: Hindu-Muslim Identities in Pre-Colonial India', *Comparative Studies in Society and History* 37, no. 4 (October 1995), p. 692.

23. In 1247, Balban, the future sultan of Delhi, had recommended raiding Indian states for precisely this purpose. See Minhaj-i Siraj Juzjani, *Tabakat-i Nasiri,* 2 vols, trans. H.G. Raverty (1881; New Delhi: Oriental Books Reprint Corp., 1970), Vol. 2, p. 816.

24. For example, a 1406 inscription records that after Sultan Firuz Shah Bahmani had defeated the forces of Vijayanagara in the much-contested Raichur doab region, 'a mosque has been converted out of a temple as a sign of religion.' It then records that the sultan himself had 'conquered this fort by the firm determination of his mind in a single attack (lit. on horseback). After the victory, the chief of chiefs, Safdar (lit. the valiant commander) of the age, received (the charge of) the fort.' *Epigraphia Indica, Arabic and Persian Supplement, 1962* (Delhi: Manager of Publications, 1964), pp. 57–8.

25. Briggs, *Rise of Mahomedan Power,* Vol. 3, p. 267. The temple's political significance, and hence the necessity of desecrating it, would have been well understood by Murahari Rao, himself a Marathi Brahman.

26. Surendra Nath Sinha, *Subah of Allahabad under the Great Mughals* (New Delhi: Jamia Millia Islamia, 1974), pp. 65–8; Catherine B. Asher, *Architecture of Mughal India,* Vol. I: 4 of *The New Cambridge History of India,* (Cambridge: Cambridge University Press, 1992), p. 254, 278; Saqi Must'ad Khan, *Ma'athir–i 'Alamgiri* (Calcutta: Bibliotheca Indica, 1871), p. 88.

27. Saqi Must'ad Khan, *Maasir–i 'Alamgiri,* trans. Jadunath Sarkar (Calcutta, 1947), pp. 57–61; Asher, *Architecture,* p. 254.

28. See Goel, *Hindu Temples*, Vol. 2, p. 78–9, 83; Sri Ram Sharma, *The Religious Policy of the Mughal Emperors*, 2nd edn (London: Asia Publishing House, 1962), pp. 132–3; Athar Ali, *The Mughal Nobility under Aurangzeb* (Bombay: Asia Publishing House, 1966), 98n.

29. Saqi Must'ad Khan, *Ma'athir-i 'Alamgiri*, text, 81. My translation. 'Ahkām-i Islām-nizām ba nāzimān-i kull-i ṣūbajāt ṣādir shud ki mudāris wa mu'ābid-i bīdīnan dast-khwash-i inhidām sāzand, wa ha ta'kid-i akīd ṭaur-i dars-o-tadrīs wa rasm-i shayū'-i madhāhib-i kufr-āyīnān bar andāzand.' Cf. Saqi Must'ad Khan, *Maasir-i 'Alamgiri: A History of the Emperor Aurangzeb – 'Alamgiri*, trans. Sir Jadunath Sarkar (Lahore: Suhail Academy, 1981), pp. 51–2.

30. Saqi Must'ad Khan, *Ma'athir-i 'Alamgiri*, p. 81. 'Ba 'arẓ-i khudāvand-i dīnparvar rasīd ki dar ṣūba-yi Thatta wa Multān khuṣūs Banāras brahminān-i baṭṭālat-nishān dar mudāris-i muqarrar ba tadrīs-i kutub-i bāṭila ishtighāl dārand, wa rāghibān wa ṭālibān az hunūd wa musulmān musāfat-hāyi ba'īda ṭaiy numūda, jihat-i taḥṣil-i 'ulūm-i shūm nazd-i ān jamā'at-i gumrāh mīāyand.' Cf. Sir Jadunath Sarkar, trans., *Maasir-i 'Ālamgīri*, p. 51.

31. Consider the swift and brutal punishment of Baha al-Din Gurshasp, a high-ranking officer in Tughluq imperial service and a governor in the Deccan. In 1327, Gurshasp joined forces with the raja of Kampila in an unsuccessful rebellion against Sultan Muhammad bin Tughluq. When captured, the raja, who had never sworn allegiance to Tughluq authority, got the relatively light punishment of a beheading. But the rebel governor, who was not only a former Tughluq officer but the emperor's first cousin, was spat upon by his female relatives and flayed alive; then his skin was stuffed with straw and paraded throughout the imperial provinces as a cautionary tale to the public, while his body was mixed with rice and fed to elephants. See 'Isami, *Futuhu's-salatin*, trans., Vol. 3, pp. 658–89; Mahdi Husain, trans., *The Rehla of Ibn Battuta (India, Maldive Islands, and Ceylon)* (Baroda: Oriental Institute, 1953), p. 96. As a final indignity to Gurshasp, we are told by Ibn Battuta that the elephants refused to eat the meal that had been mixed with the rebel's body.

32. Richard M. Eaton, *The Rise of Islam and the Bengal Frontier, 1204–1760* (Berkeley: University of California Press, 1993), pp. 176–7.

33. Muzaffar Alam, 'Assimilation from a Distance: Confrontation and Sufi Accommodation in Awadh Society', in R. Champakalakshmi and S. Gopal (eds), *Tradition, Dissent, and Ideology: Essays in Honour of Romila Thapar* (Delhi: Oxford University Press, 1996), 177n.

34. Examples of mosque desecrations are strikingly few in number. In 1697–8 in Sambhar, in Rajasthan's Jaipur District, Shah Sabz 'Ali built a mosque on the site of a temple. In the reign of Shah 'Alam (1707–12), however, non-Muslims came to dominate the region and demolished the mosque, which was subsequently rebuilt in the reign of Farrukh Siyar. See Z. A. Desai, *Published Muslim Inscriptions*

of Rajasthan (Jaipur, 1971), p. 157. Similarly, there is evidence that in 1680, during Aurangzeb's invasion of Rajasthan, the Rajput chief Bhim Singh, seeking to avenge the emperor's recent destruction of temples in Udaipur and elsewhere, raided Gujarat and plundered Vadnagar, Vishalnagar, and Ahmedabad, in the latter place destroying thirty smaller mosques and one large one. See *Rāja-sumudra-prasasti*, ch. 22, verse 29, an inscription composed ca. 1683, which appears in Shyamaldas Kaviraj, *Vir Vinod* (Udaipur: Rajayantralaya, 1886); cited in R.C. Majumdar (ed.), *The Mughal Empire* (Bombay: Bharatiya Vidya Bhavan, 1974), p. 351.

35. One can hardly imagine the central focus of a mosque's ritual activity, the prayer niche (*mihrāb*), being taken out of the structure and paraded around a Muslim capital by way of displaying Allah's co-sovereignty over an Indo-Muslim ruler's kingdom, in the manner that the ritual focus of a royal temple, the image of the state deity was paraded around many premodern Hindu capitals in elaborate car festivals.

36. Aiming to cast earlier invaders or rulers in the role of zealous and puritanical heroes, later chroniclers occasionally attributed to such figures the desecration of staggering numbers of temples. Mahmud of Ghazni, for example, is said to have destroyed 10,000 temples in Kanauj and 1,000 in Mathura, his grandson Ibrahim 1,000 in the Delhi Doab and another 1,000 in Malwa, Aibek 1,000 in Delhi, and Muhammad Ghuri another 1,000 in Benares—figures that Hindu nationalists like Sita Ram Goel have accepted at face value. Goel, *Hindu Temples*, p. 269.

37. 'Isami, *Futuhu's Salatin*, trans., Vol.1, pp. 66–7.

38. Davis, *Lives*, pp. 71–6.

39. Husain, *Rehla of Ibn Battuta*, p. 4.

40. Sebastião Manrique, *Travels of Fray Sebastien Manrique, 1629–1643*, trans. E. Luard and H. Hosten, 2 vols (Oxford: Hakluyt Society 1927), Vol. 1, p. 77.

41. P. Acharya, 'Bruton's Account of Cuttak and Puri', *Orissa Historical Research Journal* 10, no. 3 (1961), p. 46.

42. See Phillip B. Wagoner, '"Sultan among Hindu Kings": Dress, Titles, and the Islamicization of Hindu Culture at Vijayanagara', *Journal of Asian Studies* 55, no. 4 (November 1996), pp. 851–80; Wagoner, 'Harihara, Bukka, and the Sultan: The Delhi Sultanate in the Political Imagination of Vijayanagara', in David Gilmartin and Bruce B. Lawrence (eds), *Beyond Turk and Hindu: Rethinking Religious Identities in Islamicate South Asia* (Gainesville: University Press of Florida, 2000), pp. 300–26.

43. See Wink, *Al-Hind*, Vol. 2, pp. 294–333.

44. See Talbot, 'Inscribing the Other,' p. 701.

45. Brajadulal Chattopadhyaya, *Representing the Other? Sanskrit Sources and the Muslims* (New Delhi: Manohar, 1998), pp. 49–50, 53, 60, 84.

PART III

The Qutb Mosque, the First Friday Mosque of Delhi

The Origins of the Qutb Mosque and Qutb Minar

A nineteenth-century controversy

DEBATE BETWEEN ALEXANDER CUNNINGHAM AND J.D. BEGLAR

The following four extracts illustrate divergent views regarding the date and origins of the Qutb Minar and its adjacent mosque (Plates 1–3 and 10) among the officers of the newly-formed Archaeological Survey of India in the second half of the nineteenth century. The first extract is from a report by Alexander Cunningham, first director of the Archaeological Survey of India, published in 1865. In it, Cunningham argues, contrary to the prevailing view, that the Qutb Minar was built by the Ghurids or their agents after the conquest of Delhi in the late twelfth century, and was not a pre-existing structure. This extract is followed by three others, all taken from a report on Delhi published by the Archaeological Survey of India in 1872. This report had been commissioned from J.D. Beglar, an engineer. However, Beglar's conclusions regarding the 'Hindu' origins of the Quth complex were unacceptable to his superior, Alexander Cunningham, who had championed the (ultimately correct) view that this was a Ghurid monument. Consequently, Cunningham prefaced Beglar's report with a humiliating rebuttal of its conclusions, insisting that both the Qutb Minar and its adjoining mosque were built by Hindu masons for Muslim patrons.

The extracts reprinted here consist of a portion of Beglar's report on the Qutb followed by part of Cunningham's repudiation of it, and conclude with Beglar's response to his employer's criticisms, in which he is forced to admit his error and accept the dating proposed by Cunningham. The content and tone of this very heated and very public contretemps illustrates just how contested the question of the Qutb's date and origins were among European and Indian antiquarians and archaeologists throughout the nineteenth century.

ALEXANDER CUNNINGHAM FROM A REPORT ON DELHI*

During the present century, much speculation has been wasted as to the origin of the Kutb Minar (Plate 10), whether it is a purely Muhammadan building, or a Hindu building altered and completed by the conquerors. The latter is undoubtedly the common belief of the people, who say that the pillar was built by Rai Pithora for the purpose of giving his daughter a view of the River Jumna. Some people even say that the intention was to obtain a view of the Ganges, and that the Kutb Minar having failed to secure this, a second pillar of double the size was commenced, but the work was interrupted by the conquest of the Musalmâns. The first part of this tradition was warmly adopted by Sir T. Metcalfe, and it has since found a strong advocate in Syad Ahmad, whose remarks are quoted with approval by Mr Cooper in his recent hand-book for Delhi.[1] Syad Ahmad, however, refers only the basement storey to Rai Pithora; but this admission involves the whole design of the column, which preserves the same marked character throughout all the different storeys. The Hindu theory has found a stout opponent in Colonel Sleeman, who argues that the great slope of the building 'is the peculiar characteristic of all architecture of the Pathans,' and that the arches of the Great Mosque close by it 'all correspond in design, proportion, and execution to 'the tower.'[2]

Mr Cooper recapitulates Syad Ahmad's arguments, and finally states as his opinion that it 'remains an open question whether this magnificent pillar was commenced by the Hindus or Muhammadans.' I must confess, however, that I am myself quite satisfied that the building is entirely a Muhammadan one, both as to origin and to design; although, no doubt, many, perhaps all, of the beautiful details of the richly decorated balconies may be Hindu. To me these decorations seem to be purely Hindu, and just such as may be seen in the honey-comb enrichments of the domes of most of the old Hindu temples. The arguments brought forward in support of the Hindu origin of the column are the following:

1st—'That there is, only *one Minar*, which is contrary to the practice of the Muhammadans, who always give two minars to their masjids.' I allow that this has been the practice of the Muhammadans for the last

*Published in the *Archaeological Survey of India Reports* Volume 1, *Four Reports Made During the Years 1862–63–64–65*, pp. 189–95.

three hundred years at least, and I will even admit that the little corner turrets or pinnacles of the *Kâla,* or *Kalân, Masjid* of Firuz Shah, may be looked upon as Minars. This would extend the period of the use of two Minars to the middle of the fourteenth century; but it must be remembered that these little turrets of Firuz Shah's Masjid arc not what the Musalmâns call *Mâzinahs;* or lofty towers, from the top of which the Muazzin calls the faithful to prayer. But the Kutb Minar is a Mâzinah; and that it was the practice of the early Muhammadans to build a single tower, we have the most distinct and satisfactory proofs in the two Minars of Ghazni, which could not have belonged to one masjid, as they are half a mile apart, and of different sizes. These minars were built by Mahmud in the early part of the eleventh century, or about 180 years prior to the erection of the Kutb Minar. Another equally decisive proof of this practice is the solitary Minar at Koel, which was built in 652 AH, or 1254 AD, by Kutlugh Khan, during the reign of Nâsir-uddin Mahmud, the youngest son of Altamsh, in whose time the Kutb Minar itself was completed. These still existing minars of Ghazni and Koel show that it was the practice of the early Muhammadans to have only one minar even down to so late a date as the middle of the thirteenth century.

2nd—It is objected that the slope of the Kutb Minar is much greater than that of any other known minars. This objection has already been satisfactorily answered by Colonel Sleeman, who says truly that 'the slope is the peculiar characteristic of the architecture of the Pathans.'

3rd—Syad Ahmad argues that, if the Minar had been intended as a *Mâzinah* to the Great Mosque, it would have been erected at one end of it, instead of being at some distance from it. In reply to this objection I can point again to the Koel Minar, which occupies exactly the same detached position with regard to the Jâma Masjid of Koel as the Kutb Minar does with respect to the Great Mosque of Delhi. Both of them are placed outside the southeast corner of their respective masjids. This coincidence of position seems to me sufficient to settle the question in favour of the Kutb Minar having been intended as a Mâzinah of the Great Mosque.

4th—Syad Ahmad further argues 'that the entrance door faces the north, as the Hindus always have it,' whereas the Muhammadans invariably place it to the eastward, as may be seen in the unfinished 'Minar of Alauddin to the north of the Kutb Minar.' Once more I appeal to the Koel Minar, which, be it remembered, was erected by the son of the emperor who completed the building of the Kutb Minar, and which may, therefore, be looked upon as an almost contemporary work. In the Koel Minar the entrance door is to the north, exactly as in the Kutb Minar. In both instances, I believe that it was so placed chiefly for the convenience of the Muazzin when going to call the faithful to prayer. I think, also, that Syad Ahmad has overlooked the fact that the minars of modern days are 'engaged' towers, that is, they form the ends of the front wall of the Mosque, and, as the back wall of every mosque is to the westward, the entrances to the 'engaged' minars must necessarily be to the eastward. But the case is entirely different with a solitary disengaged minar, of which the entrance would naturally be on the side *nearest* to its Masjid. But waiving this part of the discussion, I return to the fact that the entrance of the Koel Minar is to the northward, exactly the same as in the Kutb Minar and that the entrances to the two great tombs of *Bahâwal Hak,* and *Rukn-uddin* in Multan are not to the eastward but to the southward, as are also those of the Taj Mahal, and of most other modern tombs. The only exception that I know is the tomb of Altamsh, of which the entrance is to the eastward. The argument of Syad Ahmad includes also the position of the entrance doors of Hindu buildings, which, as he says, are always placed to the northward. But this is an undoubted mistake, as a very great majority of Hindu temples have their entrances to the eastward. On referring to my note books, I find that, out of 50 temples, of which I have a record, no less than 38 have their entrances to the east, 10 to the west and only 2 to the north, both of which are in the Fort of Gwalior.

5th—Syad Ahmad further objects that 'it is customary for the Hindus to commence such buildings without any platform (or plinth), whereas the Muhammadans always erect their buildings upon a raised terrace or platform, as may be seen in the unfinished minar of Alauddin Khilji.' In this statement about the Hindu buildings, Syad Ahmad is again mistaken, as it is most undoubtedly the usual custom of the Hindus to raise their temples on plinths. I can point to the gigantic Buddhist temple at Buddha Gaya as springing from a plinth nearly 20 feet in height. The two largest temples in the fort of Gwalior, one Brahmanical and the other Jain, are both raised on plinths, so also are the elaborately sculptured temples of Kajrâha, and so are most of the temples in Kashmir. Lastly, the Great Pillar at Chitor has plinth not less than 8 or 10 feet in height, as may be seen in Fergusson's and Tod's Drawings, and which Tod describes as 'an ample terrace 42 feet square.'[3] The smaller pillar at Chitor must also have a good plinth, as Fergusson describes the entrance as at some height above the base. That the Muhammadans in India also erect their buildings on plinths or raised terraces, I readily admit; for, on the same principle that a cuckoo may be said to build a nest, the Musalmâns usually placed their buildings on the sites of Hindu temples which they had previously destroyed. The mosques at Matura, Kanoj, and Jonpur, are signal examples of this practice. The raised terrace is, therefore, only an accidental adjunct of the Muhammadan building, whereas it is a fundamental part of the Hindu structure. But the early Musalmâns did *not* place their buildings on raised terraces or platforms, as may be seen by a reference to the Drawings of mosques in Syria and Persia, which are given in Fergusson's Hand-book.[4] The Ghaznivides also, who were the more immediate predecessors of the Indian Musalmâns, built their minars at Ghazni without plinths. The contemporary tomb of Altamsh is likewise without a plinth. From all these facts I infer that the early Musalmân structures in India were usually built without plinths, and therefore that the Kutb Minar is undoubtedly a Muhammadan building.

6th—The last argument brought forward by Syad Ahmad is, that bells, which are used in Hindu worship, are found sculptured on the lower part of the basement storey of the Kutb Minar. It is true that bells are used in the daily worship of the Hindus, and also that they are a common ornament of Hindu columns, as may be seen on most of the pillars in the cloisters of the Great Mosque. But bells are no more idolatrous than flowers, which are used in such profusion in the daily service of the Hindu temples. The fact is that, where Muhammadan mosques have been built of the materials stolen from Hindus temples, such portions of architectural ornament as were free from figures either of men or of animals, were invariably made use of by the conquerors. For this reason most of the ornamentation of the early Musalmân buildings is purely Hindu. For instance, in the Jâma Masjid of Kanoj, which is built entirely of Hindu materials, the whole of the concentric circles of overlapping stones in the central dome, with only one exception, still preserve the original Hindu ornament unaltered. The exception is the lowest circle, which is completely covered with Arabic inscriptions. One of the Hindu circles is made up solely of the *Swastika* or mystic cross of the early Indians. This symbol is essentially an idolatrous one, although it is most probable that the Musalmâns were not aware significance. But if the ornamental bells of the Kutb Minar are to be taken as a proof of its Hindu origin, even so must the ornamental Swastikas of the Kanoj Masjid be accepted as evidence to the same effect. It is admitted that this masjid is built up entirely of Hindu materials, but these have been skilfully rearranged by the Moslem architect to suit the requirements of a mosque, so that the design of the building is strictly Muhammadan, while its ornamentation is purely Hindu. I may add that one of the western pillars that supports the central dome of this mosque is made up of two old shafts, both of which are decorated with the Hindu bell and suspending chain.

The strong evidence which I have brought forward in reply to the arguments of Syad Ahmad and others, appears to me to be quite conclusive as to the origin of the Kutb Minar, which is essentially a Muhammadan building. But the strongest evidence in favour of this conclusion is the fact that the Musalmâns of Ghazni had already built two separate minars of *similar design* with angular flutes, whereas the only Hindu pillar of an early date, namely, the smaller column at Chitor, is altogether dissimilar, both in plan and in detail. The entrance to this Hindu tower is at some height above the ground, while that of the Kutb Minar is absolutely on the ground level. The summit of the Hindu tower is crowned by an open pillared temple of almost the same width as the base of the building, whereas the cupola of the Kutb Minar is little more than one-sixth of the diameter of its base. But this small cupola of less than 9 feet in diameter was peculiarly adapted for one special purpose connected with the performance of the Muhammadan religion. From this narrow point the Muazzin could summon the faithful to prayer from all sides by simply turning round and repeating the *Izân*, and on all sides, he would be visible to the people. The small size of the cupola, which crowns the Kutb Minar, is a characteristic peculiar to Muhammadan towers for the special reason which I have just mentioned On this account, therefore, I conclude that the Kutb Minar is a Mâzinah or Muazzin's tower.

That the Kutb Minar was actually used as a Mâzinah, we may infer from the records of Shamsi Sirâj, who about 1380 AD, records that the magnificent minar in the Jâma Masjid of old Delhi was built by Sultan Shams-uddin Altamsh. But the fact is placed beyond all doubt by Abulfeda, who wrote about 1300 AD. He describes the Mâzinah of the Jâma Masjid at Delhi as made of red stone and very lofty, with many sides and 360 steps. Now this description can be applied only to the Kutb Minar, which as it at present stands, has actually 379 steps; but we know that the minar was struck by lightning in the reign of Firuz Shah, by whose orders it was repaired in 1368 AD. There is, therefore, nothing improbable in the account of Abulfeda that the minar in his time had only 360 steps. On the contrary I accept the statement as a valuable hint towards ascertaining the height of the original Minar as completed by the Emperor Altamsh.

The object of building this lofty column seems to me to be clear enough. The first Musalmân conquerors were an energetic race, whose conceptions were as bold and daring as their actions. When the zealous Muhammadan looked on the great city of Delhi, the metropolis of the princely Tomars and the haughty Chohans, his first wish would have been to humble the pride of the infidel; his second, to exalt the religion of his prophet Muhammad. To attain both of these objects, he built a lofty column, from whose summit the Muazzin's call to morning and evening prayer could be heard on all sides by Hindus as well as by Musalmâns. The conqueror's pride was soothed by the daily insult and indignity thus offered to the infidel, while his religious feelings were gratified by the erection of a noble monument which towered majestically over the loftiest houses in the city.

J.D. BEGLAR FROM A REPORT ON DELHI*

I now turn to the Kutb Minar (Plate 10). What most strikes the beholder is its gigantic proportions. It is built within 11 feet of the present Iltitmish's colonnade, along the outer south wall of outer enclosure. It is generally assumed to have been begun by Kutbuddin, and added to by his successors.

It has been shown already that the walls, both outer and inner, of the masjids of Kutb and Iltitmish are Hindu, that the corner dome also is Hindu, and that consequently, if the minar was constructed by the Muhammadans, its foundations were laid long after that of the walls of the temple, the present masjid: that such a gigantic structure could be built within a few feet of previously, existing structures by the barbarous Muhammadans, at a time when constructive engineering skill was far inferior to what it now is, and modern engineering appliances were unknown, without producing the most disastrous effects on these walls, appeared to me little short of incredible.[5] But this was not all. The pillar

*Published in the *Archaeological Survey of India Reports*, Volume 4, *Report for the Year 1871–72*, pp. 46–52.

is supposed to have been built up to first storey alone by Kutb, and the rest added subsequently by Iltitmish and his successors. Iltitmish also built the cloisters within 11 feet of the visible base of the minar, and yet, although immense weight was added to the original portion built by Kutb, the floor of Iltitmish's cloisters in its immediate vicinity is not appreciably distorted.

To me, this objection to its having been built by the Muhammadans appeared insurmountable, but to be consistent, I cannot admit that it was built at any time subsequent to the building of the temple; it must have either existed before, or been built simultaneously with, the temple.

The iron pillar (visible in Plate 3) proves that when its characters were engraved the temple existed; for the pillar must have been made to set up on the existing floor, and not the enormous floor built to set the iron pillar on. Therefore the minar must date to a period anterior to this.

The position of the Minar is outside of Kutb's mosque, and General Cunningham contends[6] that it was the custom then to build Mâzinah (which he supposes[7] the minar to have been) originally outside the Masjids and independent of them. Without entering into a discussion on this point, I will simply note that it is built in a position quite away from the masjid, not symmetrically placed in regard to it, and indeed, as regards its connection with Kutb Masjid alone, it may have been placed anywhere else without making its position a whit more difficult to account for than it now is. It is hard to suppose that barbarous, though the Muhammadans were, they would, in fixing the position of a structure so grand and unique, and withal so *expensive*, have not given more thought to it than they would have to the raising of a dirt pie; or why, if they selected the place after deliberation, did they select the site it stands on, which neither in direction nor distance has any conceivable dependence on the masjid to which it served as a pendant.

No one contends that the minar was founded by Iltitmish, though, if they did, there would be some sense in his placing it facing the centre arch of one wing of his extension; but although roughly it faces the centre arch, it is by no means accurately in the centre, and the quantity by which it is out of the centre position is not a few inches, which would have been allowable, or due to error in setting out, but about 3 feet, and therefore neither on the supposition of Kutb nor of Iltitmish being its founders can its peculiar and eccentric position be accounted for.

But supposing it to be a Hindu structure, how easily its position is accounted for! *Vide* previous description. Colonel Sleeman's argument that the slope of the Kutb Minar is a peculiar characteristic of Pathan buildings, and that the arches of the great mosque close to it all correspond in design, proportion, and execution to the tower is palpably erroneous; for not only is the great slope of the minar emphatically not a characteristic of the Pathan architecture of that period, or even of subsequent periods up to Toglin's reign, but the walls of the very arches, which he says correspond with it in design, proportion, and execution, have not a particle of slope all the way up; and what proportion is there between the first storey of the Kutb Minar, which alone, be it remembered, was built by Kutb, and Kutb's arches? In fact, what proportion, or possible connection is there at all between the Kutb Minar and any Muhammadan[8] structure whatever, or in the Kutb enclosures, when the builders did not understand how to proportion the large and small arches of their Masjid, as is to be seen in the existing front wall of Kutb Masjid (Plate 3), noble though it is from sheer greatness of size? How could they possibly conceive even the idea of proportioning the mazinâh to the arches of the masjid? No doubt the execution is similar in both arches and minar. But why? Because the arches were built, the mechanical part of the work there was done by Hindu workmen, probably descendants of the very men who previously built the minar, for in India professions and trades are hereditary.

The Minar or Lat is a tapering shaft ornamented at intervals by bands and balconies (Plate 10). It will be noticed on examining the minar that the first three storeys and a portion and the fourth are cased with red sandstone on the exterior, and higher up with marble and sandstone in irregular widths.

That the style of ornamentation used in the first three storeys, whether we take the bands, the balconies, or the flutings of the shaft itself, is widely different to the style of ornamentation of the other two existing storeys; this difference is so great, so utterly irreconcileable, that, in the absence of every other argument in favour of the supposition, it alone would justify a belief that the three lower storeys belong to a period widely distant from the date of the upper two.

But the difference between them is not confined to the exterior or the ornamentation above; the internal construction presents a difference still more radical; this difference is, that whereas in the lower three storeys the openings for light are constructed on the same principle as the windows in the outer south wall of the Kutb enclosure, that is, by an arch of overlapping stones, extending a part of the way into the body of the wall, to be replaced by the bracket and architrave construction, in the upper two storeys this construction is not used, the change is not even gradual, it is abrupt and decisive. Further, the steps that wind round the interior are up to a portion of the fourth storey supported invariably by the usual Hindu brackets, identical in every particular with the brackets used in the temple or masjid as it is now called, whereas higher up no brackets are used. This change is likewise abrupt and decisive. Again, further, the central shaft round which the steps wind is sloping all the way up from the base to the top of the third storey, and a little way beyond,—in short, exactly to the point corresponding to the termination of the bracketted steps, whilst up above for the remainder of the fourth storey the central shaft does not taper at all, and though the shaft again tapers in the fifth, that does not in any way affect the argument. The three changes in the internal construction all occur at the same point, and are all equally abrupt and decisive.

But to add to the difference in construction in the interior, the material used also changes at that very point, all below being constructed internally of granite, all above of sandstone. Further, my examination has failed to show any mortar between the joints of the stones in the first three storeys, except a little at and near the lowest door, which having a true arch may well be considered to be a late construction, and at the other doors no instance of the true arch is seen in the structures of either Kutbuddin or Iltitmish, and the occurrence of the true arch therefore stamps the portions as later alterations; therefore, as the question of the foundation of the minar lies between Kutb, or possibly Iltitmish and the Hindus, the occurrence of these arches in no way affects the question. But to revert; although no mortar is apparently used in the joints in the first three storeys, which are internally built of granite, mortar joints are invariably the rule in the two higher storeys.

Inscriptions are more frequent in the harder material of the three lower storeys (Plates 10 and 15) than in the softer material of the upper two, which is curious.

Returning to the outside, and examining with a powerful telescope the ornamental bands of the exterior, it will be found that there is great difference in the appearance of the weathering of the stones, which are carved with bells and lotuses, and triangle patterns, and of the Arabic inscriptions. This difference is quite as great as the difference in weathering between the Arabic inscriptions and the restorations carried out not half a century ago by the British which last can, by this means, be detected with certainty.

But the difference between the bands of lotus and triangles and the bands of Arabic is not confined to the external weathering alone; the construction too is radically different, for whereas the lotus and triangles are carved on the exposed edge of a stone of the proper thickness exactly for the purpose, which stone is built into the structure with its longest dimension or bed, horizontal, as it ought to be in all good and genuine work, the stones on which the Arabic is cut are set with their longest dimensions vertical, forming only a sort of veneer on the outside; and not this alone, but the stones are not all of a size; and, further, they are in some places so thin, that in cutting out or countersinking the Arabic inscriptions, the entire thickness of the stone has been cut through.

It is clear therefore that the original design provided for the bands of lotus, bells, and triangles, but not for the deep-cut Arabic inscriptions. My opinion is, and it is only an opinion, unsupported by any facts, that where these Arabic inscriptions exist, there originally existed bold projecting bands of sculpture, and that, in cutting away the Hindu sculpture, the Muhammadans so reduced the stone in thickness as to present the characters it now does. When I first examined the minar, I had not seen the way bands of statues are executed by the Hindus. I now know how it is done, having seen the magnificent examples at Khajurâho, and remembering the fact that some of the stones in the Arabic band are set with their long dimensions horizontal (although I did not then think it worthwhile noting their positions, nor, if I had, could I have ascertained all the stones in any single band which are laid horizontally). I am inclined rather to think that the band of sculpture consisted of detached statues, or of detached but boldly projecting tablets carved with geometrical patterns, or even plain, as at the temples of Khajurâho, Mahoba or Garhwa.

The difference, however, goes a step more. Whereas the bell, lotus, and triangle bands project boldly beyond the face of the minar, the Arabic inscriptions do not project beyond the general level of the adjacent parts. The letters are indeed in high relief, but this relief is obtained by countersinking the ground of the inscriptions, and the projecting faces of the relief letters do not, in a single instance, project beyond the level or surface of the adjacent parts. In this way relief sculpture could be executed even at the present day on any part of the minar.

It will be seen from the preceding paragraphs that between the three lower and the two upper storeys there are marked differences of style, of construction, and of material. The three lower storeys correspond with each other in every respect, but are very different to the upper two, and this external difference may be seen in any photograph of the minar, or on the actual Minar, by looking at it from a distance, sufficient to give at once a view of all the storeys.

I now proceed to detail the intimate connection that exists between the minar and the temple as it stood in the Hindu period.

ALEXANDER CUNNINGHAM, PREFACE TO BEGLAR'S REPORT*

The two buildings of greatest interest in old Delhi are the Kutb Masjid with its magnificent arches and colonnades (Plates 2 and 3), and the noble Muazzin's pillar, called the Kutb Minar (Plate 10), which is nearly 250 feet in height. The erection of the masjid has always been assigned to Kutb-ud-din Aibeg, the first Muhammadan king of Delhi. Indeed this assignment is distinctly stated in the inscription over the eastern or main entrance to the masjid, with the addition of the important fact that it was built out of the material furnished by twenty-seven ruined Hindu temples. That the pillars of the colonnades are Hindu is obvious to every one; and at the same time it is equally obvious that they have been rearranged and made up to their present height by the Muhammadans, by piling the shafts of two or three pillars one over the other. This fact was equally clear to Mr Fergusson as it is to me. In the [...] report [above] Mr Beglar admits that the pillars have been more or less rearranged, but he contends that they occupy their original positions in the colonnade of a single Hindu temple, and that their present height is exactly that of the original Hindu colonnade. Consistently with this view he is obliged to condemn the record of the Muhammadan builder of the masjid regarding the destruction of twenty-seven Hindu temples as a false boast.

This opinion I consider as quite indefensible. The Muhammadan conqueror could have no possible object in publishing a false statement

*Published in the *Archaeological Survey of India Reports*, Volume 4, *Report for the Year 1871–72*, pp. i–ix.

of the number of temples destroyed, nor in recording a lie over the entrance gateway of his great masjid. I therefore accept the statement as rigidly true. It is besides amply confirmed by the made up pillars of the colonnades on three sides of the court (Plate 2), which, as I have shown in my account of Delhi, must certainly have belonged to a great number of different temples.

That the Kutb Masjid was the site of a single Hindu temple I have no doubt whatever; and before Mr Beglar began any excavations under my instructions, I stated to him my opinion that the lower portion of the surrounding walls of the raised terrace on which the masjid stands was the original undisturbed platform of a Hindu temple. The excavations made by Mr Beglar outside these walls have proved that my opinion was correct. I therefore look upon this raised terrace on which the Kutb Masjid stands as the site of the chief temple of the old Hindu city of Delhi, of which the only remains now existing *in situ* are the tall Hindu pillars immediately behind the great arch. These are true Hindu pillars, undisturbed and unaltered by the Muhammadans. I consider them *undisturbed*, because their places are marked out on the pavement by chiselled lines; and I call them *unaltered*, because they have single Hindu shafts like those of other Hindu temples, whilst *all* the pillars in the surrounding colonnades are Muhammadan compositions, made up of two or three separate pillars to obtain height. I can offer one proof as to the pillars behind the great arch being in their original positions, in the fact that the stones of the piers of the great arch are actually *cut out* so as to fit against the mouldings of the pillars. This fact seems to me to show that the arches were an after addition built by the Muhammadans *against* the pillars of the old Hindu temples, which, therefore, I conclude to be *in situ*.

In the cloisters this curious mode of fitting new work to old work is found exactly reversed in the case of one of the pilasters of the northern colonnade. Here a natural bulge on one of the wall stones is met by a corresponding hollow cut out of the pilaster. I call them pilasters because they are placed against the walls; but they are frequently full pillars with one face turned to the wall, and their bases not being reduced to bring their centres under the midlines of the shafts, these bases are projected several inches out of their true positions beyond the central lines of the shafts. I conclude, therefore, with absolute certainty that the pillars of the surrounding colonnades are not *in situ*, but were added by the Muhammadans to the old Hindu walls of the courtyard of the ruined temple.

As a further proof of the patchwork character of these incongruous pillars, I can adduce the following simple facts:

l. In the north cloister, the first pillar in the outer row to the east has an almost plain granite shaft for the lower member, which is placed *upside down*.

2. In the north cloister, two contiguous columns of the outer line are each formed of three pieces of similar pillars placed one above the other, with the same mouldings and the same ornaments. Of these six pieces four are octagons with the alternate faces indented, the other two being plain octagons; but in one the plain octagonal piece forms the top third, in the other it is the middle third.

3. Several plain octagonal shafts, as well as others with the alternate faces indented, are found resting on square blocks, which were originally intended to receive square shafts. This is clearly shown by the upper surfaces of the exposed corners of the square blocks, which are not covered by the present octagonal shafts, being still in a rough state, just as they left the mason's hand, furrowed with chisel marks.

But the proofs of rearrangement of old materials are not confined to the pillars of the colonnades. They are equally numerous and equally convincing in the domes of the gateways and corner rooms of the cloisters. These domes Mr Beglar considers to be in their original positions, but the *following* facts will show that they also have been rearranged by the Muhammadans:

1. In the southeast corner the dome springs from an octagon which rests on a square-supported by eight pillars, namely, four corner pillars and four middle pillars. The angles of the octagon, therefore, fall on the beams of the square instead of over the pillars.

2. In the dome of the northwest corner this notable fault is intensified by the spaces between the pillars being unequal, as the intermediate pillars are not placed in the middle of the sides of the square.

3. In the northeast corner the dome springs from an octagon supported on twelve pillars forming a square; but there are capitals of five brackets placed in the corners of the square, and some common capitals of four brackets in the angles of the octagon. How did these brackets get into the wrong places except by rearrangement?

4. In the great dome of the cloister of the east gateway there is the same kind of anomaly; some of the beams of the octagon resting in the angles between two brackets of common four bracket capitals, instead

of being placed on the angular bracket of a five-bracket capital. The beams also are of different kinds, some being plain and some ornamented. This dome must, therefore, have been rearranged in its present position by the Muhammadans.

5. In the smaller ceilings of the side spaces of the corner rooms, there are some square ornamented slabs with their sides cut to make them fit into oblong spaces, whilst others are uncut, but are eked out at the ends of the oblong by plain slabs to fill the blank spaces. These roofs, therefore, are certainly not in their original positions, and I conclude, without any hesitation, that they must have been arranged as they are now by the Muhammadans when the great masjid was erected by Kutb-ud-din out of the spoils of twenty-seven Hindu temples.

6. In the upper rooms of the northeast and southeast corners many of the roofing slabs appear to have been taken from a Jain temple, as the faces of several of the stones which reduce the size of the square openings by covering the angles are filled with figures of men, elephants, and horses, with a single squatted figure in the middle, *quite naked,* and with both hands lying in the lap, exactly after the fashion of Jain, statues. If then, as Mr Beglar argues, these cloisters are the colonnades of a single Hindu temple, that temple must have been dedicated to the Jain worship, a conclusion which is directly negatived by the inscription on the iron pillar standing in the midst of the courtyard, in which the pillar itself is called the 'arm of Vishnu'. It is also at variance with the several Vaishnava sculptures which are built into the surrounding walls, such as the Ten Avatârs, and Nârâyan reposing on the folds of the snake Ananta.

The conclusion which I have come to regarding the Kutb Masjid is simply this—that it was built by Hindu masons under Muhammadan supervision out of the ruins of twenty—seven Hindu temples, some of which were no doubt Jain. This would be quite sufficient to account for all the faults of construction which have been noted, as well as for the incongruous make up of the pillars of the colonnades. The object of the Muhammadans was to obtain height, and as the generality of Hindu shafts are short monoliths, they gained their object by building up a single tall column of two or three Hindu shafts piled one over the other, with portions of bases and other blocks interposed. The general effect is no doubt pleasing, but I believe this to be due solely to the profusion of ornament, which distracts the eye, and prevents it from observing the incongruity of thick shafts surmounting thin ones, of bracket projections supporting nothing, and of niche projections unsupported. If the pillars were plain, I believe that their utter want of symmetry would be signally striking, and the incongruity and want of harmony of the several pieces would be obvious at once.

The Hindu origin of the Kutb Minar is also upheld by Mr Beglar, who argues in favour of his opinion with much ingenuity. The Hindus themselves claim the pillar as their own, and assert that it was erected by Prithi Râj to enable his daughter to see the Ganges! In a former report I have stated my reasons at length for believing that the Kutb Minar is a purely Muhammadan building,[9] and I will now adduce others which have occurred to me during two separate visits to the Kutb Minar in company with Mr Beglar. On the first visit he pointed out to me the following short inscriptions in Nagari letters recorded on the lower part of the minar:

1. On plinth outside, to right of entrance – *Sam(va)t* 1256.
2. On wall of passage inside door to left – *Samvat* (1) 256.
3. On underside of lowest overlapping archstone in entrance passage – *Samvat* 1256.

I take these three inscriptions to be the records of one of the Hindu masons employed in building the minar. That they are productions of an illiterate person is shown by the omission of the letter *v* in the first, and of the figure 1 for 1,000 in the second record. These three records of the same date Samvat 1256, or 1199 AD, seem to me to point either to the foundation or to the completion of the building in that year—the repetition of the date being a common practice amongst Hindu masons. Thus, on the pillars of the Atâla Masjid at Jonpur, which is known to have been originally a Hindu temple converted to Muhammadan use by Ibrahim Shah Sharki between the years 1403 and 1440 AD, I found the date of Samvat 1464, or 1407 AD, three times repeated as follows :—

1. On right jamb of north-gate outside—

Samvat 1464 *Sumapt*
Sutradhâra Padumavi
Saï Sutradhâra Suta

'Finished in the Samvat year 1464 by the mason Padumavi, son of the mason Saï'

2. On one of the lower square pillars—*Samvat* 1464.

Buniâdipari.

'Founded in the Samvat year 1464.'

3. On one of the outer pillars on the south side—*Samvat* 1464.

But in addition to these dates, I can cite an actual record of the master mason, or builder who superintended the erection of the minar. This is cut on the south face of the plinth, and was first pointed out to me by Mr Beglar. The record is unfortunately rendered imperfect by the fracture of the stone; but the remaining letters and figures are sufficiently distinct –

x x Ma gaj $51^1/_2$—$83^1/_4$ dâranâmuni

Immediately to the right of the figures 511/2 there is a broad arrow, or long upright line with a stroke sloping downwards on each side—and about one inch to the right there is another similar mark which has been partially obliterated. Both of these lines are continued on the upper surface of the plinth. The words *dâranâmuni* I take to mean the 'exemplar line', or as we should say the 'plumb-line' of the building, which the shifting of the mark shows to have been readjusted to the extent of rather more than one inch at the time that the record was made. That this was done, by a Hindu mason is proved by the adoption of the word *gaj*, instead of the Persian *gaz*, which would certainly have been used by any one of the Muhammadan conquerors. It is curious that I found a similar mark on the projecting part of the back wall of the masjid itself immediately behind the centre, which was obviously intended for the adjustment of the midline of the masjid itself, as the mark is several inches outside of the middle of the projection.

Mr Beglar bases his opinion chiefly on two arguments:

1st—That there is a difference of style observable between the three lower storeys and the two upper storeys, from which he infers that the former must be Hindu work and the latter Muhammadan.

2nd—That the distances between the bands of ornamentation are in geometrical progression; from which he argues that as the chain of the series must have been a work of 'no ordinary labour', it could not have been discovered by the 'barbarous Muhammadan conquerors', and must therefore be the work of the intellectual Hindus.

In his first argument Mr Beglar ignores the fact that the two upper storeys were rebuilt by Firoz Tughlak, as recorded in the inscriptions, as well as in his autobiography. The difference of style is indeed very striking, but it is not necessary to suppose that it marks more than the difference of architectural taste which had taken place in a century-and-a-half that had elapsed between the times of Kutb-ud-din Aibeg and Firoz. The rich style of ornamentation of the lower balconies is in strict accordance with the lavish traceries of the arches which is seen in both the early masjids of Delhi and Ajmer, while the contrast of white marble with red sandstone was a favourite device in the time of Firoz, as may still be seen in his pillar at Hisar. That the style of ornamentation is Hindu may be admitted; but this was a simple necessity of the early Muhammadan architecture of India, as the conquerors were soldiers who were naturally obliged to employ the masons of the country in carrying out their designs. Hence came the overlapping arches as well as the Hindu ornament.

Mr Beglar's second argument, which depends on the use of a *recondite geometrical series,* I utterly repudiate as a mere fanciful guess. Even supposing it were true, it is not easy to believe that the armies of Muhammad Ghori were formed entirely of literate men when we remember that the learned Abu Rihan accompanied the still earlier expeditions of Mahmud of Ghazni. But when it is admitted that 'the chain of the series (geometrical) must alone have been a work of no ordinary labour', I must confess that I put no faith in the application of such a practically impossible series.

Mr Beglar further argues that there is a difference of projection between the bands of lotus flowers and the bands of Arabic inscriptions, the former being flush with the faces of the column, while the latter have a considerable projection. But it is only the lowest band of writing that is flush with the face, all the others being raised; and this belt has been so much injured by time and by ignorant restorations that it is now illegible, Sayid Ahmed being able to read no more than the words *Amir ul Umra,* or 'chief of the nobles'. I believe therefore that the depression of this belt is due entirely to the restorers, a conclusion which is borne out by the fact that several of the red facing stones have been cut right through so as to leave the inner core of rough stone quite visible. Now, this belt forms no part of Mr Beglar's geometrical series, and as I am quite satisfied that it was an integral part of the original ornamentation, I repudiate the whole scheme of recondite Hindu design as a mere fanciful theory.

But on this subject of the ornamentation of the Kutb Minar we now possess the most decisive evidence that it is not of Hindu origin in, the Târikh-i-Alai of Amir Khusru, a contemporary of Alauddin Khilji. Speaking of the new minar, which this king had ordered to be built, the poet adds that he also 'directed that a *new casing* and cupola should be added to the old one.'[10] According to this account, which we must remember is that of an eye witness of the fact, the whole of the present red stone facing was added by Alauddin, and to him we must assign all its exquisite balconies as well as all its ornamental bands. It was no doubt the knowledge of this entire restoration by the Pathan King that led Baber to call it the minar of Alauddin Khilji.

Having thus disposed of the Hindu origin of the ornamental bands on the face of the pillar, I will add a few words about the minar itself. In proof of the Hindu origin of the column, Sayid Ahmed states that 'there is only *one minar*, which is contrary to the practice of the Muhammadans, who always give *two* minars to their masjids.' But this statement is correct only for the custom of the last three centuries, as the following facts will show that the previous practice of the Muhammadans was to have only one minar, or mazinâh, to their masjids:—

1. The masjid of Tûlûn in Cairo, built in 876 AD, has only one minar.[11]

2, 3. The two minars of Mahmud at Ghazni, built about 1000 AD, are of different sizes, and stand half a mile apart. They therefore belonged to two different masjids.

4. The masjid of Sultan Barkût (*sic*) in Cairo, built in 1149 AD, has only one minar.[12]

5. The minar at Koël, built in 1252 AD, was a single column, and occupied exactly the same position with regard to its masjid as that of the Kutb Minar to its masjid.

6. The unfinished minar of Alauddin at Delhi is a single column built about 1300 AD.

7. Two masjids at Bayana have only *one* minar each, placed outside the courtyard of the masjid, but on the northeast corner instead of on the southeast corner as in the Kutb example. One of these bears an inscription of Naseruddin Muhammad, who was reigning in 1390 AD.

From these eight examples, which range over a period of more than five centuries down to within one hundred and sixty years of the accession of Akbar, it is clear that it was the fixed practice of the Muhammadans to have only one minar, or mazinâh, to each masjid. That the Kutb Minar was a mazinâh or Muazzin's tower we have the evidence of its inscriptions which cannot be ignored, as well as the express declaration of Abulfeda who calls it a mazinâh. That it was a Muhammadan design we have the fact, that the conquerors of Delhi were the rulers of Ghazni, where they had been familiar with the minars of Mahmûd, which are star polygons in plan, with deeply indented angles. For the Muhammadan the Kutb Minar had a purpose which was intimately connected with the daily practice of his religion. I am therefore firmly convinced that it is a purely Muhammadan building both in purpose and in design, although most, if not all, of the details of its execution, and notably its overlapping or corbelled arches, are Hindu.

J.D. BEGLAR'S RESPONSE TO CUNNINGHAM'S PREFACE TO HIS REPORT*

Until lately I held the opinions expressed in my report regarding the Kutb Masjid and Minar. Starting with the hypothesis that the foundation and such parts of the walls of the Kutb Masjid, both inner and outer enclosures, as were below the ground level, were original Hindu, the conclusion I have arrived at in the report is simply inevitable; but early in November this year, General Cunningham and I visited the Kutb remains together, and he pointed out to me various incongruities which clearly showed that the foundations of the inner and outer inclosures, as they stand, are not original Hindu, although doubtless some portion, probably the portion of the foundation of the back wall immediately behind the middle of the masjid proper, is Hindu.

It is necessary that I notice and point this out particularly. As stated in my report, the material and workmanship I have there supposed to be Hindu, are precisely similar; but in one portion of the foundation courses of the south wall of the inner enclosure are inserted not one but several stones which either have, or once had, bracket projections. In the west back wall of the masjid also General Cunningham pointed out to me sculptured stones with their sculptured faces turned inwards; and further the upper double cornice which runs along the back wall of Kutb's portion of the masjid, is carried round the corner, proving that the inner enclosure was once complete in itself, and yet the same cornice

*Published in the *Archaeological Survey of India Reports*, Volume 4, *Report for the Year 1871–72*, pp. xv–xvii.

is continued through Alitmish's extension, and the materials and workmanship of this portion so closely correspond to the portion of Kutb's masjid, as to have led me to suppose the whole to have been one continuous wall, I not having then noticed that the cornice turned the corner of Kutb's enclosure.

These which are only a few of many similar incongruities now convince me that the entire foundations and walls (with the exception *perhaps* of some small indefinite portion) of the Kutb Masjid and Alitmish's extension are Muhammadan.

This admission completely alters the application of my arguments in the body of the report, without, however, in the least affecting their coherence.

Starting from the hypothesis that the foundations were undisturbed Hindu, I proceeded to prove that the various other parts of the masjid, as it stands, could not be Muhammadan; and as the minar is most intimately connected with the masjid by a definite law, it also could not be Muhammadan. Now, as I maintain that the foundations are not Hindu, but Muhammadan, my previous arguments all tend most emphatically to establish that every other part there supposed Hindu is Muhammadan also—in short, the whole force of my argument mainly went to show that to whatever age the foundations belonged, to the same age must be as signed the minar—and having started with a wrong hypothesis, I was compelled by the conclusions to which I then was logically and necessarily driven to maintain that the minar was Hindu. At present therefore I gladly and unhesitatingly acknowledge the grave error 1 committed, and General Cunningham will find that my 'fanciful' law, as he styles it, which governs the disposition of the various parts of the structure, forms one of the strongest proofs in favour of his views.

I now accordingly hold that, whatever in the masjid and minar I have maintained in my report to be undisturbed Hindu, is Muhammadan of the period of Kutb and Alitmish, and that whatever I have there called Muhammadan is due to subsequent repair and alteration, first, by Alauddin Khilji, second, by Firoz Shah, of both of whom history distinctly records that they repaired extensively the havoc time and violence had made in the buildings, and third, of those other repairs and alterations subsequent to Firoz Shah, which must have from time to time been executed by different kings, but of which history has left no record.

The execution, however, of the entire structure as a whole is Hindu; for the simple reason that Hindu workmen were the only ones Kutb and Alitmish could have procured.

I take this opportunity of thanking General Cunningham publicly for the kindness and patience he has shown in pointing out my error to me, an error of such a nature, that no mere argument could have touched it, and which, but for our going to the spot together, would have remained uncorrected; for none of his reasonings have shaken the coherence of my arguments and of the 'fanciful' law that governs the parts of the masjid and minar.

In a future paper I shall show a similar law governing the parts of structures indisputably Hindu, such, for instance, as the superb temples in various parts of Central India. So that it is clear the law was recognized by Hindu architects, and this is my reason for supposing that although the Kutb remains were executed under the orders of Muhammadan kings, and the leading features of the structure determined by them, the arrangement of the detail, both of construction and ornamentation, was left entirely to Hindu architects.[13]

NOTES

1. G. Beresford and Frederick Cooper, *The Handbook for Delhi* (Delhi, 1863), p. 73.

2. William Henry Sleeman, *Rambles and Recollections of an Indian Official* (London, 1844), Vol. II, p. 254.

3. James Tod, *Annals and Antiquities of Rajast'han* (London, 1829–32), Vol. II, p. 761.

4. James Fergusson, *The Illustrated Handbook of Architecture* (London, 1855), Vol. I, p. 415.

5. *Note by General Cunningham*—No one has ever supposed that the minar was actually built by the Muhammadans, they employed Hindu masons as a matter of necessity.

6. *Note by General Cunningham*—I do not *contend* that it was the custom. I have *proved* it by the two examples at Ghazni, and the single example at Koïl.

7. *Note by General Cunningham*—I do not suppose that the Kutb Minar was a Māzinah. *I know* that it was so called by Abulfeda. The Kutb Minar besides occupies *exactly* the same relative position to the Kutb Masjid which the Koïl Minar did to the Koïl Masjid.

8. *Note by General Cunningham*—I have already answered this question by a reference to the kindred towers at Ghazni and Koïl, all of which are known to

have been Mâzinahs. Such a building has a special use in the daily performance of the Muhammadan religion. I may now ask Mr Beglar, what possible connexion there is between the minar and any *Hindu* building whatever. Did the Hindus ever build another structure like it, either before or after the Muhammadan conquest? And lastly, what was the purpose which the tower was designed to serve amongst the Hindus?

9. *Archeological Survey of India*, Vol. I, p. 190.

10. Târikh-i-Alai in Dowson's edition of Sir H. Elliot's *Muhammadan Historians*, Vol. III, p. 70.

11. James Fergusson, *History of the Modern Styles of Architecture* (London, 1862), Vol. II, pp. 383, 387.

12. Ibid., Vol. II, p. 387.

13. *Note by General Cunningham*—It must be obvious to every one that the distances between the different bands of ornament could not have been determined by mere rule of thumb, buy must have been arranged by some simple series of difference either in arithmetical or geometrical progression. That the series was a very simple one I have no doubt; and I believe that it has not yet been discovered owing solely to the difficulty of measuring the exact distances between the bands.

The Qutb Complex as a Social Document*

MOHAMMAD MUJEEB

The Memoirs and Reports and Lists of Delhi Monuments published by the Archaeological Survey of India contain complete and detailed information about the groups of buildings which constitute the Qutb complex and other related material which is beyond the scope of this essay. My purpose here is not to reproduce all that information in an abbreviated form. I have had to study Indian architecture for a book I wrote some eighteen years ago on ancient Indian culture and now for lectures on Indian Muslim architecture. I am not a specialist in any sense. I can only present certain methods of approach that have occurred to me in the attempt to make architecture intelligible and interesting to myself and to my students, and I have selected the Qutb complex as the subject of this essay because it is particularly useful for this purpose.

The study of my specimen of architecture consists, I feel, in reading the architect's mind to discover how he adopted techniques and selected material for the construction of the building, the purpose of which was known to him. In reading the architect's mind we are moved by the same sentiments, we participate, as it were, in the planning, in the choice of ways and means, in the execution of the plan and in the assessment of the completed work. It may bring us no joy if we feel from the start that the architect was content to imitate or to follow a fashion, to use the prevalent techniques and the most easily available material, and to look forward to no appreciation beyond what is shown by the unimaginative

*Previously published as a chapter in M. Mujeeb, *Islamic Influence on Indian Society*, Meenakshi Publications, Delhi, 1972, pp. 114–27. In the present version, some portions of the text and notes have been removed. For the complete text see the original version.

for work which did not involve exercise of the imagination. We may, on the other hand, share the rapture of the artist who discovered the most perfect harmony between purpose and design, and find that the plan, the techniques, the material and the proportions of the created work reduce themselves to a single moment of exaltation. It is this experience which assures us that the beauty of architecture is the beauty of poetry, music, painting, and sculpture, and the great artist can enable us to overcome our imperfection and realize the underlying unity of all art.

Unfortunately, we tend to impose many limitations on ourselves. In Indian architecture, for instance, we consider first the categorization—is the building Hindu or Muslim? Then we look at the size, the costliness of the material, the names and dates of the builder and the building. We also overlook certain basic facts of the history of architecture. The technique of corbelling, that is, projecting stones or bricks of the upper layer over the lower so as to make an arch or a ceiling, and the use of the beam and post, or the trabeate system, are much older and more universal than Hinduism; the use of the arch and dome, or the arcuate system, was developed by the Romans and is much older than Islam, but we have labelled one system Hindu and the other Muslim. We look everywhere for borrowed elements. I do not mean that there are no differences between Hindu and Muslim architecture or that they should be ignored. The temple and the mosque represent two different concepts of worship, and cannot, therefore, be built in the same way. But if we begin, as we should, by understanding the purpose of the structure and then attempt to read the architect's mind, we shall appreciate the beauty of the created work without being misled by irrelevant considerations.

What we have to remember, I think, when studying Indian monuments, is the difference between architecture and sculpture. While trying to explain this difference to my class, a definition of both these arts occurred to me, which my artist friends have since assured me is fairly apt and comprehensive. Architecture is creation with material; sculpture is creation out of material. The canvas of the architect is space; in space he creates a form by putting together whatever material he builds with. The canvas of the sculptor is the material itself, out of which he makes a particular form emerge. A very small building can be a specimen of architecture; a very large building, or even a complex of buildings can be an example of sculpture. Not only the Kailash Temple of Ellora, which was in fact sculptured, but many other temples have been deliberately given an outline which creates the impression that they were not built with but hewn out of stone, and are sculptures on a gigantic scale. Between the definitely architectural and the definitely sculptural we can have variations of approach. The architecture of Gujarat is generally characterized by a sculptural approach, though there are also buildings, like the Jame' Masjid of Sarkhej, where the influence of sculptural standards is completely absent. We could say that up to a certain time in Indian history the aesthetics of sculpture dominated architecture. During Muslim rule sculpture may not have been patronized to any appreciable extent, but the stone-masons and sculptors certainly did not give up their profession, and they took their time to accept the aesthetics of architecture. It would be fairer and more precise not to make distinctions on the ground of religion when the real difference lies in the degree to which the standards and aesthetic principles of sculpture and architecture have been applied in the planning, the construction and the ornamentation of a building. If we bear this in mind, a study of the Qutb complex becomes an exciting intellectual and aesthetic adventure, and gives history another perspective.

I cannot here dilate upon the purely archaeological problems. We know that the Quwwat-al-Islam mosque (Plates 1–3) grew with the Muslim population of Delhi. As constructed originally, in 1199, it would not have accommodated more than 2,000 persons. Its final extension by Alauddin would have made it sufficient for ten or fifteen times that number, if not more. These extensions have been traced out without much difficulty by archaeologists, and fairly reasonable and convincing reconstructions have been made to show what the mosque looked like after its first extension by Iltutmish and second extension by Alauddin. Here I propose to consider only what is still standing, and can be seen and judged by those who do not have the imagination and the training of the archaeologist.

The Turks who occupied Delhi came from an area in which both brick and stone were used in building, but architecture in brick, such as we see in the oldest monuments of Bukhara, would have set the standard. Along with brick structures, the art of making tiles had been developed and was making continuous progress, both aesthetically and technically. On the other hand, sculpture and stone-masonry practised in the Greek colonies of Bacteria and Gedrosia would not have died out. Thanks to Alauddin Jahansoz, we cannot now say whether Ghazni was mainly a city of brick, or of stone, or of wooden structures. But we may be certain that those who thought of building a mosque and a *minar* at Delhi were thinking in terms of architecture and not sculpture. Construction in wood was ruled out; bricks were not available; they could only build in stone.

There is an inscription above the northern entrance to the Quwwat-al-Islam mosque stating that the material of twenty-seven temples was utilized for its construction. If this was done after the people of Delhi had submitted, it was certainly against the *sharīʿah,* but there would hardly have been any among the Turks occupying Delhi whose conscience would have troubled them on that account. We must, however, unequivocally condemn the action. Some of the temples would no doubt have been damaged and desecrated during the fighting, and they would have been abandoned for that reason. But the inscription indicates that these temples were deliberately dismantled, and it was not only a matter of utilizing the material of temples destroyed as an act of war.

While the moral and legal issue is clear, however, the question of who carried out the dismantling has still to be answered. We can assume that Hindu stone-masons were forced to do it, or that Muslim masons were employed. In any case the work was done by stone-masons. If they had been Muslims brought over from the Punjab or beyond they would have known the technique of building true arches and we would [not] have had corbelled arches in the screen of the Quwwat-al-Islam mosque (Plate 3). As it is, the true arch appears for the first time in the Alai Darwaza, built in 1311. We must assume, therefore, that the stone-masons were Hindus. And not only in this first instance. It appears from an inscription on the fifth storey of the Qutb Minar (Plate 10) that the repairs and additions in the reign of Firoz Tughlaq in 1368 were carried out under the supervision of a master-mason named Nana Salba, son of Chahada Dev Tala.

The stone-masons employed for dismantling the temples and building the mosque would not all have been residents of Delhi. The city was not large enough to provide continuous employment for any considerable number of stone-masons, unless we assume that a good proportion of the twenty-seven temples mentioned was in the process of construction. Family group or communities of stone-masons and sculptors generally migrated from one place of work to another, remaining settled for as long as was necessary to complete a particular project. Many such families and groups would have been collected in haste from near and far, for the mosque had to be built soon and the minar was to follow.

What would have been the attitude of these stone-masons and sculptors to what they were asked to do? Would they have undertaken it for fear of losing their lives, with hatred seething within them? That would be the logical deduction, considering what had happened. But, then, would not their feelings have affected their work? Cunningham has pointed out some technical defects in the construction of one or two corbelled ceilings and their supports in the southwestern corner of the mosque colonnade, and attributed them to haste. But the later extensions have not stood the test of time as well as the original mosque, and instead of any evidence of slipshod work we find unimpeachable examples of free, creative effort. The stone-masons were not submissive instruments. They must have asserted themselves as technicians, and also exercised their imagination to appreciate and their skill to realize in practice the architectural values they were asked to express.

There are many mosques in India with colonnades around their courtyards, but none in which the eastern side has been so definitely emphasized. The gateway built by Iltutmish and the Alai Darwaza are on the southern side, because the city lay to the south. But the main gateway of the original mosque, like the entrance to a temple, is on the east, and the columns on this side are four deep, while those on the north and south are only three deep. Does not this imply that the stone-masons, or their chief, feeling instinctively that the eastern colonnade must represent the vestibule of a temple, insisted that this should be emphasized, and had his way? The screen, which stands opposite, was probably the central feature, following a prevalent style in mosque construction which was further developed in different parts of India. It must have been higher than the domes of the covered area behind it. What remains of the screen now is the central arch and three of the four low arches which flanked it, two on each side. Originally, one would have looked through the central arch into a shadowy interior, and felt that passing through it one would enter the world of the spirit, of calm and quiet contemplation of the divine. Now one looks through it into space and feels that in isolation and decay its beauty has acquired another and far richer meaning. I remember taking the Russian artist Magda Nachmann to the Qutb over twenty years ago. Once she had seen this arch she would look at nothing else. She stood before it in rapturous silence and wept when it became dark and we had to return. And indeed, if we look at the arch and take in its beauty, we feel that it is something that can be translated into many forms and many moods, into the peace and tranquillity of the Buddha image, into the timeless contemplation of the Trimurti of the Elephanta

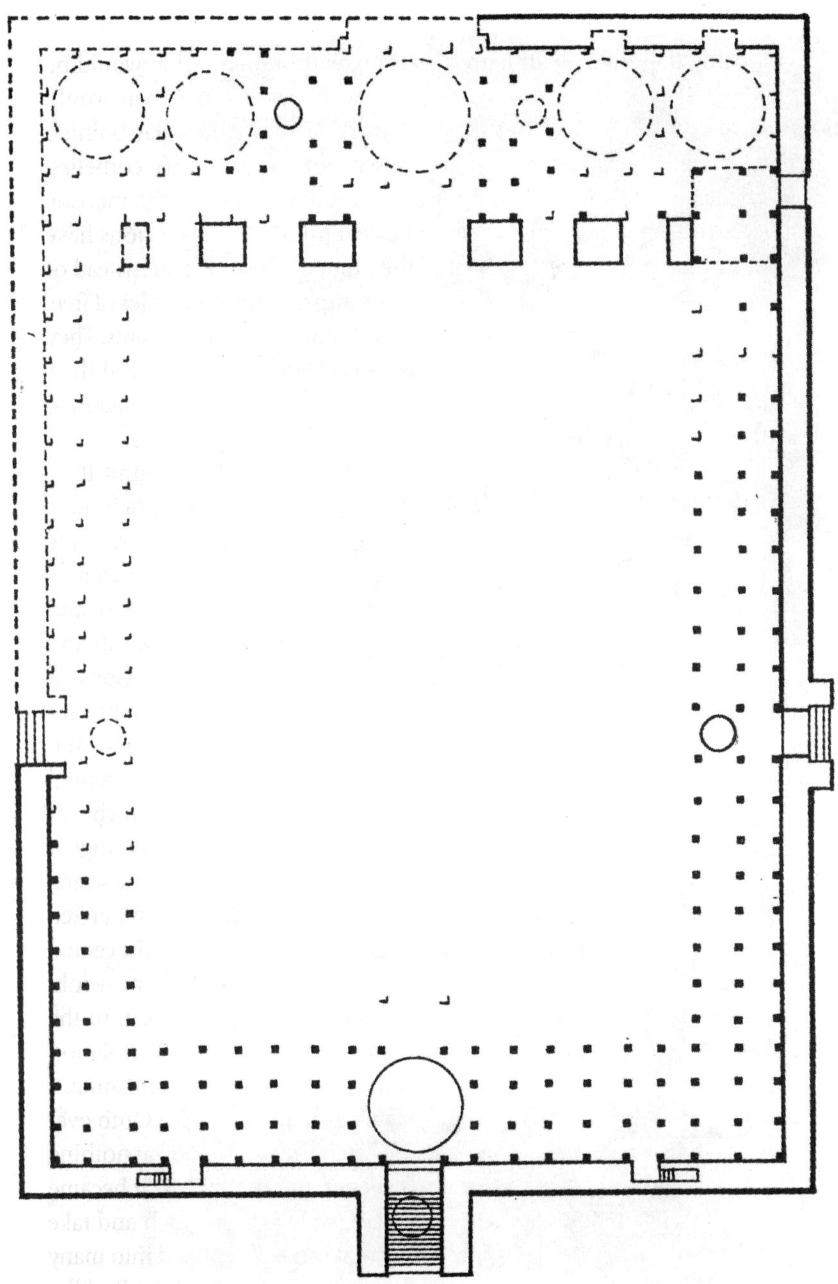

Plate 1: Qutb Mosque, Delhi, schematic plan with plan of *mulūk khāna* indicated in north-western corner of prayer-hall (top right)

Plate 2: Qutb Mosque, Delhi, reused pillars in northern colonnade (photo, Finbarr Barry Flood)

Plate 3: Qutb Mosque, Delhi, prayer-hall screen of 1198 with Iron Pillar in the foreground (photo, Finbarr Barry Flood)

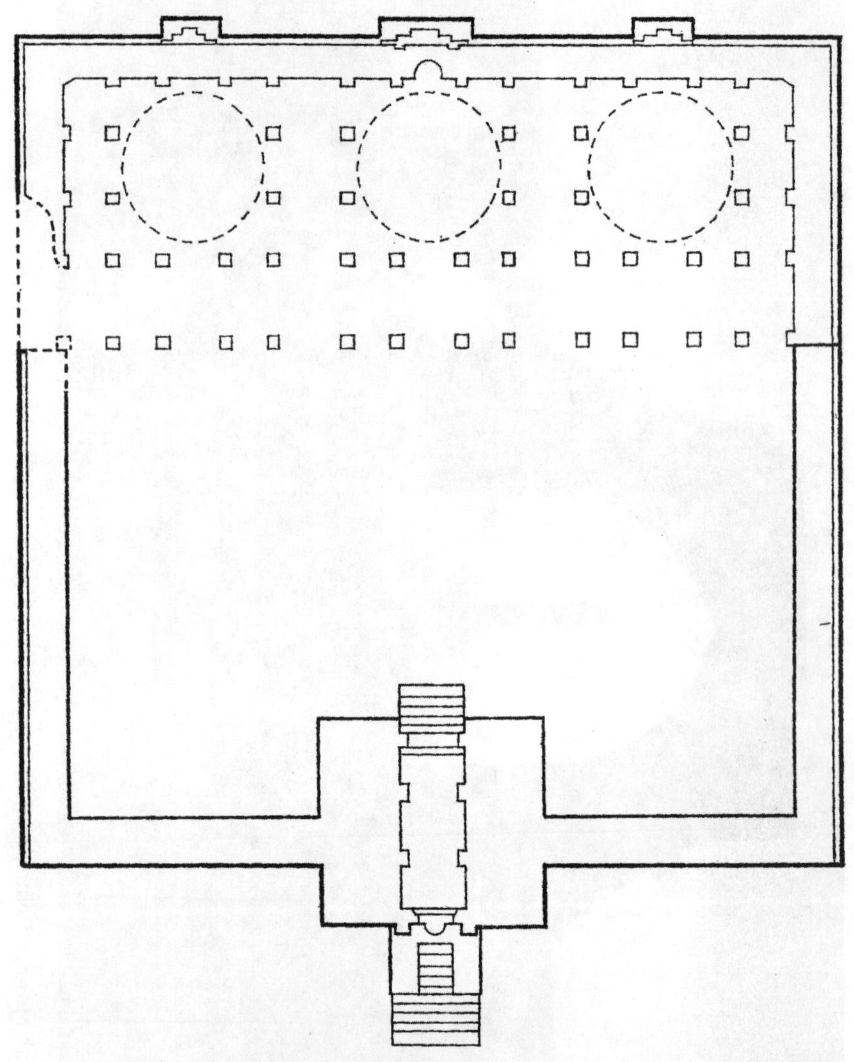

Plate 4: Shahi Masjid, Khatu, schematic plan showing domed prayer-hall on western side of courtyard

Plate 5: Arhai-din-ka-Jhonpra Mosque, Ajmir, marble mihrab
(photo, Finbarr Barry Flood)

Plate 6: Shahi Masjid, Khatu, view of main mihrab and prayer-hall (photo, Finbarr Barry Flood)

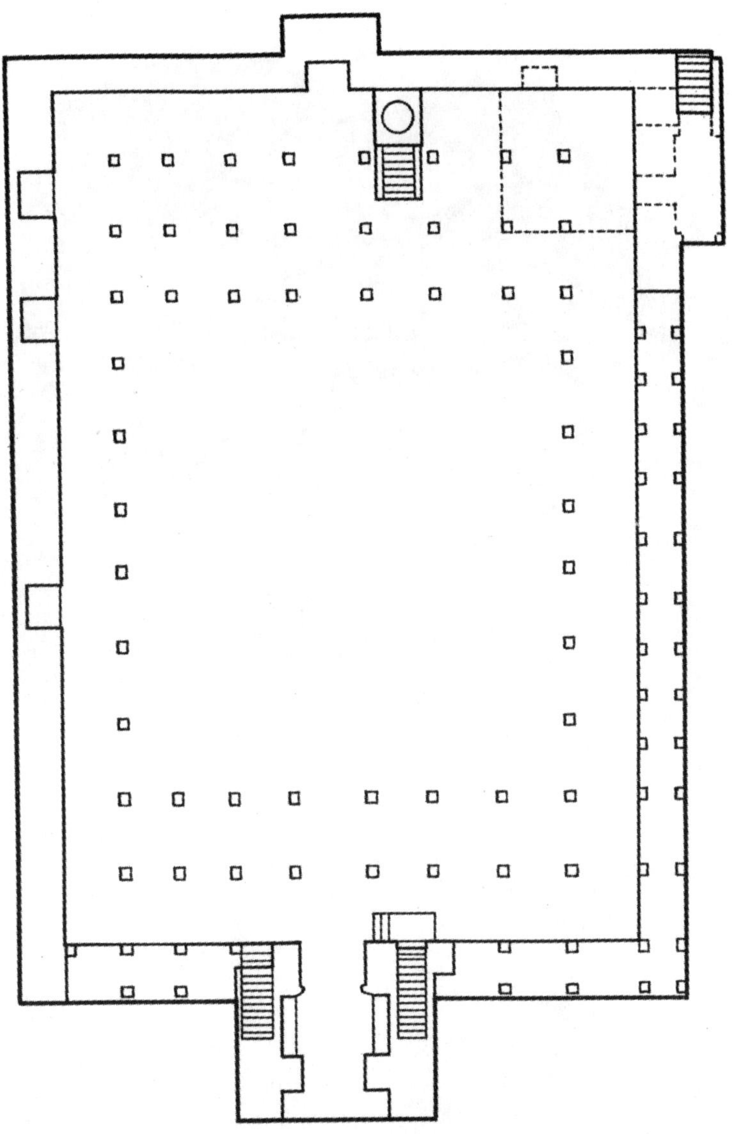

Plate 7: Chaurasi Kambha Mosque, Kaman, schematic plan showing *mulūk khāna* in north-west corner of prayer-hall (top right)

Plate 8: Shahi Masjid, Khatu, view of main entrance from the south-east (photo, Finbarr Barry Flood)

Plate 9: Chaurasi Kambha Mosque, Kaman, view from the south-east (photo, Finbarr Barry Flood)

Plate 10: Qutb Minar, Qutb Mosque, Delhi (photo, Finbarr Barry Flood)

Plate 11: Arhai-din-ka-Jhonpra Mosque, Ajmir, prayer-hall façade with screen added by sultan Iltutmish, probably in the 1220s (photo, Finbarr Barry Flood)

Plate 12: Qutb Mosque, Delhi, exterior of the entrance to the royal chamber or *mulūk khāna* (photo, Finbarr Barry Flood)

Plate 13: Chaurasi Kambha Mosque, Kaman, detail of reused pillar showing damaged *apsaras* at corners and intact *kīrttimukha* face at centre (photo, Finbarr Barry Flood)

Plate 14: Arhai-din-ka-Jhonpra Mosque, Ajmir, reused columns in prayer-hall (photo, Finbarr Barry Flood)

Plate 15: Qutb Minar, Delhi, detail of epigraphic band (photo, Finbarr Barry Flood)

Plate 16: Qutb Mosque, Delhi, detail of inscription on prayer-hall screen of 1198 (photo, Finbarr Barry Flood)

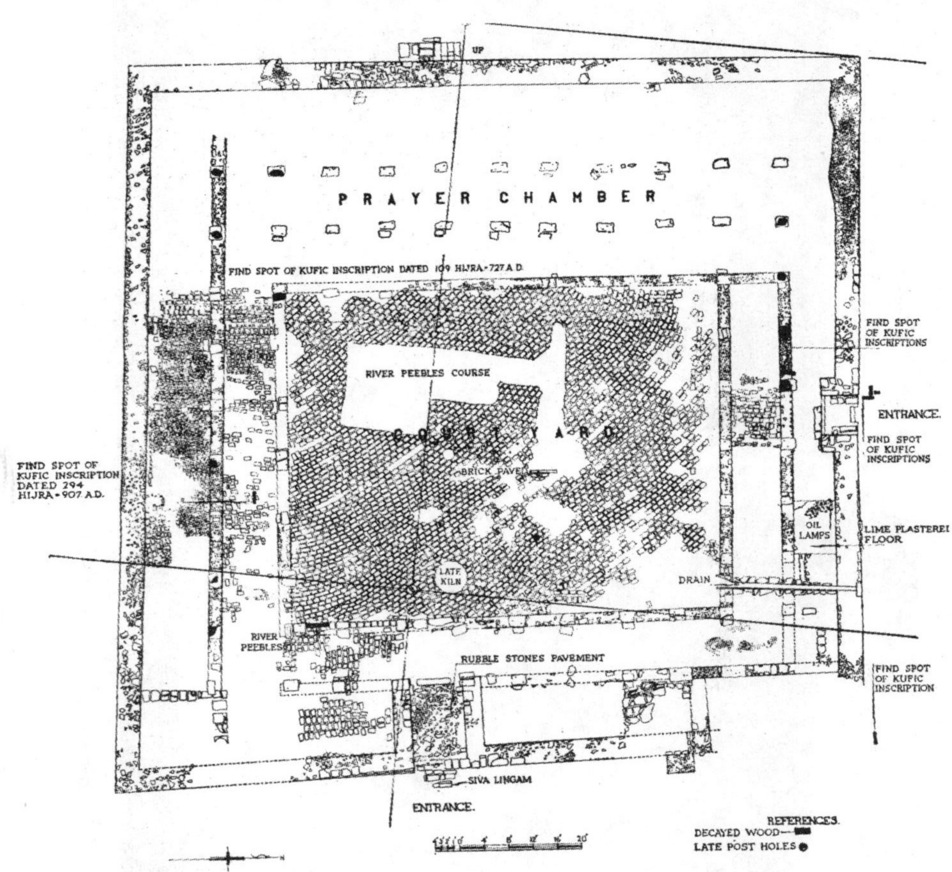

Plate 17: Great Mosque of Banbhore (probable site of Daybul), plan as excavated (after Ashfaque 1969)

Plate 18: Arhai-din-ka-Jhonpra Mosque, Ajmir, detail of ceiling (photo, Finbarr Barry Flood)

Plate 19: Arhai-din-ka-Jhonpra Mosque, Ajmir, detail of screen (photo, Michael W. Meister)

Plate 20: Mahavir temple, Osiañ, Rajasthan, sub-shrine No. 3, ca. 1025 (photo, Michael W. Meister)

Plate 21: Chaurasi Kambha Mosque, Kaman, main mihrab

Caves, the ecstasy of the *sufi*, the poet's dream of a loveliness that eludes the drapery of woods. It is something beyond architecture and beyond sculpture, a chiselling out of space that creates the framework for endless horizons of thought and feeling.

I referred earlier to reading the architect's mind in order to understand his work. Archaeologists have found inscribed, on a pillar of one of the arches of the screen (Plate 3), and again near the entrance to the minar (Plate 10), the name of Fazl-bin-abi'l-Maali as superintendent of the works. He may have been an Arab, or an Iranian, or a Turk. He may have been a genius in the art of communication as well as of architecture, able to design beautiful and impressive monuments, and to explain to masons who did not know his language how to build what he had designed. But if he were a Muslim from outside India, would he have designed corbelled arches, knowing that they could stand much less weight than true arches? We can be sure that he would not. It must have been the Hindu masons who insisted on building according to their traditional techniques, disclaiming all responsibility for the stability of the structure if any other technique was followed. And when this had been agreed to, they must have made their own calculations of the width and height and the massiveness of the supporting piers. This explains the exquisite proportions of the central arch, its quality of being eloquent and alive, its rising upward with a moving, natural grace, the two sides meeting not with a mathematical precision, but as it were by mutual attraction, with an upward tilt at the meeting point symbolic of the joy of union.

But this is only a part of the sculptors' contribution. I imagine that the suggestion of making the decorative reliefs sweep upward instead of running horizontally (Plates 3 and 16), as in temple decoration, must have appeared to the stone-masons as an exciting novelty, and their enthusiastic response is evident in their work. Among the decorative bands are verses from the Qur'an, inscribed in bold relief. The architect may have known of a mausoleum in Uzkund, built in 1187, where the Quranic inscription has a setting of flowers and foliage, and have proposed to do the same here. But while the floral setting in the Uzkund monument is stylized and repetitive, the setting in the Qutb screen is naturalistic, warm, and vocal. The Hindu sculptor did not know anything about the doctrine of revelation, he knew only about nature, and instinctively he has represented the Qur'an as an utterance of nature, the voice of leaves and flowers, the whisper of the woods.

Some thirty years later, the mosque was enlarged, and the screen extended to maintain symmetry. The arches of this screen do not have the same proportions. In the relief work on their frontage there is stiffness and austerity; the exuberant naturalism of the earlier work has given place to something severely geometrical. An archaeological expert has expressed the view that this relief work is in the Saracenic style, and must have been executed by imported craftsmen. This is unlikely. The arches are still corbelled; there is still lack of faith in the strength of the true arch. As for the ornamentation, it is doubtful if a sufficient number of skilled stone-masons would have been found in the neighbouring Muslim principalities or would have been worth recruiting when so much skill was available in India. Besides, Persian and Central Asian ornamentation is of tiles or inlay, and depends for its effectiveness very largely on colour compositions. On the screen built by Iltutmish and on the inner walls of his tomb the patterns may be similar, but they have been executed on different material. They are neither plastic nor colourful and give the impression of overloading. The craftsmen must have been Hindus or Indian Muslims, but because more than a generation had passed since the construction of the first screen, they would be new men, less imbued with the sculptural traditions of their fathers. In any case, a change was bound to come, with architecture seeking independent self-expression.

In the context of this aesthetic struggle, the Qutb Minar (Plate 10) stands midway between the first screen of the Quwwat-al-Islam mosque (Plate 3) and its extension. It was built in two stages, the first storey in 1199, and three storeys by Iltutmish about 1230. Firoz Tughlaq repaired the minar because it had been damaged by lightning, and very unwisely converted the fourth storey into two. He somewhat increased the height of the minar, but also introduced incongruous elements. Apart from the alteration made by Firoz, the minar would have been planned as a whole, Iltutmish completing what Qutubuddin Ibak had left undone. An inscription—the lower band on the second storey—states that Iltutmish ordered the completion of the minar.

What was the idea underlying the minar? It would have gratified the religious if it were called a *mazna*, a lofty tower from which the *muezzin* called the faithful to prayer. There are examples of such maznas in Muslim countries, but probably not as tall as even the first storey of the minar, which is 95 feet high. There are also examples of free-standing minars which have an architectural significance of their own. The tower we now call the Qutb Minar has not been so called in the contemporary histories. It could have been used as a mazna. But its architectural qualities most probably derive from the fact that a small group, determined to occupy and rule for all time as much territory as it could, found it necessary to create a symbol for its confidence in itself, in the stability of its power, and in its destiny. But great architecture, let us remember, is the instinctive self-assertion of man against time and death. It is the offspring of inspired moments. The purpose of a great monument cannot, therefore, be too precisely defined. It is almost always something beyond what the planners themselves could have stated in words.

The minar has a Central Asian Turkish ancestry. There is a minar at Jar Qurgan, near Termez, built in 1108–9, which has the appearance of sixteen round columns tied together, and there is a strong resemblance between it and the second storey of the Qutb, which has a pattern of rounded flutes in section. The Minar-i-Kalan, at Bukhara, built in 1127, has a round, arched clerestory at the top, supporting a cluster of arches, like three balconies of the Qutb. The minar at Ghazni consists in part of a polygon with deeply indented angles, a form of which the wedge-shaped flanges of the third storey of the Qutb could be considered a variation. An almost contemporary structure was the minar at Wabkent, built in 1196–7. All these minars have a taper. But these were examples for the Muslim architects of the Qutb, Fazl bin abi'l Maali, whose name is inscribed near the entrance, and Muhammad Amir Koh, under whom the minar was completed in the reign of Iltutmish, as appears from an inscription on the side of the doorway of the third storey. One question of basic importance would have been decided the way the Hindu craftsmen wanted it to be. These craftsmen, in accordance with their inherited notions, would have insisted that to ensure stability, horizontal pressures should be entirely eliminated. The minar has, therefore, a very pronounced taper. Its diameter is 46 feet at the base and, as it now stands, 10 feet at the top. As originally built, in four storeys, the top would have had a diameter of perhaps 12 to 15 feet. There are notations on the south face of the minar's plinth which Cunningham believes refer to an adjustment of about an inch in the plumb-line of the building. In this respect, the Hindu master-masons would have left nothing to chance. The minar at Jar Qurgan has a fairly high plinth, the Minar-i-Kalan of Bukhara, a very low one, and there would not have been much discussion if the Hindu master-masons insisted that there should be no visible plinth. They were not used to the idea of the plinth as a distinct feature of a building. The rounded flutes and wedge-shaped flanges as we see them give the minar an exquisite sculptural character, and it is my conjecture that this, too, is either entirely a contribution of the Hindu master-masons, or their interpretation of the treatment of the facing shown in the plans, or explained to them by word of mouth. The massing of inscriptional and ornamental bands and decorative mouldings below the balconies reminds us of the decorative treatment of temple walls, but the restraint shown in the spacing out of the other bands on the shafts of the three storeys of the minar is something on which the Muslim architect would have insisted. The balconies, which form one of the most attractive features of the minar are an essentially Muslim idea, and so are the clusters of miniature alcoves, or vaulted arches, which support them. But, in a network that looks like honeycombing and in the cusped tracery reminiscent of temple ceilings, there is evidently an attempt to disguise architectural forms with sculptural effects. The result of the technical and aesthetic cooperation of the Muslim architects and Hindu master-masons is one of the most striking monuments of the world. But in form as well as meaning it is not what it was probably meant to be. The Turks wanted to create a symbol of power and stability; with its upward surge, expressed in the taper and in the almost organic emergence of one storey from another, the Qutb Minar is such a symbol. But the Hindu sculptor has also put his stamp on it. You can have power, he seems to have said, but I shall so suffuse it with beauty that those who see it will know that beauty is the only power that endures. [...]

The sculptural beginnings of Indian Muslim architecture are an indication that we must revise our perspective. For while the written record of history shows the establishment of authority by force and bloodshed, we have in the architectural record unimpeachable evidence of understanding and cooperation, of joyful participation in creative work of the very highest quality. Should not this incline us to reconsider any views we may have formed of blind hostility between Muslims and Hindus in the first stages of the Turkish occupation of north India? War and destruction would have been inevitable in any case if ambitious men came from outside to displace the rulers of the country, but need we also assume that the people as a whole, Hindus as well as Muslims, were committed to this conflict, that there was no mutual appreciation and cooperation between the urban populations of north India, the Ghaznavi kingdom of the Punjab, and lands beyond the Khyber Pass? Surely the actual builders of the Qutb complex must have known, if not admired, each other, for how else could they have achieved such perfect understanding? And if we assume that they knew and admired each other, we must exercise our imagination to correct impressions created by the rhetoric of the medieval historians and the political slogans of our own times.

Architecture of the Early Sultanate Period and the Nature of the Muslim State in India*

FRITZ LEHMANN

The rich heritage of early Muslim architecture in India is now a misunderstood and neglected field of study. There are, as always, good reasons for this. Since the trauma of Partition, scholarship in both India and Pakistan on subjects dealing with Islamic society in the subcontinent has laboured under sometimes severe handicaps.[1] Neither nation has a great deal of money to spare on luxuries, so archaeological work has been limited, and has understandably been directed to the more exciting and important pre-Islamic sites; so there has been very little new archaeological work done to help enlarge our knowledge of the medieval period. In the Western countries, scholars interested in Islam tend to concentrate on the Arab world and Western Asia; scholars interested in South Asia in the humanistic disciplines tend to specialize on Hindu, or perhaps Buddhist, culture. Works which analyse the monuments of the Sultanate period in relation to the general cultural history of their time are not many, and with some exceptions to be discussed in a moment, we are still largely using books and articles written during the period of British rule, often by writers who held official appointments in the colonial regime or were closely connected with it, and often too based on the pioneer surveys of India's archaeology and antiquities done in the nineteenth century. While much of this literature is good and even still useful, it is my purpose in this essay to show by means of a few examples how this seemingly trite material can be looked at in new ways and give us some new insights into late medieval Indian society.

*Previously published in *Indica*, Vol. 15, No. 1, Heras Institute of Indian History and Culture, Mumbai, March 1978, pp. 13–31. In the present version, some portions of the text and notes have been removed. For the complete text see the original version.

First, to avoid misunderstanding, let us very briefly look at some of the recent literature. Rigid adherence to a doctrinaire 'two nation' ideology has vitiated much Pakistani scholarship as is well known, so that even, a reputable scholar like M.A. Chaghatai seemingly felt obliged to assert in print: 'Consequently we should not hesitate to assert with confidence that our Indo-Pakistan Architecture is purely of non-Hindu origin.'[2] In fairness to him, this statement is made in the context of a hasty reply to the fanatic assertions of the P.N. Oak school. Oak and his Institute for Rewriting Indian History represent the most extreme example in India of a falsification of medieval history through an over-enthusiastic projection backwards of modern ideology and concerns, the sort of thing that presumably rekindles the zeal of Pakistani two-nation ideologues but hardly deserves any notice by serious scholars.[3] But even responsible scholars who are clearly trying to maintain objectivity have some difficulties in treating the Turkish conquests of north India in the late twelfth and early thirteenth centuries. For example, even when internal weaknesses in medieval Hindu society are recognized as a cause, K.M. Munshi persists in trying to force a modern nationalist sense of identity back into the twelfth century and condemns Turkish imperialism in the north, while praising and extolling Hindu imperialism by the Cholas of the south; while P. Saran and R.C. Majumdar show an acute appreciation of the historiographical problem along with a marked unwillingness to believe that the elements of weakness in the Hindu social order which they enumerate could be the major cause for the rapid success of Turkish arms.[4] This point of view represents not just a modern repugnance for the presumed medieval humiliation inflicted on the one-time rulers of their native land, but carries with it an unwillingness to accept the presence of Muslims in Indian society from that time forward—not just because some were foreign in vaders, but precisely because many were Indian converts. To the believer in *varnāśrama dharma,* conversion to another religious and social system is as morally repugnant as collaboration with a foreign enemy is to a modern nationalist. The Indian Muslim thus partakes of the double odium of apostate and Quisling. To scholars with this outlook, it is hard to see the early Indian mosques as a new kind of Indian aesthetic achievement—since the buildings seem so clearly symbolic of events and social developments which are themselves unacceptable as *Indian* events.

A more fruitful approach will be to lift our discussion of the Sultanate monuments and events out of the very narrow and circumscribed focus on medieval India, the usual context of discussion, and see what historical analogies outside and within India might contribute to our interpretation of the Sultanate material. This essay will do so in a modest way, and then proceed to a re-examination of some of the Sultanate monuments from the point of view of their function in their own time and place. It is my belief that once we take this discussion away from the usual context of seeing all medieval Indian history exclusively in terms of *religious* conflict, we are at once in a position to make more powerful use of Sultanate mosques as evidence of the nature of Sultanate society.

One of the ways in which an overly narrow focus on India has obscured understanding of the medieval situation has been the vexed question of tearing down existing buildings and reuse of their materials. For example, A.L. Srivastava's statement that:

> ... the early conquerors almost invariably built their mosques, palaces and even tombs out of the material of Hindu and Jain temples which they had callously destroyed ... the Turkish sultans sometimes converted the Hindu and Jain temples into mosques by demolishing flat roofs and erecting domes and minarets in their places.[5]

In all pre-modern societies such plundering of earlier buildings was a commonplace phenomenon, understandable enough when one considers the labour involved in preparing building materials in the days before power tools and mechanical transport. Still, this could be done for many different purposes and it may be important to distinguish just which ones were operating. Peasant workmen on an archaeological site in southern Anatolia being explored by my university take away, with permission, larger dressed stones from the Roman town to use in their own homes for lintels, hearths, and the like. Despite abundant supplies of stone, they can ill afford such fine already-prepared building material; here it is clear their motives are purely practical and economic, with no political or cultural overtones. During World War I the Ottoman Turks drilled holes in a number of surviving Greek and Roman columns in Syria and Lebanon to extract the lead inside, to use in making bullets; here there was a political motive, but clearly one that had no reference to the builders of the original monuments. The great Charlemagne (c. 742–814) took marble columns and mosaics from Ravenna, the one-time imperial capital in north Italy, to use in building his new capital at Aachen. Dragging these materials across the Alps could hardly have been economic, and it seems obvious that his motives were political, an attempt to bring some of the prestige of the Roman, Ostrogoth, and Byzantine rulers of Ravenna to the northern town. Around the Mediterranean there are sites and even buildings which have been sacred to whole successions of religions from various local ancient cults to Greek and then Roman paganism, then to Christianity, finally to Islam. To a certain extent most of these changes in use represent a desire by the new religion to take over the existing sacred locus of the community; sometimes the actual change came from political events, new rulers imposing their religion—the Romans, for example, converting local temples to the worship of Jupiter or the cult of the emperor—in which case the motives are obviously political. But in other cases the change came about because the local population ceased to practise their former religion and largely adopted a new one—in which case the motives must have been largely religious.

In India itself, such activities were not exclusive to the late medieval Muslim rulers. The imperial Cholas of south India, for example, are well-known for their destruction of the temples of religious sects like the Jains not supported by them. One example was recorded in the Gāwarwād inscription of their Chalukyan rivals, which includes the words 'As the Chāṇḍāla Chola with wicked malignity worthy of the Kalī Age had caused to be burnt down and destroyed the dwelling of the great Jinas' ... but then records the Chalukyan's (Someśvara II) victory over the Chola and subsequent restoration of the temple.[6] The Cholas themselves recorded a parallel event in later years in rather different terms:

> The glorious king Vira-Champa, who used to win victories at the time of the completion of sleep, (and) who was the son of the glorious Chōla king—having speedily conquered all the hostile kings in battle,—*caused to be built with their treasures*, by an ascetic, called Jnānātman, a mandapa, named Bhadra (i.e., auspicious), which affords delight to Śiva, the lord of Śri-Va11a.[7]

One modern scholar interprets these events with an interesting analysis of political and economic motives at work in medieval society, showing what can be done when the old records of religious conflict are examined in a broader context.[8]

For medieval Kashmir the only major history written in Sanskrit provides unusually rich documentation of an interesting case of temple destruction by the Hindu king Harṣa (1089–1101 CE). There is a fine ironic passage in which a villain suggests to the king, who like so many ambitious monarchs of pre-modern times was always in need of cash, that he liberate (to use the modern term in its full ambiguity) a certain abandoned temple:

Let, therefore, the treasures of this (shrine), which cause the fear of theft, be taken away. Let that (image), too, freed from its captivity, enjoy its treats of flowers, lights and other (offerings). Thus urged on by him, the king acted in that way, and found thereupon a treasury full of jewels, gold and other (valuables). *And he reflected upon what riches there might be in other wealthy temples, when there was such wealth in this deserted shrine.*[9]

Harṣa, whose motives seem to bear comparison with Henry VIII's famous expropriation of the English monastic lands, went on to appoint a special officer for expropriating temple wealth for the good of the state, a 'prefect for the overthrow of divine images (*devotpāṭananāyaka*)'.[10] Was Harṣa simply a pioneer exponent of the secular state, centuries ahead of his time? The question is facetious of course, but there are a number of interesting sidelights to his career. The local corporation of priests connected to the first temple liberated and plundered by the king used the traditional device of the group fast against the king—but not to get their temple wealth restored. Instead, they demanded and got a secular reward, exemption from the forced labour of carrying loads. On another occasion Harṣa considered a proposal to bridge the Vitasta River with stones from a Śaivite temple, using its expropriated wealth to finance the building. M.A. Stein points out that permanent bridges over the Vitasta seem to have originated with Zain-al-'Abidin in the fifteenth century, leading to the question, were the Hindu architects and masons of Harṣa's time *incapable* of anything better than a bridge of boats, or was there a conscious political and social decision to put such public investment entirely into religious architecture? Harṣa was an ambitious opportunist who employed Muslim ('Turuṣhka') soldiers of fortune, but Kalhaṇa's condemnatory tone in discussing Harṣa and his reign is a response not only to his real and alleged immoral acts, but also to his deviations from the norms of medieval Hindu society.

Bearing on this theme of politically-motivated attacks on temples by Hindu rulers, Professor Ebrahim Kunju cites an interesting case from eighteenth-century Kerala. When Mārtaṇḍa Varma, King of Travancore, launched a war of conquest against his kinsmen and his northern neighbours in the 1740s, the Raja of Cochin with his petty feudatories organized a counter campaign which went too far, according to the

Peṛumpaḍappusvarupam Granthavari: 'In the course of the campaign, temples were desecrated, cows slaughtered and many other enormities committed ....'[11] In a political struggle at the dawn of the modern age, in which both sides used European allies (Dutch in Cochin and English in Travancore), temples were attacked for political reasons but one of the kings involved drew back from such complete politicization of the state, in contrast to Harṣa in late eleventh-century Kashmir.

Muslim rulers did not begin the practice of using pre-Islamic buildings as quarries for materials and non-Muslims subjects as master craftsmen and architects in twelfth century India (or even eighth century India). Indeed, these practices began in the first days of Arab Islamic architecture in Western Asia. When the Prophet Muhammad gave the unifying force of Quranic revelation to the Arab peoples in the seventh century, their only highly developed art form was poetry. Islam began with no established traditions, styles, or refined tastes in architecture, but the early Muslims did have an exuberant confidence in the universality of their religion and a keen drive to enrich and glorify it with the accumulated learning and culture of their subjects and neighbours.[12] The early Muslims had no preconceptions, no self-conscious, psychological aversion to taking over whatever pleased and suited them in existing architectural traditions. So when 'Abd al-Malik built the first great Islamic architectural masterpiece, the Dome of the Rock in Jerusalem, he did not hesitate to use local architects and workmen and the prevailing Byzantine decorative style. Similarly in Persia and Syria, as K.A.C. Creswell has pointed out, the early Muslims used existing buildings at first, even sharing portions of churches with the local Christians for their mosques. When they did build they used local architects and craftsmen who built in the local styles, and the ambition to build was chiefly political in inspiration.[13] There are some obvious parallels in the architecture of the early Turkish Sultans in India. They, too, drew on local (non-Muslim or pre-Muslim) traditions and skills for both design and execution of their monumental architecture—and why not, when Indian work in stone was widely acknowledged to be the best of that era? But in commissioning a work like the Qutb Minar (Plate 10), Qutb-ad-din Aibak and Iltutmish had some significant differences with 'Abd al-Malik's situation in Jerusalem nearly five centuries earlier. The years that separated them had seen two significant developments that affected the introduction of an Islamic architecture in India. First, in the centuries after the Dome of the Rock the Muslim world had absorbed the classical schools of architecture and produced a new synthesis, a characteristically Islamic style (or better, styles) of architecture. It is not true to state, as a Swiss art historian has done recently, that the Delhi Sultans who built the Quwwat-al-Islam mosque were not bound by any rules or traditions regarding general layout or even detail in the building of mosques.[14] There were well-developed ideas about the general plan of the mosque, although considerable freedom remained in its embellishment and decoration. Second, those same five centuries of experience which separated the Delhi builders from the builder of the Dome of the Rock had not been without effect upon the intellectual climate of Islam: the Last Day was no longer thought to be just around the corner, the urgency of missionary proselytization had been largely lost, and generation after generation of living in a world in which Islam had not become universal had had a slow, subtle, cumulative effect on Muslim thinking, even if Muslims were not prepared to abandon faith in the universality of their system.

The Turkish rulers of Delhi in the twelfth century were not the first Muslim empire builders to appear in the Indian subcontinent. Pakistani excavations at Banbhore in the Indus delta have brought to light the medieval port town of Daybul (abandoned since the thirteenth century). Here are the remains of what may be the oldest datable mosque in the sub-continent, probably founded soon after and as a consequence of Muhammad ibn Qasim's conquest in 711 CE. The mosque (Plate 17) is a relatively large building laid out in what became the usual plan for a mosque, a hollow rectangle, 128 ft x 122 ft, surrounding an open, paved courtyard (or *sahn*), enclosed on three sides by pillared cloisters and corridors *(riwāq)* and on the fourth side, here the western side—the direction of Mecca—by a larger pillared prayer chamber *(liwān)*. It appears that stone blocks from earlier buildings were reused in building the mosque, and a Hindu *lingam* (phallic stone) was set in the main doorway (visible in Plate 17) where mosque users would step on it.[15] Is this then an example of a 'typical' Muslim act of iconoclasm and insult to pagan idolatry? Perhaps, but more on this in a moment; notice, however, that the excavators also discovered an intact Hindu temple with a lingam properly installed.

M.A. Ghafur's discussion of this mosque in the light of the early Arab records of the conquest of Sind and of the fourteen inscriptions found in the Daybul mosque brings out some further interesting points.[16] At the conquest of Daybul, the Hindu ruler's major religious structure, a Śaivite temple, was the last refuge of the priests and ruling elite of the city. The Arab conqueror Muhammad ibn Qasim killed most, including at least two temple guardians, and apparently before they could burn themselves to death. The Arabs found *devadāsīs*, women who were servitors of the temple deity and temple prostitutes, who were also found in the temple at the conquest, and the conquerors treated them and their jewellery as booty of war. Subsequently the temple itself was converted to a prison and its tower or *shikara* was dismantled and the stone reused. Again, is this a 'typical' act of Muslim barbarity and desecration? Interpretations will differ of course, but in this essay an alternative explanation that seems to the writer to be at least plausible will be offered.

While very little of the mosque itself survives, we do have the very important evidence of the inscriptions. Two of these record major rebuildings or repairs of the mosque in 230 AH (844/5 CE) and 294 AH (906 CE), thus confirming the early date. Others record propaganda for what came to be the orthodox viewpoint in the controversy over the Mutazalite doctrines. This seems to me to be very important, showing that the Muslim community of Daybul or perhaps more accurately the members of the Muslim community controlling this, the principal mosque, at the time of these inscriptions, were taking an active part and showing an informed concern with a fairly complex theological controversy that was internal to the Islamic world community and centred around the court circles of the Caliph in Baghdad.

The information available to us about the conquest of Daybul and the building of this mosque admits of another explanation than the usual one of 'typical' Muslim fanaticism and intolerance. It is offered here as a tentative hypothesis that seems more plausible as an explanation of these events to me. The obvious facts are that the Arab conquerors seized, altered, and secularized the principal Hindu temple, and that they built a large mosque which in the course of time was posted with inscriptions referring to a politico-religious controversy of major international concern to the Islamic world. Are these primarily religious acts or political ones? The fact that one lingam was symbolically used in the mosque entrance but no wholesale uprooting and destruction of such Hindu symbols was carried out is significant. So is the survival of smaller temples in use after the city's main one was taken over by the new rulers. The main temple, the temple of the city's Hindu rulers and thus in some measure a public building of the old regime as well as a place of worship, was indeed taken over and removed from Hindu worshippers but local Hindu worship was, permitted to continue. The bitterly resisting Hindu rulers and, the temple guardians who in some measure at least partook of the character of public officials, employees of the state, were mostly massacred, but in circumstances indicating that they had no intention of surrendering and accommodating themselves to a subordinate status, while the mass of ordinary commoners were not killed and were accepted as subjects of the new masters. The female servants of the old temple, who were not a political or military threat to the conquerors, were simply taken over. The new mosque was itself a public building, like parallels in early Islamic Mesopotamia for instance, a part of the complex of public buildings that made up the power centre of the new Muslim regime. The lingam in its doorway is but a symbol of the downfall of one set of rulers and the seizure of power by another set. Such a symbol, I submit, and such acts were not intended to lead to a wholesale extermination of the non-Muslim local society and culture but were the concrete acts which in a more limited way publicly marked a political revolution. Why did the priests and officials retire to the temple when the invaders had got inside the city? Perhaps for the comfort of religion. Perhaps as the best site for the ritual suicide that would preserve them from defilement, or more prosaically from capture and enslavement by the hated enemy. Or perhaps even because the temple was the largest building in the city and the best place from which to continue resistance? We may not be able to answer this question, but we do have some information touching on the likely motives of the attackers. Ghafur suggests that Daybul under the Hindu kings was closely tied to Sassanid Iran and its maritime trade (a Sassanid king is supposed to have visited Daybul in the early fifth century CE), but that with the decline of the Sassanids, their trading empire contracted as well, and by the seventh century Daybul 'was infested with pirates who interrupted the sea trade between Ceylon and the Persian Gulf'.[17] Thus the expanding Arab Islamic empire that sent Muhammad ibn Qasim to Daybul in the eighth century had, in addition to religious zeal, adequate grounds for the kind of purely secular economic and political ambitions that have motivated so many imperialist adventures before and since. But in 711 neither Islamic society nor Hindu society had any concept of separating the political from the religious functions and character of the rulers.

Muhammad ibn Qasim did not stop with Daybul, for he and his men went on to conquer other cities including Multan. In Multan great quantities of gold were seized from the principal temple, but the temple itself was left intact and the temple guardians were not killed. For two centuries after the conquest the Multan Hindu temple continued to flourish under the Muslim rulers of the city, who found it a lucrative source of revenue. Only with the advent of a sectarian Muslim ideologue to power in Multan about 986 CE was the temple destroyed.[18] The contrast with Daybul is marked, and the reasons for the different policies of Qasim towards the Hindus in the two cities seem to lie in political, not religious or ideological, considerations. In Multan although fighting was just as bitter as in Daybul, the defeated old regime was willing to make a deal with the victorious new one. The apparent paradox of concurrent tolerance and bigotry (in both Hindu and Muslim society) in this period is a paradox only in the traditional narrowly-focussed approach to the medieval period as only an era of religious conflict. The conflict was not between religions, but between groups of individuals who struggled for power. They could be and were tolerant of religions other than their own as the private beliefs of submissive subjects, and could tolerate worship and ritual as long as it carried no political implications. But rulers and aspirants to power could not and did not tolerate other religions as the symbolic assertion of rival political identity.

In many respects this mosque at Daybul and the events associated with its foundation and use remarkably foreshadow the later experience of the medieval Sultanates in Hindustan. The Quwwat-al-Islam mosque at Delhi (Plates 1–3), [and] the Arhāī Din kā Jhoṅprā mosque at Ajmer (Plates 5, 11, 14, 18–19) [...] [is] each [...] an outstanding work of architecture, and each was, for its time and place, the architectural symbol of new Muslim sovereignty. Each was located on a site alleged to have been previously occupied by Hindu temples, and for differing reasons each of the two came to be thought of as having been built from the spoil of Hindu temples (not in each case accurately). Each of these mosques has been understood by historians in the nineteenth and twentieth centuries to be symbolic of the violent intrusion of Muslim rule in India, and to be evidence of the religious fanaticism of the new Muslim rulers. This understanding of these monuments is more accurate in the case of the first than the others; these views have combined fact with presumption as a result of a theoretical approach to the study of medieval India which encouraged ill-conceived assumptions which by frequent repetition have become so familiar as to seem established fact, and fine rhetoric about Indo-Islamic architecture and the nature of Sultanate government has nearly replaced study of the evidence. This attitude, to my mind, seriously distorts our understanding of medieval Indian history by underestimating the political role of these mosques and the states they served.

One physical fact is obvious about these two-mosques and common to them all. They are very large structures. Qutb-ad-din Aibak's first Quwwat-al-Islam mosque had exterior dimensions of 148 ft. 9 in. by 214 ft. (Plate 1). From the internal measurements and making a fairly generous allowance for the space required, I have calculated that it could have held about 3,800 worshippers at one time. This was not big enough, apparently for a few years later Qutb-ad-din's son-in-law Iltutmish tripled the size of the mosque and made possible the accommodation of about 11,000 worshippers. The Ajmer mosque, begun by Qutb-ad-din and completed by Iltutmish, is intermediary in size between the two stages of the Delhi mosque and probably could have held about 7,300 persons. [...] The size of these mosques, the magnitudes of the congregations they could accommodate, the quality of their design, and the richness of their execution and embellishment all serve to emphasize their importance. But we must ask ourselves, at the time that these mosques were built, in the cities where they stand, and in the societies which they served, what was the nature of that importance? What was the mixture of motives involved in building such monumental structures?

The Delhi mosque and its accompanying tower, the Qutb Minar, are especially rich in inscriptions (Plates 3, 10, 15–16).[19] Three inscriptions on the gateways of the original mosque record its construction by Qutb-ad-din at the alleged command of his sovereign Muhammad ibn Sām Ghurī, and boast that 'the materials of twenty seven temples, on each of which two million Deliwals had been spent, were used in this mosque,' and also quote from the Quran:

> Lo! Those who disbelieve, and die in disbelief, the (whole) earth full of gold would not be accepted from such a one if it were offered as a ransom (for his soul). Theirs will be a painful doom and they will have no helpers.
>
> (Quran III: 19)

> And Allah summoneth to the abode of peace, and leadeth whom He will to a straight path.
>
> (Quran X: 26)

The great bands of inscriptions which are the principal decoration of the Qutb Minar (Plate 15) are even more interesting as a mixture of political conceits and pious moralizing. There are ten of these bands, six of which are panegyrics to the builders in the most exaggerated speech: 'Lord of the necks of the people, master of the kings of Arabia and Persia, the most just of the sultans of the world' as a sample. Numbering from the bottom up, these extol Qutb-ad-din in band one, his Ghurid masters in bands two and four, and Iltutmish in bands seven, nine, and ten. The remaining four bands are inscribed with Quranic quotations and a list of the attributes of God. These bands with religious texts are placed in positions which make them far more difficult to read than the bottom two bands of panegyrics, although all the bands follow around the angles of the decorative fluting, as they must of course, which makes it impossible to read the text of any one of them without considerable effort by the observer. Band three quotes Quran XLVIII:1–6, which in verse 5 promises 'Gardens underneath which rivers flow' to believers and in verse 6 threatens hypocrites and idolaters with hell. Band five quotes Quran LIX: 22–3 on the nature of God and then lists His attributes, while band six quotes Quran II: 255–60, which includes the famous passage 'there is no compulsion in religion,' and assures those who believe that God:

.... bringeth them out of darkness into light. As for those who disbelieve, their patrons are false deities. They bring them out of light into darkness. Such are rightful owners of the Fire. They will abide therein.

Band eight, the last of the bands with religious material, quotes Quran XIV: 29–30, which promises hell to those who mislead others by setting up false rivals to God: 'Say: Enjoy life (while ye may) for lo! your journey's end will be the fire.' It also includes Quran LXII: 9–10 on the importance of responding to the call to prayer.

The inscriptions and their arrangement testify to the intertwining of political inspiration, which is perhaps dominant in this building, and religious concern. The religious texts chosen are significant insofar as they could have been read. They seem to be chosen at least in part for their appropriateness in the Indian setting with a large non-Muslim population, not so much to advertise the basic tenets of the new rulers' faith to potential converts who in any case presumably would not have been able to decipher the script let alone understand the language, but to reassure the rulers' Muslim followers of the superiority of their ideology. Notice that Creswell suggests similar considerations in Abd-al-Malik's building of the Dome of the Rock. Insofar as the texts might have been chosen with any consideration of the local population at all, these are not texts which would serve to persuade Hindus to convert, but rather texts which would reinforce those who have converted that they are now among the elect and will enjoy even greater rewards than their still pagan former fellows in the next life. But perhaps only a very few were ever expected to read the great inscriptions: for others, the majority, the sight of these beautifully carved bands of decorative lettering was intended to convey not the specific meaning of the words and sentences formed in the stone but rather the symbolic affirmation, in the Muslims' holy language and script, of the new fact of political dominance and cultural assertion. Ettinghausen's recent interesting argument that many, though not all, Islamic inscriptions were intended to serve such a symbolic role would support this view.[20]

The buildings which serve as the setting for these inscriptional symbols are significant in their own right, for as Professor Ved Prakash has written, this complex at Delhi represents an early example of a fusion of Hindu and Muslim architectural traditions.[21] The Hindu contribution is richest in details of decorative motif and in the workmanship and technique, particularly seen in the efforts to grapple with unfamiliar forms—by corbelling the great arches in the *maqsura* screen (Plate 3), for example. The Turkish patrons clearly were firm on overall design, the fairly standardized general layout of a mosque, the use of arches, mihrab niche and mimbar, but seem to have been free to local suggestions on decoration and execution, and perhaps did not know enough about building technology in the older Islamic centres to be able to provide instruction in the techniques of building the exotic Muslim forms. The boast about destroying temples and using their stones in the mosque is readily understandable as a political as well as cultural assertion, and it seems clear that the mosque is in fact built upon the site of a temple complex. But why did the iconoclastic Muslims with their Semitic horror of graven images use stones with Hindu figural sculptures in their mosque, and why did they set up in its courtyard (presumably with considerable difficulty) the Iron Pillar, a fourth century Hindu votive monument? These seemingly incongruous acts may be explained if the mosque itself is seen as a public building of a new imperium, which uses these symbols of the past to glorify itself just as the ancient empires carved representations of subject peoples in their great palaces, as for example the Persians did at Persepolis, The Hindu subject population is thus symbolically included, not excluded, in a way that recognizes past great achievements of their civilization and so subtly underscores the power and magnificence of the new rulers.

The mosque at Ajmer (Plates 5, 11, 14, 18) was also begun at the order of Qutb-ad-din and finished by Iltutmish, but the architect apparently profited from the earlier venture at Delhi. The surviving portion gives an impression of better planning and execution, and perhaps a better-integrated overall design. As in the Qutb Minar, here too the most spectacular decoration is in the bands of inscriptions, and, here too the beautifully chiselled calligraphy (Plate 19) alternates panegyrics with piety, again with the panegyrics more prominently placed. Fulsome praise of Iltutmish is recorded for posterity in the bands around the two small minarets and in the great band of decorative lettering around the inner frame of the great arch, where all beholders may learn that Iltutmish was:

> ... the high, the just, the great, the most exalted Shāhanshāh, the Lord of the necks of the people, the master of the kings of the Turks and Persians, the shadow of God in the world ... the subduer of the unbelievers and the heretics the subjugator of the evil doers and the polytheists ... the lord of the land and the master of the sea ...[22]

to select a sample of his attributes, perhaps not intended to be taken too literally. The band around the outer frame of the great arch is engraved with Quranic verses IX: 18–23, which stress the importance of belief in God and the Last Day, observance of proper worship, and support of the poor. This quotation concludes with the thought:

> Choose nor your fathers nor your brethren for friends if they take pleasure in disbelief rather than faith. Whoso of you taketh them for friends, such are wrongdoers.

Other Quranic verses are engraved around the side arches, including Sura XLVIII: 1–6 which also appears on band three of the Qutb Minar, verses LIX: 21–4 which appear in part on band five of the Qutb, verses XVII: 1–4, and verses. XXV: 62–6 which extol modest humility and prayer—somewhat incongruously next to the royal panegyrics.

Although historians have presumed that the Aṛhāī Din kā Jhoṅprā mosque was built on the site of a Hindu temple or college, this still is conjectural and remains to be confirmed by evidence. The related assertion, that the building itself, and especially the pillars and ceilings of the prayer hall, was mostly built from the spoils of Hindu temples, has recently been shown to be untrue in a brilliant article by Michael W. Meister.[23] The pleasingly light and spacious interior of the prayer hall was deliberately created by the architect who piled pillars two on one to make the ceiling high enough; but unlike the Delhi mosque where pillars from several older sources seem to have been jumbled together with no planning other than fit, here new pillars were specially commissioned for the mosque, with relatively plain finish using modified forms of traditional Hindu decorative patterns to suit the needs and taste of the new builders (Plate 14). These new, plainer pillars were used for the bottom-half of the combined double-height pillars, and the builders made up the top-half with the richly decorated Hindu pillars taken from older buildings; the whole thus gives a much more pleasing effect of orderly planning and uniformity than one sees in the pillared cloisters of the Quwwat-al-Islam mosque (Plate 2). Meister believes that the ceilings too show Hindu workmanship newly commissioned for this mosque, and even the great screen with its purely Islamic Kufic inscriptions makes use of styles of mouldings and punctuating bands with decorative motifs which the stone cutters took directly from the repertoir of contemporary temple architecture. Thus this structure at Ajmer even more than the Delhi mosque commissioned by the same patrons and built at the same time demonstrates a fusion of Muslim and Hindu ideas in architecture. Oleg Grabar has written that 'The mosque at Ajmer shows the translation of Iranian architecture into Indian stone.'[24] But the superlative quality of the Hindu workmanship executing a building designed and supervised in construction by Muslims shows that the professional skills of the two communities could be peacefully and fruitfully combined even at this early date, at the very beginning of Muslim conquest. The failure to conceive of this mosque as a major public building of a new government and the persistence of the narrow imperial-era historiographical outlook that sees only conflict and conquest has caused us to miss the significance of this (and other) buildings as a monument to synthesis and peaceful growth. [...]

The cases discussed here all share a common theme, and the key to understanding them lies in seeing these (and other) great cathedral mosques as something more than places of worship, but as great public buildings that served and glorified the medieval state in ways analagous to the post offices and courthouses of modern states. Like many public buildings today too these great state-built mosques represented an investment in public funds on a large scale, state patronage of the building industry and all its associated skilled professionals. Once again we are confronted with the danger of accepting historical evidence uncritically. Early Turkish Sultans were proud to call themselves 'Ghazis' (holy warriors) and destroyers of temples, but not to boast about their patronage of Hindu craftsmen. But they clearly did better at the second than the first. Medieval Indian society had a world reputation for skill in working stone that continued and flourished under the Sultanate regimes, and while some big, public temples were destroyed all over north India, thousands of smaller, private temples survived. Hinduism was not extirpated (compare the earlier hounding of Buddhism out of existence in India by zealous Hindu rulers) and the worship of idols which was particularly anathema to Islam was tolerated by Indian rulers who considered themselves good Muslims.

The ruling elite groups of Hindu medieval society who bore the brunt of the Sultanate conquest and lost their sovereignty were, by all accounts, an exploitative and irresponsible ruling class. The incredible stratification of Indian society under the medieval caste system left most productive workers, peasants, artisans, and service workers with little stake in the old political order and it seems the mass of the population stood by passively and accepted the change of masters apathetically. The furious conflict—and it often was furious and ruthless—between Hindu and Muslim rivals for power, that dominates the traditional view of Indian history, involved only a tiny proportion of the population, and it would not be very exaggerated to say that control and exploitation of the remaining majority was the prize they fought for. The stonecutters went on working for whoever commissioned their work; there was no sense of nationality then and it is surely anachronistic to read back into the twelfth century our ideas of the twentieth and expect Hindu peasants and artisans who were treated as chattels to fight for one set of masters against another. Many low caste artisans must have found their status and opportunities improved slightly under the Sultanate governments in any event—what concern would they have for the no-doubt humiliating loss of status of former rulers. Men in the building trades got work when rulers built temples or mosques, palaces or forts, regardless of who the ruler was.

Why did the new Muslim Sultanates need these monumental mosques, especially when most of their subjects were not Muslims? Just as the existence of thousands of small and seemingly unimportant Hindu temples in Sultanate territories during Sultanate rule is often overlooked, so too the splendour and beauty of the large cathedral mosques has obscured the existence of thousands of little, architecturally insignificant mosques which were the real centres of popular Islam. Some Muslim villages may never have had mosques at all, such as Dharkandha (in the former Shahabad district, Bihar) where the tailor caste converted to Islam in the early eighteenth century and produced a regionally-famous eclectic saint of the Kabir type; but this village as recently as 1972 still had no mosque, although it did have an open brick platform constructed in the twentieth century as an *'Id-gāh.* The Quwwat-al-Islam mosque itself has the remains of two small late Mughal period mosques of this parochial character adjoining it. Ajmer has become and long remained the principal Islamic cult centre in India, drawing thousands of pilgrims annually to the shrine complex which has grown around the tomb of Mu'in-ad-din Chishti (d. 1234) while the beautiful mosque of the early Sultans is empty and derelict, a historical monument but not a living centre of worship. These mosques were not built primarily as religious institutions. At the everyday level, the local level of village or muhalla across north India, the actual practice of both Hinduism and Islam by devout believers went on largely independent of the state and probably independent, too, of elite leadership. The political symbolism involved in building monumental temples or mosques, pulling them down or converting them operated at a completely different level. There is the interesting case of the Ukha Mandir at Bayana which went from Hindu temple to mosque and back to temple with changes in politics,[25] and the dramatic case of Ranjit Singh's symbolic conversion of the Mughal mosque at Lahore into an arsenal—an assertion of Sikh triumph over their long-time foes.

Not every mosque, or even many of them, will fit this analysis. A great many mosques were built in premodern India for many different motives and to suit a variety of needs. We can however distinguish the public, political mosque by its cathedral character, its political symbolism, and its state sponsorship. The large size and magnificent decoration of these mosques dramatically advertised the new rulers' power and reassured his inner circles that they belonged to a winning group. The mosques had a functional aspect as well—when the ruler proceeded to the Friday congregational prayers, accompanied by all his (Muslim) courtiers and retinue—again a symbolic act not necessarily invested with religious meaning. Compare the much-publicized although infrequent attendance at Sunday church services of some of the recent American presidents who were not known for piety or even church membership; or photos in the *Illustrated Weekly of India* of a recent prime minister of that country who sometimes claimed to be an agnostic, but visited the great Hindu temple at Tirupati during election campaigns. We do not have to be unduly cynical when we put medieval Sultans in this context, and interpret a congregation of many thousands at a cathedral mosque as more of a political ceremonial than an act of religious piety. We have some figures (for a slightly later period) of immense numbers of persons in the armies, court, household, and bodyguards of the Delhi Sultans,[26] and even the Jaunpur Sultans are alleged to have put armies of over 100,000 cavalry with 1,400 elephants in the field,[27] which also implies a large establishment at court. But this mass attendance at Friday prayers was essentially political in its inspiration not only for the king, but for his ambitious subjects. Without the king, his ministers and generals there was no attraction to pull thousands of men to Friday prayers in the big royal mosques—nobody's career to be advanced, no opportunities for the ambitious to make those chance encounters, to see and be seen. When the royal courts departed the huge musters at the cathedral mosques largely came to an end too, and the worldly upper classes had to pursue other chances for fame and fortune. The local Muslim population was left to carry on with the humble but ubiquitous local neighbourhood mosques, often ignored by us historians because they rarely have interesting inscriptions with dates and names for our notebooks, but themselves social institutions that reflected the more enduring reality of caste or kin small-scale social groupings.

Perhaps like the Hindu masses, the Muslim commoners too did not identify very deeply with their rulers. They, too, were given very little cause for some precocious sense of national fellow identity with immigrant Muslim elites that professed to scorn mere Indian Muslims, even if Muslim society was spared the full horrors of caste stratification and untouchability. A modern Muslim writer has written about India's greatest example of Muslim monumental architecture, not a cathedral mosque but Shah Jahan's tomb for his beloved wife:

These buildings, these mausoleums, these ramparts, and these forts,
They are the pillars supporting the structure of royal despotism,
On the pages of the world they represent the splashing of a colour
In the making of which the blood of your, and my, ancestors has gone.[28]

Sahir Ludhianvi's sentiment is modern, but the medieval peasant (Hindu or Muslim) was probably conscious of the fact that his labour paid for the glories and follies of his ruler, while the craftsmen and builders were never too proud to take the wages from whatever ruler gave them the chance to express their skills.

NOTES

*The author dedicates this article to the memory of Harindra Kanwar, mentor and friend.

1. P. Hardy, *The Muslims of British India* (Cambridge, 1972), p. 261 ff.

2. M. Abdullah Chaghatai, 'The Sources of the Pre-Mughal Architecture', *Journal of the Pakistan Historical Society,* 8 (1960), p. 289.

3. The Institute's President, P. N. Oak, a Hindu journalist, has among other accomplishments published a book entitled *The Taj Mahal is a Hindu Palace* and an article 'on the ignorance of English lexicographers about the Sanskritic origin of English'. An Institute 'campaigner' asked my university's Asian Studies faculty for opinions on this work, and subsequently wrote me (personal letter from Suva, Fiji, 2 August 1973) that the old Hindu empires included Arabia, that the Ka'aba of Mecca is a Hindu shrine, and that Timur's tomb in Samarkand is a Hindu building—but assured me that the Institute is not anti-Muslim !

4. R.C. Majumdar *et al.*, (eds), *The History and Culture of the Indian People, Volume V. The Struggle for Empire,* Second edition (Bombay 1966), pp. vii–xxi, 125–8.

5. Ashirbadi Lal Srivastava, *Medieval Indïan Culture* (Agra 1964), p. 120.

6. Lionel D. Barnett, 'Two Inscriptions from Gawarwad and Annigeri, of the Reign of Somesvara II: Saka 993 and 994', *Epigrahia Indica,* XV (1919–20), pp. 338, 346. The dates fall in 1071–72 CE.

7. (Emphasis mine) T.P. Krishnasvami, 'Three Inscriptions of Chola Chiefs', *Epigraphia Indica,* III (1894–95), p. 70.

8. R.N. Nandi, 'Origin and Nature of Saivite Monasticism: The Case of the Kalamukhas', *Indian Society: Historical Probings in Memory of D.D. Kosambi* ed. R.S. Sharma with V. Jha (eds), (New Delhi, 1974), pp. 190–201.

9. (Emphasis mine again) *Kālhana's Rājataraṇgiṇī: A Chronicle of the Kings of Kaśmīr,* trans. M.A. Stein (Delhi, 1961 reprint), Vol. I, p. 352 (verses VII: 1085–7).

10. Ibid., verse 1091.

11. A.P. Ebrahim Kunju, 'Travancore-Cochin Relations in the Eighteenth Century', *Journal of Kerala Studies,* 1 (1973), p. 9.

12. Hanna E. Kassis, 'The Rise of the Muslim Tradition of Learning', *Hikmat* I: 3 (1396/1976), pp. 16–19.

13. K.A.C. Creswell, *A Short Account of Early Muslim Architecture* (Harmondsworth, 1958), pp. 7–16.

14. Andreas Vohlwahsen, tr. Ann Keep, *Living Architecture: Islamic Indian* (New York, 1970), pp. 39–40. Note that Vohlwahsen carelessly and slavishly follows the established literature of the colonial era in asserting that these Sultanate builders, fully shared the presumed Islamic taboo on figural sculpture and hacked off 'even a small head' from Hindu pillars before using the stone. He visited the Quwwat-al-Islam site and so preferred the authority of books to the evidence of his own eyes—many complete *apsaras* and votive figures can still be seen on the pillars of the cloisters of this mosque.

15. Anonymous, 'Excavations at Banbhore', *Pakistan Archaeology* No. 1 (1964), p. 53, and Plates XV, XVII-A, XVIII.

16. M.A. Ghafur, 'Fourteen Kufic Inscriptions of Banbhore, the Site of Daybul', *Pakistan Achaeology*, No. 3 (1966), pp. 65–90.

17. Ibid., p. 68.

18. Yohannan Friedmann, 'The Temple of Multan: A note on early Muslim attitudes to idolatry', *Israel Oriental Studies*, 2 (1972), pp. 176–82.

19. J.A. Page, *An Historical Memoir of the Qutb: Delhi* (1925, reprinted Delhi, 1970), p. 29ff.

20. Richard Ettinghausen, 'Arabic Epigraphy: Communication or Symbolic Affirmation', in D.K. Kouymjian, (ed.), *Near Eastern Numismatics, Iconography, Epigraphy, and History: Studies in Honor of George C. Miles* (Beirut, 1973), pp. 297–317.

21. Ved Prakash, 'The Qutb Minar from Contemporary and Near Contemporary Sources', *Proceedings of the Indian History Congress*, Ranchi session, 1964, Part II, pp. 52–7.

22. J. Horovitz, 'Inscriptions of Muhammad ibn Sām Qutbuddin Aibeg and Iltutmish', *Epigrahia Indo-Moslemica*, (1911–12), p. 30.

23. Michael Meister, 'The "Two-and-a-half-day" Mosque', *Oriental Art*, 18 (1972), pp. 57–63. Reprinted in this volume as Chapter 9.

24. Derek Hill (photographs) and Oleg Grabar (text), *Islamic Architecture and its Decoration* AD *800–1500* (Chicago, 1965), p. 72. This quotation continues 'It was begun around 1200 and is known as the *Arhai-din-ka-jhonpra* (hut of two and-a-half days) presumably because it used to be on the site of a fair that lasted two-and-a-half days.' This may not only explain the name of the mosque but in the absence of any convincing evidence about previous buildings on the site may indicate that there was no temple or college on the spot to be taken over.

25. John Marshall, 'The Monuments of Muslim India', *Cambridge History of India* (1928, reprint Delhi, 1965), Vol. III, p. 622.

26. I H. Qureshi, *The Administration of the Sultanate of Delhi*, 5th edn. (Delhi, 1971), pp. 67–8, 141, 153, 155–6.

27. M.M. Saeed, *The Sharqi Sultanate of Jaunpur* (Karachi, 1972), pp. 72, 88, 91.

28. Abdul Haye Sahir Ludhianvi, 'Taj Mahal', *Talkhiyān* (Delhi, n.d.—1944), fifth stanza.

Quṭb and Modern Memory*

Sunil Kumar

The Quṭb Mīnār and mosque (Plates 1–3 and 10), Delhi's first masjid-i jâmi', constructed in the last decade of the twelfth century, has drawn the attention of tourists, antiquarians, and scholars over the years. The tall minaret with its elaborate balconies and intricate inscriptions has an element of what Gell called 'magic'.[1] How did people in the late twelfth and early thirteenth centuries construct something so enormous, so perfectly symmetrical, and yet so delicate? Our cultural sensibilities attuned to appreciate uniqueness, size, proportion, and the investment of money and labour, savour the immensity and beauty of the structure and marvel at the accomplishment of mortals nearly a millennium ago. The reactions of visitors to the adjoining mosque, constructed out of the rubble of twenty-seven demolished temples, are, however, more ambivalent. The starkness of the mosque is relieved only by the redeployed temple spoils (Plate 2). Temple columns, Hindu and Jain iconic motifs, some complete and many defaced idols, are beautiful in themselves but clearly out of context within the environs of the mosque. They appear to be spoils of war, the evidence of pillage, and victory in a conflict fought in the distant past. Most visitors in the mosque today are unaware of the identity of the contestants nor are the events of the conflict any clearer. But since the presence of plundered material from 'Hindu' temples within a 'Muslim' mosque is unmistakeable, the masjid confirms images of Islamic iconoclasm and fanaticism. It resurrects memories of communal

*Previously published in Suvir Kaul (ed.), *The Partitions of Memory, The Afterlife of the Division of India*, Permanent Black, New Delhi, 2001, pp. 140–82. In the present version, some portions of the text and notes have been removed. For the complete text see the original version.

distinctions and strife which almost every Indian regard as a part of his country's social history. Unlike the minaret, the mosque impresses visitors with its images of destruction, power, and might, but not 'magic'.

The manner in which visitors to the Quṭb complex understand and interpret the structures at the site is not simply shaped by their cognitive understanding of what constitutes an object of 'beauty'. It is as much a product of their socialized, historicized, understanding of the intentions of the constructors, and the meanings they presume are encoded into the structure. This [essay] seeks to study the manner in which the Quṭb complex is understood today, and the epistemological assumptions which have supported such an understanding. As I discuss in this [essay], both the builders and detractors of the mosque attached a host of meanings to the mosque in the Middle Ages, many of which were reworked in the popular imagination in the early modern period. Yet, today, only one interpretation has survived through the ages.

Historians have played a major role in the construction of this modern memory of the Quṭb. They have written extensively on the Quṭb itself, and on the political and religious conditions of the time when it was built. Their research on the Quṭb has not remained relegated to the pages of arcane tomes; it has received wide circulation in text books and the popular press. Daily, thousands of visitors are guided through the Qutb monuments by the descriptions and interpretations provided by the Archaeological Survey of India at the site of the mosque itself. These narratives were culled from the works of scholars on medieval architecture, Islam, and Indian history. Together they constitute a text through which the experience of visitors to one of the major tourist spots in north India is refracted into authoritative knowledge about the character of Islamic piety and the nature of 'Muslim rule' in medieval India. This [essay] enlarges on the complex relationship between scholastic interpretations and popular perceptions in the constitution of the Quṭb complex as a statement of the 'Might of Islam' in India, an interpretation which unfortunately consolidates the fractured communal realities of a post-Partition subcontinent.

THE DELHI MASJID-I JÂMI', ITS BUILDERS, AND ITS MAIN FEATURES[2]

The Delhi masjid-i jâmi' underwent construction on three different occasions. The first mosque, 214 by 149 feet (Plate 1), was a relatively small rectangular structure, with a central courtyard surrounded by colonnaded arcades. The construction of the mosque was begun in 587/1191–2 by Quṭb al-Dīn. Ai-Beg, and relied upon material derived from plundered temples. The temple spoils were used randomly, but very ingeniously. Column shafts, bases, and capitals, of different sizes and forms, with Hindu or Jain sculptures and iconic motifs, were placed one upon the other to attain a uniform height for the roof (Plate 2). The lack of concern for iconic symmetry, with Shaivite, Vaishnavite, and Jain motifs placed cheek-by-jowl with each other, conveys the impression of destruction, a temper which is very much a part of the construction of the first mosque. The Archaeological Survey of India helps in the consolidation of this impression. Through its tourist literature it reminds visitors that the better portion of the mosque resides on the plinth of a demolished temple. Together with other evidence of redeployment of plundered material, it is left to be assumed that the 'iron pillar' of the Gupta period (visible in Plate 3) was, another trophy of conquest placed within the centre of the mosque by Muslim invaders.[3]

Sometime later, perhaps in 595/1199, the huge arched screen was built in front of the west wall of the mosque (Plate 3). The east face of the screen was decorated with Arabic calligraphy, verses from the *Qur'ân* and the traditions of the Prophet, interspersed with floral and geometric patterns (Plate 16).

Perhaps even more dramatically than the reused temple spoils, the screen carries evidence of the handiwork of native artisans, who used familiar traditions of corbelled architecture to satisfy unusual stylistic requirements. It was around this time that work on the ground floor of the minaret (Plate 10) was also completed. Although derived from the architectural precedents established in the G͟hûrîd minaret of Khwaja Siyah Push in Sistan, the mînâr, in Quṭb al-Dîn's reign, was not very tall, and its girth lent it a rather squat appearance. Built out of red sandstone and inscribed with *Qur'ânic* inscriptions and eulogies of conquest, it served as a memorial of victory and a vantage point to call the faithful to prayer.

The second phase of construction within the masjid-i jâmi' occurred during the reign of Shams al-Dîn Iltutmish (607–33/1210–36) and was completed sometime around 627/1229–30. Although Iltutmish's additions nearly doubled the width, if not the depth, of the mosque, very little survives today of this construction. New courtyards were added to the north, south, and the east, in a form which maintained the overall stylistic symmetry of the mosque. Hence the arches and the addition to the minaret harmonized with the preexisting architecture. Since these additions are largely in ruins today, the final impact of their size and grandeur, their dwarfing of the original masjid, is completely lost upon the modern audience. Only the extended minaret, towering over the environs with three additional storeys, provides a sense of the huge transformation that Iltutmish introduced in the architectural landspace of the masjid-i jâmi. Many historians tend to obscure this intervention by suggesting that rather than altering the mosque, Iltutmish merely 'completed' it.[4]

The changes in the mosque introduced during the third phase of construction, in the reign of 'Alâ al-Dîn Khalajî (695–715/1296–1316), are also nearly lost today. But for one entrance hall, and an unfinished minaret, there is no visible trace of any Khalajî building activity within the mosque. Archaeological evidence, however, has clarified that 'Alâ' al-Dîn extended the mosque until it was twice the size of Iltutmish's, that the arches on its west wall towered over the older constructions, and if the girth of the unfinished mînâr is any indication, it would also have been twice the size of the old. Other than the size, the entrance hall on the south wall, today called the 'Alâ'î darwaza, stands as a testimony to the quality of construction during this period. Built out of red sandstone, the square silhouette of the 'darwaza' is pierced with evenly spaced rectangular windows and doors. These are outlined with marble trimmings and epigraphs carrying Qur'ânic verses and statements commemorating the achievement of the Sultan. The modern visitor needs to imagine, if he or she can, a rite of passage from the bustling world of the medieval city of Delhi, through the ornate 'Alâ'î darwaza into the relative peace of the enormous Khalajî mosque, with huge arches decorated with Qur'ânic verses on the western wall, and a new minaret under construction to balance and dwarf the old one. In sheer size and grandeur it would have been one of the most awe-inspiring mosques of its time in the world.

Since the middle of the nineteenth century, scholars and archaeologists have studied this mosque and attempted to explain its significance to a lay audience. Their writings have over the years assumed 'authoritative dimensions', until most visitors rely upon their guidance to consolidate their own opinions of the structure. The next section attempts to disaggregate this scholarship to understand how changing historical assumption and research methodologies are reflected in the study of the Quṭb monuments.

READING THE MASJID-I JÂMI' AS THE MIGHT OF ISLAM MOSQUE

The munsif of Delhi, Sayyid Ahmad Khan, was the first scholar to make a detailed study of the epigraphs and architectural form of the Quṭb complex in the 1840s. Many of his conclusions were summarized and developed in the reports of the Archaeological Survey of India written in the 1860s, and some years later in the *Epigraphica Indo-Moslemica*, a journal devoted to the study of Persian and Arabic inscriptions. Much of this information was recompiled in the 1920s in the report of the excavations and conservation efforts of the Archaeological Survey of India narrated by J.A. Page. This corpus of information provided the empirical data on the basis of which an early consensual opinion on the nature of the Quṭb complex developed.[5] The guides prepared at the turn of the century for English tourists to Delhi also relied upon these scholarly texts for their information and interpretation.

The major subject of interest in the works of all these authors was the redeployment of Hindu and Jain temple material within the masjid structure. Their narrative and line drawings focused upon the details of this aspect of the congregational mosque: what was the extent of the original plinth of the temple upon which the mosque was built; how many temple pillars were in fact used in the making of the cloisters? Alternatively their attention was drawn to the fact that 'Hindu' architectural styles continued to predominate within a 'Muslim' mosque. They noted the absence of the true arch in the great screen of the mosque and the use of a corbelled technique by indigenous craftsmen, together with the *voussoir,* to convey the impression of the 'saracenic' arch. In a similar fashion these scholars also noted the inability of the 'Hindu' craftsmen to construct domes; instead 'domes' which once again followed the corbelled technique were used from despoiled temples. Their discussion of the minaret was again largely restricted to its stylistic origins: was it of a 'Hindu' provenance, or did it have earlier Ghûrid and Ghaznavid antecedents?

Khan, Cunningham and Page's analyses suggested that in the usage of plundered temple material, which was defaced, inverted, or plastered over, the military commander, Quṭb al-Dīn Ai-Beg, made a statement of conquest and hegemony over an infidel population in north India, and conducted a ritual cleansing of profane territory. The authors also recognized the presence of temple material in the mosque as evidence of swift transposition of 'Muslim rule' in 'India' where the 'Turkish cavalry' had outdistanced the 'Muslim artisans'. Architecture in the formal 'Saracenic' tradition, constructed under the supervision of migrant 'Muslim architects' and craftsmen had to, therefore, await the later years of Iltutmish's reign (607–33/1210–36). Meanwhile the symbolic redeployment of plundered temple rubble in the masjid-i jâmi', did not merely proclaim Quṭb al-Dîn's conquest of Delhi (588/1192), it also served as a statement of Islam's victory over idolators. This point was driven home when Sayyid Ahmad Khan, Horowitz, and Page recorded in their respective scholarly publications that the name by which the congregational mosque was known in the past was 'Quwwat al-Islâm', or the 'Might of Islam'. Their self-confident assertion was surprising for the masjid-i jâmi' was not identified as Quwwat al-Islâm by any extant inscription in the mosque or referred to by this name in any Sultanate chronicle.[6] As we will see later it was the corruption of a name sometimes used for Delhi in the thirteenth century. Suffice it to note for now, that for these scholars, it was almost logical that the congregational mosque which celebrated the conquest of Delhi should be called the 'Might of Islam'. After all, the conquest of Delhi, the capital of the Sultanate, was the final, victorious culmination of a preceding series of plunder raids led by 'Muslims' into Sind, Punjab, and 'Hindustan'. In the early narrative of Indian history, where the medieval period was synonymous with the Muslim, it was entirely apposite that Delhi's first masjid-i jâmi' should be named the Quwwat al-Islâm mosque, and symbolize the beginning of a new historical epoch.

In the 1960s when a more secular' narration of the South Asian medieval past was attempted, historians like Meister, Mujeeb, and later, Husain, glossed over the 'Might of Islam' interpretation of the masjid.[7] Their writings focused instead upon the architectural characteristics of the monument where Islamic inspiration was dependent upon indigenous craftsmanship for its ultimate realization. In an effort to mute the episode of plunder and military conquest involved in the capture of Delhi, the 'Hindu' adaptation of the 'saracenic arch', or the corbelled dome, were highlighted as examples of inter-community cooperation and amity. Although these scholars continued to accept the interpretation of the masjid as the Quwwat al-Islâm, their writings suggested that this might have been merely a formal statement not to be taken very seriously. To their mind, the presence of the Hindu hand in designing and constructing the mosque needed to be given greater recognition.

Anthony Welch and Robert Hillenbrand could not disagree more with such 'secular' interpretations of the mosque.[8] Writing in the 1990s these scholars are strongly influenced by the cultural anthropological emphasis upon semiotics and ideology. Unlike scholars in the past, who were presumably guided by their anachronistic communal or secular assumptions, these scholars sought the 'native's point of view', a potentially more dangerous interpretive move in its assumption that it could capture an indigenous, native perspective. Welch found it significant that the Muslim patrons of the Hindu craftsmen never compromised with the indigenes: the Delhi Sultans forced the Hindu craftsman in their service to always conform to a 'Muslim aesthetic'. In an important passage he noted that

> the architecture of this early Turkish-dominated period is not eclectic: instead it is obsessed with imposing an aesthetic that carried comforting meaning for the conquerors. The attempt to replicate the familiar from back home is overriding: it ignores north India's established building types and twists indigenous architectural techniques to accommodate it. The resulting torque is obvious, but not surprising: without such mimetic references [Delhi] Sultanate would have appeared adrift in an all too new and unfamiliar land.[9]

In his study of the epigraphical remains in the congregational mosque, the mînâr, and Iltutmish's tomb, Welch concluded that the inscriptions were carefully located within the masjid-i jâmi' precincts bearing in mind the architectural and functional qualities of the specific structures. Thus, since the minar performed the 'symbolic function of marking the *Dâr al-Islām* (the land of Islam)' newly conquered from the infidels, and the towering structure was 'most visible to believers and non-believers outside the city walls', it carried Qur'ánic statements of conquest and warning to the heathen population.[10] The Qur'ánic and *hadi<u>th</u>* inscriptions on the qiblah screen, the direction all Muslims faced during prayer, stressed 'instead the importance of worship, of adherence to the principles of Islam, and of recognition of the obligations incumbent on believers.' While the mînâr was directed primarily to the 'Hindus' and its epigraphs proclaimed victory over heathens, the inscriptions within the sanctuary of the masjid-i jâmi' were addressed only to the Muslims and expounded 'general religious statements' concerning their conduct.[11]

Welch's analysis of the congregational mosque and its epigraphs was not far removed from that of Khan, Cunningham, or Page. While the latter had emphasized the theme of Muslim conquest and victory symbolized by the Quṭb monument, Welch developed the idea further and argued that the congregational mosque also reflected the political context in which it was created. The monument was an uncompromising Muslim celebration of conquest, and the building material, architectural form, and epigraphic texts of the congregational mosque asserted the unity and cultural uniqueness of the 'Muslims'. It distanced the conquerors from their 'Hindu' subjects while for Muslims resident in a 'foreign' land it created familiar, reassuring landmarks of Islam's superiority.[12] From a different methodological track, Welch confirmed that the Quṭb complex needed to be understood as the 'Might of Islam'.

PROVIDING THE POLITICAL CONTEXT

Welch could push his reading of 'the native's point of view' with a great deal of confidence because his arguments coincided with, and were supported by, a larger historiographical interpretation of the nature of early Sultanate society and polity in north India. In the early thirteenth century according to the author, the Turkic ruling class of the Sultanate was both 'compact and cohesive', and severely threatened by 'Hindu' opposition. The historiographical understanding of the bonds which tied the Delhi Sultan with his military commanders were worked out in the writings of a number of authors which included scholars of the stature of Habibullah, Nizami, and Nigam.[13] In the interpretations of these scholars, despite the occasions when the 'crown and the nobility' were in conflict, an underlying material self-interest, a shared Turkish ethnicity, and the religion of Islam, provided coherence and an exclusive nature to the Turkic ruling oligarchy in the thirteenth century. In this logic, the common background of the ruling elite and their Sultan made them a category apart, and in the absence of any shared affinities with the ruler, the 'Hindus' were a distinct group who were then treated indifferently as subjects. The equation, Muslim rule—Muslim state, was worked out to its full extent in the writings of Habibullah, who completed the juxtaposition by defining resistance to the Sultanate as 'Hindu aggression'.[14] In Welch's analysis this was summed up in his declaration that 'with their victory in 1192 ... [the Muslim armies] initiated an Islamic state that by the beginning of the fourteenth century encompassed nearly all of the Indian subcontinent.'[15]

In this vision of medieval history it was also argued that by the fourteenth century, the composition of the Muslim ruling elite began to alter until it started to include 'low class' indigenous Muslim converts, a process which one scholar described as the 'plebianization of the nobility.'[16] The presence of these neo-convert indigenes provided the Sultanate with cultural 'roots' in the subcontinent.[17] This was most apparent in art, architecture, literature, and ritual; but it did not affect the great chasm which separated the politically cohesive, rapacious Muslim state from the exploited peasantry. The juxtaposition of the monolithic entities—the rulers and the ruled—was perceived by scholars as an axiomatic reality throughout the middle ages. With regard to the establishment of the Delhi Sultanate, Irfan Habib, perhaps the most influential scholar writing on medieval India, noted:

> The Ghorian conquests of Northern India, leading to the establishment of the Delhi Sultanate (1206–1526) may be said to mark the true beginning of the medieval period in India ... To begin with, the new conquerors and rulers who were of a different faith (Islam) from that of their predecessors, established a regime that was in some profound respects different from the old. The Sultans achieved power that was, in terms of both territorial extent and centralisation, unprecedented (except, perhaps, for the Mauryas 1,500 years earlier) ... [Centralisation] ... ensured that the land revenue (*kharaj/mal*) demanded on their behalf should comprehend the bulk, if not the whole, of the peasant's surplus produce; and the King's bureaucracy thereby became the principal exploiting class in society.[18]

Habib shifted the argument of his peers to suggest that the fundamental contradiction within the medieval political systems constructed by Muslims in south Asia derived from class and not confessional interests. Yet, despite the presence of a variety of class interests, it was the fundamental divide between the rulers and the ruled which determined the fate of the state. [...]

POSITIVISTIC READINGS OF THE TEXT

In a historiography where the material interests of the monolithic state were threatened only by the exploited, conquered indigenous population, the discursive assertions of the authority of the state were read as reaffirmations of the existing [class] solidarity of the ruling elite. What was lost in reading a text from this perspective was the recognition that discursive texts, like Delhi's thirteenth-century masjid-i jâmi', carried the authorial voice of the patrons, the Delhi Sultans, and they would have hardly acknowledged the presence of competing centres of power or resistance in a monument that was a public statement of their authority. In a similar fashion it was hardly likely that the court chroniclers of the Delhi Sultans would organize their narratives to suggest that Delhi was not the legitimate centre of power and authority in north India. In the Persian chronicles of Minhâj-i Sirâj Jûzjânî, Ẓiyâ' al-Dîn Baranî or Abû'l-Faẓl, the power of the monarch might be challenged by his subordinates—as it certainly was when rulers were morally incompetent—but the occasional hiatus notwithstanding, there was never any alternative to the authority of Delhi or the Mughal Pâdishâh. [...]

Most contemporary, scholars forget, however, that the medieval documentation used by them, either chronicles or archival, was either produced by or for the state. For them, once we sift the encomia from these texts we remove the obvious elements of bias, and are left with a largely unaltered narrative in which the king and 'his subordinates, remain the principal actors in the history of the period. In a sense, as in the case of Ranke himself, the search for 'authoritative information' in chronicles and archives privileged the knowledge conveyed by the written word which, for the medieval period, concerned the state and governance. Information from other authors was understood to be biased unless it corroborated the product of the state. [...]

The positivist methodology which exalted documents as the pristine source for the study of the past directed scholars of medieval India to seek in their Persian documentation the secrets of the Middle Ages. But a Rankean epistemology, which elevated the state as the epitome of historical development and the proper subject of historical investigation, also led them to accept the discourse of a unitary dominion, a cohesive ruling elite, and a potentially recalcitrant peasantry, without any critical reflection. It is this epistemology which enables the reading of the Quṭb monuments today as the 'Might of Islam'.

There can be no gainsaying the fact that Persian chronicles are the extant sources available to the historian of the Middle Ages, especially for the Delhi Sultanate. There are, however, other sources of information as well: epigraphs, coins, monuments, and a voluminous literature produced in the 'courts' of the ṣūfī saints. With very few exceptions, these sources lack the coherence and chronology present in the chronicles, and they are, therefore, used as repository of facts useful to substantiate or expand the material provided by the 'histories'. Information which contradicts the 'evidence' of the court chronicles has frequently remained unexplored. The discourse of the monolithic state has therefore remained unquestioned.

It, is, however, possible to pluck the seams in this discourse. The texts of the Persian court chronicles themselves are riddled with discrepancies, with niggling inconsistencies which are significant only if the reader approaches the text with the awareness that it carries information deliberately organized to impress specific conclusions upon the reader. These discrepancies in the text are important indicators of fractures in the discourse, dissonances which need to be enlarged with the aid of other source material. But giving space to the internal dissonances within a text is not always an easy task and it certainly does not contribute to the writing of monolithic, linear histories of state systems.

POLITICAL COMPETITION AND THE DISCOURSE OF THE UNITARY STATE

The premise of the unitary Muslim state, and a composite ruling elite owing allegiance to the Sultan of Delhi, would be difficult to question if we followed the obvious conclusions of the Persian chroniclers. Fakhr-i Mudabbir's *Tâ'rîkh-i Fakhr al-Dîn Mubârak Shâh*, a text dedicated to Quṭb al-Dîn Ai-Beg, suggests, for example, that the favourite, competent military slave of Mu'izz al-Dîn, was appointed as the sole authority, the 'viceroy' of his master's dominion in north India.

> This hero and world conqueror of Hind (Quṭb al-Dîn) was addressed as Malik,[19] and was made the heir apparent, *wali'ahd,* to Hindustan; and the lands from the gates of Peshawar (Parshūr) to the limits of Hind were given to him, and the [authority] to appoint and remove, (literally, 'unfasten, and bind, *hall wa'aqd'*), the remaining commanders was entrusted with him, *ba-dû mufauwaz gardânîd* [Mu'izz al-Dîn] left [Quṭb al-Dîn] as his deputy and heir in the capital of Hindustan, *qa'im maqâm wa wali 'ahd-i khud ba-dâr al-mulk-i Hindustân ba-guzasht,* and sent him back to Delhi.[20]

The narrative of the near contemporary chronicler Minhâj-i Sirâj Jûzjânî also supported Quṭb al-Dîn's claims to be the Amîr al-Umarâ', the chief of the Mu'izzî military commanders in north India. Writing in the 660s/1260s for the Delhi Sultan, Nâṣir al-Dîn (644–64/1246–66), Jûzjânî arranged his text to suggest that Delhi and its ruler had always been the paramount power in Hindustan.

Jûzjânî's narrative, however, was organized in the more disaggregated ṭabaqât form, where each unit of the text studied 'people belonging to one layer or class in the chronological succession of generations.' As a result, the history moved beyond the sharp focus on the ruler and included accounts of social peers or dependents. Thus, the twentieth section, ṭabaqa, narrated the history of other important Mu'izzî subordinates in Hindustan without losing sight of his need to emphasize Quṭb al-Dîn's overall superiority.[21] In this section Jûzjânî provided a somewhat circumspect account of the independent ability of the Mu'izzî commanders to raise a military retinue, wage war, and sometimes compete with each other over the distribution of spoils. One such military commander was Bahâ' al-Dîn Tughril, the governor of Thangir, in the province of Bayana.

According to Jûzjânî, Bahâ' al-Dîn sought to improve the economy of his appanage by attracting merchants, *tujjar*, and well-known men, *ma'arif-i rûy*, from different parts of Hindustan and Khurasan towards his domain. In an effort to encourage trade within the Bayana region all merchants were granted accommodation and material support, *jumala-ra khānah wa asbâb bakhshîd*, by the Mu'izzî subordinate. As a result, Jûzjânî noted, Bahâ' al-Dîn Tughril made his province prosperous, an indication of which was the construction of Sulṭânkôt, a new capital to go with changed circumstances.[22] From Sulṭânkôt, Bahâ' al-Dîn commenced periodic raids towards Gwalior and was promised its territory by Mu'izz al-Dîn upon its capitulation. The seizure of Gwalior would have opened up the frontier into northern Rajasthan and Bundelkhand and brought considerable plunder and war material into the Amir's reach. Bahâ' al-Dîn's efforts to enlarge and consolidate his appanage were resisted by Quṭb al-Dîn Ai-Beg, who reacted to Bahâ' al-Dîn's increasing influence in the area by seizing Gwalior himself in 597/1200. Jûzjânî, who narrated this incident, concluded rather diplomatically that as a result of the Gwalior episode there was (not?) a little dislike, between Tughril and Quṭb al-Dîn, *miyân Malik ... wa Sulṭân andak ghabârî bûd.*[23]

Although Quṭb al-Dîn Ai-Beg may have believed and proclaimed that he was the supreme Mu'izzî commander in north India, his peers certainly did not share this opinion. Despite the predisposition of the Persian documentation towards Quṭb al-Dîn and the authority of Delhi, the presence of competing autonomous dominions could not be wholly obscured. Even the eulogy of the likes of Fakhr-i Mudabbir wore thin on occasion, and he confessed:

And although all the victories which God caused him (Quṭb al-Dîn Ai-Beg) to win are clearer than the sun, and well known to all the world: nevertheless it must not be forgotten how much was due to the care and assistance of the *Sipahsâlâr* Ḥusam al-Dîn Aḥmad 'Ali Shâh, who was the slave and officer of the King of Islam (Mu'izz al-Dîn), and was never absent from his stirrup, and was present at these victories and battles. Indeed all the generals of this court were gifted, brave and noble, and each was distinguished for his courage, and received an ample share of the fortune and prosperity of the King of Islam, who by his patronage and favour made each and all famous. To some he gave high commands, body guards, pavilions, drums, standards and districts, and each performed fine acts of service, and was duly praised ...[24]

In a political world where all the generals of Mu'izz al-Dîn's court were 'gifted, brave and noble, and each ... received an ample share of the fortune and prosperity of the King of Islam, who ... made each and all famous', there was also considerable rivalry and conflict. It is in the context of a factionalized political environment of the 'north Indian Sultanates' (certainly in the plural), rather than a unitary dominion of the Delhi Sultanate, that we need to situate Quṭb al-Dîn Ai-Beg's urgency to' appear as the unique Amîr al-Umarâ', the protector of the fortunes of the Muslim community.

The construction of the Delhi masjid-i jâmi' was a part of Quṭb al-Dîn's effort to impress the Muslim congregation of his military and pious virtues. The inscriptions on the main entrance to the mosque remarked on his unique prowess and piety as a military commander destroying infidel temples. But again, given the nature of the political competition of the age, Quṭb al-Dîn was hardly unique in making statements of this nature. His rival in Bayana, Bahâ' al-Dîn Tughril, also constructed congregational mosques which were architecturally similar in form and conception to the Delhi masjid-i jâmi'. The Bayana mosques also eulogized Bahâ' al-Dîn as the conqueror of infidels and the creator of havens for Muslim congregations. But if Quṭb al-Dîn Ai-Beg's inscriptions in the Delhi masjid-i jâmi' drew the attention of the visitor to his military and moral accomplishments as the 'viceroy' of Mu'izz al-Dîn Ghuri, the visitor to the mosques in Bayana saw evidence of the same virtues in Bahâ' al-Dîn's constructions. The only difference was that the inscriptions in the Bayana mosque went beyond Quṭb al-Dîn's claims and introduced Bahâ' al-Dîn as *Pâdishâh* and *Sulṭân.*[25]

Divorced from their assumed political context of a unitary dominion and a composite ruling elite, the discursive statements carried in texts like Delhi's masjid-i jâmi' need to be oriented to audiences beyond just the infidels. Indeed, the probity of the military commander as the paradigmatic Muslim leader, God's choice of a shepherd for his flock, was an important theme in the epigraphs in the mosque, but these statements seem to have been directed to the Muslims who visited the congregational mosques, and were aimed at displacing rival claims made by Mu'izzî peers.

THE CONGREGATIONAL MOSQUE AND THE 'HINDUS'

The Delhi masjid-i jâmi', like other congregational mosques, differed from ordinary mosques in its size and function. Where the latter served purpose of performing prayer for a limited number of people, the Delhi masjid-i jâmi' was a huge public monument created for the purposes of a congregational gathering of Muslims. Through the performance of prayer in congregation, Muslims acknowledged the fact that they were one united community who had submitted to the will of Allah. In the normal course of events, unbelievers, especially profane idolaters, would not have been allowed within the precincts of the Delhi masjid-i jâmi' and, as a result they may have only possessed a general sense of the manner in which temple spoils were redeployed within the mosque. The architectural composition of the mosque however, would-have impressed the congregation of believers, who would have seen in it the evidence of their Amir's ability to defeat infidels and provide a sanctuary for Islam.

Despite their ignorance of the precise architectural form in the interior of the Delhi masjid-i jâmi', it would be naive to assume that the 'idolators' were unmoved by the destruction of their places of worship. But certainly within Delhi itself, there is no epigraphic record of rancour or sorrow at the destruction of temples, not even in the devnagiri graffiti inscribed by Hindu artisans in the nooks and crannies of Quṭb al-Dîn's mosque.[26] Instead, one early inscription in a local dialect identifies the minaret as 'the pillar of Malikdin. May it bring good fortune.' Another anonymous artisan in 'Alâ al-Dîn's reign (695–715/1296–1316) had no hesitation in recognizing the minaret as Shrî Sultan Alâvadî Vijayasthamb, the Sultan's pillar of victory. In Muhammad Shâh Tughluq's reign (725–52/1325–51) the architects Nânâ and Sâlhâ recorded their contribution to the repairs of the minaret in an inscription which also celebrated the completion of their work 'by the grace of Sri Visvakarma'.[27]

Sultanate court chronicles and the inscriptions on the masjid-i jâmi' seek to create the impression that the righteous Muslim Sultans of Delhi. obliterated all evidence of temples and Hindu habitation in the vicinity of Delhi. Historians who have conscientiously followed these narratives have ignored evidence to the contrary just eight hundred metres away from the Quṭb. A stone's throw from the site of iconoclastic destruction was a large garden, known as the bâgh-i Jasrath. Jasrath's garden was described by Niẓâm al-Dîn Awliyâ' as a landmark, and the memory of its owner was fresh even at the turn of the thirteenth century. Adjoining the garden was a reservoir which was built by a 'Hindu' queen prior to the capture of Delhi. Not merely was the reservoir the site of several court ceremonies in the thirteenth century, but the memory of the original infidel constructor was preserved in its name: the Queen's reservoir, *ḥauẓ-i Rânî*, an interesting admixture of languages (Arabic>Persian: ḥauẓ; Sanskrit>vernacular: Rânî) which passed quite unremarked in the literature of the period. In other words, in the immediate vicinity of iconoclastic destruction, there were other important areas built and patronized by 'Hindus', some large enough to be major landmarks in the city, others which were sites of public congregation.[28] Unlike the destruction and reconstruction within the Quṭb complex, 'Muslim' conquest of Delhi left these areas undisturbed. In fact, their original 'profane' identities were preserved in public memory in their names. The extent of the rupture caused by 'Muslim' conquest in 'Hindu' society certainly deserves to be recontextualized more carefully.

Although the destruction, desecration, and appropriation of temple artifacts was an unexceptional event during conflict between rival 'Hindu' kingdoms in the Middle Ages (and it is perfectly possible that Quṭb al-Dîn's conduct drew a reaction from the local population quite dissimilar from ours today), we need to nevertheless remember that the actions of the Mu'izzî commanders differed from those of the precedents set by the 'Hindu' rulers. When 'Hindu' rajas pillaged each other's temples, the authority of the vanquished lord was either appropriated or reconstituted within the temple shrine of the conqueror. The statements of conquest embodied in the process of destruction and reconstruction of imperial temples, was carried out within ritually homologous forms of Hindu kingship.[29] By contrast, Quṭb al-Dîn's statements of conquest in the masjid-i jâmi' redeployed temple spoils, but there was no sense of appropriation of authority. It signified instead the arrival of alternate traditions of governance in Delhi. This carried larger social and moral implications for the constitution of authority in Delhi since the royal temples were also the sites of redistributive and transactional relationships between the king, his subordinate chieftains and the larger subject population. Quṭb al-Dîn's conquest, the destruction of temples and the construction of a mosque in their stead, fractured the relationship between the king and his subordinate chieftains. This development need not necessarily imply, however, a concomitant distancing of the subordinate echelon of rural chieftains from newly emerging structures of Sultanate authority. It is certainly worth querying whether the Mu'izzî governors constructed new, but different, relationships with these local political regimes in the countryside.[30]

The discourse of the Persian chronicles and the nature of the masjid-i jâmi' would suggest that this was not the case; political authority remained the exclusive preserve of the new Muslim Turkish elite and 'Hindus' were hunted, not recruited, in the new political order. Stray references within the same chronicles, however, would suggest that this was hardly universally true. The author of an early Muslim epic of conquest, Fakhr-i Mudabbir, mentioned that *râtkan wa tâkran/rautagân wa thakurân*, petty ['Hindu'] chieftains and their military subordinates, were present within the ranks of the pillaging armies of Quṭb al-Dîn Ai-Beg.[31] We lack a sense of numbers and roles occupied by these subordinates within the new dispensation, but their sheer presence forces us to reevaluate the relationships between the different ruling elites in ways more complicated than those suggested by a simple confessional divide.

The efforts of Quṭb al-Dîn, and other Mu'izzî commanders, towards consolidating relationships with 'Hindu' chieftains only becomes clearer when we turn to other source material. In their ability to reach a far larger audience, the coinage of the Mu'izzî governors, even more than the masjid-i jâmi' in Delhi (or Bayana), served as effective discursive statements of conquest. Unlike the congregational mosque, however, the coinage carried statements of both conquest and reassurance to the conquered people. To begin with, the coins were unequivocal in their announcement of a new political order, and they introduced the masters, the Mu'izzî Amîrs, as Shrî Hammirah; the Persian titles of the new lords stamped in the locally comprehensible devnagiri script.

The presence of the new political order, however, did not seem to suggest any evidence of material change. The conquerors made no effort to alter the weight and purity of the precious metals in their coins which harmonized perfectly with existing circulating mediums. Deliberate attempts seem to have been made to emphasize continuity with the older patterns of fiscal and commercial exchange. Perhaps even more impressive was the confessional ambiguity in the sigilla of Mu'zzî coins of this period. Emblems of a previous political regime, the image of God Shiva's vehicle, the *nandî* bull and the 'Chauhan horseman' were stamped on the coins together with the title of Shrî Hammirah. Even more significant were the gold coins which carried both the outline of Lakshmi, the Hindu Goddess of wealth, and the Sultan's title in the devnagiri script. As discursive statements, these coins made deliberate attempts to incorporate the conquered people within the newly established political and economic systems, not through pillage and mayhem, but through reassuring measures and symbols that suggested continuity with a preceding regime. These statements would suggest that 'Muslim conquest' did not seek to traumatize the subject population and it certainly did not wish to create any major disjunctions in their material life. As the hoard evidence from north India confirms, Mu'izzî coins were valued as much as the earlier Rajput currencies and were fully assimilated within an economic world unimpressed with transitions in the political realm.[32]

Without devaluing the statement of plunder and conquest conveyed by the Delhi masjid-i jâmi', it should not be forgotten that it is the Persian chronicles and the epigraphs in the mosque that make much of the eposide of temple destruction. It is these texts which saw in the mosque the incumbent ruler's piety, a statement directed to the Muslim congregation in the mosque. From a different aspect, the destruction of the temple of the 'Hindu' Raja was also necessary to break the social and political networks which sustained the old regimes. The ideology of iconoclasm, even within a 'Hindu' context, carried the familiar sense of conquest and valour, but the construction of the masjid-i jâmi' denied a reconstitution of authority along old 'familiar' lines. Within the new Sultanate regimes, 'Hindu' subordinates might have been ritually distanced, but the sigilla on the coinage points to the presence of discourses—different 'non-monumental' structures—which eased the political transition and sought to construct new, stable, productive relationships with the *rautagân wa thakurân*. The trauma of the political change was assuaged somewhat by the remarkably restrained and confessionally ambiguous ways in which the new regime intruded into the life of a second rung of 'Hindu' political commanders. Within the context of their own discursive statements, this was a fact that the Persian chronicles and the Delhi masjid-i jâmi' would not wish to recognize [....]

CONCLUSION: 'OBJECTIVE' HISTORY AND THE MEMORY OF THE QUṬB

At the time of its construction, the Delhi masjid-i jâmi' left a variety of different impressions upon visitors. For many it was a symbol of a flourishing Muslim community abiding by the tenets of the sharî'a, triumphant over its idolatorous opponents, secured by the energetic, armed interventions of its Sultans. For others, it was a haven for 'scholars', who were concerned less with the spiritual fate of their congregations and more with a coercive regimen of rituals, pecuniary gain, and their own authority. These claims and counter-claims were very much a part of the history of Delhi's first masjid-i jâmi' in the thirteenth and fourteenth centuries. Events after the thirteenth century consolidated rival interpretations of the congregational mosque and the modern memory of the Quṭb was strongly impressed with these conflicting images.

For over three centuries after 'Alâ' al-Dîn Khalajî's death (715/1316), the old masjid-i jâmi' was sporadically associated with the authority of the rulers of Delhi. But this was not at the expense of the ṣūfîs whose influence remained undiminished during this period. In the fourteenth century itself, the tomb of Niẓâm al-Dîn Awliyâ' emerged as the most venerated shrine in the region of Delhi completely eclipsing the Delhi masjid-i jâmi'. The area around his shrine was blessed by the grace of the saint and his disciples chose to be buried in 'proximity of their pîr, their intercessor with God on the day of judgement. Amongst many others buried in this necropolis was the Mughal emperor Humayun (died 963/1556). A pilgrimage to the dargâh, or the 'court' of Niẓâm al-Dîn Awliyâ', was a part of the Mughal itinerary whenever the rulers of the dynasty visited Delhi.[33] Mughal patronage to the shrine, paradoxically, 'controlled' the saint's discourse against the inadequacies of temporal government. The Mughals did not hesitate to appear as disciples of mystic saints and incorporated strains of mysticism within the ideological baggage explaining their rites of kingship.

The example of Niẓâm al-Dîn Awliyâ' notwithstanding, not all ṣûfî shrines were equally hegemonized by the Mughals. To the south of Delhi, near the old masjid-i jâmi', the dargah of Quṭb al-Dîn Bakhtiyâr Kâkî (died 634/1235) was also an important ṣûfî shrine. Although he was not an unusually influential saint in his own life time, Ba<u>kh</u>tiyâr Kâkî was the pîr of Bâbâ Farîd, Niẓâm al-Dîn Awliyâ's spiritual master, and the renown of the student had certainly accrued to his teacher as well.[34] The record of royal visitations to the dargâh suggests that Ba<u>kh</u>tiyâr Kâkî's shrine emerged as a pilgrimage site as early as the late fourteenth and early fifteenth centuries.[35] In 932/1526 it was included in Babūr's tour of significant areas worthy of a visit in Delhi and in the mid, 1150s/early 1740s Dargâh Qulî <u>Kh</u>ân commenced his account of Delhi's ṣûfî shrines, with a narration of Ba<u>kh</u>tiyâr Kâkî's dargâh.[36] Ba<u>kh</u>tiyâr Kâkî may have lacked the popularity of Niẓâm al-Dîn Awliyâ', but in the eighteenth and nineteenth centuries, his mystical powers were considered so commanding thàt the Mughal emperors Shâh 'Âlam Bahâdur Shâh (1119–24/1707–12), Jalâl al Dîn Shâh 'Âlam (1173–1121/1760–1806) and Mu'în-al-Dîn Akbar (1221–53/1806–37) chose to be buried near the dargâh. The wish of the last Mughal ruler, Bahâdur Shâh 'Zafar' (1253–74/1837–58), to be buried near the saint remained unfulfilled; he was deported to Rangoon by the British where he died.[37]

Unlike Niẓâm al-Dîn's dargâh, Ba<u>kh</u>tiyâr Kâkî's charisma did not materially alter the prestige of the Mughal emperors. This was not because of any shortcoming in the saint's popularity. By the end of the eighteenth century, Mughal might had not survived the onslaught of the Afghan, Maratha, and British incursions and its capacity to command obedience was in obvious decline. The Mughal ability to access the increasing popularity of Ba<u>kh</u>tiyâr Kâkî's shrine for its own ends was also severely limited. In the eighteenth century many people in Delhi regarded Quṭb al-Dîn Ba<u>kh</u>tiyâr Kâkî as senior most in the 'hierarchy of saints', the Quṭb al-aqṭâb, specially chosen by God to maintain order in the world. The actual extent of his influence is uncertain, but at least within a local, popular cosmology evident in Delhi in the late eighteenth, early nineteenth century, Ba<u>kh</u>tiyâr Kâkî was regarded as the Quṭb, the axis, around whom the world revolved. This interpretation was also provided an iconic representation when the mînar of the neighbouring, thirteenth-century masjid-i jâmi', was described as *Quṭb ṣâḥib kî lâth*. In other words, the minaret was believed to represent the staff of Quṭb al-Dîn Ba<u>kh</u>tiyâr Kâkî which pierced the sky, and like the pîr himself, connected heaven with earth, providing stability and shelter to mortals on earth.[38] In this reworked popular cosmology, it was the saint who was the *qubbat al-*

Islâm, the 'sanctuary of Islam' and not the congregational mosque. It was in acknowledgement of the pîr's charisma, that the minaret of the mosque was christened the Quṭb mînâr, the name which it still carries today.

The reason why we have any information at all about the later developments in the meaning of the masjid-i jâmiʿ is because of attempts made in the nineteenth and twentieth centuries to correct some 'errors'. In 1263/1846–47 the judge (*munsif*) employed with the British East India Company, Sayyid Ahmad Khan, wrote his famous topographical monograph on Delhi, the *Âṣâr al-Sanâdîd*. At that stage in his life, Sayyid Ahmad was strongly influenced by the emerging positivistic historiographical methodologies gaining currency in the west. In his research on Delhi's monuments, the scholar was extremely careful in citing his literary and archaeological evidence, and in ascertaining chronological, geographical, and lexicographical details. Subsequent to the *Âṣâr al-Sanâdîd*, Sayyid Ahmad Khan published critical editions of Abû'l-Faẓl's *Â'în-i Akbarî*, Ẓiyâ' al-Dîn Baranî' *Târîkh-i Fîruz Shâhî*, and Jahangir's *Tûzuk-i Jahângîrî*, all medieval Persian chronicles on which he had started work several years before. The course of his research was charted by his belief that 'only a correct and sober presentation of the facts can convey a true sense of direction in history and enable the Indians to arrive at a realistic assessment of their situation.'[39] The documentary record of the court chronicles was an important source for the historian, and Sayyid Ahmad Khan carefully selected texts which were, in his opinion, repositories of reliable, objective information.

His concern to recount the 'correct facts' about the capital of the Sultans and the Mughals motivated Sayyid Ahmad Khan to write the most comprehensive text on the monuments of Delhi. In his account of Delhi's old congregational mosque, he did mention that one of the names for the minaret was 'Quṭb ṣâḥib kî lâth', and, amongst other names, the masjid was also called Quwwat al-Islâm.[40] Presumably because these names belonged to the realm of an oral, popular culture and not to an 'objective', 'scientific', verifiable, documentary record, there was no discussion of why the, mosque and the mînâr were ascribed such intriguing names. Sayyid Ahmad Khan's text led the reader away from these names towards the more 'relevant' subject of the architectural and epigraphical content of the monument and Sultan's contribution to its construction.

In its own turn, the *Âṣâr al-Sanâdîd* was regarded as an 'authoritative' text because it carried all the evidence of sound historical research.

Archaeologists and historians of a later generation were dependent upon Sayyid Ahmad Khan's collection of data, his readings of the epigraphs, bibliography of sources, and discussion of the authorship and architectural significance of the mosque. The major development in the early twentieth century occured when the analysis of the congregational mosque was further elaborated by an emerging consensus about the history of the Delhi Sultanate. Ironically, in their research in this area as well, scholars continued to be dependent upon Sayyid Ahmad Khan's scholarship. It was his editions of the Persian chronicles which became the staple diet for most medievalists, because their factual account[s], scholars in the twentieth century noted, were 'correct in all substantive matters'.

There is no doubt that the scholarship on the medieval period today bears little resemblance to that of Sayyid Ahmad's time. Irfan Habib's work in itself has inspired research into questions concerning material culture, agricultural production, and the structures of the state. These developments notwithstanding, historians are still wary of examining medieval Persian texts as discursive constructions of evidence, or as images which sought to shape reality. In the absence of such interrogation, a circular logic which first locates 'authoritative' sources and then reconstructs a 'definitive' history of the Middle Ages, has led to the writing of histories which have in different ways remained congruent with the fortunes of the state.

This methodology has left little space for the presence of local histories, popular memories or contesting discourses in the history of medieval India.[41] For the Quṭb mosque, it led to the 'clarification' that the minaret was not named after the ṣûfî saint Quṭb al-Dîn Ba<u>kh</u>tiyâr Kâkî, but the military commander Quṭb al-Dîn Ai-Beg. The term *Qubbat al-Islâm*, or the 'sanctuary of-Islam', which was at first ambiguouly used by Jûzjânî for Iltutmish's Delhi and later applied to define the spiritual domain of Ba<u>kh</u>tiyâr Kâkî, was transformed into Quwwat al-Islâm, or the 'Might of Islam' and used for Quṭb al-Dîn's mosque. This name coincided more closely with the military persona of the first constructor of the mosque and his proclamation of a new political order built out of the rubble of temples. Despite all the other developments in research on medieval Indian history, this interpretation of the mosque has remained unquestioned. In that sense, the problem before us today is not a simple one of reinterpreting the significance of the Quṭb monuments. We need to be aware that it is the epistemologies dominant in the study of medieval Indian history that enable the interpretation of the Quṭb monuments as the 'Quwwat al-Islâm' mosque.

As purveyors of 'information', historians shape the contours of India's past, in history textbooks, school and college syllabi and the popular media. Despite the best intentions of many of these practitioners, their work only serves to consolidate popular misconceptions concerning the monolithic character of Hindu and Muslim social structures in the medieval period. Historians may no longer use the term 'Muslim period' to refer to the subcontinent's Middle Ages, but their histories still consider the Delhi Sultans and the Mughal pâdishâhs as the principal actors in the history of medieval India. The different rulers and their structures of administration, revenue, and diplomatic policies are studied as the agencies which introduced social and economic change in the subcontinent. Marxist analyses of relations of exploitation and dominance in Sultanate and Mughal society, confirm the image of a monolithic ruling elite, predominantly Muslim and obsessed with 'a' Persian culture. This static and undifferentiated account is disturbed only occasionally by the bhaktî, sometimes the ṣûfî, perhaps even by groups such as the Mahdawîs. But these are often discussed as dissenting groups, 'non-conformist movements', related to, but outside the pale of two well contoured religions. During this entire period 'Muslims' remained the politically dominant group within the subcontinent. The relationship of these historiographies to the memory of the Quṭb is extremely important. The events and individuals—Quṭb al-Dîn Ai-Beg or Quṭb al-Dîn Ba<u>kh</u>tiyâr Kâkî, for example, are not terribly significant in themselves, but once situated within larger contextual frames of signification they recall a host of memories. The Quṭb is one of those historic sites which can extend beyond its own historical moment to carry a much larger symbolic statement.

Part of its importance lies in the manner in which it has been preserved and 'done up' into a national and world heritage monument. In one of its advertisement campaigns, the *Hindustan Times*, a national newspaper, asked its readers the rhetorical question: 'Can you imagine Delhi without the Quṭb?' Its ruins are presented today as a part of 'Indian' antiquity, a part of each citizen's, inheritance which he or she can cherish. One mosque out of several from the twelfth century has gained this doubtful honour. Indians are asked to take pride in 'their' mînâr—we are told that it is one of the tallest free standing minarets built out of stone and mortar. Nationalist pride, however, is shortlived and the Quṭb monuments lead to a host of ambivalent reactions.

If the minaret is wonderful, what of the mosque? Responses vary. For many, especially children, the monument is an incredibly beautiful and grandiose palace or a larger congregational hall. That it is a mosque escapes most of them. Other, more 'discerning' visitors, remain disconcerted by the statues, pillars, and elaborate carvings, so obviously of a Hindu/ Jain provenance situated within a congregational mosque. Still others may see in the mosque evidence of the might and dominance of 'their community' in the affairs of the subcontinent in the near past.

Since it is a major tourist site, the Archaeological Survey of India has placed short descriptions inscribed on stone near the several monuments to 'guide' visitors through the Quṭb complex. These inscriptions provide the name, the physical properties, functions and significance of the respective monuments. These are facts; there is no hint of doubt, speculation, or debate concerning the multiple interpretations of these sites or the changing historical contexts in which they were built. Instead the self-confident recounting of undisputed information is in itself reassuring to the visitors. It is presented as the wisdom of the professional body of historians and archaeologists, the 'authorities' whose knowledge should be above doubt.

Once armed with the crucial information that the Quwwat al-Islâm masjid celebrates the conquest of Hindustan by the Muslim Sultans of Delhi, the nature of the monument itself leaves little space to visitors for doubt. Even as they function as historians themselves, the 'evidence' of plunder before them is 'proof' sufficient of Muslim iconoclasm and a bigoted hatred of Hindus and their religious beliefs. Their empirical conclusions are not very far from a seamless historiography of medieval Indian history which has provided little to contest the overriding impression of the hegemony of the Muslim state.[42] As a result, the Quṭb serves as a catalyst which resurrects a host of memories about Muslims and their governance: from casual stories concerning Muslim fanaticism and violence, to history lessons where Muslim rulers and their subordinates monopolized power and exploited Hindu subjects. Within the mosque the visitor is struck by the juxtaposition of the great monolithic communities, a divide which the Quṭb suggests commenced from the very intrusion of Islam into India. A Partition which from its very first encounter was remarkable for its violence.

More than any large tome or pedagogical instruction, the Quṭb provides an opportunity, to educate visitors about the complex, fragmented political and religious world of India's Middle Ages, a time when there was considerable disunity and contestation within the groups defined as 'Hindus' and 'Muslims'. It is this frame of reference which should also guide us to reflect upon the manner in which discursive constructions of knowledge were formed in the Middle Ages. The Quwwat al-Islâm mosque was built to represent a unity of belief and conduct to a Muslim congregation who not only remained quite unimpressed with Sultanate statements of piety and power but also produced their own contesting discursive texts. The spoils of the Hindu and Jain temples are only a small part of the story of the Quṭb; Mu'izzî *Amîrs* such as Bahâ' al-Dîn Tughril, ṣûfî *derwishes* like Nûr Turk, *shaykh*s like Niẓâm al-Dîn Awliyâ', the popular veneration of Quṭb al-Dîn Bakhtiyâr Kâkî and the historiography of Sayyid Ahmad Khan and his successors are all ingredients that should be used to explain the multi-levelled history of the mosque and minaret to visitors. Instead it is the extreme nationalist ideologies prevalent in India which filter our understanding of the Quṭb. This unfortunately also burdens visitors with unequivocal evidence of wrongs inflicted in the past upon the Hindu community, wrongs that are in need of correction today. As a result, the Quṭb stands as an icon, encapsulating the trâuma of 1947 and acting as a historical exoneration for the acts of December 1992. What is tragic is the manner in which historians of medieval India have provided 'proof' and 'evidence' supporting the reading of this icon.

NOTES

This is an abbreviated version of a paper presented at the Indo-French Seminar (sponsored by the University Grants Commission, Indian Council of Historical Research and the Maison des Sciences de l'Homme) held at the School of Social Science, Jawaharlal Nehru University, 14–16 February 1994. I am currently revising the paper, for publication as a monograph entitled 'Defining and Contesting Territory: The Delhi Masjid-i Jâmi' in the thirteenth century'. The paper has profited from the comments of Anjali Kumar, David Gilmartin, Dilip Menon, Ebba Koch, Gail Minault, Suvir Kaul, and Tanika Sarkar, none of whom necessarily share the opinions of the author expressed here.

1. Alfred Gell, 'The Technology of Enchantment and the Enchantment of Technology', in *Anthropology, Art and Aesthetics,* (ed.) J. Coote and Anthony Shelton (Oxford: Oxford University Press, 1992), pp. 40–63.

2. For details on the spatial, architectural and epigraphic information, other than my own field surveys, I am reliant on the research of Sayyid Ahmad Khan, Alexander Cunningham, J. Horowitz, J.A. Page, A.B.M. Husain, M.A. Husain, and Ebba Koch. The full bibliographical citations are given below.

3. Although there is absolutely no evidence to warrant such an assumption, all historians and archaeologists have concluded that it was the Muslims who placed the iron pillar within the Quṭb mosque. Their conclusions might have been guided by the fact that later rulers like Firûz Shâh Tughluq and Akbar transported Asokan pillars and placed them as trophies in Delhi and Allahabad respectively. As Richard H. Davis has pointed out, ('Indian Art Objects as Loot', *Journal of Asian Studies,* 52 (1993), pp. 22–48) however, temples were also plundered by Hindu rulers, and their idols were frequently treated as war trophies and publicly displayed as statements of conquest. A similar effort at embellishing his own authority may well have guided the Tomara ruler Anangpal sometime around 1052: at least according to popular legend, it was this ruler who placed the fourth century iron pillar at its current site. See Alexander Cunningham, 'Four Reports made during the years 1862–65', *Archaeological Survey of India Reports,* Simla: Archaeological Survey of India, Government Press, 1871, Vol. 1, pp. 171–5.

4. See, for example, the opinion of H.C. Fanshawe, *Shah Jahan's Delhi—Past and Present* (Delhi: Sumit Publications, 1979 [1902]), p. 257.

5. See Sayyid Ahmad Khan, *Âṣâr al-Sanâdîd,* (ed.) Khaliq Anjum (Delhi: Urdu Academy Delhi, 1990 [1847]); Alexander Cunningham, 'Four Reports'; J. Horowitz, 'The Inscriptions of Muhammad ibn Sam, Qutbuddin Aibeg and Iltutmish', *Epigraphia Indo-Moslemica* (1911–12), pp. 12–34; J. Yazdani, 'Inscriptions of the Khaljî Sultans of Delhi and their contemporaries in Bengal,' *Epigraphia Indo-Moslemica,* 1917–18, pp. 23–30; J.A. Page, *An Historical Memoir on the Qutb,* Calcutta: Memoirs of the Archaeological Survey of India, no. 22, Government of India Central Publication Branch, 1926.

6. As far as I have been able to date it, Sayyid Ahmad Khan was the first author to refer to the Delhi Masjid-i Jâmiʿ as the 'Quwwat al-Islâm' mosque. S.A. Khan, *Âṣâr al-Sanâdîd,* Vol. 1, p. 310, provided three names for the mosque; *Masjid-i Adîna Dehlî ya* (or) *Masjid-i jâmiʿ Dehli ya* (or) *Quwwat al-Islâm.* Cunningham (1871) either misread Quwwat al-Islâm in Khan's text as *Quṭb al-Islâm* or, as is more likely (see below), he relied upon a locally current source for his reading. Literature on Delhi produced for English tourists at the turn of the century always referred to the mosque as Quwwat al-Islâm. See H.C. Fanshawe, *Delhi—Past and Present,* p. 258, and Gordon Risley Hearn, *The Seven Cities of Delhi* (New Delhi:

SBW Publishers, 1986 [1906]), pp. 51, 54, 94. Some years later, the widely cited Horowitz, 'Inscriptions', 1911–12 and J.A. Page, *A Historical Memoir on the Qutb*, (1926), informed scholars that Quwwat al-Islâm was the name of this mosque. It was a fateful christening for it was to eventually become the 'official' name of the mosque. From two edges of the historiographical spectrum where this is used for the masjid-i jâmi', see: J. Burton Page, 'Dihli', *Encyclopaedia of Islam*, (eds) C.E. Bosworth *et al.* (Leiden: E.J. Brill, second edition, 1956), Vol. 2, pp. 225–6, as representing the 'Islamicist' tradition, and Y.D. Sharma, *Delhi and Its neighbourhood*, New Delhi: Director General Archaeological Survey of India, 1982, rpt., pp. 17–19, 52–9, amongst the better tourist guide literature.

7. Michael W. Meister, 'The Two-and-a-half day Mosque', *Oriental Art* 18 n.s. (1972), pp. 57–63, reprinted as Chapter 9 in this volume. Mohammad Mujeeb, 'The Qutb Complex as a Social Document', in *Islamic Influence on Indian Society* (Delhi: Meenakshi Prakashan, 1972), pp. 114–27, reprinted as Chapter 5 in this volume; and A.B.M. Husain, *The Manara in Indo-Muslim Architecture* (Dhaka: Asiatic Society of Pakistan, Publication no. 25, 1970).

8. Robert Hillenbrand, 'Political Symbolism in Early Indo-Islamic Mosque Architecture: The Case of Ajmir', *Iran* 26 (1988), pp. 105–17, reprinted as Chapter 10 in this volume; Anthony Welch, 'Architectural Patronage and the Past: The Tughluq Sultans of India', *Muqarnas* 10 (1993), pp. 311–22.

9. Welch, 'Architectural Patronage...', p. 314.

10. Anthony Welch, '*Qur'ân* and Tomb: The Religious Epigraphs of Two Early Sultanate Tombs in Delhi' in *Indian Epigraphy: Its bearings on the History of Art*, (eds) Frederick M. Asher and G.S. Ghai (New Delhi: Oxford and IBH Publishing Co., American Institute of Indian Studies, 1985), pp. 257, 260. Welch summarized the argument which he presented in another article, published as Chapter 8 in this volume.

11. Ibid., p. 257.

12. Welch, 'Architectural Patronage....' pp. 311–14. Welch suggests that: 'Building types—mosques, tombs, madrasas, and mînârs—as well as forms are also at the same time assertively alien to the Hindu majority, and in their strident distinctiveness from indigenous buildings, they proclaim Islam's universal aspirations and its distance from the polytheism of the subject population', pp. 312–3.

13. A.B.M. Habibullah, *The Foundation of Muslim Rule in India* (Allahabad: Central Book Depot, 1976 rpt.); Khaliq Ahmad Nizami, *Some Aspects of Religion and Politics in the Thirteenth Century* (Delhi: Idarah-i Adabiyat-i Delhi, 1974 rpt.); S.B.P. Nigam, *Nobility Under the Sultans of Delhi*, AD *1206–1398* (Delhi: Munshiram Manoharlal, 1968).

14. Habibullah, *Foundation of Muslim Rule*, Chapter VI, pp. 120–34.

15. Welch, 'Architectural Patronage ...', p. 311.

16. 'The plebianization of the nobility', a clumsy formulation at best, has several proponents but was first suggested by Mohammad Habib, 'The Governing Class', in *The Political Theory of the Delhi Sultanate* (Allahabad: Ketab Mahal, n.d.), pp. 144–51, and later developed by Irfan Habib, 'Baranî's Theory of the Delhi Sultanate', *Indian Historical Review* 7 (1980–1), p. 109.

17. For the architectural consequences of this development see Welch, 'Architectural Patronage and the Past', pp. 314–5. Here the author argues that since the Tughluqs were [more?] secular rulers, governing a pan-Indian state, their architecture was also less 'saracenic' and more eclectic.

18. Irfan Habib, 'The Social Distribution of Landed Property in Pre-British India: A Historical Survey', *Enquiry* n.s. 2 (1965), p. 45.

19. *'In pahwan (?) wa jahândâr-i Hind-ra Malik khitab farmûd'. 'Pahwân'*, in the Persian edition of the *Tâ'rîkh* must be a mistake for *'pahalwan'*.

20. Fakhr-i Mudabbir, *Tâ'rîkh-i Fakhr al-Dîn Mubârak Shâh*, (ed.) E.D. Ross (London: Royal Asiatic Society, 1927), pp. 28–9.

21. On the ṭabaqât form as a historical genre of writing see Franz Rosenthal, *History of Muslim Historiography* (Leiden: E.J. Brill, 1969), pp. 93–5 and Louise Marlow, *Hierarchy and Egalitarianism in Islamic Thought* (Cambridge: Cambridge University Press, 1997), pp. 9–10. For the Mu'izzî subordinates in Hindustan, see Minhâj-i Sirâj Jûzjânî, *Ṭabaqât-i Nâṣirī*, (ed.) Abdul Hayy Habibi (Kabul: Anjuman-i Târîkh-i Afghanistan, 1963–64), Vol. 1, pp. 415–38.

22. Jûzjânî, *Ṭabaqât* ..., Vol. 1, p. 421.

23. Ibid., Vol. 1, p. 421. Notice also the titulature and Jûzjânî's attempt to communicate his sense of the hierarchical relationship: Malik was used for Bahâ' al-Dîn and Sultan for Quṭb al-Dîn.

24. Fakhr-i Mudabbir, *Târîkh-i Fakhr al-Dîn Mubârak Shâh*, pp. 25–6. I have used the translation of E.D. Ross, 'The genealogies of *Fakhr al-Dîn Mubârak Shâh*', in *'Aja'ib Namah: A volume of Oriental Studies presented to E.G. Browne on his Sixtieth Birthday*, (eds) T.W. Arnold and R.A. Nicholson (Cambridge: Cambridge University Press, 1922), p. 399.

25. For Bahâ' al-Dîn's inscription in the 'Chaurasi Khamba' mosque in Kaman, see Mehrdad and Natalie H. Shokoohy, 'The Architecture of Bahâ' al-Dîn Tughrul [*sic*] in the Region of Bayana, Rajasthan', *Muqarnas* 4 (1987), p. 115.

26. But note the graffiti on the right-hand jamb of the eleventh slit window on the stairway in the minaret: 'May your mother be ravished by a donkey!' See Page, *The Qutb* ..., p. 40. This may have been a response to the destruction of temples, but at least equally, if not more likely, a venting of frustrated resentment by an artisan at a personal injury caused by an aggressive supervisor at work.

27. See Page, *The Qutb* ..., pp. 39–40, 41, 43. I have followed the revised and edited translation of Pushpa Prasad, *Sanskrit Inscriptions of Delhi Sulṭanate*

1191–1526 (Delhi: Oxford University Press, 1990), pp. 3, 19, 35. I concur with Pushpa Prasad's reading of the inscription from Muhammad Shah Tug͟hluq's reign. But for an alternate reading see Carl W. Ernst, *Eternal Garden; Mysticism, History and Politics at a South Asian Sûfî Center* (Albany: State University of New York, 1992), pp. 32–3.

28. On the bâg͟h-i Jasrath, see Amîr Hasan Sijzî, *Fawâ'id al-Fu'âd*, (ed.) Hazan Sani Nizami Dihlawi (Delhi: Urdu Academy, 1990), p. 242. On the *ḥauẓ-i Rânî*, see ibid.; Amîr K͟hurd, *Siyar al-Awliyâ'*, (ed.) S.M. Ghuri (Lahore: Marqaz-i Tahqiqat-i Farsi Iran wa Pakistan, 1978), p. 120; and Jûzjânî, *Ṭabaqât-i Nâṣirî*, Vol. 1, p. 469, Vol. 2, p. 27. For a fuller description see Sunil Kumar, 'A Medieval Reservoir and Modern Urban Planning, Local History and the Ḥauẓ-i Rānī', in Sunil Kumar, *The Present in Delhi's Pasts*, (Delhi: 3 Essays Collective, 2nd edition, 2008), pp. 62–94.

29. See Davis, 'Indian Art Objects as Loot', pp. 22–48.

30. Peter Hardy, 'Growth of Authority Over a Conquered Political Elite: Early Delhi Sultanate as a Possible Case Study', in *Kingship and Authority in South Asia*, (ed.) J.F. Richards (Delhi: Oxford University Press, 1998 rpt.), pp. 216–41, had studied a similar set of questions years ago without much success. Significantly his research was based primarily on the textual evidence of the thirteenth and fourteenth centuries.

31. Fak͟hr-i Mudabbir, *Tâ'rîk͟h* ..., p. 33; Hardy, 'Authority Over a Conquered Political Elite', p. 238.

32. See John S. Deyell, *Living Without Silver* (Delhi: Oxford University Press, 1990), pp. 193–206, 318.

33. See Ebba Koch, 'The Delhi of the Mughals Prior to Shahjahanabad as Reflected in the Patterns of Imperial Visits', in *Art and Culture*, (eds) A.J. Qaisar and S.P. Verma (Jaipur: Publication Scheme Press, 1993).

34. In contrast to the very full account of Bâbâ Farîd, the *Fawā'id al-Fu'ād* provides occasional references to Bak͟htiyâr Kâkî's life and teachings: pp. 42–3, 87–8, 104–5, 132, 184–5, 212–3, 246, 268, 315–6, 336, 407, 420. It was in Amîr K͟hwurd's *Siyar al-Awliyâ'*, (ed.) Sayyid Mahdi Ghuri (Lahore: Markaz-i Tahqiqat-i Farsi Iran wa Pakistan, no. 23, Mu'assi-yi Intisharat-i Islami, 1978), pp. 48–56, a late fourteenth century biographical compendium, that the spiritual genealogy of the Chishtî mystical order was clearly worked out, and Bak͟htiyâr Kâkî's position in the descent of Chishtî saints confirmed.

35. According to Ibn Baṭṭûṭa's evidence, Bak͟htiyâr Kâki's grave had already become a place of pilgrimage when he visited it in the mid or late 730s/1330s. Ibn Battuta, *The Travels of Ibn Battuta*, Vol. 3, trans. H.A.R. Gibb (Cambridge: Cambridge University Press, Hakluyt Society, second series, no. 141, 1971), pp. 625–6. In 800/1398 the agreement between Mallu Iqbâl K͟hân and Sultan Nâsir

al-Dîn Mahmâd Shâh (795–801/1393–99) was reached in the dargâh of Bakhtiyâr Kâkî: see Yahyâ Sîhrindî, *Tâ'rîkh-i Mubârak Shâhî*, (ed.) M. Hidayat Hosain (Calcutta: Bibliotheca Indica, 1931), p. 163. Faced with the threat of Husain Shâh Sharqî's invasions in 883/1478, Bahlul Lôdî prayed at the dargâh of the saint. See Shaikh Rizqullâh Mushtâqî, *Waqî'at-i Mushtâqî*, trans. and (ed.) I.H. Siddiqui (New Delhi: Indian Council of Historical Research, 1993), p. 11.

36. Babūr, *Babūr nâmah*, Vol. 2, p 474. Dargâh Qulî Khân, *Muraqqa'-i-Dihlî* (ed.) and trans. Nural Hasan Ansari (Delhi: Urdu Department, University of Delhi Press, 1982), pp. 23–5, 119–21. The description of Bakhtiyâr Kâkî's dargâh followed accounts of shrines venerating the Prophet's and Ali's footprints and it preceded an account of Nizâm al-Dîn Awliyâ's tomb.

37. Mughal construction within the dargâh is in evidence from the eighteenth century during the reigns of Shâh 'Alam Bahâdur Shâh (1119–24/1707–12) and Farrukh Siyar (1124–31/1713–19). See Sayyid Ahmad Khan, *Âṣâr al-Sanâdîd*, Vol. 1, p. 335. The author makes no mention of the floral multi-coloured tiles presumed to have been fixed in the shrine by Aurangzeb, for which see Y.D. Sharma, *Delhi and its Neighbourhood*, pp. 62–3.

38. Sayyid Ahmad Khan, *Âṣâr al-Sanâdîd*, (ed.) Khaliq Anjum (Delhi: Urdu Board, 1990 rpt.), Vol. 1, p. 312.

39. Christian W. Troll, *Sayyid Ahmad Khan: A Reinterpretation of Muslim Theology* (Karachi: Oxford University Press, 1978–79), p. 105, and for his scholarship in the context of the *Âṣâr al-Sanâdîd* see Troll, 'A Note on an Early Topographical Work of Saiyid Ahmad Khan: Athar as-Sanadid', *Journal of the Royal Asiatic Society* (1972), pp. 135–46.

40. Sayyid Ahmad Khan, *Âṣâr al-Sanâdîd*, Vol. 1, pp. 310–12.

41. It is also one of the reasons why medieval Indian history is so weak in social as well as women's history.

42. This is not to suggest that no historian has questioned the interpretation of the monolithic state and its ruling elite in the medieval period. The writings of scholars such as Muzaffar Alam and Sanjay Subrahmanyam are, however, restricted to the Mughals. For their most recent contribution see Muzaffar Alam and Sanjay Subrahmanyam, eds. *The Mughal State* (Delhi: Oxford University Press, 1998). The writings of Alam, Subrahmanyam and others, however, have not received the circulation they deserve. Their fate seems to be determined by what Peter Hardy described as 'a kind of Gresham's Law' (which continues to operate for the Sultanate period) where 'one or two text-books of political history ... drive out of intellectual circulation many articles on cultural history in learned periodicals'. Peter Hardy, *Historians of Medieval India: Studies in Indo-Muslim Historical Writing* (London: Luzac and Company, 1966 rpt.), pp. 4–5.

Epigraphs, Scripture, and Architecture in the Early Delhi Sultanate*

ANTHONY WELCH, HUSSEIN KESHANI, AND ALEXANDRA BAIN

The Dome of the Rock (691) in Jerusalem was the first expensive, aesthetically oriented religious structure in Islamic history. It was also the first to use architectural inscriptions as part of its overall theme and decoration. Though these inscriptions were small and difficult to see in the dimly lit interior, they offered several themes that had direct bearing on the social and religious functions of this shrine in a city with a Christian population that was both large and powerful and took notable pride in its many splendid monuments. The Arab traveller al-Muqaddasi noted in 985 that it was vital for Islam in its first century to construct magnificent structures that would match and transform the inherited architectural environment. Thus the epigraphic programme of the Dome of the Rock makes explicit references to Islam's unyielding monotheism, to its rejection of Christ's divinity but its acceptance of Christ's role as a prophet, and its belief in Muhammad's unique role as Allah's Messenger bearing the final revelation. It has been convincingly argued that there was nothing haphazard about the selection of the Qur'anic verses that make up the larger part of these epigraphs and that it was the written word that was considered the suitable vehicle for these central beliefs.[1] The Dome of the Rock is not alone in having a specific and very carefully chosen epigraphic programme.

In significant ways Islam's subsequent experience in late-twelfth and early-thirteenth-century India paralleled seventh-century Syria and Palestine. The vast majority of the population of the Delhi Sultanate in

*Previously published in *Muqarnas*, Vol. 19, Brill, Leiden, 2002, pp.12–43. In the present version, some portions of the text, notes, and illustrations have been removed. For the complete text see the original version.

its first 128 years of existence under the Mu'izzi and Khalji sultans from 1192 to 1320 consisted of non-Muslims who adhered to faiths possessing rich figural traditions in the arts and architecture, and the visual landscape abounded in monuments erected to display the tenets of these other faiths. But there were also important differences: Islam came to India under Ghurid leadership, not as a recently revealed faith, but rather as a long-established religion that had a five-hundred-year-old culture with complex theologies and a vital architectural heritage of its own. Islam brought not only the distinctive, identifying traditions of architecture necessary to create structures symbolizing an enduring state, but also its own, virtually unique means of demonstrating central religious convictions through the use of monumental epigraphy. It is this particular facet of architectural history that will be explored here, not in terms of stylistic development, but instead as a means of investigating and elucidating the political, social, and religious history of medieval Sultanate India through its visual culture.[2]

The central monument for the early history of Islam in northern India is the early jami' masjid of Delhi, begun in the late twelfth century during the reign of Sultan Mu'izz al-Din and continued by his Mu'izzi and Khalji successors (Plates 1–3, 10, 12).[3] Both in its architectural style and in its extensive epigraphs it owes much to Ghaznavid and Ghurid precedents. This chapter will examine all of the extant inscriptions in or near this complex and in the jami' masjid of Ajmer. Given the diversity of religious currents in Central Asia and northern India, then, this study can only be regarded as an initial foray into unravelling theological and social complexities and pointing to possible future research directions. Its underlying premise is that inscriptions were carefully selected to set out key doctrinal points and to support, emphasize, and elucidate recent history and contemporary events.

STATE, FAITH, AND ARCHITECTURAL EPIGRAPHS UNDER THE GHAZNAVIDS AND GHURIDS OF AFGHANISTAN

The spheres of Ghaznavid and Ghurid authority in the eleventh and twelfth centuries included the regions of Ghur, Ghazna, Sind, and Punjab. Sultan Mahmud of Ghazna (r. 998–1030) conducted more than twenty raids into northern India between 1001 and 1027. The Ghurids continued this strategy in the last quarter of the eleventh century and often met defeat until their victory at the second battle of Tarain in 1192.

As elsewhere in Islam, disputation loomed large in intellectual and social life under the Ghaznavids and Ghurids, and the religious environment was complex. The Hanafi *madhhab* (school) probably had the greatest influence under both dynasties. The Shiʿa, including an Ismaʿili community, in Ghazna and Firuzkuh had their own intellectual and theological traditions. The Shafiʿi scholar and philosopher Fakhr al-Din Razi, who had influence at the Ghurid court in Firuzkuh, was intimately familiar with Greek philosophy and with Ibn Sina's thought, and he struggled against Karamiyya theologians.[4] Shafiʿi scholars with their rigorous testing of prophetic tradition rejected many purported hadith that the Hanafis relied upon and therefore challenged their authority. Sufis seem to have had substantial followings in Khurasan, and if al-Hujwiri's writings are any indication, Ghazna was a centre of sufi activity. Some rejected the prescriptive approaches of the *madhhab,* while others rigorously advocated them. Relatively unorganized, the sufis were early on also vulnerable to penetration by Ghaznavid spies who were suspicious of their activities.[5] The Ghurids inherited these tensions. Accordingly, the mainly Hanafi religious officials of the Ghaznavid and Ghurid state had to defend their views on four fronts. First, they had to respond to Shafiʿi criticism that the Hanafi school was too lax in its identification of valid hadith. Second, their methods of reasoning had to appear rigorous enough to compete with the philosophers in the Greek tradition. Third, they had to accommodate many of the established Shiʿa, while responding harshly to Ismaʿilis and some sufis who were thought to have strayed too far from orthodox faith and practice. And fourth, they had to deal with Karamiyya criticism of traditional Sunni and Shiʿa doctrines.

The Ghaznavids were active architectural patrons. Literary sources offer a number of references to their buildings. With the plunder from his northern Indian campaigns, Sultan Mahmud commissioned in Ghazna a new mosque, the Arus al-Falak, and a madrasa; a palace, the Gawshak-i Kuhan-i Mahmudi; and a garden, the Bagh-i Mahmudi. He is also credited with building a number of other gardens and palaces: the Bagh-i Sad Hazara, the Bagh-i Firuzi, the Gawshak-i Dawlat, and the Gawshak-i Sapid, as well as elephant stables, irrigation canals, and dams. Outside Ghazna,

Mahmud built a palace in Balkh, while his brother Yusuf commissioned the al-Sa'idi madrasa in Nishapur in 999–1000.[6] Mahmud's son, Mas'ud, took an active interest in the design of buildings and commissioned his own palace, the Gawshak-i Mas'udi, which he had decorated with spoils from Indian campaigns.[7]

Surviving Ghaznavid architectural remains can be found in Ghazna, Bust, and Sangbast. In Ghazna there are the minars of Mas'ud III and Bahram Shah, the palace of Mas'ud III, remains of the houses of prominent men, as well as fragments and funerary structures.[8] Mahmud's waterworks project, the Band-i Sultan, has survived north of Ghazna.[9] In the suburbs of Bust, three Ghaznavid palaces in ruins at Lashkar-i Bazar have been surveyed.[10] Finally, in Sangbast, the domed square 'mausoleum' of Mahmud's governor Arslan Jadhib has been documented.[11]

The two most celebrated figures of the Ghurid empire are the brothers Shams al-Din Muhammad (later Ghiyath al-Din) b. Sam, who ruled from the Ghurid heartland of Firuzkuh between 1163 and 1203, and Shihab al-Din Muhammad (later Mu'izz al-Din) b. Sam, who ruled from Ghazna between 1173 and 1206. Both initially adhered to the Karamiyya doctrines widespread in Ghur, but as they extended their power, they were increasingly inclined towards the Shafi'i and Hanafi madhhabs.[12] Ghiyath al-Din was also partial to the Shafi'i *faqīh* and philosopher Fakhr al-Din al-Razi, who angered the Karamiyya ulema dominant in Ghiyath al-Din's court at Firuzkuh. Another clue to Mu'izz al-Din and his court's religious outlook on Islam is his attempt to eliminate the Qarmatians (Isma'ilīs) in Multan in 1175.[13]

The architecture of Ghur, for which there is relatively little textual and archaeological evidence, has only been briefly summarized thus far by K.A. Nizami and warrants further elaboration.[14] We are somewhat more fortunate when it comes to knowing the architectural efforts that took place during the reigns of Ghiyath al-Din and Mu'izz al-Din. Ghiyath al-Din ordered the construction of a madrasa for Fakhr al-Din al-Razi in Herat and contributed to the Friday mosque.[15] In Chisht, he appears to have supported the development of a mosque and madrasa. In Khurasan, he commissioned mosques, madrasas, and caravanserais.[16] At his capital Firuzkuh, he commissioned the minar of Jam.[17] It is also said that he funded several Shafi'i colleges throughout his territories.[18] Only the fragments at Chisht and the minar of Firuzkuh have been identified and studied.[19] An immense madrasa attributed to a female patron was also completed in 1175–6 during Ghiyath al-Din's reign in Gargistan (northwestern Afghanistan) of which fragments have survived.[20] Mu'izz al-Din commissioned a fortress at Sialkot near Lahore,[21] as well as mosques and madrasas at Ajmer. He is also associated by name with the minar and the first stage of the jami' masjid in Delhi.[22]

In what is believed to be the Ghurid capital city of Firuzkuh between Chisht and Ahangaran stands the great minar erected during the reign of Ghiyath al-Din Muhammad and inscribed with the entire chapter Maryam (Qur'an 19: 1–98) in the intertwining vertical bands of the minar's lower half.[23] The chapter refers to the revelations sent by God to his messengers John, Jesus, Abraham, Moses, Ishmael, Idris, and Noah. The message eventually went unheeded, and humanity is chastised for its waywardness and ignorance of God. Mary's immaculate conception is affirmed, but the notion that God would have a son is seen as an affront that will be addressed on the Day of Resurrection.

Four Kufic inscriptions in bands are located on the upper half of the minar.[24] The first is the profession of faith *(shahāda)*: '1 bear witness that there is no god but God and that Muhammad is the Messenger of God.' The second inscription is Qur'an 61: 13–14: 'Help from Allah and present victory. Give good tidings (O Muhammad) to believers! O ye who believe.' The third inscription gives the ruler's name: 'The magnificent Sultan Ghiyath al-Dunya wa'l-Din Abu'l-Fath Muhammad b. Sam.' The fourth inscription provides his honorifics: 'The magnificent Sultan, the august king of kings, Ghiyath al-Dunya wa'l-Din, who exalts Islam and Muslims, Abu'l-Fath Muhammad b. Sam, the agent of the Commander of the Faithful, may God preserve his rule!' Other fragments on the minar mention the work of 'Ali and Abu'l-Fath.

The body of extant Ghaznavid and Ghurid epigraphs is limited, and it is difficult to draw from it any substantive conclusions about epigraphy. Many of the inscriptions are funerary and predictably speak to the universal experience of death. It is really only the inscriptions on Ghiyath al-Din's minar at Firuzkuh that invite broader inquiry, and there the range of possibilities is intriguing. Do the selections demonstrate the tensions within and between Hanafi, Shafi'i, and Karamiyya thought? With their references to biblical history do they reflect the influential Jewish presence in Ghur?[25] More importantly, is it appropriate to see the minar, not as the end of an architectural and epigraphic Ghaznavid–Ghurid tradition in Afghanistan, but rather as the first monument of a new Ghurid tradition that will subsequently flourish under the dynasty and its descendants in northern India?

If one considers these inscriptions along with the elaborate inscriptions at the early jami' masjid complex of Delhi, then there is an impressive body of evidence suggesting that architectural epigraphy had signal importance for the Ghurids. Complex inscriptions could only have been made by individuals who were profoundly learned, alert to current affairs, and functioning at high official levels. With their knowledge of the Qur'an, hadith (Sayings of the Messenger Muhammad), *tafsīr* (exegesis), shari'a (religious law), and contemporary social, political, and religious issues, senior *qadis* (canon lawyers and judges) would have been the logical choice to consult about appropriate epigraphic selections for new buildings. More significantly, qadis had real authority to resolve issues not only of the faith but also of *awqāf* (charitable endowments), water distribution, and property ownership and development. Along with their legal and spiritual duties, they were key regulators of the built environment.

Scholars and Texts

The following observations are an initial attempt to make more tangible the interplay of texts and personalities that enlivened the complex intellectual environments at the Ghurid courts in Ghazna, Firuzkuh, and Delhi. Much research still needs to be done. At this point it is only possible to touch on a few of the works that charged Hanafi-Traditionist and Maturidi perspectives on the meanings of the Qur'an and influenced the qadis in the employ of Mu'izz al-Din and Qutb al-Din Aybak. Through them we can gain some idea of the complexities behind the selection of Qur'anic inscriptions.[26]

One of the earliest and most comprehensive collections of hadith, the *al-Jāmi' al-ṣaḥīḥ* (Collection of Sound Tradition) of al-Bukhari, has a chapter devoted to instances where the Prophet explained the significance of certain passages from the Qur'an. Along with the collection of Muslim, it was available to Mawlana Razi al-Din al-Hasan al-Saghani (d. 1252) of Badaon who settled in Iltutmish's court at Delhi in 1220 and popularized both compilations of hadith in his *Mashāriq al-anwār* (Sunrise of Lights), a rearrangement and editing of Bukhari and Muslim that became the standard work in Indian madrasas. The eighth-century *al-Fiqh al-Akbar I* (Greater Jurisprudence) was widely known, and it established general Hanafi principles of belief. It appears in Rukn al-Din al-Kashani's bibliography.[27]

It is possible that the Qur'an commentary of al-Tabari was known to the Delhi ulema since it was translated into Persian for the Samanid ruler Abu Salih Mansur b. Nuh, who ruled over Transoxania and Khurasan from 961 to 976, but no mention of it is found in the later historical literature. The scholar/mystic al-Hujwiri (d. 465–69), who was forced to move from Ghazna to Lahore, speaks of the popular but incomplete tafsīr by the Hanafi legal scholar Abu 'Âbd Allah Muhammad b. 'Ali al-Tirmidhi and says that it was widely circulated among theologians. Al-Maturidi himself wrote a commentary entitled *The Book of Commentary on the Qur'an.*[28] Though there is no clear evidence that it was read, Rukn al-Din al-Kashani's bibliography demonstrates that the works of Maturidi's students were known in the Delhi Sultanate.

The *Testament (Waṣīya)* of Abu Hanifa was seen as part of standard, traditionist Hanafi doctrine in the eleventh and twelfth centuries. In the early tenth century AD, the *Fiqh Akbar II,* probably written by al-Ash'ari (d. 935), provided a model for the writings of later Maturidi scholars.[29] The writings of al-Ghazali were well known in the Delhi Sultanate as well. One of the most significant texts on the Hanafi–Maturidi position is the creed (*'aqīda*) of Najm al-Din al-Nasafi (d. 1142), though only *al-Manẓūma al-Nasafiyya* fi *al-khilāfātiyya* ('Nasafi's Didactic Poem on the Caliphate') by the same author is mentioned by Rukn al-Din al-Kashani.

The tafsīr that was probably the most widely read by the ulema when the early jami' masjid of Delhi was constructed was the recently completed work by the Mu'tazili al-Zamakhshari (1070–1144), who was from Khiva.[30] Despite the anti-Mu'tazili sentiment of Maturidi and Ash'ari scholars, al-Zamakhshari's tafsīr was sufficiently learned and subtle to be considered as a valuable resource to the ulema, who were well versed in their opponents' points of views. Al-Juzjani makes no mention of al-Zamakhshari, but the date of his work and its known popularity in the later Delhi Sultanate strongly suggest that it was read. The Chishti shaykh Hamid al-Din Nagawri (d. 1276), a contemporary of Sultan Iltutmish, is recorded as having said, 'Whatever is given in other works is from this book; whatever the people have liked, they have copied from it and have compiled a separate work in their own name.'[31] One of the most celebrated of all Chishti shaykhs, Nizam al-Din Awliya' (d. 1325), studied fiqh and hadith in Badaon and Delhi between roughly 1240 and 1250 AD. He was also familiar with al-Zamakhshari's tafsīr but, because of the anti-Mu'tazili sentiment of the ulema and sufis of the period, felt that its author was to be consigned to hell. Al-Juzjani mentions the celebrated Fakhr al-Din Muhammad al-Razi (d. 1209), who was patronized by Sultan Ghiyath al-Din and his nephew Baha' al-Din in Ghazna and Herat. Al-Razi is thought to have died before completing his tafsīr, so it would not have been in circulation when the epigraphs of Mu'izz al-Din's and Aybak's portions of the jami' masjid and minar were being selected, but it may have been available when Iltutmish made his additions later.

The Hanafi legal texts of the period that may have been widely read are the works of Abu'l-Hasan Ahmad b. Muhammad al-Quduri (972–1037) and the *Hidāya* of Mawlana Burhan al-Din Abu'l-Hasan 'Ali al-Marghinani (1135–97). Both are mentioned as being part of Nizâm al-Dîn Awliya's education in Badaon and Delhi.[32] In fact, the *Hidāya* is generally considered to be the principal text in the application of Islamic law in India to the present day.

THE GHURIDS IN INDIA AND THE FOUNDATION OF THE DELHI SULTANATE

Defeated by the Rajput confederacy under Rai Pithora in 1191 in the first battle of Tarain, the Ghurid sultan Mu'izz al-Din b. Sam returned in the following year and emerged victorious from the second battle of Tarain. In the words of the most important contemporary chronicler, 'Almighty God gave the victory to Islam, and the infidel host was overthrown.'[33] The sultan returned to Ghazna and appointed his general Qutb al-Din Aybak to rule as his deputy. Qutb al-Din rapidly took Mirath, Delhi, Gwalior, and Badaun so that by 1195 a great part of northern India was under Ghurid control. The city of Delhi was established as the administrative centre of the new Indian domain, and at first its population consisted largely of soldiers. Muslim merchants, ulema, qadis, scribes, and officials began to migrate to Delhi, drawn by opportunities offered by members of the new ruling class like Malik Baha' al-Din Tughril. Appointed administrator of the territory of Thankar eighty kilometres southwest of Agra, Malik Baha' al-Din actively encouraged the settlement of merchants and men of credit from Khurasan and Hindustan by giving them land and houses.[34]

Even after the establishment of a sultanate in Delhi in 1206, the sectarian debates that flourished in the Ghurid homelands informed the thinking of Muslim officials. Religious currents there seem to have been strongly influenced by Hanafi scholars subscribing to Maturidi doctrine. Competing with Mu'tazili, Karamiyya, Traditionist, and Shi'i ideas, this *kalām* had developed in Samarqand and spread westward with the Seljuq Turks. A key feature of Maturidi thought was the definition of faith as dependent primarily upon inner assent, but it also emphasized the doctrine of the qualities of God, the existence of God's throne, and the actuality of Muhammad's ascension (*mi'rāj*) and vision of God. Hanafi–Maturidi religious intellectuals were numerous and powerful in Ghazna, first under Ghaznavid rule and then under the Ghurids. Since Ghazna was Mu'izz al-Din's seat of power, it is reasonable to assume that he endorsed the views of Hanafi–Maturidi officials.[35]

In 1206 Mu'izz al-Din died, and Qutb al-Din was declared the ruler of an independent Delhi Sultanate. When he in turn died in 1210, the leadership of the Sultanate appointed another former mercenary slave, Iltutmish (r. 1211–36), as his successor after a brief interregnum, and it was during his long reign that Delhi became the centre of Islamic political, religious, and cultural life in India. With some lapses it retained that position of primacy until the middle of the sixteenth century. In its first two centuries the Sultanate vigorously and steadily expanded to the east, south, and west, coming into constant conflict with Hindu principalities. In part, the Sultanate defined itself by its aggressive confrontations in the Abode of War *(dār al-ḥarb)* in the Indian subcontinent, and so sought regular recognition from Baghdad and, later, Cairo through formal submission to the Abbasid caliph. Though Muslim immigrants came from the west and northwest and spoke Persian, Arabic, or Turkish, it was Persian that was the language of court and recordkeeping. Persian administrative structures set the patterns of governance, at least at the high court level. After the onset of the Mongol invasions into Central Asia and Iran, many more immigrants came to India, where life was more secure and economic opportunities were greater, so that by the end of the thirteenth century the Sultanate had a diverse and numerous Muslim population. Delhi with its population of Muslims, Hindus, Jains, and Parsis became the most heterogeneous major city anywhere under Islamic rule.

Qutb al-Din Aybak was inclined toward Hanafi scholars. Coming as a youth from the slave markets of Turkestan, he served the chief qadi and governor of Nishapur under Seljuq rule, Fakhr al-Din 'Abd al-'Aziz, who claimed descent from Abu Hanifa. Al-Juzjani reports that Aybak studied the Qur'an with the qadi's sons: 'in attendance on, and along with his sons, he read the Word of God, and acquired instruction in horsemanship, and shooting with the bow and arrow, so that, in a short time, he became commended and favorably spoken of for his manly bearing.'[36]

His successor, Iltutmish, had grown up in the family of the chief qadi of Bukhara, lived some years of his early life in Ghazna and Baghdad, and was later purchased in Delhi by Qutb al-Din Aybak. After his ascent to the throne, he devoted several years to subduing rivals, and in 1229 welcomed an emissary, bearing robes of honour and formal recognition from the Abbasid caliph in Baghdad. In 1234 he defeated the Hindu rulers of Malwa and demolished the sacred temple of Mahakali, one of the great religious centres of northern India. In the same year members of the Isma'ili population in Delhi made an attempt on his life during Friday prayer; in retaliation, Iltutmish not only drove them out of Delhi but also marched on Multan, where they had settled after being expelled from Ghazna by Sultan Muhammad Ghuri. The sultan died in 1236.

The deteriorating political situation in Khurasan and Transoxania resulting from the disintegration of the Ghurid empire, Genghis Khan's Mongol invasions of the region in 1220, and the retreat of the Khwarazmian army to Lahore accelerated the migration of the ulema, sufis, and notables from these afflicted regions to Delhi. Al-Juzjani writes that Delhi became a place of retreat for the learned and virtuous fleeing the advancing Mongol conquests of the provinces and cities of the west.[37] Immigration must have also been stimulated by Iltutmish's patronage of religious scholars and mystics. A qadi himself, al-Juzjani appreciated Iltutmish's generous support:

> From the very outset of his reign, and the dawn of the morning of his sovereignty, in the congregating of eminent doctors of religion and law, venerable Sayyids, Maliks, Amirs, Sadrs, and [other] great men, the Sultan used, yearly, to expend about ten millions; and people from various parts of the world he gathered together at the capital city of Dihli, which is the seat of government of Hindustan, and the centre of the circle of Islam, the sanctuary of the mandates and inhibitions of the law, the kernel of the Muhammadi religion, the marrow of Ahmadi belief, and the tabernacle of the eastern parts of the universe—Guard it, O God, from calamities and molestations.[38]

Distinguished members of the ulema were attracted to Delhi. For example, al-Saghani, a famous scholar of hadith, originally hailed from Badaun, went to Baghdad, and then moved to Delhi. His text became standard in the curriculum of religious scholars. Awfī, the author of the history *Jāmi' al-ḥikāyāt,* which is dedicated to Iltutmish's minister Nizam al-Mulk Muhammad b. Abi Sa'id Junaydi, studied at a madrasa in Bukhara before settling in Delhi. Al-Juzjani came from Khurasan to Delhi via Ghazna, Mitha, and Uch during Iltutmish's reign.

The immigration of sufis was also important. The Chishti mystic Qutb al-Din Bakhtiyâr Kâkî travelled from Farghana to Baghdad, and from there to Multan and Delhi. In keeping with Chishti abhorrence of state sponsorship, he is portrayed in later hagiographical accounts as nobly resisting Sultan Iltutmish's offers of employment. There were, of course, disagreements between the Sunni ulema and the mystics as al-Hujwiri's writings and the controversy over the legitimacy of singing of mystical poetry (*samā'*) in the Delhi Sultanate period shows. Given the influx of refugees from Khurasan and beyond, most of the doctrinal disputes and conflicts of Khurasan, Ghazna, and Sind under the Ghaznavids and Ghurids were probably continued in Delhi.

MONUMENTS AND INSCRIPTIONS

The Early Jami' Masjid of Delhi

Central to this inquiry into early Sultanate epigraphy is the architectural complex of the early jami' masjid of Delhi (Plates 1–3, 10, 12): its great masjid, minar, madrasa, and two early tombs were the visible centre of Islamic power in India from 1192 until the rise of the Tughluq dynasty in 1320 . Before the advent of the Ghurids, the whole site had been dominated by the Hindu Rajput citadel of Lal Kot, and the immediate area of the mosque had been occupied by the citadel's Vaishnavite temple. Thus the founding of a mosque in this spot by Sultan Mu'izz al-Din and his general Qutb al-Din Aybak meant not only the destruction of the existing temple, it also signified the symbolic appropriation of the land itself. Like the Temple Mount in Jerusalem, this location already had the aura of holiness, and now, reused for an architectural statement of the new order of politics, government, and religion, it became a sign of the conquest.[39]

Qutb al-Din Aybak was the true force behind the jami' masjid complex. Writing during the reign of Iltutmish, Hasan Nizami records that Mu'izz al-Din commanded the demolition of temples in Ajmer and then ordered the construction of mosques and madrasas from their ruins.[40] However, Hasan Nizami clearly credits Qutb al-Din with the construction of the Delhi jami' and its epigraphs: 'Qutb al-Din built the Jami' Masjid at

Delhi and adorned it with stones and gold obtained from the temples which had been demolished by elephants, and covered it with inscriptions in *tughra*, containing the divine commands.'[41] The historical inscriptions in the mosque give credit to both Aybak as its builder in 1192 and Muʿizz al-Din as its patron in 1197, but Qutb al-Din was appropriately recognizing his suzerain.

This architectural complex used a form, the hypostyle mosque, classic in Islam to the west but new to Delhi and its environs. Constructed for the most part out of red sandstone with some decorative marble facing, it also made use of pillars and other materials taken from twenty-seven destroyed Hindu and Jain temples in the vicinity. But these structural elements supported a great number of figural sculptures and were not immediately appropriate for a Muslim place of worship: therefore most of the images were chiselled off, and the rest were concealed under layers of plaster. Through this pragmatic recycling of temple architecture the imprint of the old faith was diminished, a first step in transforming this part of the *dār al-ḥarb* into the *dār al-Islām*. Specific parts of the demolished temples were, however, preserved—most notably the Iron Pillar directly in front of the central arch of the qibla. Stone blocks with figural sculptures were also imbedded in walls and were even used as steps in the mosque's entrances so that the images of the past would be trod underfoot by Muslims coming to pray, a clear sign of the triumph of the new faith and the establishment of a new ruling class, a major theme in the epigraphic programme of the jamiʿ masjid complex over the 128 years of development examined here.

The principal entrances into Qutb al-Din's original mosque are on the east and north sides (Plate 1), and each bears an important Qur'anic inscription in *naskhī* script. At the eastern entrance are two verses from the Qur'an (3: 91–92) that refer to the non-Muslims on the outside and then address the Muslims who enter the mosque:

> Lo! those who disbelieve, and die in disbelief, the (whole) earth full of gold would not be accepted from such a one if it were offered as a ransom (for his soul). Theirs will be a painful doom, and they will have no helpers.
>
> Ye will not attain unto piety until ye spend of that which ye love. And whatsoever ye spend, Allah is aware thereof.[42]

On the inner lintel is a historical inscription in Persian:

This fort was conquered and this jami' masjid was built (in the months of) the year 587 (1191–92) by the amir, the great and glorious commander of the army, Qutb al-Dawlat wa al-Din Aybak Sultani, may God strengthen his helpers. The materials of twenty-seven temples on each of which 2,000,000 deliwals had been spent, were used in this mosque. May God the great and glorious have mercy upon him who should pray for the faith of the good builder.[43]

An additional Persian inscription repeats this information on the arch of the east gate: 'This mosque was built by Qutb al-Din Aybak. May God have mercy on him who should pray for the faith of this good builder.' Historical and Qur'anic epigraphs should be understood as a unity of mutually supporting parts: both verse 91 and the historical information about the source of building materials refer to the conquered Hindu and Jain population and implicitly condemn them for their disbelief. Encouraging spending on pious works, verse 92 reinforces the two historical inscriptions that identify the pious benefactor, Qutb al-Din Aybak.

Qur'an 10: 26 is inscribed over the north entrance and is a promise of salvation and paradise for those who do good. As at the east gate, there is an additional historical inscription in Arabic. It and the Qur'anic citation once again present the Ghurid ruler as someone who is doing good and will inherit paradise: 'In the year [5]92 (1197) this building was erected by the high order of the exalted Sultan Mu'izz al-Dunya wa'l-Din Muhammad b. Sam, the helper of the prince of the faithful.'

These inscriptions are only a small part of the extensive epigraphic programme in virtually every part of the mosque complex. The selection of Qur'anic verses is extremely diverse and complex, the work of religious officials in the army and government of sultans Qutb al-Din and Iltutmish. A notable example of such an important dignitary was al-Juzjani's own father, Mawlana Saraj al-Din Minhaj, who in 1186, five years before the first Ghurid invasion of northern India, 'became the qadi of the forces of Hindustan, and, dressed in an honorary robe, conferred upon him by Sultan Mu'izz al-Din, in the audience hall [or tent] of the camp he established his Court of Judicature.'[44] Although Mawlana Saraj al-Din may not have been still serving as army qadi during the occupation of Delhi, whoever occupied the office would have been the most senior religious official present in the city and the most likely candidate for selection as qadi of Delhi. The development of an epigraphic programme for the new capital's jami' masjid would have come under such an official's authority.

The Minar

Located 10.2 metres from the qibla wall and immediately in front of its central and largest arch is the famous Iron Pillar (visible in Plate 3), cast in the fourth century: it was probably set in place here in front of the site's original Vaishnavite shrine in the middle of the eleventh century and was topped with an image of Garuda, the Hindu god of victory. With the sculpture of the deity removed by Qutb al-Din's builders (presumably the victorious Muslim commander was aware of the irony), the pillar became a suitable, though highly unusual embellishment for the mosque around it and served as another symbolic expression of the displacement of Jain and Hindu faiths by Islam.[45]

This symbol of the conquest was amplified in a more traditional way by the construction of the great minar against the mosque's southern wall, for the minar as a Muslim form functions not only as a *ma'dhana* from which the faithful may be called to prayer, but also as a visible commemoration of victory and as a means of marking a landscape as part of the dār al-Islām (Plate 10). The immediate precursor in the Ghurid lands to the north was the great minar of Jam, slightly shorter and uniformly cylindrical, without the fluting and wedge-shaped articulation of its counterpart in Delhi. Apart from its historical inscription ascribing its construction to Qutb al-Din's overlord, Mu'izz al-Din Muhammad b. Sam, its epigraphic content, as we have noted, consists largely of Qur'an 19 (Maryam).

These preceding, largely non-epigraphic observations are central to an understanding of the inscriptions on the Delhi minar (Plate 15) and jami' masjid (Plate 16), for Qutb al-Din and Iltutmish's construction is a remarkably unified creation. But it is important to remember the construction chronology. The first story was completed under the authority of Mu'izz al-Din b. Sam and Qutb al-Din Aybak. The second, third, and fourth storeys were, according to their historical inscriptions, constructed under the patronage of Sultan Iltutmish as a sign of his devotion to a noted holy man in Delhi, Khwaja Qutb al-Din Bakhtiyar Kaki. The present fifth and final story resulted from extensive repairs to the original fourth storey, damaged by lightning during the reign of Firuz Shah Tughluq (1351–88).

The minar's essential religious epigraphs appear on the first storey in six bands (Plate 15). The styles and disposition of script recall epigraphic achievements in twelfth-century Khurasan and suggest that the designers of these inscriptions were Khurasani or Khurasani-trained calligraphers, who also designed the inscriptions elsewhere in the jami' complex and in the contemporary jami' masjid of Ajmer. The first band has been badly disturbed by later restorations. A fragment of a Persian historical inscription refers to 'the amir, the commander of the army, the glorious, the great.' In addition, parts of two chapters from the Qur'an (6: 11 and 13: 1) can be identified. Both passages refer to disbelievers who do not accept the revelation of Islam, a theme that will recur on the minar and other structures in the complex. In addition, with its distinct reference to the Qur'an itself, 13: 1 points to the actual presence of scripture on the minar itself:

> Alif. Lām. Mīm. Rā. These are verses of the Scripture.
> That which is revealed unto thee from thy Lord is the
> Truth, but most of mankind believe not.

The second band on the minar's first storey offers two inscriptions. The first (59: 21–2) is a basic statement of God's uniqueness and omniscience. It is combined with an Arabic historical inscription referring to the victorious Ghurid ruler:

> ... necks of the people, master of the kings of Arabia and Persia, the most just of the sultans of the world, Mu'izz al-Dunya wa'l-Din ... the kings and sultan, the propagator of justice and kindness ... the shadow of God in east and west, the shepherd of the servants of God, the defender of the countries of God ... the firm ... sky, victorious against the enemies .... the glory of the magnificent nation, the sky of merits ... the sultan of land and sea, the guard of the kingdoms of the world, the proclaimer of the word of God, which is the highest, and the second Alexander (named) Abu'l-Muzaffar Muhammad b. Sam, may God perpetuate his kingdom and rule, and Allah is high, beside Whom there is no God, Who knows what is hidden and what is revealed. He is compassionate and merciful ....

The third band is from Qur'an 48: 1–6 (al-Fath) and begins with a statement relevant both to Islam's recent conquest and to the architectural function of the minar:

> Lo! We have given thee a signal victory,
>
> That Allah may forgive thee of thy sin that which is past and that which is to come, and may perfect His favour unto thee, and may guide thee on a right path,
>
> And that Allah may help thee with strong help—
>
> He it is Who sent down peace of reassurance into the hearts of the believers that they might add faith unto their faith. Allah's are the hosts of the heavens and the earth, and Allah is ever Knowing, Wise—

That He may bring the believing men and the believing women into Gardens underneath which rivers flow, wherein they will abide, and may remit from them their evil deeds—That, in the sight of Allah, is the supreme triumph—

And may punish the hypocritical men and the hypocritical women, and the idolatrous men and the idolatrous women, who think an evil thought concerning Allah. For them is the evil turn of fortune, and Allah is wroth against them and hath cursed them, and hath made ready for them hell, a hapless journey's end.

These six verses promise Allah's guidance, reassurance, and assistance to believers, and offer a very tangible vision of the paradise awaiting the faithful. With their reference to the 'heavens and the earth', they also describe the minar itself, resting on the earth but stretching into the heavens. They end, however, by warning of the fate awaiting not simply disbelievers, but, more specifically, idolators: Hindus and Jains were not among the 'people of the book' belonging to the monotheistic faiths of Judaism, Christianity, and Islam. Thus this third band of epigraphy on the great minar focuses on three main points: God has given Muslims a great victory; God will stand by and support the faithful; God will punish the hypocrites and the idolators.

These verses appear to have been selected with care in order to offer the most direct scriptural reference to the particular situation in which Qutb al-Din Aybak and his followers found themselves. In 629 Muhammad and his followers had been refused permission to enter Mecca. After the Treaty of al-Hudaybiya in the following year the Muslims were allowed into Mecca, and the Prophet ordered the destruction of the idols in the Ka'ba. The 'signal victory' is a reference to these events.[46] The person responsible for selecting these verses for the Delhi minar was therefore drawing an exact parallel between the Prophet's actions in Mecca and the situation in contemporary northern India. In 1191 Sultan Mu'izz al-Din and his general Qutb al-Din Aybak had been defeated at the first battle of Tarain and had been forced to retreat to the Ghurid homeland. On their return in 1192 they were triumphant, and they also destroyed the 'idols', namely, the Hindu and Jain temples of Delhi from whose materials the jami' masjid was built. The parallel with the Meccan experience 562 years earlier was evidence of the unfolding of a divine plan. References to defeat followed by victory will occur again and again in the inscriptions in the complex.

On the fourth band is an Arabic historical epigraph praising Sultan Ghiyath al-Din b. Sam Ghuri, Mu'izz al-Din's older brother and the distant ruler of these new domains, and briefly referring to the loyal younger brother:[47]

The greatest sultan, the most exalted emperor, the lord of the necks of the people, the master of the kings of Arabia and Persia, the sultan of the sultans of the world, Ghiyath al-Dunya wa al-Din, who rendered Islam and the Muslims powerful, the reviver of justice in the worlds, the grandeur of the victorious government ... of the magnificent, the bright blaze of the Caliphate, the propagator of kindness and mercy amongst created beings, the shadow of God in east and west, the defender of the countries of God, the shepherd of the servants of God, the guard of the kingdoms of the world, and the proclaimer of the word of God, which is the highest, Abu ... b. Sam, an ally of the prince of the faithful, may God illumine his proofs.

The fifth band presents chapter 59: 22–3:

He is Allah, than Whom there is no other God, the Knower of the Invisible and the Visible. He is the Beneficent, the Merciful.

He is Allah, than Whom there is no other God, the Sovereign Lord, the Holy One, Peace, the Keeper of Faith, the Guardian, the Majestic, the Compeller, the Superb. Glorified be Allah from all that they ascribe as partner (unto Him).

These verses are followed by all the *asmā' al-ḥusnā,* God's ninety-nine most beautiful names. Their use appears to assert the validity of the doctrine of attributes *(ṣifāt)* of God as an extension of the oneness of God *(tawḥīd),* an important topic in Maturidi thought. The citation of 59: 22–3 and the names of God can be seen as offering Qur'anic support for the compatibility of the doctrines of *tawḥīd* and the attributes of God since the verses assert the oneness of God and then begin the listing of His names. The importance of this doctrine is reinforced by its placement high on the first storey.

Occupying the sixth band is a long inscription from Qur'an 2: 255–60 (al-Baqara):

Allah! There is no God save Him, the Alive, the Eternal. Neither slumber nor sleep overtaketh Him. Unto Him belongeth whatsoever is in the heavens and whatsoever is in the earth. Who is he that intercedeth with Him save by His leave? He knoweth that which is in front of them and that which is behind them, while they encompass nothing of His knowledge save what He will. His throne includeth the heavens and the earth, and He is never weary of preserving them. He is the Sublime, the Tremendous.

There is no compulsion in religion. The right direction is henceforth distinct from error. And he who rejecteth false deities and believeth in Allah hath grasped a firm hand hold which will never break. Allah is Hearer, Knower.

Allah is the Protecting Friend of those who believe. He bringeth them out of darkness into light. As for those who disbelieve, their patrons are false deities. They bring them out of light into darkness. Such are rightful owners of the Fire. They will abide therein.

Bethink thee of him who had an argument with Abraham about his Lord, because Allah had given him the kingdom; how, when Abraham said: My Lord is He Who giveth life and causeth death, he answered: I give life and cause death. Abraham said: Lo! Allah causeth the sun to rise in the East, so do thou cause it to come up from the West. Thus was the disbeliever abashed. And Allah guideth not wrongdoing folk.

Or (bethink thee of) the like of him who, passing by a township which had fallen into utter ruin, exclaimed: How shall Allah give this township life after its death? And Allah made him die a hundred years, then brought him back to life. He said: How long hast thou tarried? (The man) said: I have tarried a day or part of a day. (He) said: Nay, but thou hast tarried for a hundred years.

Just look at thy food and drink which have rotted! Look at thine ass! And, that We may make thee a token unto mankind, look at the bones, how We adjust them and then cover them with flesh! And when (the matter) became clear unto him, he said: I know now that Allah is Able to do all things.

And when Abraham said (unto his Lord): My lord! Show me how Thou givest life to the dead, He said: Dost thou not believe? Abraham said: Yea, but (I ask) in order that my heart may be at ease. (His Lord) said: Take four of the birds and cause them to incline unto thee, then place a part of them on each hill, then call them, they will come to thee in haste. And know that Allah is Mighty, Wise.

Particularly verse 255 (the Throne Verse, which appears with great frequency on buildings and objects throughout the Islamic world) stresses Allah's omnipotence. As in the use of the chapter al-Fath in the third band, the mention of the heavens and the earth once again refers to the minar that linked them. The later verses return to the theme of disbelievers. Verse 256 refers to false deities; verse 257 threatens the disbelievers; verses 258–60 record Abraham's conversation with an unbeliever and describe the divine power to create and maintain life.

Here are compelling allusions to the contemporary social, political, and religious situation. The citation on the sixth band (2: 256: 'There is no compulsion in religion') can be interpreted as a reference to the religious policy that the Muslims saw themselves adopting toward the Hindu/Jain populace. The following verse encourages them to reject polytheism, making faith a matter of free choice but underscoring the punishment awaiting idol-worshipers who disparage Allah. The final three verses turn to Abraham whose devotion to monotheism and whose destruction of idols must have seemed an appropriate object lesson for the polytheists in northern India. These references to the resurrection of life and townships were also evocative allusions to the reuse of sites and materials to build the jami' masjid and minar.

The historical references and naming of patrons constitute a clear hierarchy of authority at the time of the building's construction. On the first band is the phrase, 'The amir, the commander of the army, the glorious, the great,' a reference to Qutb al-Din Aybak. On the second band are Mu'izz al-Din's name and honorifics, and there is a clear allusion to his military successes, notably the victory at Tarain. He is described as 'victorious against the enemies ... the sultan of land and sea ... and the second Alexander.' The third band divides the two brothers' names with a citation from the Qur'an, and Ghiyath al-Din's name appears on the fourth band. Whereas Mu'izz al-Din is 'the most just of the sultans of the world,' Ghiyath al-Din is described as 'the sultan of the sultans of the world' and as 'an ally of the commander of the faithful,' clear reflections of his superior authority, reinforced by the higher placement of his name on the minar. The fifth band includes the names of God and is subordinate to the sixth and highest band that bears the Throne Verse and proclaims that God is the supreme authority.

The lower band on the second story is an Arabic historical inscription and recounts the names, titles, and requisite praises of Iltutmish, the patron responsible for storeys two, three, and four:

> The most exalted sultan, the great emperor, the lord of the necks of the people, the pride of the kings of Arabia and Persia, the shadow of God in the world, Shams al-Dunya wa'l-Din, the help of Islam and the Muslims, the crown of kings and sultans, ... in the worlds, the grandeur of the victorious government, the majesty of the shining religion, helped from the heavens, victorious over his enemies, the bright meteor of the sky of the caliphate, the propagator of justice and kindness, the guard of the kingdoms of the world and the proclaimer of the word of the High God, Abu'l-Muzaffar Iltutmish al-Sultani, the helper of the prince of the faithful, may God perpetuate his kingdom and rule and increase his power and rank.

Over the doorway is a shorter but similar Arabic inscription:

> The completion of this building was commanded by the king, who is helped from the heavens, Shams al-Haqq wa'l-Din Iltutmish-i Qutbi, the helper of the prince of the faithful.

Above these historical inscriptions on the second storey is a band presenting the final two Qur'anic citations on the minar. The first comes back to a central theme by presenting verses 29–30 of chapter 14:

> [verse 28: Hast thou not seen those who gave the grace of Allah in exchange for thanklessness and led their people astray to the Abode of Loss],
>
> (Even to) hell? They are exposed thereto. A hapless end!
>
> And they set up rivals to Allah that they may mislead (men) from His way. Say: Enjoy life (while ye may), for lo! your journey's end will be the Fire.

With its emphasis on the story of Abraham and its several rejections of idolatry, this chapter must have had particular resonance for the Muslim leadership in Delhi. The second Qur'anic selection consists of two verses (62: 9–10) that affirm directly the importance of congregational prayer and the call to prayer from the minar.

The epigraphs on the first two storeys of the great minar present several themes, underlining Allah's omnipotence, the importance of prayer and faithful adherence to Islam, and the pain and anguish awaiting disbelievers and idolators. It is this latter theme which is the constantly recurring message. The selected verses had precise bearing on the new Muslim state in northern India. These significant verses are all confined to the lower storeys, where literate and sharp-eyed persons, familiar with the Kufic and naskhi scripts, could have read them. The remaining Arabic inscriptions on the upper three storeys are solely historical epigraphs, referring to rulers and their works.[48]

Qutb al-Din's Qibla Screen

Under the patronage of Qutb al-Din and Iltutmish a great stone screen was erected on the west side of the mosque's courtyard in order to provide a suitably imposing façade for the mosque's qibla (Plate 3). Designed to resemble qiblas from mosques to the west, it effectively concealed the pillars taken from Hindu and Jain temples (Plate 2) and provided a surface for one of the most extensive epigraphic programmes in Islamic history. Immediately to the west of the famous Iron Pillar stands the screen's high central arch flanked on each side by two lower arches. This area, then, forms the core of the earliest part of the mosque. On the south side of the central arch is the date 594 (1198–9). Late in his reign Iltutmish expanded the jami' masjid and provided a substantial extension of the original screen with three additional arches on each of its sides. On the south of the southernmost of these later arches is the date 627 (1229–30).

It is immediately apparent that the inscriptions, which form a major part of the decorative surface on Qutb al-Din's screen, differ in important ways from the inscriptions on the minar: architectural position therefore seems to have been an important factor in the selection of epigraphs. Briefly, the hadith and Qur'anic verses that are used on the qibla screen put much less emphasis on the punishment awaiting disbelievers and stress instead the importance of worship, the obligations incumbent upon believers, and the power of God.

The screen is like an open book, held vertically in front of its readers (the faithful gathered in worship) to present carefully selected passages from the Qur'an and hadith (Plate 16). Visual support for the imam-khatib leading the community in prayer and delivering a sermon, it is scripture in stone and should be 'read' from right to left in keeping with the movement of the Arabic script. Therefore, anyone facing the screen should begin with the northernmost arch of Qutb al-Din's original mosque. This arch's inscriptions combine three hadiths and a passage from the Qur'an. The first hadith can be found in the al-Bukhari and Muslim collections of hadith. The source of the other two is not known.

> In the name of God, the Merciful, the Compassionate. The Prophet, peace be on him, said: 'Islam is founded on five basic principles: there is no god but God, and Muhammad is the Prophet of God; the offering of prayer; the giving away of the poor-rate; the keeping of fast during Ramadan; the pilgrimage to the House (of God at Mecca) enjoined on those who can afford it.'
>
> And the Prophet, peace he on him, said, 'The mosques are built for God, the Most High.'
>
> And the Prophet, peace be on him, said, 'Whoever visited ... a mosque visited (so to say) the Most High God (Himself), and it is incumbent on the one thus visited to bless the visitor. And all praise is due to God ...'

The principles of Islam are expounded in a clear form, and reference is made to the importance of the mosque as a building of special worth and importance. For the early rulers of Muslim India it was an unquestioned necessity to build mosques of imposing size in order to counter the physical presence of Hindu and Jain temples and to transform the architectural content and outline of the landscape. These three hadiths then can be viewed as a theoretical justification for the building programme undertaken by the Muʿizzi sultans.

The Qur'anic portion of this arch's inscriptions is from chapter 3: 189–93, and these particular verses emphasize God's omnipotence and the need to believe. 3: 189 begins with sovereignty: 'Unto Allah belongeth the Sovereignty of the heavens and the earth. Allah is able to do all things.' Appropriately, it may have been the passage most visible to the worshipping ruler, since the *maqsura* was most often to the right of the main *mihrab*, here the central arch. If this hypothesis is correct, then social authority may have been one of the determinants of an epigraph's placement.

The second arch, immediately to the left, presents the theme of disbelief and destruction in the form of historical examples from chapter 25: 36–9:

> Then We said: Go together unto the folk who have denied Our revelations. Then We destroyed them, a complete destruction.
>
> And Noah's folk, when they denied the messengers, We drowned them and made of them a portent for mankind. We have prepared a painful doom for evil-doers.
>
> And (the tribes of) ʿAād and Thamūd, and the dwellers in Ar-Rass, and many generations in between.
>
> Each (of them) We warned by examples, and each (of them) We brought to utter ruin.

The allusion to the defeat of the non-Muslim peoples of India is obvious, and historical references to Noah's community and to ʿAd and Thamud make it clear that that will be the fate of all those who deny the Revelation. But the arch is thematically balanced by further verses from the same chapter (25: 61–7), which turn to the subject of belief and the blessedness enjoyed by believers. The destruction visited upon disbelievers and the blessedness awaiting believers are therefore thematic opposites on the arch. Faith and prayer were also the themes of the Qur'anic verses on the remaining portion of the southernmost arch of Qutb al-Din's original mosque.

The central, large arch (Plate 3), immediately to the west of the Iron Pillar, bears the date of the arch and portions of two chapters. The first six verses of chapter al-Isra' (17: 1–6) include the famous description of the miʿrāj of the Prophet and go on to deal with the revelation to Moses and the punishment of the Children of Israel for their lapses from it. The fact that these verses ornament the high, central arch immediately in front of the mihrab indicates how very significant they were for the patrons:

Glorified be He Who carried His servant by night from the inviolable Place of Worship to the Far Distant Place of Worship, the neighbourhood whereof We have blessed, that We might show him of Our tokens! Lo! He, only He, is the Hearer, the Seer.

We gave unto Moses the Scripture, and We appointed it a guidance for the Children of Israel, saying: Choose no guardian beside Me.

(They were) the seed of those whom We carried (in the ship) along with Noah. Lo! he was a grateful slave.

And We decreed for the Children of Israel in the Scripture: Ye verily will work corruption in the earth twice, and ye will become great tyrants.

So when the time for the first of the two came, We roused against you slaves of Ours of great might who ravaged (your) country, and it was a threat performed.

Then We gave you once again your turn against them, and We aided you with wealth and children and made you more in soldiery.

To the Muʿizzi patrons verses 4–6 must have offered particularly prophetic references. Muslim Turkish armies, as slaves of God, had invaded India in 1191 under Muʿizz al-Din. Though they had emerged victorious then, the Hindu rulers had not accepted this divine warning. Accordingly, the second Muslim invasion in 1192 ended in Islam's victory, and northern India was ravaged and occupied. The defeated Hindu armies, enjoying such great numerical superiority, were overcome through the fact that they were ignorant of the Revelation and did not have divine support. To the Muslim army and its leadership they were idolators who did not possess a scripture and whose religious practices were the antithesis of their own. As we shall subsequently see, these key verses from chapter 17 preoccupy the three major patrons of the mosque and are central to understanding not only the role epigraphy plays in defining the function of this whole architectural complex, but also the political and religious attitudes of the early Delhi sultans toward their Hindu subjects.

The rest of the central arch supports chapter 23: 1–14, verses that define the obligations of believers and God's role as sole Creator. Together the two Qur'anic selections emphasize divine power, either as destroyer of those who neglect or reject the Revelation or as creator of life and protector of the faithful. Their specific reference to the revelation and to prayer suggests that the mosque's minbar was placed in the immediate vicinity of the central arch.[49]

The adjoining arch to the left supports additional verses from chapter al-Isra' (17: 78–82). The first three verses again deal with the obligations and times of prayer; but verses 81 and 82 turn to a different theme:

And say: Truth hath come and falsehood hath vanished away. Lo! falsehood is ever bound to vanish.

And We reveal of the Qur'ān that which is a healing and a mercy for believers though it increase the evil-doers in naught save ruin.

It was verse 81 that was recited by the Prophet Muhammad as he watched the destruction of the idols around the Ka'ba after the Muslim conquest of Mecca in 630. In India, to the Muslims a country of idol worshippers, it was singularly appropriate. Having coexisted largely with People of the Book in the Muslim lands to the west, this new situation must have seemed similar to the transition from the Days of Ignorance before Islam (the Jahiliyya). Inviting comparison between the Prophet's actions and those of the Ghurids, this verse stated Muslim aspirations and presaged their intent. Verse 82 underscores this point by its reference to the Revelation of the Qur'an, a boon for the faithful in contrast to the destruction toward which the idolators were heading.

Also included on the same arch are the initial verses of the chapter al-Fath (48: 1–5). Verses 1–6 had also been inscribed on the third band of the first story of the minar. Here, however, only verses 1–5 are used—referring to God's victory, support for believers, and promise of paradise–but verse 6, which specifically cites and threatens the hypocrites and idolators, is omitted, so that the inscription focuses on the virtues of belief rather than the punishments awaiting disbelief. This makes good sense, for those to whom it would have been visible would have been the Muslim faithful in the mosque.

Only a portion of the badly damaged southernmost arch is still extant. On it is written one of the more frequently cited hadith: 'In the name of Allah, the Beneficent, the Merciful. The Prophet, peace be upon him, said, "The mosques are the Divine courtyards and structures. The Most High Allah orders their erection confers blessings on their inmates."' In addition, two verses from chapter 30: 17–18 are used that define the times of prayer. Through its epigraphs this arch therefore states the importance of mosques as structures and the need to build them; it then identifies when the faithful should pray. Like the first and northernmost arch of

Qutb al-Din's original screen, this arch combines hadith and Qur'an, a balanced placement that was the result of careful planning. Not only in their combination of hadith and Qur'an, but also in their reiteration of similar themes, the southernmost and northernmost arches form a pair, an integral unit framing and binding together the whole prayer wall screen.

Iltutmish's Extensions to the Qibla Screen

As with the minar, Qutb al-Din's mosque was extended by the third Mu'izzi sultan, Iltutmish, in order to accommodate the growth of the Muslim population in Delhi and to commemorate his many military victories. These 1229–30 extensions are also densely inscribed, and the inscriptions continue the basic tenor of the earlier epigraphs on the original qibla screen. In 1229–30 under his patronage two sections of three arches each were joined to the north and the south of Qutb al-Din's qibla screen, while the outer walls of the mosque on the north, east, and south were extended, more than tripling the area of the building to accommodate the rapid growth of Delhi's population. His own tomb may have been begun at this time, for it is behind the northwest corner and is aligned with the expanded mosque's north wall. As a result of this expansion, the great minar was now situated in the southeast corner within the walls of the enlarged mosque.

The northernmost arch, immediately in front of Iltutmish's tomb (ca. 1235), is in ruinous condition, and only retains some portions of chapter 67: 10–15 explicitly concerned with obedience to Allah and salvation for the righteous. The second and middle arch of Iltutmish's northern extension presents two Qur'anic inscriptions that may have special significance, though for different reasons. Two verses from chapter al-Fath (48: 15–16) that referred to half-hearted followers of the Prophet in the seventh century seem to have been directed here at recent converts to Islam, or to less than enthusiastic Muslims in Iltutmish's own army, or possibly also to the Rajput forces ('a folk of mighty prowess') opposing the Mu'izzis:

> Those who were left behind will say, when ye set forth to capture booty: Let us go with you. They fain would change the verdict of Allah. Say (unto them, O Muhammad): Ye shall not go with us. Thus hath Allah said beforehand. Then they will say: Ye are envious of us. Nay, but they understand not, save a little.

Say unto those of the wandering Arabs who were left behind: Ye will be called against a folk of mighty prowess, to fight them until they surrender; and if ye obey, Allah will give you a fair reward; but if ye turn away as ye did turn away before, He will punish you with a painful doom.

A second long inscription appears on the same arch.

It is composed of ten verses from chapter Ya Sin (36: 1–10):

Ya Sin.

By the wise Qur'an.

Lo! thou art of those Sent

On a straight path,

A revelation of the Mighty, the Merciful,

That thou mayst warn a folk whose fathers were not warned, so that they are heedless.

Already hath the word proved true of most of them, for they believe not.

Lo! We have put on their necks carcans reaching into their chins, so that they are made stiff-necked.

And We have set a bar before them and a bar behind them, and (thus) have covered them so that they see not.

Whether thou warn them or thou warn them not, it is alike for them ....

Its significance here may be quite personal, for these verses with their image of the bound and collared enemies of Islam seem to have been particular favourites of Sultan Iltutmish, the pious warrior. They are unique in appearing also on his ca. 1235 tomb behind the qibla of the northernmost part of his extension of the mosque and on the 1231 mausoleum for his son, Nasir al-Din Mahmud, some five kilometres to the west of the mosque. The two Qur'anic selections are brilliantly juxtaposed. The first passage inveighs against cowardice in the face of a powerful and experienced enemy (the Rajputs); the second presents the utter defeat and surrender of this enemy to whom the Revelation had not been brought before and who are now overcome and shamefully bound. The pious warrior sultan, Iltutmish, is following the example of the Messenger Muhammad, sent to bring the Revelation to those who had not been warned. From its compelling reference to military struggle and victory we may infer that Iltutmish's maqsura in the expanded mosque was located directly in front of this arch.

The third arch, immediately to the north (and right) of Qutb al-Din's original qibla screen, linked it to Iltutmish's extension. Because of this special significance, it bears a historical epigraph dating it to 1223–4. But the greater part of its surface is inscribed with several Qur'anic selections (3: 18; 33: 40–4; 55: 1–3; and 9: 18–19). Together these passages set out key aspects of Islam: divine oneness, Muhammad's unique role as Messenger, God's power to protect human beings, God's infinite creative power, and the duties of prayer, belief, and right action.

The arch immediately to the south (and left) of Qutb al-Din's screen (Plate 3) provides a promise of paradise, a statement of divine omnipotence, and references to the Ka'ba in Mecca, the importance of pilgrimage, and the necessity of belief in the revelation (61: 12–13). Two citations, both from the third chapter (3: 1–4 and 96–102) also appear. To reinforce their proclamation of the final Revelation and their warning not to fall into disbelief by adhering to old faiths, the arch also includes hadith relating to the importance of prayer and a fragmentary hadith pointedly referring to outsiders: '(The Prophet), peace be on him said, "... non-Arabs, none can acquire excellence except through righteousness."'

The second south arch presents some of the asmā' al-ḥusnā, and through selections from three chapters (9: 112; 35: 1–2; 35: 7–12; 3: 132–6; 3: 146–50) largely focuses on the themes of divine creative power, human submission to it, the punishment awaiting those who disbelieve, and God's mercy and forgiveness.

The third, southernmost arch of the south extension returns to chapter Nuh in which Noah warns those who do not serve God (71: 1–5). Verses 6–9 are then omitted, even though they continue this theme with powerful descriptive language. Perhaps there was insufficient space, but it is more likely that it was important to move on to the second theme, namely, an expression of divine creative power and an enumeration of God's blessings in 71: 10–18. On the same arch are verses from chapter al-Isra' (17: 1–6 and 10–12). 17: 1–5 had already been used on the central arch of Qutb al-Din's screen (Plate 3) to refer to the first sultan's victory over the Rajput confederacy in the second battle of Tarain. With notable success Iltutmish had continued this struggle to expand the dar al-Islām into the dar al-ḥarb. With its actual reference to the Bani Isra'il, verse 17: 6 must have seemed a striking metaphoric reference to the power, wealth, and population of the non-Muslim opponents of Iltutmish: 'Then We gave you once again your turn against them, and We aided you with wealth and children and made you more in soldiery.' The comparison is emphasized by the addition of 17: 10–12, since this selection begins by threatening disbelievers with a 'painful doom' and then asserts the divine power that they neglect to acknowledge.

These citations are the finale to the epigraphs that Iltutmish added to the original qibla. They deserve close scrutiny, not only for their content but also for the light they may shed on the reasons behind their selection. Through their references they sum up the sultan's achievement and his place in the Sultanate's history. Iltutmish had spent much of his reign consolidating the military and administrative achievements of Qutb al-Din. He had repulsed Mongol incursions and suppressed vassals who had withdrawn their allegiance after Qutb al-Din's death. Hindu power in northern India had been humbled just as the Bani Isra'il, cited in the Qur'an, had been overcome by a 'people of mighty prowess.' Those who knew the Qur'an would have been so aware of verse 17: 7 (used neither on Qutb al-Din's nor Iltutmish's screen) that it was not necessary to inscribe it. They bore it in their memories:

> (Saying): If ye do good, ye do good for your own souls, and if ye do evil, it is for them (in like manner). So, when the time for the second (of the judgments) came, (We roused against you others of Our slaves) to ravage you, and to enter the Temple even as they entered it the first time, and to lay waste all that they conquered with an utter wasting.

Of the twenty-two sets of Qur'anic inscriptions on Iltutmish's qibla screen, twenty-one are new, used here for the first time in the new Sultanate of Delhi.[50] That he or his theologian chose to repeat verses 17: 1–5 from Qutb al-Din's central arch underscores its importance. This is the only instance in which Iltutmish's additions repeat an inscription already employed on Qutb al-Din's screen. The Ghurids' victory was the victory of God and Muslims ('slaves of Ours,' as God refers to them in 17: 5) that laid the basis for the Sultanate and that offered non-believers the opportunity to accept Islam.

The Tomb of Sultan Iltutmish

The sultan died in 633 (1236), and his tomb is located at the northwest corner of his extension of the qibla screen.[51] Square in ground plan, the building measures fourteen metres on a side. It was originally domed and has entrances on the south, east, and north sides. Exterior facing that may have carried inscriptions is no longer extant, but the mausoleum's interior walls are richly adorned with passages from the Qur'an and hadith, which make it one of the most densely inscribed surfaces anywhere in the Islamic world.

A total of thirty different Qur'anic selections line the interior. A visitor was intended to begin with the east wall, which was opposite the qibla and accordingly provided the primary entrance into the mosque. The inscriptions were meant to be read in sequence and counterclockwise: verses from chapter Ya Sin (36: 1–11) provide the key as to how it should be read. On the north side of the east entrance are the first two verses of the chapter (36: 1–2), which subsequently connects to the east side of the north entrance (36: 3–4), to the west side of the north entrance (36: 5–6), over the main mihrab on the west wall (36: 7–8), then to a band west of the south entrance (36: 9) and a band east of the south entrance (36: 10 and the first three words of 36: 11). The final words of 36: 11 occur to the south of the entrance in the east wall. Thus there is a complete sequence of chapter 36: 1–11 wrapping around the interior at the same eye level: visitors to the tomb first face the mosque (and the back of its qibla) and then turn to the left in a complete circle until they are back where they started. The inscriptions in the tomb give spatial direction and bind the four walls together. The words referring to the Qur'an and to those who heed its message are on the east side facing toward the mosque, while the words of warning and punishment directed toward non-believers are on the walls facing the world beyond the mosque. These words from chapter Ya Sin had also been used on the great minar. They appear on the 1231 tomb of Nasir al-Din Mahmud, too. With their explicit reference to the Qur'an and to the capture and bondage of unbelievers, they must have seemed particularly apt to the rulers of the early Sultanate.

The initial verses of three other chapters are on the east wall, but they are not continued on the other walls. Two of the selections had already been used on the mosque's qibla screen: Chapter al-Fath (48: 1–5) is a promise of paradise to believers; chapter al-Isra' (17: 1–4) begins with the description of the mi'rāj of the Prophet and continues with references to the scripture given to Moses; and chapter al-Qadr (97: 1–3) focuses on the power of the Revelation, a regular theme throughout the Delhi mosque complex and singularly appropriate in a land where the great majority of the population were not People of the Book:

Lo! We revealed it on the Night of Power.
Ah, what will convey unto thee what the Night of Power is!
The Night of Power is better than a thousand months.

The last four verses from chapter al-An'am (6: 62–165) focus on monotheism and divine omnipotence and complete the east wall. The final verse must have seemed especially appropriate for sultan Iltutmish whose reputation for piety was noted by contemporary and later chroniclers.

He it is who hath placed you as viceroys of the earth and hath exalted some of you in rank above others, that He may try you by (the test of) that which He hath given you. Lo! Thy Lord is swift in prosecution, and lo! He verily is Forgiving, Merciful.

Chapter Nuh begins on the north wall (71: 1–4), continues on the east wall (71: 5 to the first four words of 71: 7), and ends on the north wall again (remaining words of 71: 7). It is largely a warning to those who do not listen to God's prophet, and like chapter Ya Sin this passage links the interior's walls with a sustained message of warning to disbelievers. During his long rule Iltutmish had vigorously expanded the Sultanate and had seen at first hand the reluctance of the Hindu population to accept the new faith. Thus the particularly powerful image in 71: 7 may have seemed to the sultan and the Muslim ruling class like a prophetic description of the conquered peoples of northern India:

And lo! whenever I call unto them that Thou mayst pardon them they thrust their fingers in their ears and cover themselves with their garments and persist (in their refusal) and magnify themselves in pride.

In a more poignant and personal reference, 71: 4 from the north wall was repeated on the south wall. Its words of forgiveness were especially appropriate for the tomb of the sultan:

That He may forgive you somewhat of your sins and respite you to an appointed term. Lo! the term of Allah, when it cometh, cannot be delayed, if ye but knew.

Three other themes are limited to the north wall: the obligations of Muslim believers (chapter 23: 1–21), the oneness of Allah (chapter 112: 1–4, and the already cited passages from chapters 71 and 36) that warn disbelievers of the punishments awaiting them.

The west wall supports the tomb's most extensive epigraphic programme, and in keeping with their location on the qibla, the Qur'anic selections focus on the theme of faith rather than warnings and punishment. On the qibla's three mihrabs appear passages dealing with the revelation (chapter 20: 1–12; chapter 56: 77–80), the promise of paradise (chapter 18: 107–10; chapter 61: 12), prayer (chapter 3: 38), and Allah's power to take life (chapter 2: 155–6; chapter 3: 143–6). These last verses are notably relevant to Islam's situation in northern India, since they deal not only with death and the hereafter but also with martyrdom:

> And verily ye used to wish for death before ye met it (in the field). Now ye have seen it with your eyes!
>
> Muhammad is but a messenger, messengers (the like of whom) have passed away before him. Will it be that, when he dieth or is slain, ye will turn back on your heels? He who turneth back on his heels doth no hurt to Allah, and Allah will reward the thankful.
>
> No soul can ever die except by Allah's leave and at a term appointed. Whoso desireth the reward of the world, We bestow on him thereof; and whoso desireth the reward of the Hereafter, We bestow on him thereof. We shall reward the thankful.
>
> And with how many a prophet have there been a number of devoted men who fought (beside him). They quailed not for aught that befell them in the way of Allah, nor did they weaken, nor were they brought low. Allah loveth the steadfast.

Muslim ghazis had brought the jihad to India, and martyrdom with its promise of immediate paradise was a powerful force behind its expansion. Verse 3: 144 in particular had been recited by Abu Bakr after the Prophet's death, and its use here could be seen as an implicit comparison between the Prophet and the deceased sultan, celebrated for his piety and for his devotion to the sunna.

Above and beside the three mihrabs are many Qur'anic selections focusing on a number of different themes. Two verses from 55: 26–7 speak of the ephemeral nature of life as opposed to the eternity of Allah, while the Throne Verse (2: 255) asserts the fact of divine omnipotence. God as unique and all-powerful judge is presented in two selections from chapter 3: 17–18 and 25–6. The obligations of belief are set out in chapter 2: 278–9. Verses 59: 22–3 appear twice on the qibla, each time in association with all or many of the asmā' al-ḥusnā, and may well indicate the influence of Hanafi/Maturidi thought at the sultan's court:

> He is Allah, than Whom there is no other God, the Knower of the Invisible and the Visible. He is the Beneficent, the Merciful.
>
> He is Allah, than Whom there is no other God, the Sovereign Lord, the Holy One, Peace, the Keeper of Faith, the Guardian, the Majestic, the Compeller, the Superb. Glorified be Allah from all that they ascribe as partner (unto Him)!

Those who deny the role of the Messenger, as the Hindus and Jains were doing in not accepting Islam, are described in a single verse, 3: 184: 'And if they deny thee, even so did they deny messengers who were before thee, who came with miracles and with the Psalms and with the Scripture giving light.' To drive this point home, the non-Muslim population of northern India is addressed even more explicitly through the example of the prophet Abraham in 16: 120–3:

Lo! Abraham was a nation obedient to Allah, by nature upright, and he was not of the idolaters;

Thankful for His bounties; He chose him and He guided him unto a straight path.

And We gave him good in the world, and in the Hereafter he is among the righteous.

And afterward We inspired thee (Muhammad, saying): Follow the religion of Abraham, as one by nature upright. He was not of the idolaters.

After all, it was Abraham who had rejected the idolatry in which he had been brought up, had become a devout and fervent monotheist, and had built the Ka'ba in Mecca, the first temple to Allah in Arabia, just as the early jami' masjid of Delhi was the first temple to God in northern India.

The naskhī inscription over the octagonal zone of transition begins, as did 36: 1–11, over the east wall and ends over the south wall. It presents all of chapter al-Mulk (67: 1–30) with its vivid depictions of Allah's creative and sustaining powers, the warning presented to the world through the revelation, and the eternal pains awaiting disbelievers. Above the zone of transition was the base of the dome, only a fragment of which survives over the south entrance. It bears a naskhī inscription containing portions of two verses 3: 26–27:

... Thou withdrawest [sovereignty] from whom Thou wilt. Thou exaltest whom Thou wilt, and Thou abasest whom Thou wilt. In Thy hand is the good. Lo! Thou art Able to do all things.

Thou causest the night to pass into the day, and Thou causest the day to pass into the night. And Thou bringest forth the living from the dead, and Thou bringest forth the dead from the living ....

If, as seems most plausible, the inscription immediately under the dome also supported verses from a single chapter and this inscription also began on the east and ended on the south side, then this fragment represents the conclusion of a lengthy selection from the third chapter which ought to have run from verses 3: 1–28. In that case the dome's base would have presented one of the Qur'an's strongest statements of divine power and the beauty of paradise (both utterly suitable for their placement in the sultan's tomb) as well as one of the most powerful indictments of the disbelief and idolatry that the pious sultan had been determined to root out. In essence, themes articulated throughout the tomb would have been summed up in the dome's base [...]

The Tomb of Nasir al-Din Mahmud

Two major buildings done under Iltutmish's patronage lie outside the confines of the early jami' masjid of Delhi. The first is the tomb of his son and heir apparent who died before him; the second is the so-called Arhai-din-ka-jhompra masjid in Ajmer, an important centre of Mu'izzi power. Both structures are significantly inscribed, and an analysis of them may test some of the hypotheses and conclusions we have advanced about the epigraphic programme of the Delhi mosque.

Sultan Iltutmish's son, Nasir al-Din Mahmud, died in 1231, according to an Arabic inscription on the marble gateway of the prince's tomb that identifies the sultan as the patron in the year 629 (1231–2).[52] Located about five kilometres to the southwest of the early jami' masjid of Delhi, the square building resembles a fortress and served as the centre of a madrasa community that survived well into the Mughal era. A broad flight of steps leads from the stony ground up to the marble-framed entrance. It and the mihrab are the two areas that are inscribed. [...]

The [Qutb] minar 'spoke' to those beyond the mosque's walls, namely, the non-Muslim majority, and its reference to idolators was inscribed with conscious design. The qibla inscriptions in the tomb of Nasir al-Din Mahmud, however, like those in Qutb al-Din's mosque and in Iltutmish's tomb, were planned for the Muslim minority praying and facing the qibla: they were more concerned with the results of prayer and the promise of paradise than with the fate meted out to idolators. The only epigraphs referring to disbelievers in the tomb of Nasir al–Din Mahmud occur in the entrance inscriptions which faced the outside world; and as we have noted, that area offers prominent references to sovereignty, a theme frequently associated with monumental gateways. Disbelievers are not mentioned on the qibla, and any mention of them appears to he deliberately avoided. Instead, the mihrab inside was dedicated to the needs and desires of believers through inscriptions that focussed on God's power to give and take life, pilgrimage, the centrality of monotheism and worship of the one God, and the promise of paradise for the faithful.

The Arhai-Din-Ka-Jhompra Mosque in Ajmer

Qutb al-Din's and Iltutmish's architectural patronage was not limited to the confines of Delhi,[53] and during the same period an even larger mosque was commissioned, the so-called Arhai-din-ka-jhompra masjid in Ajmer (Plate 11).[54] Founded around 1100, the city of Ajmer in Rajasthan had fallen to Ghurid forces in 1192 soon after the second Battle of Tarain. One of the greatest of sufi saints, Mu'in al-Din Chishti, came to Ajmer from Iran in the same year, and his tomb, built around 1455, is a major Muslim place of pilgrimage. An Arabic inscription on the central mihrab combines the date of the mosque's construction (March–April 1199) with one of the Prophet's hadith.[55] Writing during the reign of Iltutmish, Hasan Nizami credits Sultan Mu'izz al-Din with ordering the demolition of temples in Ajmer and the construction of mosques and madrasas from their ruins following the Battle of Tarain in 1192.[56]

A historical inscription on the dome behind the mihrab (Plate 5) gives an additional date for the construction of the original mosque as Dhu'l Hijja 596 (September–October 1200) and cites the builder, Abu Bakr b. Ahmad Khalu al-Hirawi. Two verses from chapter 9: 18–19 frame the mihrab and its arch and deal with the identification and obligations of believers. They appear, too, on lltutmish's extension of Qutb al-Din's jami' masjid in Delhi. According to al-Bukhari, they were among the last chapters to be revealed, and 'Ali b. Abi Talib was instructed to recite them in order to prohibit pagan worship at the Ka'ba.[57] With their identification of the obligations of believers, they offer a powerful historical allusion: the older religious sites of Ajmer had been recently destroyed, in effect preventing Hindus and Jains from worshipping where Muslims now gathered in prayer. They are followed by a hadith that also focuses on prayer: 'Be timely with your prayer before (the time for it) goes by, and be timely with repentance before death (takes you).'

In 627 (1229–30) Sultan Iltutmish ordered the construction of a qibla facade for the Ajmer mosque, similar to its counterpart in Delhi but consisting of seven arches (Plate 11). Two small minars, both now badly damaged, top the central arch. The screen is also heavily inscribed, though its epigraphic programme is less extensive than that in the Qutb mosque in Delhi. The Ajmer inscriptions are restricted in location to the right-hand (north) minar and to the central and two flanking arches.

On the northern minar remnant are two inscriptions. On the lower half is a historical record in naskhī script that identifies Iltutmish as the patron.[58] On the upper half is a citation from chapter 41: 31–4 that emphasizes God's protection, the importance of prayer, the value of submission to God, and the need for forgiveness. This citation does not appear in the early jami' masjid of Delhi.

On the arch flanking the right (north) side of the central arch is a historical inscription citing the individual who may have been the scribe, 'Ali Ahmad, There are also six verses from chapter 49: 1–6 that focus on proper decorum and on wise behaviour. These verses also do not appear on the Delhi mosque. According to al-Bukhari, these verses refer to the controversy between Abu Bakr and 'Umar over the appointment of the governor of the Banu Tamim. They instruct the two to defer to the Prophet's judgment. In this light, the presence of these verses may allude to the controversy surrounding the governance of Ajmer, which Qutb al-Din had assigned to Rai Pithora's son. A second Qur'anic citation, however, is one of the most widely used, namely, the first four verses of chapter 17, which present the Prophet's mi'rāj and describe the faithlessness of the children of Israel. They also embellish Qutb al-Din's qibla screen, Iltutmish's extension of it, and Iltutmish's tomb.

The screen's central arch is inscribed, like the flanking arches, in Kufic, naskhī, and *thuluth* scripts. Unlike the original jami' masjid in Delhi that was built under the patronage of Qutb al-Din, the central arch does not present a citation from the Qur'an. Instead, it gives pride of place to the sultan and patron himself, and bears a very lengthy historical inscription in his praise:

> This construction has been ordered by the sultan, the high, the just, the exalted, the most high shahanshah, the master of the necks of nations, the lord of the kings of the Turks and the Persians, the shadow of God on earth, Shams al-Dunya wa'l-Din, the refuge of Islam and of Muslims, the crown of kings and of sultans, the subjugator of infidels and of heretics, the vanquisher of transgressors and of polytheists, the defender of Islam, the elevation of the triumphant empire and the brilliant nation, the possessor of victory, the amir of the continent, the sovereign of the sea ... the sultan of the East, the fortified by God, the (one who is) victorious over his enemies, Abu'l-Muzaffar Iltutmish al-Sultani, the helper of the caliph

of God, the defender of the amir of the believers, may God elevate his position and make his proof to appear at all times. This (has been completed) on the twentieth of Rabi' II of the year ....

The flanking arch to the left (south) of the central arch is provided with two Qur'anic selections. Six verses from chapter 25: 61–6 exalt God and urge pious and modest behaviour from the faithful.[59] The other passage is chapter 59: 21–4. It also appears in the tomb of Iltutmish in Delhi and focuses on the names of God, a key point of Maturidi doctrine. Thus the content of the inscriptions on the Ajmer screen turns essentially to the same themes as those at Delhi. Two Qur'anic selections (25: 61–6 and 17: 1–4) at Ajmer were obviously particular favourites, either of Sultan Iltutmish or of the person responsible for choosing the inscriptions, since they appear on Qutb al-Din's original qibla screen in Delhi, Iltutmish's extension of it, and on the Ajmer mosque.[60] With their themes of revelation, submission to divine power, and the history of the Children of Israel, they underscore the new social and religious order that the Mu'izzi rulers had brought to northern India.

The epigraphs also offer guidance in the practice of the faith, for they instruct the believer to walk modestly, spend the night in prayer, beg to be spared from Hell, maintain regular prayers, pay the poor rate, and conduct righteous actions. Finally, there are some more direct allusions to the actual structure. The use of the first verses of chapter al-Isra' suggests a parallel between Ajmer and sacred sites in Jerusalem and Mecca. Chapter 9: 18 speaks of those who attend God's sanctuaries, while verse 25: 64 refers to prayer itself. And the mosque's builders refer to the Qur'anic inscriptions themselves on the mosque's qibla with 59: 21, which speaks of a Qur'an descending to humankind.

WORDS AND MEANINGS

For many centuries India had been a land of immigration, remarkable for its ability to absorb newcomers, and this capacity was a vital asset for governance under the sultans. Muslims were no longer simply raiding and looting northern India; they were striving to create an Islamic society. In this endeavour, however, they were confronted by a 'folk of mighty prowess' who were vast in number and far different in religion from the Christians, Jews, and Zoroastrians with whom Muslims had earlier been in contact. They did not accept Islam with anything like the alacrity of the non-believers in the lands to the west, and the Sultanate of Delhi had to depend far more upon the immigration of people of skill and knowledge than upon rapid conversion.

The inscriptions of the Delhi jamiʿ masjid and associated buildings were designed to proclaim Islam's domination and new dominion. They were also selected within the framework of the Hanafi madhhab. Since Qutb al-Din had been raised in the home of a Hanafi jurist and educated with his sons, he was familiar not only with the Qur'an but also with contemporary Hanafi doctrine. Bearing three dates over a seven-year period from 1192 to 1199, the jamiʿ masjid was built during a period of immigration of Muslims from lands to the west. The city's population was diverse, including not only soldiers, but also Muslim merchants, scribes, artisans, and notables, and this migration increased substantially after the Mongol onslaught into Central Asia and Iran began. But initially the core population would have been the army, who settled with their families in and around Delhi and other towns with grants of lands. The army's legal and spiritual guidance would have come from its qadi who, like al Juzjani's father, must have been Hanafi. It was the army qadi, perhaps also appointed as qadi of Delhi, who would have had the requisite knowledge and authority to provide advice on the inscriptions to be used on the jamiʿ masjid, where he also officiated.

Al-Juzjani's work is infused with awareness that God's plan is unfolding in the new Sultanate in India, a view of history that he must have shared with his father. God was present, closer to human beings 'than their jugular veins,' and was guiding them in what was the greatest expansion of the dar al-Islam since the seventh and eighth centuries. The chapters of God's Book resonated throughout their daily lives, and events were unfolding as part of a divine plan that human beings could sometimes perceive in the eternal words of the Qur'an. What might have appeared to be a disaster, like the Hindu victory in the first battle of Tarain, turned out to be a demonstration of God's authority and intent after the stunning defeat of the Rajput confederacy a year later. Scholars could find the evidence of divine omniscience and foreknowledge in the words of chapters like al-Isra' and al-Fath. For the threatened and insecure Sultanate with its tiny population, such proofs were of the utmost importance, and because they had enduring resonance for generations of patrons, they were repeated on monuments and reapplied to fit different occasions. They justified Muslim action, and they were a security, deposited by God for the reassurance of the community. So, it was essential that the Qur'an, with its capacity to explain the past and present and its potential to reveal the future, be made visible and serve as a sermon in stone providing the most relevant texts, whether or not the community was present. It needed to take on monumental form in keeping with the grandeur of the Book. Set up in centres of authority and population, like Delhi and Ajmer, the Word needed to face the faithful and to tower above the nonbelievers. Even if most people could not read the passages, the words were still there, forms that surpassed in beauty and meaning any figural imagery.

In a normative culture it was necessary to set out how people should live. Thus the qibla screens in Delhi and Ajmer (Plates 3 and 11) served as visual presentations of the Law. A righteous society rested on Qur'an, hadith, and shari'a. In a land that in the eyes of the newcomers did not possess a scripture, the new order of things had to be proclaimed, not only orally through the recitation of the Qur'an and through the disputations and explications of legal scholars, but also through the monumental rendering of God's Word. In no other period of Islamic history is monumental epigraphy so abundant, so strident, and so complex as it was here in a still largely Hindu and Jain environment. If the qibla screens looked like huge books held up before their communities, it was because they were.

Viewed in their entirety, the epigraphs on Qutb al-Din's mosque. the extensions and additions by Iltutmish, and those on the Ajmer mosque focus on several themes: divine power; the principles of Islam; the act of worship; the importance of actual mosque structures; and God's support for the faithful and His punishment of unbelievers, particularly through the references in chapter al-Isra' to the destruction of Israel and its temples. There is no specific reference on either the Delhi or Ajmer screens to idolators, the class of unbelievers most strongly attacked on the Delhi minar. Thus we could say that the two mosque screens use pointed references to expound more general religious statements, while the minar in its function as landmark and victory tower is the logical bearer of messages aimed directly at the conquered Hindus and Jains outside the mosque and the community of the faithful. In their prominent epigraphic form these messages underscore the vast distance separating Islam from these other faiths and their figural, hence idolatrous, arts. Even if the Delhi jami' masjid and minar had developed over more than a century and under different patrons, inscriptions were intended to go in some places and not others, for different architectural elements required different epigraphs. Similarly, the two tombs were favoured with passages promising forgiveness and paradise for the deceased.

To the designers and patrons of the early Delhi Sultanate architectural epigraphs had signal importance, as is evident when they are used again and again. Theological issues were of central significance and could be presented in architecture, as the use of the asmā' al-husnā on the minar and on the screen may suggest. The prominence of the Maturidi Kalam and the Hanafi madhhab influenced the selection of epigraphs and would have been important for legal scholars and for the governing elite, but at our remove the reasons for selection are difficult to decipher. Contemporary political history also had a pronounced impact on the selection of appropriately metaphoric inscriptions, like those from the chapter al-Isra'. Such political allusions are probably easier for us to identify now than are the theological references.

Furthermore, these are not rote inscriptions. Instead, they identify those issues that were of central importance to the Delhi sultans and the Muslim ruling class. Whether we regard the architecture of the Ghurid homeland, of neighbouring and influential Iran, or of the many dozens of later Sultanate and Mughal buildings with complex epigraphic programmes, there is no instance of one building's inscriptions exactly repeating another. While individual Qur'anic passages or hadith may be used more than once (as we have seen here in the appearance of the initial verses of the chapter al-Fath on both the minar and mosque), in its totality each epigraphic scheme is unique. If it has content and function, then script on buildings was presumably meant to be read (at least by some of the devout) as well as to be seen. Its appearance, particularly in monumental Kufic and thuluth script styles, undoubtedly lent an aura of sanctity to a site, but it is also clear that God's words and those of Muhammad were carefully chosen in order to convey specific ideas of central importance to the patrons of architecture and to the wider community of the faithful. Not all of those who worshiped there could read the words, of course, but by analogy very few of their French contemporaries had any inkling of the intricate theology that gave intellectual and religious life to the figural sculptures of Chartres cathedral. Epigraphs—or, perhaps more accurately, epigraphic sculpture—functioned on levels dependent upon the worshipper's capabilities and were designed to enhance religious life and elevate the soul.

NOTES

Authors' note: The authors have individually received assistance in their research from one or more of the following sources which they gratefully acknowledge: the University of Victoria, its Centre for Studies in Religion and Society, its Centre for Asia-Pacific Initiatives, the Shastri Indo-Canadian Institute, and the Social Sciences and Humanities Research Council of Canada.

1. For the Dome of the Rock and its inscriptions, see S.D. Goitein, 'The Historical Background of the Erection of the Dome of the Rock,' *Journal of the American Oriental Society* 70 (1950), esp. p. 106; Oleg Grabar, 'The Umayyad Dome of the Rock in Jerusalem', *Art Orientalis* 3 (1959), pp. 33–62; Erica C. Dodd, 'The Image of the World: Notes on the Religions Iconography of Islam', *Berytus* 18 (1969), pp. 35–58; Miriam Rosen-Ayalon, *The Early Islamic Monuments of al-Haram al-Sharif, Jerusalem: An Iconographic Study* (1989); Julian Raby and Jermy Johns, eds, *Bayt at-Maqdis, Part I: 'Abd al-Malik's Jerusalem,* Oxford Studies in Islamic Art, Vol. 9 (1993); and Jeremy Johns, (ed.), *Bay-al-Maqdis, part II: Jerusalem and Early Islam,* Oxford Studies in Islamic Art, Vol. 9 (2000).

2. India is not alone, of course, in having a Muslim ruling class governing a religiously mixed population and in favouring impressive monumental epigraphy. Spain under the Umayyads and Seljuq Anatolia with its rich pre-Islamic figural traditions offer history and monuments that could he usefully compared with early Sultanate buildings in northern India. Like the jami' masjid of Delhi, the Great Mosque of Cordoba is a creation over time, and both monuments experience successive enlargements to provide for gradually growing Muslim populations.

3. Throughout this chapter we refer to this first jami' masjid of Delhi as the 'early' jami' masjid in order to distinguish it from Shah Jahan's great seventeenth-century jami' masjid in Delhi. Locally, the early jami' masjid is referred to as the Qutb mosque (a name derived either from the Iron Pillar or from the first sultan's name) or the Quwwat al-Islam mosque, a much later name of uncertain derivation.

4. C.E. Bosworth, 'The Early Islamic History of Ghur,' *Central Asiatic Journal* 6 (1961): 132.

5. C.E. Bosworth, *The Ghaznavids* (Edinburgh: Edinburgh University Press, 1963), p. 94.

6. R. Hillenbrand, *Islamic Architecture* (New York: Columbia University Press, 1994), p. 174.

7. Arthur U. Pope, *A Survey of Persian Art*, 6 vols (Oxford, 1939), Vol. 2, p. 978.

8. J. Sourdel-Thomine, 'Deux minars d'époque seljoukide en Afghanistan,' *Syria* 30 (1953): 108–21; and A. Bombaci, *The Kufic Inscriptions in Persian Verses in the Court of the Royal Palace of Mas'ud III at Ghazni* (Rome, 1966).

9. Bosworth, 'Ghazna', *The Encyclopaedia of Islam,* 2nd edn (1955), Vol. 2, pp. 1049–50.

10. Daniel Schlumberger, 'Le palais Ghaznevide de Lashkari Bazaar', *Syria* 29 (1952), pp. 251–70, Daniel Schlumberger, et al., *Laskari Bazar: une residence royale ghaznevide et ghoride,* Mémoires de la delégation archéologique, 2 Vols. (1963).

11. J. Sourdel-Thomine, 'Ghaznawids: Art and Monuments', *Encyclopaedia of Islam,* 2nd (ed.) (1965), Vol. 2, p. 1054.

12. The historical accounts of lbn al-Athir and al-Juzjani confirm that Ghiyath al-Din in particular favoured the Shafi'i *madhhab* under the influence of the Shafi'i *faqīh* (legal scholar) Shaykh Wajih at-Din Abu'l-Fath Muhammad b. al -Marvarrudhi, who was critical of the Karamiyya. Bosworth discusses both accounts in 'The Early Islamic History of Ghur', *Central Asiatic Journal* 6 (1961), pp. 130–3.

13. Minhāj al-Sirāj al-Jūzjānī, *Ṭabāqāt-i Nāṣirī,* trans. H.G. Raverty as *Tabakat-i Nasiri: A General History of the Muhammadan Dynasties of Asia,* 2 vols (1881; repr. New Delhi, 1971), pp. 449–51. The term Qarmatians loosely refers to Isma'ilis or various splinter groups of the Isma'ilis .

14. K.A. Nizami, 'The Ghurids', in *History of Civilizations of Central Asia,* (ed.) M.S. Asimov and C.E. Bosworth (Paris: UNESCO 1998), Vol. 4, p. 189.

15. Bosworth, 'The Early Islamic History of Ghur', p. 132.

16. C.E. Bosworth, 'Ghurids', *Encyclopaedia of Islam,* 2nd edn, Vol. 2, p. 1103.

17. A. Maricq and G. Wiet, *Le Minar de Djam, Mémoires de la delegation archéologique française en Afghanistan* (Paris: Librairie C. Klinseck, 1959).

18. K.A. Nizami, 'The Ghurids', p. 189.

19. See Maricq and Wiet, *Minar de Djam,* pp. 69–70.

20. M.J. Casimir and B. Glatzer, 'Sāh-i Māshad: A Recently-Discovered Madrasa of the Ghurid Period in Gargistan (Afghanistan)', *East and West,* Rome [N.S.] 21 (1971), pp. 53–68. For a brief summary of the site and reproduction of its plan, see Hillenbrand, *Islamic Architecture,* pp. 182 and 508.

21. Jūzjānī, *Ṭabāqāt,* p. 453.

22. J.A. Page. *An Historical Memoir an the Qutb: Delhi,* Memoirs of the Archaeological Survey of India, Vol. 22 (Calcutta, 1926).

23. Maricq and Wiet, *Minar de Djam,* p. 25.

24. Ibid., pp. 26–28.

25. Hebrew inscriptions have been found near Ghur that testify to the existence of Jewish colonies, which managed much of Ghurid trade. See André Wink, *Al-Hind: The Making of the Indo-Islamic World, Volume II, The Slave Kings and the Islamic Conquest, 11th-13th Centuries* (Leiden: Brill, 1997), p. 135.

26. The term Maturidi is derived from the tenth-century scholar al-Maturidi who wrote on the Hanafi tradition in Samarqand. Contemporary scholars even referred to this intellectual tradition as the doctrine of the 'ulema of Samarqand' or the 'ahl al-sunna wa'l-jamā'a.'

27. Carl W. Ernst, *Eternal Garden: Mysticism, History, and Politics at a South Asian Sufi Centre* (Albany: SUNY Press, 1992), pp. 25–41 (no. 46).

28. Al-Māturidī, *Kitāb Ta'wīlāt al-Qur'ān,* (ed.), Ibrahim 'Awadayn and al-Sayyid 'Awadayn, Vol. 1 (Cairo, 1971).

29. A. j. Wensinck, *The Muslim Creed* (London: Frank Cass and Co., 1965), pp. 2–3, and p. 246.

30. Abu'l-Qāsim Maḥmūd al-Ẓamakhsharī, *Al-Kashshāf 'an Haqā'iq al-Tanzīl wa-'Uyān al-Aqāwil fī Wujūh al-Ta'wīl,* Vol. 1 (Cairo: Mustafa al-Babi al-Halabi, 1966).

31. K.A. Nizami, 'The Ghurids', p. 42.

32. Ibid., p. 24.

33. Jūzjānī, *Ṭabaqāt,* p. 468.

34. Ibid., pp. 544–5.

35. Along with Samarqand, Bukhara also became a centre of the Maturidi *kalām,* later favoured by most Hanafi scholars opposed to the Ash'ari *kalām* of Shafi'i scholars. For more detailed analysis of the Maturidi presence and role in the Ghurid domains, see Bosworth, *Ghaznavids,* and Wilferd Madelung. 'The Spread of Maturidism and the Turks,' in *Religious Schools and Sects in Medieval Islam* (London: Variorum Reprints, 1985).

36. Jūzjānī, *Ṭabaqāt,* p. 5l3.

37. Ibid., p. 598.

38. Ibid., pp. 598–9.

39. Several inscriptions provide dates for the construction of the mosque. On the east gate an inscription states that the amir, Qutb al-Din Aybak, built the mosque in 1191–2. On the north gate is a second inscription saying that the mosque was built by Sultan Mu'izz al-Din in 1197. On the central arch of the qibla screen is the date 1198–99, suggesting that the screen, which bears most of the building's inscriptions, was added to the original mosque at that time. Inscriptions on the minar mention the names and titles of Sultans Ghiyath al-Din and Mu'izz al-Din, while Nagari inscriptions on the minar give the date 1199, indicating that the minar and the screen were completed in the same year and that Hindu/Jain workers were employed in the complex's construction. Writing during the reign of Iltutmish (1206–35). Hasan Nizami credits Qutb al-Din with the construction of the jami' masjid at Delhi and with adorning it 'with stones and gold obtained from the temples which had been demolished by elephants, and covered it with inscriptions in *tughra,* containing the divine commands'.

(Hasan Niẓāmī in H.M. Elliot and J. Dowson, *The History of India as Told by its Own Historians,* 8 vols [Allahabad: Kitab Mahal, 1963], Vol. 2, p. 222).

40. K.A. Nizami, 'The Ghurids', p. 69.

41. Ibid., p. 76.

42. M.A. Husain, *A Record of All the Qur'anic and Non-Historical Epigraphs on the Protected Monuments in the Delhi Province,* Memoirs of the Archaeoloical Survey of India, No. 47 (Calcutta: Superintendent Government Printing, 1936) is an essential source for any study of Sultanate epigraphy. Historical inscriptions in the complex are published in Page, *Historical Memoir.* All quotations from the Qur'an are from Marmaduke Pickthall, *The Glorious Koran* (London: George Allen and Unwin, 1976).

43. For Persian original and translation, see Page, *Historical Memoir,* p. 29. 'Twenty-seven temples' may not reflect the actual scale of destruction, but instead the system of lunar mansions.

44. Jūzjānī, *Ṭabāqāt,* p. 46.

45. For translations of the Nagari inscriptions on the pillar, see Page, *Historical Memoir* pp. 44–5.

46. Al-Bukhārī cites the following hadith by Anas: 'Verily, We have given you (O Muhammad) a signal victory', which refers to the al-Hudaybiya Peace treaty. Bukhārī, *Collection of the Hadith,* trans. M. Muhsin Khan, MSA/USC Hadith, on-line database, no. 6.60.358 (*http://www.usc.edtt/dept/MSA/reference/searchhadith. html*).

47. For the historical inscriptions and a study of the early jamiʿ masjid site, see Page, *Historical Memoir.*

48, Ibid., pp. 32–34. The uppermost band on the third storey identifies the building supervisor as Muhammad Amir Kuh. The inscriptions on the third and fourth storeys identify Iltutmish as the patron. The upper part of the minar was damaged by lightning in 1369 and was repaired on the instruction of Sultan Firuz Shah, the third ruler of the Tughluq dynasty.

49. On a pillar near the central arch is an inscription identifying the project's supervisor, Fadl b. Abu'l-Maʿali.

50. Many of these inscriptions are, however, repeated on the Tomb of Iltutmish located to the west of the mosque's qibla and discussed later.

51. For an earlier analysis of this building and its inscriptions, see A. Welch, 'Qur'an and Tomb: The Religious Epigraphs of Two Early Sultanate Tombs in Delhi', in *Epigraphy: Its Bearings on the History of Art,* (eds) F. M. Asher and G.S. Gai (New Delhi: Oxford University Press and the American Institute of Indian Studies, 1985), pp. 257–67.

52. This building and its epigraphs have been examined in A. Welch, 'Qur'an and Tomb', pp. 257–267.

53. For another contemporary mosque in Kaman, see Michael Meister, 'Indian Islam's Lotus Throne', in *Islam and Indian Regions,* (ed.), A. Dallapiccola (Stuttgart: Franz Steiner Verlag. 1993), pp. 445–53. Reproduced as Chapter 11 in this volume.

54. See Michael W. Meister, 'The Two-and-a-Half Day Mosque', *Oriental Art* n.s. 18 (1972): 57–63; Robert Hillenbrand, 'Political Symbolism in Early Indo-Islamic Mosque Architecture: The Case of Ajmir', *Iran* 18 (1988), pp. 105–17, reproduced as Chapters 9 and 10 in this volume. The mosque's present popular name, 'Two-and-a-half Day Mosque', comes from the local tradition that it was built in that span of time.

55. 'Built ... (in) Jumada II of the year 595. The Prophet, on whom may be God's blessings, said: Be speedy with your prayers before (its time) elapses and be speedy with repentance before death (intervenes).' Cited in J. Horovitz, 'The Inscriptions of Muhammad ibn Sam, Qutbuddin Aibeg, and Iltutmish', *Epigraphica Indo-Moslemica* (1911–12), pp. 12–34; esp. p. 15.

56. Hasan Nizami in trans. Elliot and Dowson, *The History of India,* Vol. 2, p. 222.

57. Bukhārī, *Collection,* no. 6.60.179.

58. 'The sultan of the sultans of the East, Abu'l-Muzaffar Iltutmish al-Sultani, the defender of the amir of the believers, May God make his kingship and his sovereignty eternal, and may He raise his situation on the horizons' *(Repertoire chronologique d'épigraphie arabe* 10 [1941], no. 4092). The same source also provides the lengthier inscription below from the central arch.

59. Verses 61–7 were also used on Qutb al-Din's screen.

60. Chapter 17: 1–4 are also used on Iltutmish's tomb.

PART IV

Early Mosques in Rajasthan

The 'Two-and-a-half-day' Mosque*

MICHAEL W. MEISTER

Arab Muslims first invaded India in the eighth century, only to be driven back to strongholds in Sind where, for ten generations, they maintained an uneasy truce with the Hindu dynasties of western India. During that period Hindu art flourished, unaware or unreceptive of the art of Islam; and Islam itself only uneasily and for plunder looked toward the great temples of Hindu India.

Yet for a single generation after the Ghoris had finally established a foothold on the plains of Hindustan late in the twelfth century, Hindu and Muslim artistry mixed, before the flood of foreign blood could take the building of monuments out of the hands of local workmen (and of provincial dynasts), and turn Muslim architecture in India to reflect the styles and dynasties ruling elsewhere in the Islamic world.

This paper wishes to introduce one mosque, the Adhāī-din-ka-Jhoṁprā at Ajmer (Plate 11), built in that first grey edge of cultural contact, partly to redraw attention to so fine an example of Indian craftsmanship, and partly to open slightly the door to an evaluation of how and in what ways invading cultures interact.[1]

The Ajmer mosque is the second built by the Slave Dynasty, following the Quwwatu'l-Islam mosque in Delhi. Both used the spoils of Hindu temples in the construction of their pillared halls; both added massive arched screens in front of the lower 'Hindu' halls behind. Yet what had seemed but an expedient in Delhi, shows calculation at Ajmer. Considerable non-Hindu (or 'neo-Hindu') material has been combined with plundered pillars to form the hall, and an organization reflecting a calculated conception of space as an aesthetic medium has made itself apparent. The screen,

*Previously published in *Oriental Art*, Vol. 18, No. 1, 1972, pp. 57–63.

more so than Delhi's, shows, not only a mixing of motifs, but also an aesthetic balancing between the decorative styles of Hindu India and Islamic styles most probably of Afghanistan and Russian Turkistan.

Inscriptions give some sequence to the building of this mosque. On the central *mihrāb* (Plate 5), at the back of the hall is an inscription of AH 595, Jumādā II = AD 1199 April. On the back wall under the roof of the second dome from the centre to the north is an inscription of AH 596 Dhu'l Hijja = 1200 AD September/October, recording the name of Abū Bakr ibn Aḥmed Khālū (?) al-Hirawī as supervisor of construction. On the central arch of the screen an inscription assigns the construction to Iltutmish (ruled 1210–36), and two inscriptions from the northern minaret also refer to Iltutmish of the Mamluk dynasty, giving the usual titles for the Sultan. Behind the second arch from the south an inscription refers to the supervision of one Aḥmed ibn Muḥammad al-Ārid.[2]

That Muslims supervised construction throughout can be gathered from the above inscriptions. That Hindu workmen continued to work for the new Muslim rulers can be determined quickly from the material remains. Previous writers, enamoured of the plunder recorded by the Mamlūks in their building of the mosque in Delhi, have largely called the pillars of the great hall 'Hindu'.[3] They are 'Hindu', but they are not all plundered, a new order having been created by Hindu workmen for their iconoclastic rulers and combined with plundered pillars (images defaced), piled two on one, to give a new height to form the hall.

This new order, the plain-shafted (square to octagonal) pillars in Plate 14, which support the ornate Hindu pillars above, follow Hindu patterns in details: in the ornate pediment to the large diamond pattern, in the down-turned leaf pattern supporting the upper diamond-filled niches. Their starkness and form, however, are new, and not merely rough hewn. The tall foliate diamonds are themselves borrowed from Hindu architecture, but used here to fill niches meant, on truly Hindu pillars, for images of deities and sub-deities.

That such a new order was created, and used in a consistent way to support, tone down, and lend sobriety to the plundered Hindu pillars used above—a use consistent throughout the mosque—is in marked contrast to the disordered plunder in Delhi's Might-of-Islam mosque (Plate 2). That this new order is combined with *two* layers of plundered pillars to give a height and airiness no Hindu interior had then achieved is a sign of the creative impulses stirring in the hearts both of the plunderers and of the plundered.

The lintels in the interior, like the older pillars, show workmanship closely connected with that of the Cāhamāna dynasty defeated by the invading Muslims. So also the ceilings, yet in the ceilings especially there are details which indicate new work combined with old. The central lotuses in several of the ceilings (Plate 18), while certainly made by Hindu workmen, are not used as they would have been in Hindu structures, but are substituted for the deep (and occasionally figured) pendants of the Hindu tradition.[4]

Even the great central ceiling, so closely related to Hindu ceilings, and so much a creation of the Hindu tradition that none but Hindu workmen could have made it, still seems to this author, from certain of its details, a work commissioned for the Muslim overlords. No provision is made for the bracket figures required of any Hindu ceiling of this dimension. Instead, small lotuses figure where the upper sockets for the brackets would have been, and the lower bases are absent entirely. The excessive use of the tall-diamond motif between the cusped clusters of the upper ceiling, and especially the inclusion of a band of these diamond niches between the two lower cusped courses of the ceiling (the band where bracket bases should have appeared, and where custom normally puts figured niches) are not consistent with pure Hindu tradition, but have some consistency with other material which, to this author, seems to have been made newly for this mosque.[5]

Of the great screen, of course, there is no doubt. Built for Iltutmish, its Kufic inscriptions and quotations from the Koran leave no doubt of its Islamic origin. Some of its decoration is related to that on the towers of Ghazni; and the crisp and repetitive Kufic patterns (Fig. 6. centre) particularly refer to contemporaneous brick decoration in Islamic Turkistan[6]).

Many of the arabesque and filagree floral and foliate patterns, also, seem certainly out of Islamic pattern-books; their geometric symmetry, drawn in fine and balanced lines against the dark background of shadow, remind one of later Persian tile-work. Yet not all the decorative work is made so, and though earlier Hindu floral work was marked by great plasticity,[7] it is the shadow filagree that marks this work aesthetically apart from the Hindu, and not its flatness. The right of centre band (Plate 19), with its flat foliage accented by shadow rather than set against it, still closely reflects Hindu patterns at Nāgdā in the late tenth century, or the crisp, dry, but elegant patterning of the Kacchapaghāta Sās-Bahu temple at Gwalior dated 1093 AD.[8]

The cusped arches of this screen (Plate 11) while reminding us and perhaps the Muslim supervisors of certain Arab arches, must probably have reminded the Hindu carvers of the *toraṇa* arches of their own tradition; and many of the punctuating bands and mouldings are taken directly from the temple wall. In Plate 19, two important temple mouldings appear, used vertically rather than horizontally as on the temple, but clearly from that source. One is the *kalaśa*, or round moulding covered with *ratna* or diamond pattern; the other the knife-edge moulding (*karṇikā*) used at the base of the medieval temple (compare Plates 19 and 20). The dot-and-diamond, recess with sunk stepped-diamond, and the chain-of-buds motif are also commonly found in the Hindu temple's decorative repertoir.

To sum up: the Aḍhāī-din-kā-Jhoṁpra mosque at Ajmer, built by the first Islamic dynasty to settle in India, and at the capital city of the strongest Hindu dynasty with which they had had to fight,[9] continued to employ Hindu workmen, who not only rendered new patterns provided by their Islamic patrons, but modified and transformed elements from the Hindu tradition.

If we can gain evidence from this example for a discussion of cultural interaction, our conclusions might be as follows: Material borrowed by the Islamic rulers from Hindu sources were several. First was material plundered and reused; second, material borrowed and modified, as the ceilings at Ajmer. Other concepts were transferred, as the toraṇa arch or the temple mouldings: both examples of a sort of empathetic response of local workmen, finding similes between elements in the local tradition and alien demands. Plunder, compromise, and simile modifying the dominant tradition: and finally, Hindu workmen themselves found stimulus from new requirements, bringing to fruition certain trends potential in their own tradition. One such is the tendency toward an etched, non-plastic, stencilled decoration; another, a desire for height and space, without heaviness, which Hindu temple *maṇḍapa*s had sought for but not fully realized.

A further conclusion might be that such blending occurs only where a culturally weak power conquers a culturally strong one. The 'Slave' kings did not carry much cultural baggage when they first built their dynasty, and the Cāhamānas they conquered at Ajmer had an active, developed, and refined artistic tradition. But as the Delhi sultanate settled into power—even by the end of Iltutmish's reign—its lines of communication with Islamic cultures elsewhere strengthened and it turned away from its early flirtation with, and dependency on, its dependent people.

The 'two-and-a-half-day' mosque thus was a short-lived phenomenon, unproductive, but the kinds of mixing rawly visible in its art, more subtly operate throughout the history of Islamic India. In one later instance—that of Gujarat in the fourteenth and fifteenth centuries—where conditions of an artistically weak conqueror ruling over a strong living tradition again occurred, and persisted, a major and successful mutation was produced.[10]

NOTES

1. Dr Oleg Grabar first gave the author an opportunity to think over these questions by inviting a lecture on early Islamic architecture in India for his course at Harvard University.

2. Z.A. Desai, 'List of Published Muslim Inscriptions of Rajasthan', *The Researcher, A Bulletin of Rajasthan's Archaeology and Museums*, X–XI, 1970–71, pp. 1–3. Also *Epigraphia Indo-Moslemica*, 1911–12, pp. 15, 29–30, 33.

3. For the Delhi mosque and inscriptions see J.A. Page, 'An Historical Memoir on the Qutb: Delhi', *Archaeological Survey of India, Memoir No.* 22, 1926. James Tod called the mosque a Jain temple (*Annals and Antiquities of Rajasthan*, 1827, Vol. I, p. 779); James Fergusson, *History of Indian and Eastern Architecture*, 1910, Vol. II, p. 211, comments: 'Like the remains at Old Delhi, the entire plan is Moslim, whilst the columns and roofs are the spoils of Hindu temples.' Because important inscriptions of the Cāhamānas referring to a Sanskrit college were unearthed in the Ajmer mosque in 1875–76 AD, many have written of the mosque as a converted Sanskrit college. For one version of this opinion see D.B. Har Bilas Sarda, *Ajmer: Historical and Descriptive*, Ajmer, 1941, chapter VII.

4. Some question should be raised of the possibility of 'restoration' in the nineteenth century also. The Archaeological Survey had at least, at that time, changed the conical outer shapes of the domes (see Fergusson, History of Indian and Eastern Architecture, Fig. 377 and Footnote 1) to 'better hemispherical ones'.

5. My suspicions about these ceilings I have checked with Sri M.A. Dhaky, whose book, *The Ceilings in the Temples of Gujrat*, (Baroda, 1963), is the most authoritative study of Hindu (and of course Jain) decorative ceilings.

6. For comparative material see Derek Hill and Oleg Grabar, *Islamic Architecture*

and its Decoration, (London, 1964); Alessio Bombaci, 'Introduction to the Excavations at Ghazni', *East and West,* New Series, 10, 1–2, March–June 1959; A.U. Pope, *A Survey of Persian Art,* (London, 1939), plates.

7. The 'plasticity' of the vegetal patterns on the Delhi-mosque screen leads Percy Brown to see Hindu workmen behind it, while he finds that the Ajmer decoration 'has become rigid under the more strict application of the Koranic prohibition' (*Indian Architecture: Muslim,* Bombay, no date, p. 13).

8. Oleg Grabar's comment that 'the mosque at Ajmir shows the translation of Iranian architecture into Indian stone' (Hill and Grabar, *Islamic Architecture and its Decoration,* p. 72), while somewhat facile, is not inapt.

9. The Cāhamānas and the Mamlūks struggled over Ajmer for several years, with the Muslims or their feudatories conquering and losing the city more than once. The Muslims were at times allied with various factions of the Hindu rulers, and for some time placed one of the Cāhamāna families as feudatory at Ajmer. For their history, see Dasharatha Sharma, *Early Chauhan Dynasties,* Delhi, 1959.

10. M.A. Dhaky, 'The Minarets of the H̲ilāl K̲h̲ān Qaẓi Mosque, Dholka' in press with the *Journal of the Asiatic Society,* 14, no. 1, 1972, pp. 18–24, discusses the formal interaction between Islamic and Indian forms in the minaret of one of the Gujarat mosques.

Political Symbolism in Early Indo-Islamic Mosque Architecture: The Case of Ajmīr*

ROBERT HILLENBRAND

In studies of Indo-Islamic architecture, pride of place has traditionally and justifiably been accorded to the Mughal period. In their imperial scale and quality these buildings yield nothing to the best that Ottoman Turkey and Safavid Iran could produce. In the sixteenth- and seventeenth-century monuments of Lahore, Delhi, and Āgra, Indo-Islamic architecture has unquestionably attained maturity in an assured blend of indigenous and western Islamic traditions. The ready accessibility of these sites has ensured that they receive ample exposure. But this very celebrity has tended to rob pre-Mughal Islamic buildings of their place in the sun. This is intrinsically a pity, for Sultanate architecture is a rich field of study in its own right.[1] Such neglect is not merely a minor hiccup in the steady process whereby Indo-Islamic architecture is at last becoming better known. More seriously, it also means that the process of acculturation which, in the field of architecture, culminated in the Mughal buildings,[2] is still insufficiently explored. The various false starts in this evolutionary process have not all been identified, and there is even some doubt as to the principal landmarks along the way.

Obviously, some features of Hindu, Buddhist, and Jain architecture were totally unsuitable for Islamic purposes, and were from the very beginning rejected out of hand.[3] Others could be adopted without a second thought.[4] In yet other cases, a period of experiment seems to have been required before the element in question was accepted or rejected. Thus progress was by fits and starts. The political fragmentation of the

*Previously published in *Iran*, Vol. 26, The British Institute of Persian Studies, 1988, pp. 105–18. In the present version, some portions of the text, notes, and illustrations have been removed. For the complete text see the original version.

subcontinent in the Sultanate period (1191–1526) could only accentuate the spasmodic nature of this development. In some areas, such as Delhi, where building continued virtually without interruption for centuries, an integrated style had time to emerge. Elsewhere the efforts of an energetic patron or dynasty would generate some distinctively local response to the problem of fusing indigenous architectural traditions with those deriving from the more thoroughly Islamicized areas to the west, notably Afghanistan, Iran, and Central Asia.[5] It is a measure of the relatively neglected state of this field that the portmanteau term 'Sultanate architecture' still has general currency. Yet it covers a period of well over three centuries and an area which at its furthest extent measures 2,000 miles from west to east and over 1,000 miles from north to south.[6]

Within this extensive continuum of time and space, some areas are of course plotted relatively better than others. This is especially true of Delhi throughout the Sultanate period[7] Even so, the crucial first generation of Muslim dominance in northern India has yet to receive the full attention it deserves. This is curious on three counts. First, common sense argues that this first encounter between two broadly-speaking incompatible building traditions would set the tone for what was to follow, and the direction taken at this time is therefore of crucial importance to the historian. Second, the initial encounter between these two disparate traditions is intrinsically worthy of study.[8] Third, the number of surviving monuments which date to this period[9] is very scanty indeed. Chief among them are the mosque at Kanauj, popularly known as *Sitā-ki Rasoī* or 'Sitā's Kitchen';[10] the Shāhī Masjid in Khatū;[11] the Chaurasī Khamba mosque in Kamān;[12] the Quwwat al-Islām mosque in Delhi, with the Quṭb Minār attached;[13] and the Arhāī-din-kā-jhonprā mosque in Ajmīr. Among the slightly later buildings which could be brought into the discussion are the mausolea in Delhi datable to the period of Iltutmish;[14] the buildings at Bada'ūn;[15] a gateway at Nagaur;[16] and the Ukhā Mandīr at Bayāna.[17] It is with the mosque at Ajmīr that the present article is concerned.

One aim of the analysis which follows is to disentangle local elements from those which have been imported, while identifying those features of the design which may claim to be original. It will be seen that what is either imported or original is of much greater moment in the design that what is local, and this finding has implications which extend beyond the remit of architecture alone. Indeed, the principal remit of the discussion will be to attempt to show that there was a psychological, even a propaganda, dimension to the building. This element is frequently encountered in the very first monuments erected by Muslims in recently conquered territory. Cases as diverse as the Dome of the Rock, the Great Mosque of Damascus, and the Ottoman mosques of Istanbul come to mind. So too, but with a slightly different emphasis, do the Quṭb Minār and the minaret of Jām. The relevance of these parallels will be explored shortly.

The mosque at Ajmīr (Plate 11) bears a curious title, 'The two-and-a-half days', which refers to a fair of that duration formerly held on the spot and has nothing to do, as local tradition would have it, with the miraculous completion of the mosque within so short a space of time.[18] It may be noted parenthetically that the standard location of a mosque in the mediaeval Islamic world was amidst bazars; so in this respect the Ajmīr mosque conforms to type. Its *miḥrāb* inscription (Plate 5) states that it was built in Jumādā II 595/March–April 1199, which puts it in the reign of Quṭb al-Dīn Aibak, a *ghulām* of the Ghūrid ruler Muḥammād b. Sām and the first sultan of Delhi, who may well have been the patron responsible for its erection.[19] In form the mosque comprises a square enclosure entered by a main portal to the east and a subsidiary porch to the south, both centrally placed. Within that enclosure, only the western sector has remained in a tolerably good state of repair. It consists of a *muṣallā* which in its present state measures some 79 by 17 m. and whose roof, which includes five large and five small domes, is carried on seventy pillars or pilasters (Plate 14); from the exterior, however, all this is masked by a great seven-arched screen (Plate 11). This was a slightly later addition to the original mosque and was erected, probably *c.* 627/1229–30,[20] by order of Iltutmish, the son-in-law of Quṭb al-Dīn Aibak and his successor as Sultan. It clearly had as its model the similar screen which that same Quṭb al-Dīn Aibak had placed in front of the muṣallā in his embellishment of the primitive Quwwat al-Islām mosque in 594/1197[21] (Plate 3) and its extension in 627/1229–30 by Iltutmish.[22] Multi-flanged towers were placed at three of the four corners; the fourth corner abutted on a rocky outcrop. This brief description should suffice to set the context for the discussion which follows; much additional relevant information, which there is no need to recapitulate here, is available in the articles devoted to the building by Cunningham,[23] Garrick,[24] and Meister.[25]

Despite the extensive restoration of the mosque under British rule in 1875–8 and again in 1900–3,[27] there seems to be no published record of excavations on the site. Thus there is no archaeological confirmation, highly desirable though this would be, of the literary tradition that the mosque was built upon the ruins of a Jain college erected in 1153 and already damaged by the ruler of Ghūr, Muḥammad b. Sām.[28] The lavish use of Jain spolia in the muṣallā is certainly strong circumstantial evidence that the literary tradition is well founded; but it is scarcely conclusive in itself. The material could easily have come from other Jain buildings in the vicinity. There is even some doubt, in published references to the mosque, as to whether the domes were built to order, or were also spolia[29]—for their corbelled construction would have made it a simple matter to dismantle and re-erect them. Given the strong likelihood that in either case the craftsmen were native Hindus, the distinction, though worth making, is perhaps not crucial. More to the point, perhaps, is the fact that the mosque in its original state was so un-Islamic that it could be taken for a Jain temple.[30] Yet these reservations are not enough to discredit the literary tradition that the mosque was founded on the site of a Jain temple, and the accuracy of that tradition will therefore be assumed in what follows.

For if the psychological dimensions of this building in its own time are considered, it will be seen that the Jain college provided an ideal site. It was, after all, almost brand new. To judge by the spolia now incorporated in the mosque, it was a splendid building and its stonework was of high quality. To demolish such a very recent building, a monument of the local religion, and to use its material to build a new religious monument, this time of the conquering Islamic faith, and to usurp the very site of the vanished Jain college for the purpose, had an unmistakable significance both political and military. It was an affirmation in stone and mortar that Islam had come to stay, and it served notice on the local people that the new faith was implacably intolerant of the local religion. The Jains, after all, did not share with Christians and Jews, whose scriptures the Muslims revered, the preferential religious, social and financial status *of dhimmīs*.

In this context, the method whereby spolia were employed (Plate 14) deserves notice. It would no doubt have been simpler, quicker, and cheaper to leave parts of the Jain college standing, as was indeed done in other, non-Indian, contexts, like the Iranian village of Yazd-i Khwāst, where a fire temple was left largely intact but for the addition of a miḥrāb.[31] Similarly, at Hagia Sophia and in the Gothic cathedral of Famagusta in Cyprus, a miḥrāb and *minbar* sufficed to assert the Islamic presence.

Why was this not done at Ajmīr? It may be suggested that the situation in northern India at the time was highly volatile and permanent Muslim settlement of the territory was not a foregone conclusion.[32] The situation called for a show of strength, a clear statement of intent, Compromises were dangerous.

The same situation applied at Kamān (Plates 9 and 13), at the Ukhā Mandīr, and, most significantly, Delhi. There the first mosque, erected by the selfsame Quṭb al-Dīn Aibak, was constructed of spolia from not one but from twenty-seven[33] Jain (and in this case also Hindu) temples, and it bore the telling name Quwwat al-Islām 'Might of Islam'. That might was given still more striking expression by the gigantic Quṭb Minār (Plate 10), which is labelled a 'pillar of victory' not in its Arabic but in its Nagāri inscriptions[34] and which bears on its lowest storey—and therefore in a more legible location than most of the other inscriptions—the first verses of the Sūra of Victory (XLVIII, 1–6).[35] Its message to the local non-Muslims could scarcely be more explicit. The case of Delhi thus sheds much light on that of Ajmīr. The root-and-branch destruction of the Jain building there was surely intended to convey the full power of the Muslim commitment to this newly-won land. So thorough was the destruction, indeed, that the Jain columns were not reused just as they were but were sawn apart and then re-erected on top of each other, as if to underline the total triumph of Islam.[36] Elsewhere in the mosque, fine pieces of carving were reemployed as secondary building material, and thus by implication despised. The dismemberment of the columns was carefully done so as to winnow out areas of carving with human figures on them.[37] These have subsequently been found in the area of the mosque and are currently preserved in a hall on the east side of the courtyard. In much the same way, the sacred lingam of the god Shīva was reused on the threshold of the mosque at Banbhore,[38] so that every Muslim entering the building should trample the hated image underfoot, an example followed some three centuries later by Mahmūd of Ghazna, who sent fragments of the lingam of Shīva at Somnath to Ghaznī to form steps at the entrance of his own palace and of the Friday Mosque, while other portions were sent to Mecca and Medina to be set into public thoroughfares.[39] Much further to the west, the same motive caused Pharaonic reliefs to be used to deck the thresholds of some mediaeval Egyptian buildings.[40]

These remarks should help to clarify the role of the mosque as a metaphor of domination at this particular time and place. If they are well founded, the location of the mosque *vis-à-vis* the town itself will fall into place as a secondary consideration. Nevertheless, it too may have been a contributory factor to the Muslim decision to build the mosque on this particular spot. Ajmīr is a city of many hills, and the mosque is advantageously set in a small declivity halfway up one such hill. Its position is thus commanding without being isolated or unduly difficult of access.

Four flights of stairs, totalling thirty-four steps in all, create a suitably imposing processional approach to the mosque; similarly, the original Quwwat al-Islām mosque in Delhi had two such flights of stairs leading to the entrance (visible in Plate 1), as did the mosque at Bari Khatū (Plate 8). Such a feature seems to have been borrowed from the Western Indian temple tradition.[41] At all events, it was to become a favoured device in Indian mosques, possibly because it connoted a sense of solemn anticipation and—like the platform on which these mosques were so often built[42]—an appropriate separation of the sacred from the profane. At the time the Ajmīr mosque was built, this development of course lay far in the future. Nevertheless, it may be suggested that its introduction here was a deliberate part of the general policy to exalt the mosque and thus the new faith and polity which it represented.

The lack of excavation referred to above makes any conjectural reconstruction of the mosque in its first phase somewhat hazardous. The columns and domes of the *muṣallā* (Plate 14)are the only elements which may confidently be assigned to this period. Since a *miḥrāb* would have been required from the beginning, that feature (Plate 5) is probably contemporary with the pillars and domes. It is in the highest degree unlikely that the original mosque was no larger than this. It would scarcely have had the desirable psychological impact had it been so diminutive. Rather would it accord with normal Muslim precedent if the muṣallā had had a courtyard, complete with enclosing wall adjoining it directly to the east. Again, normal precedent would have dictated an enclosing wall close to the northernmost and southernmost files of columns in the muṣallā. No traces of such walls exist, but against this it must be noted that a gap of some 30 m. between the outer extension of a muṣallā and the exterior wall of the mosque is apparently unprecedented in Islamic architecture at this time, though it was frequently to occur later in Indian mosques. It seems preferable to hypothesize that the mosque was not nearly so wide originally as it is now, and that the enclosing walls were removed when the portal screen (Plate 11) was added because the latter was too wide to be accommodated within them. It must be admitted, however, that no break in bond can be detected at the key spots on the inner and outer faces of the *qibla* wall. This difficulty, in turn, need not prove insuperable, for the construction of the mosque walls within their ashlar facing is of roughly worked stones, and thus the face of the wall only, rather than the entire wall itself, could have been rebuilt at the time that the mosque was extended *c.* 1200.

Thus there seem to be essentially three possibilities: first, that the original mosque comprised only the pillared muṣallā; second, that it comprised the pillared muṣallā plus a courtyard, the whole enclosed by a perimeter wall, now largely or wholly gone;[43] and third, that it was identical with the present mosque minus the screen in front of the muṣallā. The second of these possibilities accords most closely with the norms of mediaeval mosque architecture and therefore seems the most likely solution; it would also reflect the form of a Jain temple most closely.[44] The conjectural restored plan made by Cunningham incorporates these assumptions, with the addition of a *riwāq* of domed bays encircling the courtyard. Nevertheless, there is almost as much to recommend the third possibility.[45]

The question that naturally arises at this point is, why it was deemed desirable not only to extend the mosque within a decade but also to give the extension a much more pronounced Islamic character? If the tentative conclusion reached in the previous paragraph is the correct one, the extension would have involved also the entire perimeter wall complete with corner towers and processional staircase preceding the entrance. That this was no random exercise of patronage is shown by the parallel and exactly contemporary case of the Quwwat al-Islām mosque at Delhi.[46] There, too, a mosque built of Hindu or Jain materials (as was, incidentally, another of the very early mosques, also sited in a major centre of Hindu power, that of Kanauj) was within a decade given an arcaded screen in front of the muṣallā. Such a proceeding is not entirely without precedent in Islamic architecture. One might, for example, cite the case of the Iṣfahān *jāmi*ʿ, where the courtyard was simultaneously reduced and embellished in Būyid times by a continuous screen, a mere one bay in depth, which was tacked on to the existing façade.[47] But at Ajmīr and Delhi it is hard to believe that the motif for such an expensive facelift was mere embellishment. It seems preferable to suggest that these two mosques, both erected in cities of major strategic importance which had been selected as the principal capitals of the new Muslim state, were perceived as still being too Hindu or Jain in character, and that Iltutmish was therefore concerned to make them much more obviously Islamic. In that case, the refurbishing of both mosques, no less than their original construction, can be seen to have a politico-religious dimension. Thus to begin with, the mere construction of a mosque, an alien building in that environment, was enough to announce the new dispensation; the bold expansion of the building and the addition of these elaborate expensive screens document the next stage in the ongoing process of Islamization. This point will be developed in more detail later.

Given that the fall of the three capitals of the major empires of northern India—Delhi in Dhu 'l-Ḥijja 588 to Muḥarram 589/December 1192 to January 1193,[48] Ajmīr in 589/1193[49] and Kanauj in 595/1198[50]—was followed in short order by the erection of ambitious mosques in these cities, it is hard to avoid the conclusion that such mosques were intended to serve not only as places of worship but as highly visible symbols of the conquering faith. Obviously, their effectiveness in this role was directly proportionate to their size and to the location as well as the splendour of their decoration.

The inscriptions confirm this interpretation. There is no evidence that the original mosque bore any Islamic inscriptions at all, apart from those in the miḥrāb, and the craftsman's inscription of 596 AH discussed below. The contrast with the work of Iltutmish is indeed striking. As with that ruler's work at the Quṭb Minār,[51] inscriptions proliferate. Two inscription bands decorate the main entrance, and their central location as it were elbows aside the ornament in the local style; the portal screen to the muṣallā has no less than six inscription bands (Plate 11); a craftsman's signature, almost assuredly not in its original place, has been let into the back wall of the muṣallā immediately under the roof; and the better-preserved northern minaret of the screen has a further two[52] which presumably had their counterparts on the southern minaret, which is now a mere stump. Finally, there are two inscription bands in the miḥrāb (Plate 5) which have already been mentioned. Of these fourteen inscriptions—which do not include the fragmentary epigraphs found in the courtyard, which presumably also had their place on the building[53]—more than half are long bands. Most of these are as broad as the bands of abstract ornament next to them, and they have a correspondingly powerful visual impact. All are in Arabic. This plethora of inscriptions, which finds no relevant contemporary parallel in Iran proper, an area that is otherwise the source for so much of the distinctively Islamic element in the earliest Sultanate architecture, is nevertheless a major feature of such later twelfth-century Ghūrid monuments as the minaret of Jam,[54] the mausolea of Chisht[55] and the Shāh-i Mashhad *madrasa*.[56] In the remote area of Afghanistan where these last are to be found, Islam was still a relatively recent phenomenon,[57] and the repeated emphasis on these alien but striking inscriptions served to proclaim the new order. Similar conditions applied in contemporary northern India. The principal difference between the two areas was that Ghūr had previously been pagan whereas northern India had been a meeting point of many religions for millennia. The existence of well-established local religions at Ajmīr and Delhi perhaps made it expedient to impose the physical presence of Islam in a more gradual way. If so, the first stage was to build mosques of material looted from local places of worship; the second was to add further elements of structure and decoration which were more purely Islamic. The first stage may conveniently be interpreted as a naked assertion of power at the expense of the vanquished; but considerations of time, to say nothing of expense and political expediency, may also have led to this initial solution of the problem of providing the Muslims of Ajmīr with a permanent and impressive place of worship. As soon as the situation had stabilized sufficiently, the way was open for a more subtle approach whereby the view faith might advertise itself in a more worthy and characteristic fashion. The first stage asserts; the second persuades. It is this second stage that was carried out by Iltutmish and in which inscriptions played so central a role. It comes as no surprise that the mausoleum of one who understood the symbolic power of the written word so well should also be festooned with inscriptions to an inordinate degree.[58]

In this context, the role of the miḥrāb (Plate 5) calls for some discussion. If, as suggested above, the main entrance dates from the time of Iltutmish, and if the miḥrāb would have been required from the outset for liturgical reasons, its Arabic inscriptions might well have been the only ones in the mosque. Certainly, the first stage of the mosque cannot have had the same degree of emphasis on epigraphy as did the extension of Iltutmish, and it follows that the impact of the miḥrāb would have been correspondingly greater in the primitive mosque than it could have been a generation later. What could be more fitting than to have the Arabic inscriptions concentrated on the very spot which marked the prime religious focus of the mosque? Appropriately enough, the inscriptions comprise, besides the brief reference to the date of construction, a quotation from the Qur'ān and a *ḥadīth.*[59] The Qur'ānic passage is IX, 18–9, of which the first verse is perhaps the most popular passage in all of Qur'ānic monumental epigraphy:[60] 'He only shall tend Allah's sanctuaries who believeth in Allah and the Last Day and observeth proper worship and payeth the poor-due and feareth none save Allah. For such (only) is it possible that they can be of the rightly guided.' The ḥadīth is equally *à propos:* 'Be speedy with your prayer before (its time) elapses and be speedy with repentance before death (intervenes).' The content of these inscriptions seems clearly designed to assert the fundamental duty of *ṣalāt,* one of the pillars of Islam. Significantly enough, the Qur'ānic inscription of the great screen drives home this point by dint of repeating the very same words but within a fuller context (IX, 18–23).[61]

It is, moreover, not only by its inscriptions that the *miḥrāb* stands out so to speak in high relief from the rest of the *muṣallā*. Where the *muṣallā* as a whole bespeaks a painfully literal translation of wooden construction techniques into stone, the *miḥrāb* has a cinquefoil arch, and thus proclaims itself the product of a completely different architectural tradition. Its sources are clearly in the twelfth-century architecture of Afghanistan.[62] Finally, by colour and material alike it is set apart from its surroundings. It is the only part of the mosque which uses white marble as distinct from the grey and ochre stone used everywhere else. White marble flooring also marks the place of the *imām* or *pīsh-namāz.* There is no need to rehearse the reasons which dictated this multiple emphasis on the most quintessentially Muslim component of the mosque; clearly such an emphasis is of a piece with the intricate nexus of political and religious factors which motivated the construction of this particular mosque in the first place.

Before the interplay of Jain and Islamic features is discussed in detail, one further general question remains. This concerns the screen (Plates 11 and 19). It needs to be emphasized that there is not the slightest liturgical need for such a feature. Its role of intensifying the Islamic character of the mosque, and of achieving this by the blandishments of beauty rather than by a brutal *Diktat,* has already been sufficiently remarked. But its function extends beyond these purposes. It is very literally a screen, and thus it is meant to conceal what lies behind. It does so all the more effectively because it extends beyond the muṣallā by an extra bay on each side. Thus it renews the attack on Jain traditions which was begun in the first stage of the mosque. Even the Muslim-inspired domes of the muṣallā are rendered invisible by it. Presumably it was not extended to the full breadth of the courtyard because the pillared muṣallā did not extend even as far as its own outer extremities. In the cases of Delhi and Ajmīr alike, the initial decision to build a mosque of spolia which were easily recognizable as such seriously limited the options of subsequent patrons. Both mosques were substantial and to rebuild them would have been a major undertaking, and a very wasteful one given that these mosques had only just been built. Hence Iltutmish had to content himself with adapting an established plan whose essentials were immutable. The device of the screen did, however, ensure that he derived maximum benefit from what was only a slight readjustment of the design. Nevertheless, the importance he attached to this feature is revealed by the fact that he went to the trouble of extending the screen at Delhi which had been erected by his predecessor, so that its final length was some 116 m. Only some 44 m. of this screen mask the muṣallā proper; it may be deduced, therefore, that the prime purpose of an extension to the screen which almost tripled its length was to cordon off from all taint of Hindu influence that part of the mosque which was closest to Mecca. The screen at Ajmīr measures 61 m.; in both cases the proportions are carefully harmonized with the size of the courtyard.[63] Incidentally, the mosque at Bāri Khatū, which was probably built a crucial decade or two later than the first mosques at Delhi and Ajmīr, shows that the device of the screen was not needed when the mosque was built from the outset in a more thoroughly Islamic style.

Finally, the placing of the screen was an integral and indeed crucial part of its intended purpose. It could have adorned the façade of the building or the sides of the courtyard. Neither of these locations, however, was selected. Instead, it cloaks the sanctuary itself, the very heart of the mosque. To anyone entering the mosque for the first time, the alien air of the muṣallā is not visible; the natural, though mistaken, assumption is that its style matches that of the screen. In short, the screen is strategically positioned to give an unmistakably Islamic colouring to the nerve-centre of the mosque. It must be admitted, however, that its potential is not exploited as fully as that of its counterpart at Delhi, which follows a custom long established elsewhere in the Islamic world thereby the central element of the muṣallā façade led into a wider aisle, thus accentuating the axis of the miḥrāb . In the Iranian world this central element was an *īwān*. When viewed head-on, the great central arch certainly resembles an īwān, and at Delhi the illusion continues as one passes underneath it. Not so at Ajmīr.

The prevalence of indigenous traditions of material, structure, and decoration in the Ajmīr mosque has been thoroughly investigated by earlier scholars and the salient points are recapitulated here briefly only as an *aide-mémoire.* At a time when the eastern Islamic world had long adopted vaulting as the standard method for roofing mosques, the dependence of the Ajmīr muṣallā and courtyard portico on trabeate construction is an obvious concession to local custom. Carpentry techniques are boldly translated into stonework, most notably in the roof of the muṣallā, with its many joists, cross-beams, lintels, chamfered corners and brackets. Yet this battery of devices rooted in wood construction is pressed into service as a support for domes, including the dome over the porch on the south side. Large domes erected without any apparent knowledge of vaulting techniques but placed directly on a latticed framework, constitute a pretty paradox. The same bizarre inconsistency may be seen at the Quwwat al-Islām mosque in Delhi, where some of the domes are solid hemispheres—proof positive, if any were needed, that the masons were executing a form whose implications they did not grasp. At Ajmīr the domes do not give the impression of a masonry shell with added ornament, but instead look as if a solid hemisphere had been partially excavated from within and the ornament sculpted out of it rather than incrusted on it. The decoration used on these domes and on the underside of the flat roof is predominantly Jain in character, with a répertoire of lotus petals, rosettes, sunbursts, and lozenges among other motifs (Plate 18).[64] The exteriors of the domes, with their knob-like finials and radiating leaf patterns, have the same source. Even the miḥrāb incorporates some of these details, for example in its coping. Jain decorative motifs are found of course on the spolia in the muṣallā and the two main entrance porches, but also on the exterior corner towers. The trabeate principle, moreover, extends beyond the muṣallā to the portico on the east side of the courtyard, where the lintels are carried on doubly-stepped capitals. Such Jain forms do not so much coexist as collide with Islamic ones. The juxtaposition of these two mutually antipathetic traditions can be observed at its most abrupt in the rear façade of the east entrance-way and in the elaborate but non-functional brackets which project in their multiple tiers beyond and below the springing of the Islamic arch to which they are uselessly attached.

Equally local is the stone which provides the exclusive building material. Eastern Islamic architecture at this time was overwhelmingly in brick, though stone was commonly employed in Egypt, the Levant, and Anatolia. The stereotomy in the muṣallā area is of high quality, despite the fact that stone blocks of widely differing height, length, and width are employed. The mortar joints are minimal, and though small patching blocks are sometimes used, it is standard practice for blocks to fit sweetly no matter how awkward their angles and re-entrants. This stone has taken a series of tints: grey, red, and a deep amber. Quite different is the stonework of the north and south façades of the courtyard, which comprises stones so roughly cut as to resemble rubble, and coarsely bonded by lavish applications of greyish-black mortar. Presumably these façades were originally covered, or intended to be covered, with ashlar facing. One further detail consonant with a developed tradition of stone-working, but with no place in brick architecture, may be noted: the presence of elaborately detailed mouldings both as stylobates and brackets. The bases of the piers in the muṣallā screen have the best examples.

There is no lack of imported Islamic ideas to set beside this evidence of the continuity, of local traditions. Thus a glance at the rear of the muṣallā screen reveals that the arches are constructed with true voussoirs set in thin mortar beds, presumably a technique translated from the brickwork of the Iranian world, though such stone voussoirs are of course known still further to the west. The minarets flanking the central arch of the screen have alternating flanges and engaged columns like Saljuq minarets and tomb towers in Iran,[65] and the resemblance extends even to the use of encircling inscription bands. The treatment of these minarets as an articulating device on either side of the main archway is a feature which was to characterize the later architecture of Iran and Anatolia but was still in its infancy in Iran at this time. More unusual, and therefore more interesting, than this is the use of that same reeded and flanged elevation on a more spacious scale, and with a much richer array of mouldings, for the corner buttresses of the building. Here, too, Iranian parallels could be cited—for example, the Gunbad-i ʿAlawiyyān at Hamadān[66]—but it must be conceded that the architect at Ajmīr gave this theme a power and stateliness beyond anything known in the Iranian world. Yet even here the busy articulation of this imported form by means of multiple mouldings might be thought to coexist somewhat uneasily with the lavish applied ornament in Jain style. These various borrowings are only to he expected in a building whose construction was supervised by a man from Herat.

A much more significant borrowing manifests itself in the elevation of the muṣallā. First, the exterior qibla wall has the emplacement of the miḥrāb marked by a richly carved projecting rectangular buttress, and similar but lesser buttresses are disposed at intervals along the qibla wall, possibly to correspond to subsidiary miḥrābs within. This custom was later to establish itself in the subcontinent as a means of proclaiming the sanctity of the miḥrāb externally, and perhaps also, as some suggest, to obviate the possibility of the wall being used as a lavatory. But its origins lie in the west, sc. in the Maghrib, Egypt and, most significantly, Iran. The second, and rather more important, feature of this elevation is the emphasis accorded to the domes, and here too parallels throughout. the early mediaeval Islamic world could be cited. Sometimes, as at Cordova,[67] the domes are spread out above the aisle adjoining the qibla and parallel to it; in other cases, as as Qairawān,[68] the domes are disposed along the central aisle of the muṣallā, perpendicular to the qibla. In yet other cases, such as the Iṣfahān Jāimiʿ, a single dome at the centre of the sanctuary might be surrounded by a plethora of smaller ones.[69] At all events, the principle of singling out the muṣallā by means of domes was well established throughout the Islamic world, and it was only to be expected that at Ajmīr too the dome should figure in some way.

Finally, attention should be drawn to the implications of using the arch form in such a dominating way. Much ink has been spilled on explaining how the arches in this building and in other contemporary north Indian mosques are not true arches at all, but merely corbelled approximations of that form.[70] Yet to emphasize this technical detail is to miss the psychological point; for it seems likely that the arch was fully intended to be an alien import. It had a certain shock value to the inhabitants of northern India, who were unfamiliar with that form. indeed, it would be fair to say that in this particular context the arch symbolized Islam. When that basic arcuated form was itself variegated, as at Ajmīr, by a series of decorative profiles, and then—for good measure—the screen itself crowned by two tall and equally alien minarets, it is easy to imagine that the impact on the conquered population would be profound. So much, then, for the role of straightforward borrowing from Islamic tradition in this mosque.

In fact, however, the architect went well beyond any known model in his articulation of the muṣallā. The remainder of this article will therefore be devoted to an assessment of the originality of the Ajmīr mosque, first in the role of the muṣallā domes and then in various other features of the building. The novelty of the Ajmīr muṣallā goes beyond the conflation of the dome with an architecture otherwise resolutely trabeate; for it must be repeated that there is no arch in the muṣallā proper. It extends also to the number, size, and disposition of the domes. There are ten in all, which is an unusually high number given that five of them are large, with a diameter of some 7 m. or more. A group of five small domes, all of equal size (barely 2 m. in diameter), are placed at regular intervals directly behind the muṣallā screen and parallel with it. The other five domes are so placed as to straddle the three bays perpendicular to the qibla. Four are of equal size; the fifth, which is directly aligned to the miḥrāb, is larger, as custom would dictate, but paradoxically simpler than its counterparts in the matter of ornament. There is no lack of parallels for a narrow aisle adjoining the qibla and a broader one outside it, but when domes are used in this penultimate aisle the practice is for them to correspond to its width. The larger domes at Ajmīr depart from this norm by spreading into both adjoining aisles. They were of course designed to be seen from the courtyard,[71] but the muṣallā screen put paid to that and their full effect can only be appreciated from the hill behind and above the mosque. In this emphasis on muṣallā domes, as in several other ways, Ajmīr is prophetic of later mosques in the subcontinent.

No other feature in the mosque can lay a stronger claim to originality than this unusual articulation of the muṣallā, but other aspects run it close. The screen, for instance, used as a self-contained prop in mosque design as at Ajmīr and Delhi, is something new. Its basic form, of course, had long been familiar in Islamic architecture, but hitherto it had always been integrated with what lay behind. The effect here is analogous to the eighteenth-century habit of tacking a classical façade on to an Elizabethan or Jacobean house. Such a cavalier indifference to the proprieties of architectural style undeniably has something engaging about it; but though it has its parallels in the Muslim world, notably in the Umayyad period, it is by no means typically Islamic. The detailing of the screen also deserves some brief notice. Four different arch profiles are used, one for the central arch and three for the six flanking arches. All were well established in the vocabulary of eastern Islamic architecture,[72] but to use them all in a single arcade is unprecedented, all the more so when the arch profiles of the courtyard façade, which add yet another type, are taken into account. The pointed multifoil arch of the miḥrāb increases the total still further. Here too, then, Ajmīr foreshadows later developments, since a penchant for variegated arch profiles was to remain a constant of Indo-Islamic architecture.

It is hard to make quite such a hold claim for the decoration used as infill in some of the windows of the mosque, though it would be tempting to do so. Latticework and other geometrically conceived screens in stone or marble are commonplace in Sultanate and Mughal architecture. But some caution is imperative here. Geometric window grills had been known in Islamic buildings as early as the Umayyad period, but their use cannot be traced uninterruptedly up to the late twelfth century. Moreover, the designs at Ajmīr, with their crude juxtaposition of swastikas and lozenges, scarcely offer a basis for the much more sophisticated grills and screens of later periods. Nevertheless, they may justly claim the interest that attaches to any early experiment in a genre hat was to have a distinguished future.

Much the same applies to an apparently trivial detail of the muṣallā which nevertheless serves to demarcate the pillared section from the areas to either side of it and from the courtyard itself. The means of achieving this are simple: a slight raising of the floor level. It is merely one of several ways in which distinctions can be drawn between the component parts of the muṣallā The provision of a roof, different types of vaulting, variations in height, and extra intensity of ornament may all be cited in this connection, and indeed all are used at Ajmīr. This raising of the muṣallā remained a popular device in Indian mosques though it was normally a little more accentuated than at Ajmīr, where some 6 cm. were enough. Jain columns are built into the walls of the northern and southern extremities of the muṣallā, suggesting thereby a kinship with the main body of the muṣallā with its total of 124 such columns.[73] Perhaps these unroofed areas were intended as overflow facilities.

Virtually none of the applied decoration in the Ajmīr mosque can lay a convincing claim to originality. The interior of the domes is very richly carved but it is hard to detect any specifically Islamic element in this ornament; while the epigraphy and abstract patterning of the great screen is wholly in the orbit of late Saljuq Khurāsānī architecture. It is only the miḥrāb (Plate 5) which refuses to fit into this pattern. The rosettes in its spandrels would not look out of place amid the Jain decoration elsewhere in the mosque and its band of arabesques had no special claim to distinction, but its epigraphy is unusual. The main inscription is allotted an unexpectedly narrow band, which it fills in a strangely disproportionate manner. The shafts of the letters, which display curious two-pronged terminations, are cut short rather than developing to the length appropriate for a band of these reduced dimensions. The letters also slope backwards, a practice which became common in monumental epigraphy only at a much later date. Altogether the epigraphy makes a somewhat uncouth impression, as if it had been copied by a stone mason who did not know the Arabic alphabet.

The foregoing discussion will have shown that a remarkable number of borrowings from other Islamic traditions, and of apparently new ideas only tentatively tried out at Ajmīr, had a rich future in store for them. By contrast, Jain architecture seems to have struck no responsive chord in the Muslims. They made use of it at the very beginning, for strictly practical reasons. Nevertheless, in a very short space of time they ostentatiously turned their backs on it in favour of ideas and traditions which originated in Iran, Afghanistan, and Central Asia. When local traditions resurfaced, as they were bound to do, it was only to play a secondary role, typically as architectural detailing. But this revanche was not to take place in the time of Iltutmish. When viewed in a wider historical perspective than the thirteenth century affords, his patronage can be seen to have been motivated to an important extent by forces of piety, reaction, and conservatism. His attempt to transplant the Saljuq architectural style to northern India certainly enjoyed initial success, but in the longer term it miscarried because it ignored the strength and persistence of local traditions. For him, it seems, architecture, including its epigraphy,[75] was at least in part a weapon in the campaign to establish Islam in India. His zealous use of that weapon, as expressed at Ajmīr and Delhi, certainly accelerated the development of a distinctive Indo-Islamic architecture. Even so, it may be thought that he made his architecture bear a weight of meaning which it could not well support. In that sense he was a patron ahead of his time; but his failure was glorious.

NOTES

1. The point is well demonstrated in a recent article which constitutes a landmark in the study of Islamic architecture in India: A. Welch and H. Crane, 'The Tughluqs: Master Builders of the Delhi Sultanate', *Muqarnas* I (1983), pp. 123–66.

2. For an exploration of this topic, see A. Chaghtai, 'What India owes to Central Asia in Architecture', *Islamic Culture VIII* (1934), pp. 55–65; A. Chaghtai, 'Indian Links with Central Asia in Architecture', *Indian Art and Letters* XI/2 (1937), pp. 85–94; L. Golombek, 'From Tamerlane to the Taj Mahal', in *Essays in Islamic Art and Architecture in Honor of Katharina Otto-Dors,* (ed.), A. Daneshvari (Malibu, 1981), pp. 43–50. See also my paper 'Persian Influences in Mughal Architecture', to be published in the proceedings of the conference of the Societas Iranologica Europea held in Turin in September 1987.

3. Examples are figural sculpture and the gopura form.

4. For example, the emphasis on stone rather than brick as the material of construction and decoration.

5. The Tughluqid buildings of Multān, Delhi, and elsewhere are a case in point; see n. 1 above.

6. See J. Burton-Page in *EI*[2] art. 'Hind. Architecture', for a concise survey of this material.

7. T. Yamamoto, M. Ara, and T. Tsukinowa, *Delhi: Architectural Remains of the Sultanate Period,* 3 vols (Tokyo, 1968–70).

8. The problem is eloquently set out by Sir John Marshall in 'The Monuments of Muslim India', in *The Cambridge History of India. III. Turks and Afghans* (Cambridge, 1928), pp. 368–73.

9. There are in addition very few monuments which predate this period, such as the very early Indian mosques of Banbhore [F.A. Khan, *Banbhore. A Preliminary Report on the Recent Archaeological Excavations at Banbhore* (Karachi, 1976), pp. 24–30]; Manṣūra [H. Cousens, 'Brahmanabad—Mansura in Sind', *Archaeological Survey of India: Annual Reports. 1903–4* (Calcutta, 1906), pp. 132–44; H. Cousens, 'Excavations at Brahmanabad—Mansura, Sind', *ASIAR, 1908–9* (Calcutta, 1912), pp. 79–87; H. Cousens, *The Antiquities of Sind. With Historical Outline,* in *Archaeological Survey of India. Imperial Series,* XLVI (Calcutta, 1929), pp. 48–7]; the twelfth-century buildings of Bhadreśvar; and a series of apparently tenth-to twelfth-century monuments, mainly mausolea, recently surveyed by Holly Edwards in Sind [Mehrdad Shokoohy, *Bhadreśvar, The Oldest Islamic Monuments in India* (Leiden, 1988); Holly Edwards, 'The Genesis of Islamic Architecture in the Indus Valley'. Unpublished D.Phil. Thesis, (New York University, 1990)]. Virtually all of the buildings enumerated above, however, predate the Ghūrid conquest of northern India and thus do not belong to the same political context as the earliest mosques at Delhi and Ajmīr and the buildings most closely related to them.

10. A. Cunningham, *Four Reports Made During the Years 1862–63–64–65* (Simla, 1871), p. 287; J. Fergusson, *History of Indian and Eastern Architecture. Revised and Edited, with Additions ... by J. Burgess and ... R.P. Spiers* (London, 1910) Vol. II, pp. 68–9, 229.

11. Succinctly described by Z.A. Desai, *Mosques of India* (Delhi, 1971), p. 28; it shares with the Ajmīr mosque its setting on a platform, its stairway leading to

the entrance porch, its *muṣallā* of pillars and domes in Hindu style and its white marble *miḥrāb* with a five-lobed arch.

12. Cunningham, *Report of a Tour in Eastern Rajputana in 1882–83*, Archaeological Survey of India, XX, (Calcutta, 1885), p. 56.

13. The most convenient accounts are those of Marshall, 'The Monuments of Muslim India', pp. 575–9; P. Brown, *Indian Architecture* (*Islamic Period*) (Bombay, repr. 1968), pp. 9–12; and J.A. Page, *An Historical Memoir on the Qutb: Delhi*, Memoirs of the Archaeological Survey of India, no. 22, (Calcutta, 1926).

14. Brown, *Indian Architecture,* pp. 13–15; F. Wetzel, *Islamische Grabbauten in Indien aus der Zeit der Soldatenkaiser 1320–1440* (Leipzig, 1918), pp. 105–7.

15. The major publication is by J.F. Blakiston, *The Jāmiʿ Masjid at Budaun (Memoirs of the Archaeological Survey of India, no. 19*) (Calcutta, 1926).

16. Brown, *Indian Architecture,* p. 14; Burton-Page 'Hind Architecture', p. 441.

17. Cunningham, *Eastern Rajputana,* pp. 71–4; Marshall, 'The Monuments of Muslim India', p. 622, and pl. 35, no. 71.

18. Marshall, 'The Monuments of Muslim India', p. 581; S. Digby, 'Iletmish or Iltutmish? A Reconsideration of the Name of the Delhi Sultan', *Iran* VIII (1970), p. 62. Fergusson suggests that the two-and-a-half days might have referred to the time that was needed to clear away the temples (*History of Indian and Eastern Architecture,* p. 211); Cunningham, computing the number of looted columns used in the mosque as no less than 700, concludes that this represents the spoil from between 20 and 30 temples (*Four Reports,* p. 262).

19. Nevertheless, this is not specifically mentioned in the miḥrāb inscription bearing this date, which states merely that it (whether the mosque or the miḥrāb is not clear) was built in Jumādā II 595, that is, March–April 1199. In the Quwwat al-Islām mosque in Delhi, on the other hand, Quṭb al-Dīn Aibak is twice mentioned by name as the founder [J. Horovitz, 'The Inscriptions of Muhammad ibn Sam, Qutbuddin Aibeg, and Iltutmish', *Epigraphia Indo-Moslemica. 1911–12* (1914), pp. 13–4].

20. For the full text of the inscription, which has lost the crucial words after 'on 20 Rabiʿ II of the year', see Horovitz, 'The Inscriptions of Muhammad ibn Sam', p. 30 and pl. XXIII.

21. The exact date given on the screen itself is 20 Dhuʿ l-Qaʿda 594/23 September 1198 (Horovitz, 'The Inscriptions of Muhammad ibn Sam', p. 15 and p.1, XII/2). For a discussion of the controversy about the exact date of the work in the earliest mosque, see ibid., pp. 13–14. The published accounts of the mosque tend to skate over these difficulties. See, however, Page, *Historical Memoir on the Qutb,* p. 29, n. I; and R.H. Pinder-Wilson, 'The Minaret of Masʿūd III at Ghazni', in *Studies in Islamic Art* (London, 1985), p. 102, n. 23.

22. Horovitz, 'The Inscriptions of Muhammad ibn Sam', p. 23 and pl. XIII/1.

23. Cunningham, *Four Reports* (Simla, 1871) II, pp. 258–63.

24. H.B.W. Garrick, *Report of a Tour in the Panjab and Rajputana in 1883–84 (Archaeological Survey of India,* XXIII) (Calcutta, 1887), pp. 34–8.

25. M.W. Meister, 'The "Two-and-a-half-day" Mosque', *Oriental Art,* N.S. XVIII/1 (1972), pp. 57–63. Reprinted as Chapter 9 in this volume.

26. Garrick, *Tour in the Panjab and Rajputana,* pp. 35–6.

27. J.H. Marshall, 'Conservation', *Archaeological Survey of India. Annual Report, 1902–03* (Calcutta, 1904), pp. 29–30; A.L.P. Tucker, 'Restoration Work in Ajmīr', in ibid., pp. 80–3.

28. D.B. Har Silas Sarda, *Ajmer: Historical and Descriptive* (Ajmer, 1941), ch. VII.

29. Meister, 'The "Two-and-a-half day" Mosque', pp. 57, 61, and 63, n. 5; he concludes that these ceilings were ordered to be built by the Muslims.

30. J. Tod, *Annals and Antiquities of Rajasthan,* (ed.), W. Crooke (repr. Oxford, 1920), pp. 896–7; cf. Fergusson, *History of Indian and Eastern Architecture,* p. 211. As Sir John Marshall justly remarks ('The Monuments of Muslim India', p. 576), the Quwwat al-Islām mosque, as originally designed, looked Hindu from both the inside and the outside.

31. M.B. Smith, 'Three Monuments at Yazd-i Khwast', *Ars Islamica* VII (1940), pp. 104–6; M. Siroux, 'La Mosquée Djum'a de Yezd-i-Khast', *Bulletin de l'Institut français d'Archéologie orientale* XLIV (1947), pp. 101–48.

32. Indeed, Ajmīr itself was briefly lost to Hemraj, the brother of Prithvi Raj, in 590/1194 [Wolseley Haig, *Cambridge History of India,* Volume 3: *Turks and Afghans* (Cambridge, 1928), p. 43].

33. This is the proud boast of the foundation inscription (*bīst u haft ... butkhāna ... dar īn masjid bi-kār basta shūda ast*); see Horovitz, 'The Inscriptions of Muhammad ibn Sam', p. 13.

34. Viz. *jayastambha* ('pillar of victory') and *kirtistambha* ('pillar of fame'); see Page, *Historical Memoir on the Qutb,* pp. 39–40 (no. 7) and 41 (no. 20).

35. Ibid., p. 31.

36. This was also done in other mosques which employed plundered materials, such as the Great Mosque of Cordova and—more relevant to the present discussion—the Ukhā Mandīr, the mosque at Kamān and that at Bārī Khatū. Thus, for all that the muṣallā of the Ajmīr mosque has the appearance of a Jain temple, its columns have been rearranged by craftsmen working for a Muslim patron, as was done at the Quwwat al-Islām mosque (Fergusson, *History of Indian and Eastern Architecture,* pp. 201–2).

37. It may be doubted whether this was entirely successful, for Cunningham found four-armed figures on some of the pillars at Ajmīr (*Four Reports,* p. 259); while here and there on the underside of the roof of the Quwwat al-Islām mosque can he glimpsed the cross-legged figures of Jain saints (Fergusson, *History of Indian and Eastern Architecture,* p. 203). Similarly, as Dr Shokoohy has noted, in the upper reaches of a dome at Bārī Khatū is a frieze of ducks, and elephant capitals,

demeaned by their reuse as column bases, occur at the mosque at Kamān. The case of the early mosque at Iṣṭakhr in southern Iran, whose bull-headed capitals were noted by al-Maqdisī, springs to mind [K.A.C. Creswell, *Early Muslim Architecture. Umayyads.* AD *622–750* (Oxford, 1969) I/1, p. 21].

38. Khan, *Banbhore*, pp. 25–7.

39. Haig, *Turks and Afghans*, p. 25.

40. J. M. Rogers, *The Spread of Islam* (Oxford, 1976), p. 67.

41. J.C. Harle, *The Art and Architecture of the Indian Subcontinent* (Harmondsworth, 1986), figs. 164, 174, 176–7, 182–3.

42. For example, the mosque at Bārī Khatū and the Quwwat al-Islām mosque.

43. It should be noted that this theory could accommodate the notion that the present eastern portal is part of the original mosque, since that portal is on the axis of the *miḥrāb*; but the width of the mosque would have been much less than it is now.

44. Fergusson, *History of Indian and Eastern Architecture*, p. 197.

45. It will be noted that to adopt the second possibility assumes that the changes made by Iltutmish were much more than cosmetic, and that the eastern and southern entrances, plus the corner bastions, were all part of this later building campaign. Nevertheless, because the time gap between the two campaigns is only a generation, there is nothing stylistically improbable about these features dating to the period *c.* 1200.

46. There the changes are better documented, and it makes good sense that in this respect—as in the building of a screen—the work at Ajmir took its inspiration from that at Delhi. Moreover, the dimensions cited by Cunningham (*Four Reports*, p. 260), demonstrate beyond doubt that the Ajmīr mosque represented a deliberate attempt to outdo its counterpart in Delhi.

47. E. Galdieri, *Isfahan: Masgid-i Guma'a. 2. Il periodo al-i Buyide* (Rome, 1973).

48. Haig, Turks and Afghans, pp. 41–2.

49. Firishta, *History of the Rise of Mahomedan Power in India Till the Year 1612*, tr. J. Briggs (1829) I, p. 177; Haig, Turks and Afghans, p. 43.

50. M. Longworth Dames and J. Burton-Page, *EI*^{2} art. 'Kanawdj.'

51. Horovitz, 'The Inscriptions of Muhammad ibn Sam', pp. 15–16 and pl. XXVII/1.

52. Ibid., 29–30 and pl. XXVI; it has Sūra XLI, 31–4 (ibid., p. 30).

53. Horovitz, 'The Inscriptions of Muhammad ibn Sam', p. 29 and p. 1. XXV.

54. A. Maricq and G. Wiet, *Le minaret de Djam* (Paris, 1959), pls I–VIII.

55. A.S. Melikian-Chirvani, 'Eastern Iranian Architecture: Apropos of the Ghūrid Parts of the Great Mosque of Harāt', *BSOAS* XXXIII (1970), pl. 9; S.S. Blair, 'The Madrasa at Zuzan', *Muqarnas* III (1985), pls 11–13, 15.

56. M.J. Casimir and B. Glatzer, 'The Madrasa of Šāh-i Maśhad in Ġarğistān', *East and West*, N.S. XXIII (1971), pp. 51–68.

57. C.E. Bosworth, 'The Early Islamic History of Ghūr', *Central Asiatic Journal* VI (1961), pp. 122–8.

58. Assuming, as seems reasonable, that the conventional attribution to him of the mausoleum beside the Quwwat al-Islām mosque is well substantiated.

59. Horovitz, 'The Inscriptions of Muhammad ibn Sam', p. 15 and p1. XXIV.

60. See my paper 'Qur'anic Epigraphy in Medieval Islamic Architecture', *Revue des Études Islamiques*, LIX (1991), pp. 171–87.

61. Horovitz, 'The Inscriptions of Muhammad ibn Sam', p. 30 and pl. XXIII.

62. Cf. the material presented in J. Sourdel-Thomine, 'Stèles arabes de Bust (Afghanistan)', *Arabica* III (1956), pls III–VI.

63. Fergusson, *History of Indian and Eastern Architecture*, p. 198.

64. Cf. n. 29 above.

65. See A.U. Pope, *Persian Architecture* (London, 1965), figs 82, 86–91.

66. E. Herzfeld, 'Die Gumbadh-i 'Alawiyyân und die Baukunst der Ilkhane in Iran', in *A Volume of Oriental Studies Presented to E.G. Browne* (Cambridge, 1922), fig. 1.

67. F. Goitia, *La moschea di Cordova* (Milan, 1968), pl. III.

68. O. Grabar, *The Formation of Islamic Art* (New Haven, 1973), aerial view on pl. 20.

69. Pope, *Persian Architecture*, figs 105, 124.

70. Fergusson, *History of Indian and Eastern Architecture*, pp. 203–4; Marshall, 'Muslim Monuments', p. 582.

71. They might also have been conical originally; their profile was made hemispherical in the restorations of 1875–6 (Fergusson, *History of Indian and Eastern Architecture*, p. 213 and fig. 377 for a view of the conical profile they had at this time).

72. See n. 62 above.

73. Following Fergusson, not Cunningham, whose figure of 124 columns refers to his reconstructed version of the muṣallā; he believes it to have extended the full width of the mosque.

74. See, however, ns. 43 and 45 above.

75. The early Sultanate buildings in India use Qur'ānic inscriptions on a scale not encountered elsewhere in the Islamic world. The reasons for this phenomenon deserve detailed scrutiny.

Indian Islam's Lotus Throne: Kaman and Khatu Kalan*

Michael W. Meister

'Accommodation', 'assimilation', and 'synthesis' may not provide the most productive framework by which to discuss Islam in the context of India, nor, I believe, can the originality and independence of 'regional varieties' of Islam—the original topic for this seminar—best be defined by such terms. I might suggest a different metaphor, that of permeability through a membrane, for the interaction between Islam and Hindu India; which cultural forms prove to be permeable and which do not may provide a more interesting litmus for cultural interaction than a discussion of 'syncretism'. Categories governing such cultural osmosis from both sides in different periods can be determined only by undertaking specific case studies. In this essay, I wish to examine briefly two mosques from the earliest phase of Islamic building within India as such an example.[1]

The Causat Kambhā or Caurāsī Kambhā mosque at Kaman (Plates 7 and 9), near Bharatpur, Rajasthan, is among the earliest of the Islamic monuments built in India under Ghūrid occupation, before Quṭbu'd-dīn Aibak established his dynasty in 1206 AD. Unlike the Qutb mosque in Delhi (Plates 1–3) and the Aḍhāī-dīn-kā-Jhompra mosque in Ajmer (Plate 11), the Caurāsī Kambhā had no *qibla* screen added in front of its *liwan* and was neither altered nor enlarged under Quṭbu'd-dīn's successor, Iltutmish.[2]

The structure, as it now survives, consists of a rectangular court, enclosed by a colonnade, entered through a projecting masonry gateway on the east (Plates 7 and 9). Two rows of columns stand behind this gateway on

*Previously published in A.L. Dallapiccola and S. Zingel-Avé Lallemant (eds), *Islam and Indian Regions*, Ergon-Verlag, Stuttgart, 1993, pp. 445–52. In the present version, some portions of the text, notes, and illustrations have been removed. For the complete text see the original version.

the east of the court; on the west is a hall of twenty seven bays with a single central *miḥrāb* set in the back wall.

On the south and west, the structure is enclosed by solid masonry walls. On the east and north, an airy open cloister with paired columns set above a low terrace forms the periphery.[3] A Sanskrit inscription written on a pillar reused as part of the masonry wall of the mosque's interior documents the lineage of an earlier local Śūrasena dynasty.[4] A second recently uncovered inscription dated 869 AD, built into the base of the exterior wall on the southeast corner, records the excavation of a step-well and the construction of a *maṭha* (either monastery or temple).[5]

The bold arched masonry gate to the mosque on the east (Plate 9) has an Arabic inscription surrounding its inner rectilinear doorway. Alexander Cunningham in the nineteenth century thought this referred to 'Sultan lltitmish.'[6] More recent published readings, however, by Z.A. Desai report that the sultan's name has been obliterated and note a date in the inscription of *hijra* 600/1204 AD, which was two years before Quṭbu'd-dīn Aibak severed his connections with the Ghurids and assumed supreme power over their Indian territories in 1206 AD.[7] One significant even more recent report suggests that this mosque was built a few years earlier than this date by a rival Muslim prince in Bayana, Baha' al-Dīn Tughrul, but this has not, in my view, yet fully been demonstrated, in light of Desai's observation of an exact date.[8]

One of the earliest of *in situ* miḥrāb inscriptions in India surrounds this mosque's centrally placed single miḥrāb (Plate 21).[9] Its choice of a Quranic text seems particularly significant in light of the extensive, and ideologically potent, epigraphic programmes found on some other early Islamic monuments in the subcontinent.[10]

The scribe has chosen verses 1–5 from chapter 68 of the *Qur'ān:*[11]

> I call to witness the pen and what they inscribe:
> You are not demented by the grace of your Lord,
> There is surely reward unending for you,
> For you are verily born of sublime nature,
> So you will see, and they will realise [...]

No better description could have been found for the utility of an epigraphic programme on an Islamic monument, nor perhaps a subtler statement of the implied threat to a non-believer: 'So you will see, and they will realise [...]'

A reader of the Qur'ān would have known the subsequent verse as well, which continues:[12]

> Verily your Lord knows those who have gone astray from His Path,
> and He knows those who are guided on the way.

In view of the date to which this mosque can be ascribed, I would certainly wish to reiterate Percy Brown's remark that: 'in view of the rarity of these early examples of Indo-Islamic style, every building erected during the supremacy of the Slave kings possesses interest and value.'[13] The Caurāsī Kambhā mosque at Kaman, in fact, comes closest of all the surviving Islamic monuments that precede the establishment of Quṭbu'd-dīn Aibak's dynasty in India to preserving what R. Nath has called 'the humble mosque which Aibak could have hastily assembled. [...]'[14] It does not, however, represent simple plunder, nor have its Hindu elements been thoughtlessly reassembled. It preserves for us a clear model of the elements thought essential for a mosque at the opening edge of Islamic occupation in India and gives some suggestion of the aesthetic judgement exercised by the artisans and engineers then employed.[15]

My own interest in Kaman stemmed from the extensive Hindu materials from which this mosque has been constructed.[16] Building materials for the mosque were removed from a variety of structures—pavilions and monasteries *(maṭhas)* in addition to temples—built during the rule of the early Śūrasena dynasty. The Caurāsī Kambhā's foundation inscription in 1204 AD as well as a later inscription of 1271 AD, in fact, repeat a claim begun in earlier Hindu inscriptions to have made or further renovated a well at Kaman.[17] In contrast to most other early Islamic monuments in India from regions where plunder (or *spolia*) could serve both as a convenient source for building materials and as a political act, those who assembled this mosque seized elements, not from recently built Hindu structures, but rather—with what would seem to have been calculated consistency—from monuments built four or five centuries earlier (Plate 13). While this act may merely have represented the antiquity and sanctity of Kaman's resources, the results produced had explicit, exploitable, aesthetic consequences.

These borrowed Hindu elements include ornamented square pillar-shafts of several varieties, figural brackets, carved lintels, a massive overdoor, elephant-brackets, fencing, ornamental ceilings, fragments of wall-mouldings, and even plain building blocks. These have been reorganized to fit a new Islamic building programme, yet in a manner still substantially expressing a Hindu sensibility. It does not surprise me that R.D. Banerji found in 1919 that the Caurāsī Kambhā was 'no longer a Masjid' but was used, instead, 'for the *Dolayatra* ceremony during the Holi festivaL'[18]

The ancient Hindu pillars rebuilt into the interior of the Kaman mosque are primarily either square or offset and resemble mid-eighth century examples from Gwalior and eastern Rajasthan.[19] These have been piled up, one shaft above another, their ornament carefully matched. In some places, the upper shafts have either been shortened or smaller pieces added to adjust to the necessary height.

The pattern of reuse of pillars and other parts suggests a defined attempt to create a hierarchy of ornament within the new mosque. The north colonnade, for example, primarily uses nearly plain, square, pillars decorated with simple lotus-medallions; the central pair, however, are ornamented with *ghaṭapallava*s and are accentuated by being offset. The four large pillars that parallel the entry gateway on the east (visible in Plate 7) also are offset, with elaborately detailed ornamentation. The front pillars of the liwan also suggest a centralizing hierarchy.

The short ashlar wall on the north that frames the liwan is pierced by a doorway leading from a raised entry platform approached by a flight of steps from the west (visible in Plate 7, top right). This reuses Hindu pilasters with mutilated guardian figures to either side, pillars with hanging ribbons and chains and garland-bearers on the brackets, seat-slabs, and elephant-head braces meant to hold an enclosing seat-back.

Within the hall, this entry leads to a raised private platform once enclosed by perforated screens (visible in Plate 7, top right). This gallery probably acted as a *maqsurah* (or royal chamber) rather than as a *zenāna* as found in many later sultanate mosques. Such a maqsurah here survives for the first time in South Asia.[20]

In the aisle north of the central miḥrāb in the liwan is a remarkable pulpit *(minbar)* made entirely out of ancient Hindu elements. Three levels of *vedikā* fencing, consisting of small pillarets with foliated slabs between, support long beams ornamented with foliage. These frame a stairway leading to a platform, ornamented on its edges by a bold chequer pattern, with a passage beneath.

Two square pilasters and two front octagonal columns joined by lintels form a pavilion above this platform, surrounded by a straight-edged awning and roofed by a cusped dome. Above this pavilion, as ceiling for the bay, is a further flat lotus-ceiling.

Another cusped Hindu ceiling has been placed at the exterior entrance to the maqsurah and a corbelled dome—with sockets at its corners to receive now missing bracket-figures—has been used in front of the miḥrāb.

Lintels in the liwan show lotus patterns on their soffits and diamond, bell-and-garland, creeper, and other Hindu patterns on their faces. These ornamented pieces stand parallel to examples from early and mid-eighth century Hindu sites such as Osian and Chittorgarh in Rajasthan.

The buff ashlar masonry used both for the entry gateway and for the north wall of the Caurāsī Kambha mosque incorporates a number of carved pillars and other Hindu pieces and seems made up entirely of plundered stones. Particularly on the northwest, near the maqsurah's entry, buff and pink sandstone pieces have been combined to give a colouristic effect found also on some early Hindu structures such as the Kālikāmātā temple at Chittor. To this Hindu material, a minimum of new masonry was added at the time of the mosque's composition.

Strikingly different in technique from the ashlar masonry of the other walls is the red-sandstone facing, using a stretcher and header technology common to later Islamic construction, that covers the exterior of the mosque on the south and west as well as part of the interior of the eastern gateway. While it is possible that this facing represents a later renovation, even so late as the Mughal period, its fabric has, in fact, been carefully tied into the ashlar masonry of the north wall at the northwest corner, where the two technologies meet, as well as to the ashlar walls on the interior on the west and south.

Cunningham had also questioned the originality of the south wall, writing that 'at first I thought that the southern side of the quadrangle might have fallen down and have been repaired. [...] But,' he continues, 'when I examined the south wall I was satisfied that it was a part of the original structure.'[21]

I might also raise the question of whether the arched portion of the east gateway (Plate 9) might represent a later Islamic rebuilding. The use of long slabs to establish an arcuate structure, however, bears some resemblance to the Quṭb mosque's use of sloping slabs at the top of otherwise corbelled arches in the qibla screen (and none to the elaborate voussoir system found in the next century at Bayana).

E.B. Havell exaggerated considerably when he wrote in 1913 that 'the whole of Muhammadan architecture in India bears the distinctive impress of the soil to which it belongs—its structural ideas and symbolism are nearly always essentially Indian. [....]'[22] We see significantly at Kaman, however, the beginning of a process by which local craft traditions were assimilated—not only subordinated—to Islamic usage. That this is permissible is part of the nature of Islam and its expansion—as of Islamic architecture's typological base. Without it, much of later sultanate architecture would not have been possible.

It seems remarkable, for example, that the rectangular entry through the east gateway at Kaman combines the bold *naskhī* foundation inscription with a large ancient Hindu overdoor. The architectural motifs of this early eighth-century overdoor, however, would not have seemed, to its patrons, to have compromised the mosque's modality or Islamic purpose in any way.

The principal ornamental feature made fresh for the Caurāsī Kambhā mosque in the early thirteenth century was the miḥrāb in the western hall (Plate 21). Here also the craftsmen were Indian, carving ornamentation partly from Islamic pattern books (or textiles) but also clearly improvizing from Hindu sources.

The back wall of this miḥrāb preserves a badly damaged arched niche with a slight ogee point. Of its two broad ornamental bands, the inner rests above a moulded base, taking the form of a Hindu pillared jamb *(stambhaśākhā)* faced, however, by a symmetrical leaf-pattern of Central Asian origin.

The miḥrāb's outer face shows a rectangular frame, with two bands of ornament, supporting a battlement of spade-like merlons. The outer jamb shows a symmetrical sharply-cut pattern of interlaced leaves; the inner bears the long naskhī inscription from the Qur'ān, with a single vine wandering its way through it. Thin pillars support a perforated vine-scroll arch framing the miḥrāb's opening. Perhaps most remarkable as ornament are the pillars' capitals, which directly repeat fluted *laśuna-ghaṭa-bharaṇī* elements found on early thirteenth century Hindu pillars (Plate 21). A flat plank is placed above, with leaves pendant at the corners, and a block ornamented with an unmistakable and distinctive Hindu pattern—that of the interlocked 'moon-windows' (*candraśālā*s) that typically cover a temple's tower and act as pediments over niches.

Constructed early in the thirteenth century by Hindu craftsmen under Muslim patronage, the Kaman mosque shows a coherent integration of Hindu craftsmanship and ordering with an imported Islamic modality for use. Few other monuments in this early period show so successful an adaptation of Hindu elements as at Kaman.

Though the miḥrāb made for the Shahī Jamiʿ mosque at Bari Khatu (Khatu Kalan) in Nagaur District, Rajasthan (Plates 4, 6, and 8), for example—a mosque also of the early thirteenth century and made largely from plundered Hindu material—shares decorative patterns with that at Kaman, that monument, as a whole, lacks much of Kaman's architectural and decorative integrity.[23] Actual adaptation of an existing structure at Bari Khatu, much more so than at Kaman, seems to have been a political act, plunder becoming a means to demonstrate Islamic control.

The entry gate at Bari Khatu, with an upper storey presented as an open pavilion (Plate 8) represents reuse of an existing temple gateway, substituting only new jambs ornamented by large diamonds for the original Hindu śākhās with figures. The gate, however, now has steps placed within it, and the level for the mosque's raised platform is placed at the upper level of the earlier entry.

The three buttresses placed on the back wall of this monument mark the presence of miḥrābs on the interior but represent reuse of mouldings from contemporaneous Hindu temples. The central set of mouldings may in fact represent an existing monument whose *maṇḍapa* ceiling also has been reused within the hall. A lintel carved with Hindu deities had, in the process of rebuilding, conspicuously been turned so that its images face into the rubble fill of the dome over this ceiling; these are visible now only because of the structure's partial collapse.

Such a site, austere in its sense of 'occupation', gives a bottom-line to issues of plunder, reuse, and appropriation. Islamic supervisors here have felt no shame in shaping what to them was a hermeneutically effective and canonical mosque out of remains of an existing Hindu temple. Bari Khatu does not fix the rule, however. It rather stands in contrast to the rapid exploration of collaborative and creative possibilities—architectural, decorative, and aesthetic—found in less fortified contexts. At Kaman or Ajmer, architects combined old pieces with a sense of their aesthetic coherence; by integrating them to fit a new programme, they have been able to create a new unified statement for Islam in India.[24]

By the end of the thirteenth century, new ideas from Central Asia would require further acts of accommodation by architects on the subcontinent. If Indo-Islamic architecture at its beginning rooted itself in local conditions, it also appropriately opened its branches to a variety of breezes from elsewhere in the Islamic world.

Developing regional schools of Indo-Islamic architecture continued to depend on local architects and available craft traditions in creative ways. Jaunpur, Gujarat, and Bengal each create an Islamic architecture that acts as an independent regional expression. Without both seed and soil, the architecture of India's growing Islamic world could not so readily have flourished. Perhaps only in its earliest phase, however, is the delicate soil of Indian Islam's lotus throne made so self-evident.

NOTES

1. A preliminary version of this essay covering only Kaman was given to M.C. Joshi for his B.K. Thapar felicitation volume.

2. A. Cunningham, *Archaeological Survey of India*, Vol. 10, *report of a tour in eastern Rajputana in 1882–1883*, (repr. Delhi 1969), pp. 54–60 and plates XI–XII; Banerji, R.D.: *Archaeological Survey of India, western circle, progress report 1918–1919*, 1919, pp. 64–5 and plates XXII–XXVII; Mehrdad Shokoohy and Natalie H. Shokoohy, 'The architecture of Baha Al-Din Tughrul in the region of Bayana, Rajasthan', in *Muqarnas* 4, 1987, pp. 114–32.

3. *Vedikā*-fencing, heavily plastered, can be seen between these pillars in a photograph from 1919. This need not, however, have been part of the original structure (Banerji, *Progress Report 1918–1919*, plate XXII).

4. *Indian Antiquary* 10, 1881, p. 34; *Epigraphia Indica* 24, 1937–8, pp. 329–36.

5. *Epigraphia India* 36, 1965–6, pp. 52–6.

6. Cunningham, *Archaeological Survey*, 10, p. 56; Banerji, *Progress Report 1918–1919*, p. 64, reported that 'most of the inscription on the entrance has disappeared and the inscriptions on the central Mihrab are also fairly nearly gone.'

7. *Annual Report of Indian Epigraphy* 1965–1966, no. D, 320; Z.A. Desai, *Published Muslim Inscriptions of Rajasthan*, Jaipur 1971, p. 96, no. 303.

8. Shokoohy and Shokoohy, *'The architecture of Baha Al-Din Tughrul'*, in Mehrdad Shokoohy, *Rajasthan I (Corpus inscriptionum lranicarum* 4, Vol. 49), London 1986, pp. 50–3.

9. *Annual Report of Indian Epigraphy* 1965–1966, no. D. 321; Desai: *Muslim Inscriptions*, p. 304.

10. Anthony Welch, 'Qur'ān and tomb: The religious epigraphs of two early

sultanate tombs in Delhi' in *Indian Epigraphy, its Bearing on the History of Art.* eds Frederick M. Asher and G.S. Gai, (New Delhi 1985), pp. 257–67.

11. *Al-Qur'ān, a Contemporary Translation by Ahmed Ali,* Princeton 1984, p. 497.

12. *Al-Qur'ān,* v. 7.

13. Percy Brown, *Indian Architecture (Islamic period),* Bombay 1942, p. 11. He, however, is referring to the Ukhā Mandir at Bayana; Z.A. Desai, 'Islamic inscriptions: their bearing on monuments' in *Indian Epigraphy, its Bearing on the History of Art,* eds Frederick M. Asher and G.S. Gai, (New Delhi 1985), p. 252, further comments on the Kaman mosque that, 'though known, this mosque has been overlooked by writers on, and students of, Indo-Islamic architecture.'

14. R. Nath, *History of Sultanate Architecture,* (Delhi 1978), p. 15; he is, however, referring to the interior structure of the Adhai-din-ka-Jhompra mosque at Ajmer, Desai: *Islamic Inscriptions,* p. 252, comments that 'the *in situ* epigraph dated AH 600/1204 AD from Kaman [...] adds one more to the very small number of Mamluk monuments. Though known, this mosque has been overlooked by writers on, and students of, Indo-Islamic architecture.'

15. I have elsewhere explored this creative confrontation of Islamic and Hindu perquisites in Michael W. Meister, 'The two-and-a-half-day mosque' in *Oriental Art* N.S. 14, 1968, pp. 107–13. Reprinted in this volume as Chapter 9.

16. 'Śūrasenas of Śrīpatha' in *Encyclopaedia of Indian Temple Architecture* 2, part 2: *North India, period of early maturity,* (eds) Michael W. Meister and M.A. Dhaky, (New Delhi, 1991).

17. Jain, Kailash Chand, *Ancient Cities and Towns of Rajasthan,* (Delhi, 1972), pp. 266–70.

18. Banerji, *Progress Report 1918–1919,* p. 64.

19. In particular, see the wall-pilasters on the Telī-kā-mandir at Gwalior (ca. 725–750) and the eighth-century *ghaṭapallava* pillars in the later *maṭha* at Menal, Rajasthan.

20. Shokoohy and Shokoohy, *The Architecture of Baha Al-Din Tughrul.* p. 125, refer to this as *a zenāna.* This they correct in their *Hiṣār-i Fīrūza,* (London 1958), p. 36, where they use the term *mulūk khāna,* citing Shams Sirāj.

21. Cunningham: *Archaeological Survey,* p. 55. He points out also a similar arrangement of solid north and west walls at Bayana.

22. E.B. Havell, *Indian Architecture,* (London, first edition 1913, second edition 1927), p. 51.

23. Desai, *Islamic Inscriptions,* p. 163, refers to the 'undated mosque at Baṛi Khāṭu' as 'dating to this early phase, though its "referent" inscription eloquently mentions its renovation in the time of Akbar.' Shokoohy, *Rajasthan I,* pp. 54–6.

24. *Cf.* Meister, *Two-and-a half-day mosque.* Also of great interest are the mid-eleventh century monuments at Bhadreshvar documented by Mehrdad Shokoohy,

Bhadreśvar, the Oldest Islamic Monuments in India (Supplement to *Muqarnas* 2), Leiden, 1988. These represent structures made by local Hindu builders in coastal Gujarat to suit several different programmes for use by Islamic merchants and provide a pre-Imperial model for the sort of craft and patronage relationships and interactions between local craft conventions and new typologies that also must have underlain the building of monuments early in the period of Islamic political occupation.

Index

Acknowledgements

The editor and the publisher acknowledge the following for permission to include the articles/extracts in this volume:

Brill Academic Publishers for André Wink, *'The Idols of Hind'*, from *Al-Hind*, Vol. II (Leiden, 1997), pp. 294–334, and Anthony Welch, Hussein Keshani, and Alexandra Bain, 'Epigraphs, Scripture, and Architecture in the Early Sultanate of Delhi', *Muqarnas* 19, 2002, pp. 12–43.

The University Press of Florida for Richard M. Eaton, 'Temple Desecration and Indo-Muslim States', in David Gilmartin and Bruce B. Lawrence (eds), *Beyond Hindu and Turk, Rethinking Religious Identities in Islamicate South Asia* (Gainesville, 2000), pp. 246–81.

Heras Institute of Indian History and Culture, Mumbai, for Fritz Lehmann, 'Architecture of the Early Sultanate Period and the Nature of the Muslim State in India', *Indica* 15/1, 1978, pp. 13–31.

Meenakshi Publications for Mohammad Mujeeb, 'The Qutb Complex as a Social Document' from his *Islamic Influence on Indian Society* (Delhi, 1972), pp. 114–27.

Permanent Black for Sunil Kumar, 'Qutb and Modern Memory', in Suvir Kaul (ed.), *The Partitions of Memory: The Afterlife of the Division of India* (New Delhi, 2001), pp. 140–82.

The British Institute of Persian Studies and the editors of *Iran* for Robert Hillenbrand, 'Political Symbolism in Early Indo-Islamic Mosque Architecture: The Case of Ajmīr', *Iran* 26, 1988, pp. 105–18.

Michael W. Meister and the editors of *Oriental Art* for Michael W. Meister, 'The "Two-and-a-half-day" Mosque', *Oriental Art* 18/1, 1972, pp. 57–63.

Michael W. Meister and Ergon-Verlag, Würzburg for Michael W. Meister, 'Indian Islam's Lotus Throne: Kaman and Khatu Kalan', in A.L. Dallapiccola and S. Zingel-Avé Lallemant (eds), *Islam and Indian Regions* (Stuttgart, 1993), pp. 445–52.

The volume editor would specially like to thank Professors Sabayasachi Bhattacharya, Brajadulal Chattopadhyaya, and Richard Eaton for their comments, suggestions, and support, and the editorial team at Oxford University Press India for overseeing the production of the book.

Contributors

ALEXANDRA BAIN completed a PhD dissertation entitled 'The Late Ottoman *En'am-i Serif*: Sacred Text and Images in an Islamic Prayer Book,' in the Department of the History in Art, University of Victoria in 1999. Her master's thesis, completed in the same department in 1993 was entitled 'Qur'anic Epigraphy in the Delhi Sultanate: The 'Alai Darwaza.'

J.D. BEGLAR (d. 1907) was an archaeologist, engineer, and photographer. He worked closely with Alexander Cunningham in the 1860s and 1870s to prepare reports on Indian antiquities and monuments for the nascent Archaeological Survey of India.

ALEXANDER CUNNINGHAM (d. 1893) was a British archaeologist and army engineer who had a particular interest in the study of the Buddhist monuments of India. In 1861 he was appointed first director of the newly-founded Archaeological Survey of India. With the exception of a brief interlude between 1865 and 1870, Cunningham held this position until 1885. In addition to several essays and reports on South Asian architecture, history, and numismatics, his major publication was *The Stûpa of Barhut* (1879).

RICHARD M. EATON is Professor of History at the University of Arizona. His research interests focus on the social and cultural history of premodern India (1000–1800), and especially on the various interactions between the Islamic and Indian civilizations. Among his many publications on these topics are *The Rise of Islam and the Bengal Frontier, 1204–1760* (1993) and *A Social History of the Deccan, 1300–1761: Eight Indian Lives* (2005).

FINBARR BARRY FLOOD is Associate Professor in the Institute of Fine Arts and Department of Art History, New York University. In addition to a range of articles on Islamic and South Asian material culture and its historiography, he is the author of *The Great Mosque of Damascus: Studies on the Making of an Umayyad Visual Culture* (2001), and *Objects of Translation: Material Culture and Medieval 'Hindu-Muslim' Encounter* (forthcoming 2009).

ROBERT HILLENBRAND is Professor of Islamic Art and Director of the Centre for the Advanced Study of the Arab World at the University of Edinburgh. Among his recent publications on Islamic art and architecture are *The Architecture of Ottoman Jerusalem* (2002) and the prize-winning *Islamic Architecture: Form, Function and Meaning* (1994).

HUSSEIN KESHANI is Assistant Professor of Art History in the University of British Columbia, Okanagan. In 2005, he was awarded the Margaret B. Sevčenko Prize for the best essay on Islamic art and architecture by a young scholar. The essay, published in *Muqarnas*, drew upon his 2003 dissertation on architecture and ritual in eighteenth-century Lucknow.

SUNIL KUMAR is Professor of Medieval History at Delhi University and editor of the *Indian Economic and Social History Review*. He has published widely on South Asian premodern history. His recent publications include *The Emergence of the Delhi Sultanate: 1192–1286* (2007) and *The Present in Delhi's Pasts* (2nd edn., 2008).

FRITZ LEHMANN (d. 1994) was an American scholar who taught in the Department of History, University of British Columbia. His area of special interest was the history of South Asia, in particular the role of Islam in the region, technology and its relation to the region's culture and development, and Urdu language and literature.

MICHAEL W. MEISTER is Norman W. Brown Professor of South Asia Studies in the Department of Art History, University of Pennsylvania. His research focuses on temple architecture, the morphology of meaning, and other aspects of the art of the Indian subcontinent. Among his many publications is Volume 2 of the *Encyclopædia of Indian Temple Architecture*, co-authored with M. A. Dhaky.

MOHAMMAD MUJEEB (d. 1985) was the Vice Chancellor of Jamia Millia Islamia in Delhi between 1948 and 1973. He published widely in both English and Urdu on subjects ranging from Indian history to Russian literature. He was a delegate of the Indian government to the United Nations (1949) and UNESCO (1954). In 1965, he was awarded the Padma Bhushan by the Government of India.

ALKA PATEL is Assistant Professor in the Department of Art History, University of California, Irvine. In addition to various scholarly articles on South Asian architecture, she has published *Building Communities in Gujarat: Architecture and Society during the Twelfth through Fourteenth Centuries* (2004), and *The Architecture of the Indian Sultanates*, co-authored with Abha Narain Lambah (2006).

ANTHONY WELCH is Professor of Islamic Art and Architecture in the Department of the History in Art, University of Victoria. He has published numerous articles and books on Islamic art, including *Shah 'Abbas and the Arts of Isfahan* (1973), *Arts of the Islamic Book*, co-authored with S.C. Welch (1982), and *The Travels and Journal of Ambrosio Bembo* (2007). He is currently preparing a monograph on the architectural patronage of the fourteenth-century Tughluq sultans of Delhi.

ANDRÉ WINK is Professor of History at the University of Wisconsin-Madison. His research focuses on India and the Indian Ocean area in the medieval and early modern age. Among his many books are *Land and Sovereignty in India: Agrarian Society and Politics under the Eighteenth-Century Maratha Svarājya* (1986), the 3-volume *Al-Hind, The Making of the Indo-Islamic World* (1990–2004), and *Akbar* (forthcoming) for the series *Makers of the Muslim World*.